WHEN FIRMS CHANGE DIRECTION

WHEN FIRMS CHANGE DIRECTION

Anne Sigismund Huff

James Oran Huff

with Pamela S. Barr

OXFORD
UNIVERSITY PRESS

2000

OXFORD

UNIVERSITY PRESS

Oxford New York

Athens Auckland Bangkok Bogotá Buenos Aires Calcutta
Cape Town Chennai Dar es Salaam Delhi Florence Hong Kong Istanbul
Karachi Kuala Lumpur Madrid Melbourne Mexico City Mumbai
Nairobi Paris São Paulo Shanghai Singapore Taipei Tokyo Toronto Warsaw

and associated companies in
Berlin Ibadan

Library of Congress Cataloging-in-Publication Data
Huff, Anne Sigismund.
    When firms change direction / Anne Sigismund Huff, James Oran Huff
with Pamela S. Barr.
      p. cm.
    Includes bibliographical references and index.
    ISBN 0-19-513643-8
    1. Organizational change. 2. Corporate reorganizations. 3. Corporate culture.
  4. Crisis management. I. Huff, James Oran. II. Barr, Pamela S. III. Title.

    HD58.8.H824 2000
    302.3'5—dc21   00-044582

With the permission of the publisher, portions of chapter 4 are drawn from James O. Huff and
Anne S. Huff, "Recent Developments in the Modeling of Strategy Reformulation," in Manfred M.
Fischer and Arthur Getis, eds., *Recent Developments in Spatial Analysis*, pp. 253–271. (Berlin: Springer-
Verlag, 1997.)

9 8 7 6 5 4 3 2 1

Printed in the United States of America
on acid-free paper

TO DAVID AND BETSY

Introduction and Acknowledgments

All is flux; nothing stays still.
Heraclitus (c. 540–480 B.C.)

Plus ça change, plus c'est la même chose.
Karr (1849)

Hamel and Prahalad (1994), D'Aveni (1994), Brown and Eisenhardt (1997, 1998), and many others contend that continuous change will characterize firms that survive in a globalizing world. The rhetoric of these and other authors is compelling, not only to researchers but also to organization leaders whose own works have titles like *Crisis and Renewal* (Hurst, 1995) and *Only the Paranoid Survive* (Grove, 1996). There is an urgency to the claims that stability is neither possible nor desirable, and companies like Microsoft provide tangible evidence that aggressive agility pays.

At the same time, a more cautionary tale is available. Floyd and Wooldridge (1992, 2000) observe that the implementation of change often fails. Their studies show that mid-level managers frequently do not understand the enthusiasms of elites, nor do they have the means to create desired changes. Widely regarded levers, including CEO replacement, are often insufficient (Fondas & Wiersema, 1997). Conflict and politics easily derail ambitious efforts (Denis, Langley & Cazale, 1996). Reengineering and other programs adopted with enthusiasm across industries are repeatedly discarded as expensive failures (O'Neill, Pouder & Buchholtz, 1998). In short, there is convincing evidence that organizations do not change easily (Miles & Snow, 1978; Oster, 1982; Miller & Friesen, 1984; Tushman & Romanelli, 1985; Zajac & Shortell, 1989; Barr & Huff, 1997).

This book is the result of our strong desire to bring the demands and evidence for change *and* continuity into a single framework. The theoretic and empirical chapters that follow sequentially address change in individual-, group-, firm-, and industry-level processes. In sum, they provide an integrated account of when and why firms change direction, and where and how much they will move.

The cognitively anchored theory we develop incorporates behavioral and economic concerns. We begin with processes that are more micro than those observed in many previous studies of strategic change and end with industry-level influences that are more macro than many studies consider. While process dominates, attending to content is facilitated by focusing on changes within a specific industry setting—the pharmaceutical industry. We consider qualitative as well as quantitative data, and develop descriptive as well as formal models.

Our efforts have a long history. Rooted more than 25 years ago in graduate student conversations about decision making, this book began to take form over coffee and tea during a 1987-1988 sabbatical from the University of Illinois. Jim had been working on models of household relocation. Anne became interested in the company applications of these models—which weighed the current residence's attractions (compatible neighbors, mature landscaping, remodeling investments...) against household dissatisfactions (too few bedrooms, too far from new jobs, etc.). The obvious questions of interest were "When and why does a company 'move' to a new location?" and "Don't they, too, weigh the attractions of a current strategy against dissatisfactions?"

What started as a brief conversation on an interesting analogy turned into a National Science Foundation proposal which we asked Howard Thomas (then on the strategy faculty at Illinois, now the dean of the College of Commerce at Illinois) to join. Howard and several of his doctoral students had been working on a database in the pharmaceutical industry that seemed as if it would provide interesting longitudinal data to test our models. His work on risk, competitive strategy, and other topics was also highly relevant to the endeavor. Unfortunately, the database took other directions, the three of us were slow to make theoretic progress, and Howard's many other commitments led him away from this project. Various public sources were used to compile the data found in this book, but Howard is coauthor of an article in *Strategic Management Journal* that serves as the basis for chapter 4.

Our efforts also were influenced by a number of integrative, longitudinal studies of change in context. Work by Bower (1970), Pettigrew (1973, 1987, 1990, 1991), March and Olsen (1976), Mintzberg (1978), Quinn (1980), McCaskey (1982), and others had painted complex pictures of how strategic change could be conceptualized and studied at the time we began our research. Weick (1976, 1979), Hedberg and Jönsson (1978), Starbuck (1983), and others had asserted that action to discover intention accounts for a great deal. Lou Pondy (1978), Donald Schön (1967, 1983), Gerry Johnson (1988), Magoroh Maruyama (1992, 1994), and Leif Melin (1992) were among those adding psychological, cultural, social, and international variables to the study of organization change. Michel Bougon (1983) was helping people understand their own knowledge patterns with "self-questionnaires." Colin Eden and his colleagues (Sims & Eden, 1984; Eden, 1990b, 1992; Ackermann, 1992) were helping groups interactively "map" the possibilities for new strategies.

The last cognitively oriented work was particularly exciting. Hall's (1984) paper suggested new, cognitive explanations for the failure of the *Saturday Evening Post*. In the same year, Bartunek (1984) suggested that positive changes in organizations also had a cognitive foundation. Sims and Gioia's (1986) book, *The Thinking Organization*, outlined many other applications of cognitive science. A new interest group on managerial and organizational behavior was formed at the Academy of Management that provided an ongoing forum. Within a decade, Walsh (1995) was able to summarize work in organization behavior, organization theory, and strategy that established the importance of individual-, group-, firm-, and industry-level knowledge structures.

As participants in this expanding area, we were excited but increasingly dissatisfied with what a cognitive perspective, by itself, had to offer. Others also become concerned with cognition's social and political context (Ginsberg, 1994; Eden & Ackermann, 1998) and broadened their concerns to topics like organizational identity (Whetten & Godfrey, 1998), organizational learning (Crossan, Lane & White, 1999), and the competitive consequences of cognitive processes (Ginsberg, 1994).

This book is the result of trying to link the exciting work of the 1980s and 1990s in cognition with other perspectives, and to put the resulting synthesis into a more dynamic framework. By the end of the 1990s, we were joining researchers emphasizing nonlinear outcomes of organizational activities (Stacey, 1995; Brown & Eisenhardt, 1998; Teece, Pisano & Shuen, 1997; Van de Ven, Polley, Garud & Venkataraman, 1999). Our work has now consumed more than 10 years, a great deal of intense conversation, and a number of efforts not represented in this volume.

Fortunately, other colleagues joined us. Two chapters in this book reflect Pam Barr's University of Illinois dissertation and subsequent research on strategic change in the pharmaceutical industry in the 1970s. In fact, we have extensively discussed many ideas in this book, as well as working independently on models of stress and inaction. It was a pleasure to have her as a fellow traveler.

Kurt Heppard and Jim Blasick, at the time graduate students at the University of Colorado, extended the industry history Pam began in her dissertation. Gail James, also a doctorate student at Colorado, provided a useful chapter on alliances between established firms and new biotech companies based on her dissertation. We became interested in the interaction of incumbents and newcomers in response to Larry Stimpert's research, and we report on this work in the last chapter of the book.

Many other people have directly contributed to our thinking about strategic change and lack of change, often in extended and delightful conversation. Though we know we are forgetting many formative exchanges, we would like to give special thanks to Stu Alpert, Charles Baden-Fuller, Julia Balogun, Jay Barney, Jean Bartunek, Kim Boal, Michel Bougon, Ned Bowman, Roland Calori, Bala Chakravarthy, David Chappell, Julie Chesley, Karl Cool, Tom Dandridge, T.K. Das, Andre Delbeq, Irene Duhaime, Jane Dutton, Colin Eden, Kathy Eisenhardt, Roger Evered, Liam Fahey, Avi Fiegenbaum, Marlene Fiol, Steve Floyd, Peter Frost, Ragu Garud, Denny Gioia, Alan Glassman, Rob Grant, Peter Grinyer, Stuart Hart, Gerard Hodgkinson, Veronica Hope-Hailey, David Hurst, Dale Jasinski, Mark Jenkins, Gerry Johnson, Phyl Johnson, Georg von Krogh, Mauri Laukkanen, Arie Lewin, Meryl Lewis, Craig Lundberg, Marjorie Lyles, Joe Mahoney, Livia Markóczy, Joanne Martin, Dick Mason, Leif Melin, Henry Mintzberg, Ian Mitroff, Michael Moch, Margie Peteraf, Andrew Pettigrew, Lou Pondy, Joe Porac, Rhonda Reger, Johan Roos, Dick Rumelt, Ron Sanchez, Yolanda Sarason, Charles Schwenk, Paul Shrivastava, Jitendra Singh, J.C. Spender, Bill Starbuck, Murray Steele, Raymond Thiétart, Bill Torbert, Andy Van de Ven, Jim Walsh, Karl Weick, David Whetten, Alan Wilkins, Eric Wiseman, Aks Zaher, and Sri Zaher.

In addition, we appreciate support from the National Science Foundation (SES-8822358) and are pleased to acknowledge the importance of the University of Illinois and the departments of business administration and geography as a productive intellectual home for most of the period in which the work was being developed. The University of Colorado and Cranfield School of Management sheltered the production of the book itself. Many people from each of these institutions were helpful discussants of aspects of this work, as were audiences at various presentations made at the Academy of Management, the American Association of Geographers, the Strategic Management Society, the University of Auckland, the ESSEC workshop on Action, Structure and Organizations, the European Institute for Advanced Studies in Management, Jönköping University, the Minnesota Conference on Strategy Process, Otago University, and the Workshop on Managerial Thinking in Business Environments.

We also were very fortunate to have the assistance and friendship of Mary Oberg, who over a period of at least 6 years supported drafting and redrafting most of the chapters found here and who prepared the first draft of the reference section as well. Russell Huff discussed and programmed early versions of models used in the empirical section of the book. Connie Luoto, Heidi Neck, and Andrew Corbett proofed chapter drafts. David Cook prepared early maps of competitors, which Jim Robb skillfully transformed into a systematic format. Keith Brigham and Heidi Neck did a wonderful job of integrating the bibliography, chasing down missing references, and otherwise supporting the completion of the manuscript.

Families tend to be last in these necessarily incomplete lists of supporters, but they are often the most important. We appreciate a large and loving family and dedicate this book to Betsy and David, because living with them is more meaningful and rewarding than academic conversation and research—though certainly we bored them often enough by carrying out this work at home.

Contents

WHEN FIRMS CHANGE DIRECTION

1

Economic, Behavioral, and Cognitive Contributions to Strategy Theory

This book is written with several partially overlapping audiences in mind. Most broadly, our argument to the strategy field is that cognitive theories should be placed alongside economic and behavioral theories as a foundation for the field. This chapter summarizes major contributions from each of these theoretic perspectives as alternative theories of the firm.

Our particular interest is cognitive theory. We hope those taking a cognitive approach will find our theory of change an interesting example of the benefits of explicitly anchoring individual cognition in social, political, and economic contexts. This chapter provides an overview of cognitive research that gives particular attention to work that leads in this integrative direction.

Most of all, however, we want to converse with those who are interested in strategic change. This chapter establishes an interest in individual, group, firm, and industry levels of analysis and introduces stress and inertia, first and second order change, position, and opportunity as concepts that can be integratively defined across these levels of analysis. Our objective is to use this platform to answer four critical questions in the rest of the book:

- When is a firm likely to change strategic direction?
- Why does it undertake significant redirection?
- In what direction is it likely to move?
- How much is it likely to change?

THE SEARCH FOR STRATEGY THEORY

A simple observation has helped shape the strategy field: firms within the same competitive environment respond in idiosyncratic ways to changing environmental conditions. Such differences were of little interest to traditional economic theory (Nelson,

1991), while those with behavioral concerns found them of central importance. Carroll (1993) points to dispositional, situational, organizational, and environmental sources of difference in firm behavior but also finds the literature in this area not very cohesive because it responds to different subjects of interest. Nor does this disparate literature address many specific questions that diversity raises for strategists.

For example, the observation of difference among firms suggests questions about their differential capacity to change. Yet, in our opinion, the strategy field does not yet have a satisfactory answer to the question of *when* a given firm is likely to change its strategic position, relative to others with similar activities. Though familiar with work on the triggers of change, we also think more must be done to understand *why* firms change strategy. Another neglected question is *where* a firm making a change in strategy will relocate itself. Equally important, *how much* will a given firm change in a given time period? These are the basic questions we address in this book.

We believe that cognitive theory must be considered when such questions are answered and that this contribution can be developed at multiple levels of analysis. However, cognitive theory alone is not enough. As noted in the introduction, the cognitively *anchored* theory we develop incorporates behavioral and economic concerns. As we tried to bring economic, behavioral, and cognitive traditions together in one account of strategic change, we mirrored other observers of the strategy field. Richard Bettis was complaining that most strategy research was "prematurely stuck in a 'normal science straightjacket'" (1991, 315). His concerns focused on the field's inattention to critical issues of relevance to managers, but he also recommended that "strong, logical, and interesting theory" should be a part of "any empirical paper, no matter how large the sample or statistically sophisticated the analysis" (1991, 318). Rumelt, Schendel, and Teece similarly concluded "in looking back over [the last] three decades" that "what comes into focus is the search, sometimes in vain, for theoretical explanations of very complex phenomena" (1994, 24).

Rumelt, Schendel, and Teece also raised the question of which disciplines are the appropriate foundation for theoretic endeavors in the strategy field, noting that "during the last decade strategic management research has increasingly relied on the theories and methods of economics and organizational sociology, as well as (but to a lesser extent) on political science and psychology" (1994, 24). Prahalad and Hamel more explicitly suggested:

> that the I/O paradigm may at best provide us partial answers . . . [this implicit recognition is] forcing the field to search for new paradigms(s). Should the field rally behind I/O economics? game theory? sociology? or behavioral science? What is an appropriate theoretical lens to the study of strategy appears to us as a premature question. . . . Strategy as a field has an abundance of issues which can be studied from a multiplicity of theoretical vantage points. There is no need to limit variation in approaches at this time. (1994, 15)

Cognitive theory is not prominent in this and many other lists. We believe it should be placed alongside economics and behavioral science as a theoretic foundation for the strategy field. The cognitive perspective is not new to strategy research (Shrivastava & Mitroff, 1983; Schwenk, 1984, 1988; Sims & Gioia, 1986; Stubbart, 1989; Lyles, 1990;

Mintzberg, 1991; Zajac, 1992), yet this expanding body of research often is not recognized (e.g., Schoemaker, 1993; Porter, 1994; Bowman, 1995; Schendel, 1995; Grant, 1996; Baum, 1998). One impediment seems to be that management theories as well as their influencing social science disciplines have long developed in isolation (Rajagopalan & Spreitzer, 1996). With an eye toward establishing common ground, this chapter places our cognitively anchored efforts in the disciplining framework provided by economic and behavioral theories of the firm.

ECONOMIC THEORIES OF THE FIRM

Seth and Thomas (1994) outlined seven major economic theories of the firm, beginning with the neoclassical interest in predicting price and quantities of goods produced by idealized firms in a well-specified environment. A review of Table 1.1 indicates four important moves away from the initial modeling constraints of classic economics in this work:

1. *Increasing complexity in the description of the **firm** itself.* From an early focus on production issues, more recent economic theories have portrayed firms in terms of ownership and control, contractual relationships, competitive interaction, and governance arrangements.
2. *Increasing realism in specifying **managerial motives and behavior**.* Although economic man is still simplistic from behavioral and cognitive points of view, the move from dispassionate rationality to the rationality of self-interest has led to interesting theoretic speculations about the difficulty of achieving mutually beneficial cooperation. Nonetheless, economic theories typically assume that analysis will be followed by effective action in an unproblematic way.
3. *Elaboration in **firm goals**.* While profit maximization continues to dominate and supports a defining interest in performance among strategy researchers, the insight that owners and managers are separate entities with disparate interests is an important advance in understanding goal setting.
4. *Assumption of a more complex, uncertain **environment**.* Initial definitions of deterministic certainty have been replaced by descriptions of the firm's environment that admit differences in resource availability and sometimes predict outcomes contingent upon competitor actions.

Seth and Thomas (1994,184) assert that no single approach is adequate for modeling complex firm and industry phenomena; rather, a range of alternative assumptions about rationality and opportunism are of value. We agree, and note that especially interesting work from a strategy perspective has been done from transaction cost and game theory perspectives (Camerer, 1991; Saloner, 1991). In our view, however, the strictures of the economic tradition, despite the developments noted previously, severely limit the utility of economic theories of the firm as a basis for investigating many topics of interest to strategists and strategy researchers, including the questions of change that are particularly compelling today.

Table 1.1 Economic Theories of the Firm

Theory	Orientation	Process of Discovery	Central Research Problem	Theoretic Conceptualization of Firm	Manager's Motives/Behavior	Goals of Firm	Nature of Environment
1. Neoclassical microeconomics	Positive	Deductive	Market behavior	Production function	Maximize profits/rational	Maximize profits	Certain, deterministic
2. Traditional industrial organization	Normative	Inductive	Industry structure, conduct, and performance	Shaped by industry structure	Maximize profits/rational	Maximize profits	Certain, deterministic
3. Managerial	Positive	Deductive	Managerial decisionmaking	Separate ownership and management	Self-interest/rational	Maximize managerial utility	Uncertain
4. Transactions cost	Positive	Deductive	Choice between markets and hierarchies	Nexus of contracts	Control/source of administrative costs	Minimize costs, maximize profits	Uncertain, complex
5. New industrial organization	Positive	Deductive/inductive	Market behavior	Game player	Maximize payoffs/mutual rationality	Maximize payoffs	Contingent
6. Agency	Positive/normative	Deductive	Optimal contracting relationships	Governance structure	Self-interest/minimize effort, maximize gain	Maximize shareholder wealth (positive agency theory)	Uncertain, asymmetrical information

Modification of Seth & Thomas, 1994, 168.

BEHAVIORAL THEORIES OF THE FIRM

The theories that we find most interesting for understanding strategic change focus attention on managerial and firm behaviors and their implication for outcomes within more realistic internal and external environments. Five theoretic perspectives that have these defining characteristics are summarized in Table 1.2. These more behavioral approaches mark a distinct departure from economic theories of the firm, though most refer back to their economic predecessors. In general, behavioral theories are much more internally oriented, more concerned with differences among firms than similarities, and more interested in dynamics than in expected equilibrium. In briefly outlining them, we give special attention to their contribution to understanding strategic change and mention related work with similar basic assumptions.

Cyert and March's Political Theory of the Firm and Its Successors

The pivotal departure from previous economic theories of the firm made by Cyert and March (1963) is to assume inherent differences in individual interests and goals. As a result, firm outcomes are valued differently by members of the organization. As noted in Table 1.2, Cyert and March established a political theory by defining the firm as a coalition of interest groups stabilized by a satisficing distribution of benefits. The theory predicts that decisions will be made via problemistic search and quasi resolution of conflict. In their initial studies, Cyert, March, and their colleagues closely follow the framework of economic theories of the firm by predicting production, but they do so by focusing on expectations, the choice process, and goal definition.

One important descendant of this work is the study of "stakeholders," both within the organization and outside its boundaries (Mitroff, 1983; Freeman, 1984). A relatively small but persistent stream of work (Pettigrew, 1973; Hirsch, 1975; MacMillan, 1978; Huff, 1980b, 1988; Narayanan & Fahey, 1982; Mintzberg, 1983; Tichy, 1983a, b; Gray & Ariss, 1985; Schwenk, 1989; Hardy, 1996a, 1996b) considers political implications of unresolvable differences in expectations and self-interest among stakeholders, and the consequent difficulty of moving away from current firm activities. However, some authors (e.g., Eisenhardt & Bourgeois, 1988; Fombrun & Ginsberg, 1990; Russo, 1992; Doz, 1996; Eden & Ackermann, 1998) reject Cyert and March's conservative predictions that satisficing coalitions tend toward gridlock. Attention is now being drawn to the importance of external turbulence, individual power, and the capacity to create new coalitions that increase the probability of change. Research on alliances and the advantages of other cooperative behavior is a further development that can be linked to this line of inquiry (Harrigan, 1988; Hagendorn, 1995; Deeds & Hill, 1996).

The garbage can model of decision making (March & Olsen, 1976) provides another refinement of Cyert and March's initial theoretic perspective. This work makes a convincing case that the capacity of individuals and groups to affect outcomes varies over time. Decision (and, by extension, strategic change) depends not only on individual interests and the content of problems needing attention but also on the availability of solutions and opportunities to act. Work by Van de Ven (1990) and his colleagues (Garud

Table 1.2 Behavioral Theories (and Potential Theories) of the Firm

Theory	Orientation	Process of Discovery	Central Research Problem	Theoretic Conceptualization of the Firm	Manager's Motives/Behavior	Goals of Firm	Nature of Environment
Political	Positive	Inductive and deductive	The sociopolitical requirements for collective output	Coalition of diverse interests and goals	Satisfy self-interests/boundedly rational, risk adverse, satisficing	Continued existence in the face of diverse interests	Exceeds human comprehension, has differential
Evolutionary	Positive	Inductive and deductive	The dynamic process by which firm behavior and market outcomes (including firm failure) are jointly determined over time	Source of routinized technical and administrative knowledge, including the capacity to change routines	Routinize success/capable of learning in the face of novel stimuli	Survival, stability	Selective impacts
Configurational	Positive	Primarily deductive	Enduring patterns in firm characteristics, actions, and outcomes over time, and their transformation	Configuration of cognitive, social, and economic relationships	Survival/typically seeking continuity, occasionally seeking radical transformation	Not definitive, equifinality assumed	Becoming more complex and demanding
Dynamic/analytic	Positive	Deductive	The timing of competitive moves as the result of the diffusion of information	Processing information to act and respond to competitor actions in specific competitive races	To gain advantage/rational	Profit; other goals will have varied effects on action, response, and timing	Information-rich, desirable positions are limited
Resource-based	Positive	Inductive	Identifying the sources of unique, sustainable competitive advance	Bundle of resources and capabilities	Growth, competitive position/an important source of inimitable advantage	Maximize rents	Source of heterogeneous resources and rivalry

& Van de Ven, 1989; Van de Ven, Polley, Garud & Venkataraman, 1999) on innovation and change comes to similar conclusions about the complexities of organizing. Careful longitudinal study points to the differential impact of contextual factors on the shape and outcome of purposeful action and again suggests that the influence of actors, solutions, and problems on decision outcomes will vary over time. The basic argument is summarized in Table 1.2: organizations are collections of diverse interests and goals; the external environment is similarly complex; the possibility of coordinated action and changes in commitment are therefore central problems worthy of interest.

The Evolutionary Theory of the Firm and Other Theories of Routinized Behavior

While each of the behavioral theories we will outline pays some allegiance to economic theory, perhaps the greatest overlap involves Nelson and Winter's (1982) evolutionary theory of the firm. This work continues to assume that "economic actors are rational in the sense that they optimize" (1982, 8) and to be primarily concerned with the behavior of industries (1982, 18). We categorize this study as "behavioral" because organization researchers have used its description of routinized policies and procedures to understand the conservative nature of organizations (e.g., Pentland & Rueter, 1994) and because Nelson and Winter "dispense with all three components of the maximization model—the global objective function, the well-defined choice set, and the maximizing choice rationalization of firms' actions" (1982, 14). Their "core concern . . . [is] with the dynamic process by which firm behavior patterns and market outcomes are *jointly* determined over time" (1982, 18, emphasis added).

Nelson and Winter point out that many organizational arrangements are no longer being negotiated but have been formalized into day-to-day procedures that allow individuals to come and go with little disruption to the flow of work. They identify three kinds of routines: those that relate "to what a firm does at any time, given its prevailing stock of plant, equipment, and other factors of production," those that "determine the period- by-period augmentation or diminution of the firm's capital stock," and those that "operate to modify over time various aspects of [the firm's] operating characteristics" (1982, 16–17).

Similar ideas can be found in other evolutionary theories that describe strategy in terms of stocks and flows (Dierickx & Cool, 1987) or ongoing processes of variation, selection, and retention (Weick, 1979; Poole, Ven de Ven, Dooley & Holmes, 1999). Biological evolution is the primary source for understanding these processes: variation is often described as a random process, while selection is competitive, and retention has to do with the continuance of form.

Evolutionary work is appearing with increasingly frequency in the strategy literature, as illustrated in the 1996 special issue of the *Strategic Management Journal*, edited by Barnett and Burgelman, and in Joel Baum and Jitendra Singh's (1994) edited volume. Not all of this work should be included in a review of theories of the firm. Rumult, Schendel, and Teece note that "because evolutionary economics posits a firm that cannot change its strategy or its structure easily or quickly, the field has a very close affinity to population ecology views on organization theory" (1994, 31). But Charles Fombrun (1994) points out that the logic of inherent variation typically used at a population level offers the possibility of managerially led variation or deliberate change attempts.

While attending to institutional arguments (DiMaggio & Powell, 1983; Scott, 1995) about structural inertia (Hannan & Freeman, 1984), attention now is being focused on departures from established behavior. Kelly and Amburgey (1991) offer evidence that younger firms are more likely to make significant changes. Haveman (1994) suggests that size is a factor. Barnett, Breve, and Park (1994), Burgelman (1996), and others emphasize that competition not only triggers selection but also promotes learning, especially in single- unit firms. Chang (1996) broadens the learning logic to explain corporate diversification success.

The overall point is that, despite the selection benefits associated with stability, some firms are able to reposition themselves in changing environments (Ruef, 1997). Thus, evolutionary theorists are joining a group of strategy researchers who emphasize the importance, and likelihood, of strategic adaptation (Zajac & Shortell, 1989; Zajac & Kraatz, 1993) or strategic renewal (Chakravarthy, 1992; Huff, Huff & Thomas, 1992; Das & Moch, 1998).

Configurational Theories

Empirical studies by Miles and Snow (1978), Mintzberg (1979, 1983), Miller and Friesen (1984), Greenwood and Hinings (1988, 1993), and others, though not cast as formal theories of the firm, make interesting assertions about the decision-making task, firm differences, and their implications for strategic change. This work attempts to identify types of organizations and stages of development within types (see Fig. 1.2). Meyer, Tsui, and Hining's (1993) introduction to a special issue on configurational approaches in the *Academy of Management Journal* relates this effort to earlier, more static contingency studies (Donaldson, 1986), as well as to taxonomic approaches exemplified by McKelvey (1982) and Rich (1992).

Configurational work, narrowly defined, is rooted in empirical study of firm decision making over time. These studies show that (at least in the past) significant change in the configuration of firm actions is relatively rare (Mintzberg & Waters, 1982, 1984). Grinyer, Mayes, and McKiernan (1988) similarly argue for the infrequence of significant improvements in performance. In explanation, configurationalists point to the limited number of operationally viable combinations and emphasize shared ideologies (e.g., Hinings & Greenwood, 1988; Meyer, 1982b). Bureaucratic routines and institutional factors already flagged by evolutionary theory are also issues, but configurationalists are more likely to predict incremental adaptation "punctuated" (Gersick, 1991) by occasional, more radical transformation of the organization.

Interest in transformation, when major change occurs, also connects this work to the growing body of research on organizational learning (Mintzberg, Ahlstrand & Lampel, 1998), though learning models are much less likely to expect types and stages in emergent strategy. A large body of research on organization life cycles (Greiner, 1972) also can be put under the general rubric of configurational studies because these studies attempt to find patterned sequences in patterned positions. Hurst's (1995) "ecocyle" approach is particularly interesting because it is grounded in his managerial experiences.

Other studies in what Mintzberg et al. (1998) call the "positioning school" of strategic thought, exemplified by Porter (1980, 1996) and Hatten and Schendel (1977), also have a conceptual link to configuration studies. The overall assumptions of the positioning school are that (1) "only a few key . . . positions in the economic marketplace are desirable in any given industry" and (2) strategy formulation is "a controlled, conscious process that produce[s] full-blown deliberate strategies" (Mintzberg et al., 1998, 83–84). Configurational studies agree. They go beyond positioning in their interest in less deliberate emergent strategizing, but they, too, emphasize the limited number of viable alternatives available to decision makers.

Dynamic/Analytic Theories

Smith, Grimm, and Gannon's (1992) *Dynamics of Competitive Strategy* marks another approach to understanding strategic activities. This book emphasizes interaction with competitors. Moving away from the modeling limits of transactions cost and game theory, it draws primarily on communication theory (McPhee & Thompkins, 1985; Jablin, Putnam, Roberts & Porter, 1987) but extends the communication focus to flows among firms. Strategy is "a series of races against the clock" (Smith et al., 1992, xi) because "information spreads irregularly through a system, arriving at different locations at different times" (1992, 16). The critical problems to be solved include the competitive advantages of timing, especially order of entry. These have been topics of interest in I/O economics, but Smith et al.'s overall model recasts this work by looking at actors/action/channel/responder/response in a competitive industry environment (1992, 15).

Other studies of competitive dynamics can be placed under the analytic/dynamic heading because of their interest in competitive interaction. For example, Ian MacMillan participated in an interesting series of studies that considered preemptive strategies (1983a), competitor responses (MacMillan, McCaffrey & Van Wijk, 1985; Olivia, Day & MacMillan, 1988), and control by initiative (1988).

Another quite disparate group of studies focus on information (e.g., Wegner, Giuliano & Hertel, 1985; Donnellon, Gray & Bougon, 1986; Nayyar & Kazanjian, 1993;), but it is surprising that information models have not been more widely used in strategy and related fields. Similarly, the implications of communication itself (Putnam, Phillips & Chapman, 1996) could be more widely applied to strategy. Presumably, these approaches will have increasing importance as e-commerce becomes more pervasive. In a Web-connected world, useful information can be especially hard to identify (Stinchcomb, 1990), and the effects of more information are not always positive (Glazer, Stekel & Winer, 1992).

Resource-Based Theory

The attention of many strategy theorists has been captured by various formulations of resource-based theory (Penrose, 1959; Pfeffer & Salancik, 1978; Wernerfelt, 1984, 1995;

Dierickx & Cool, 1989; Barney, 1991; Grant, 1991b; Mahoney & Pandian, 1992; Conner & Prahalad, 1996). The central problem of this perspective is why some firms are persistently more profitable than others. Although theorists have looked at external imperfections in the market as an explanation (Peteraf, 1993), a critical argument is that external markets are increasingly efficient, and thus organizations must turn to internal sources of advantage. Differences in research and development (R&D) (Helfat, 1997), production capabilities (Itami, 1987; McGrath, MacMillan & Tushman, 1992), and other skills (Miller & Shamsie, 1996) have been examined, but intangible differences in culture (Barney & Zajac, 1994), organization identity (Fiol, 1991), tacit knowledge (Ambrosini & Bowman, 1998), and trust (Barney, 1997) have been highlighted. Kogut and Zander (1996) capture the essence of this work when they point to affiliations that make an organization a distinct "social community."

Competitors have the capacity to acquire new resources and imitate success, even though the ability to imitate is not assured (Lippman & Rumelt, 1982). Leonard-Barton (1992) cautions that "core capabilities" can become "core rigidities," echoing a longstanding concern of strategy theorists. Jay Barney (1991, 1995) developed the VIRO acronym to emphasize the idea that resources capable of providing a sustainable advantage must not only be of *v*alue to consumers, but *i*nimitable by competitors, *r*are, and capable of being exploited by the *o*rganization. Adherents to resource-based theory have also branched out to consider the match between the firm and industry determinants of success (Amit & Schoemaker, 1993). Resource similarities have been sought within strategic groups (Peteraf & Shanley, 1994; Fiegenbaum & Thomas, 1995) and alliances (Eisenhardt & Schoonhoven, 1996). An example of the increasing permeability of theoretic boundaries also can be found in Christine Oliver's (1997) arguments for the union of resource-based and institutional perspectives, which she suggests highlight the importance of "institutional capital."

Defining Characteristics of Behavioral Theories of the Firm

The five behavioral perspectives just summarized make several important extensions in the liberalizing trend already attributed to economic theories of the firm. Perhaps most important, they specify more inner relationships among managerial behavior, firm characteristics and goals, and environmental forces than economic theories of the firm. Within each area, they also make important advances.

1. *Firms are inherently diverse.* Cyert and March's (1963) attention to organization politics has been augmented by bureaucratic, resource, information, and other issues. Although these complexities make it more difficult to predict outcomes, behavioral theories of the firm have found theoretically interesting ways to categorize diverse firms.
2. *Diverse managerial motives and behavior are a primary source of firm differences.* The recognition of individual-level differences is an important contribution of these theories. However, with the exception of analytic and resource-based theories, most behavioral theories continue to emphasize the conservative aspects of managerial motives and behavior in an organizational setting.

3. *With few exceptions, **firm goals** still tend to stress profit maximization and survival in behavioral theories.* Dynamic/analytic and resource-based theories assume profit-making goals familiar from economic theory. Evolutionary theorists and configuration theorists often assume survival is the overall objective. Followers of Cyert and March (1963) are more likely to assume diverse and incommensurate goals.

4. *Descriptions of the **environment** focus on dynamic exchange.* Although behavioral theorists tend to focus on internal phenomena, environmental stimuli are more problematic than in economic theories of the firm. Complexity in the description of the firm is matched by complexity in the environment, and several behavioral theories describe important interconnections between the two. Dynamic and resource-based theories are particularly important for strategy theorists because they draw attention to competition with other firms that have their own behavioral profiles.

Clearly, the set of theories just discussed has more to say about firm-level change than economic theories, though change is not always the focus of attention. We agree with Cyert and March (1963) and their followers that the interests and will of individuals vary, and therefore the firm's overall capacity for coordinated change is diminished. Evolutionary theories helpfully draw attention to institutionalized processes that make change less likely and to mimetic forces that channel the form of change when it does occur. Configurational theories highlight interconnections within organizations that also structure organization activities and limit change options, though they also record occasional dramatic redirection. The work we have classified as dynamic/analytic emphasizes timing and competitive interaction as important considerations. Finally, we agree with resource-based theory that superior performance often requires distinctive, sheltered resources.

Despite these and other important insights, which we draw upon in the rest of the book, several intrinsic limitations of behavioral theories trouble us. First, there is *more emphasis on organizational forces than on individual purpose as the source of firm change.* Economic theories often treat the firm as a "quasi individual," implicitly assuming that the aggregation of individuals within the firm is not problematic. Although some behavioral theories are more attentive to individual actors, the individual remains a "black box." This is true even of resource-based theory, which identifies individual abilities as a primary source of firm advantages.

A related concern is that behavioral theories typically take an *overly rational view of individual decision makers.* "Bounded rationality" and self-interest, a legacy from economic theories, continue to be assumed. With the exception of work on learning and some resource-based and configuration theories, there is too little room for intuition or creativity, and little attention to the source and transformation of insight. Emotion also is neglected, though it plays a background role in political models we discussed as following Cyert and March's (1963) behavioral theory of the firm.

A third problem is that, with the exception of a few configuration studies, the behavioral approaches just outlined are *restricted to one or two levels of analysis.* In this they are similar to almost all strategic theorizing to date, but expansion and integration are needed. Even more problematic, relatively few theorists have followed up on the idea that individuals, groups, organizations, industries, and other social systems "enact" (Weick, 1979, 1995) circumstances around them.

Finally, there is *relatively little attention to the consequences of firm activity over time*. Many studies in the evolution tradition are interested in time-based data, but death is often the simplistic (though compelling) consequence of interest. A few dynamic/analytic studies and some configuration studies, especially Mintzberg's work with Waters (1982, 1984) and studies by Miller and his colleagues (1996; Miller & Friesen, 1980, 1984; Miller & Shamsie, 1996), point the way toward theories that include changing options and more complex interactions.

Some cognitive theories can be criticized along the same lines. However, as a whole, we believe they have the potential to extend the theory of the firm in each of these areas.

CONTRIBUTIONS FROM A COGNITIVE PERSPECTIVE

Economic theories of the firm began with questions of "Why do firms exist?" "What determines their output?" and "What is their optimal form?" Behavioral theories consider "What are the social and political requirements of organizing?" and raise the question of "Why do firms differ?" Cognitive theories can elaborate on explanations of firm difference and are uniquely equipped to ask, "How do individuals and collectives uniquely interpret complex and changing environments, and how does this knowledge inform action?" As a consequence of asking this question, we believe it is possible to give more satisfactory answers to questions of particular importance to the strategy field, especially "When and why will a specific firm deliberately change course?" and "In what direction and how far will it move?"[1]

The cognitive perspective is not new to the strategy literature. Both Mintzberg (1990) and Lyles (1990) included cognitive work in reviews of the field a decade ago, and it is increasingly likely that strategy research, particularly in the behavioral traditions just mentioned, will give some attention to cognition. Nonetheless, the contributions of a cognitive perspective are not well established. Mintzberg, Ahlstrand, and Lampel's recent review of 10 different schools of thought in strategy suggests that the cognitive perspective is one of three areas of increasing activity (1998, 353) but asserts that this work "is characterized more by its potential than its contribution" (1998, 172). They wish that extensive studies of decision bias, for example, were augmented by evidence of how complex inputs are integrated. They would like those who take a subjective approach to say more about the consequences of creative solutions and request more work on collective cognitive processes. This book addresses each of these important issues, while arguing more generally for the complementarity of economic, behavioral, and cognitive approaches.

Social Psychology Sources for Understanding Cognition in Organizations

Cognition, "the action or faculty of knowing taken in its widest sense" (*Oxford English Dictionary*, 1971, 596), is of interest in many disciplines. Organization scholars have been particularly attentive to work from social psychology, which "considers how people ask questions about the world, and organize the answers, so that they are able to act in, and on, those worlds" (Hosking & Morley, 1991, 20). Inquiry into "acting in the world" has obvious attractions for a professional discipline, and the growth of cognitive psychology came at a fortuitous time. Jim Walsh suggests that:

> During the 1970s, we saw the rise of resource dependence . . . population ecology . . . and transaction cost economics . . . as explanations for firm behavior. These three theoretical perspectives shifted the focus away from individual managers as a locus of firm performance. . . . What was lacking was a fresh theoretical perspective to consider how managers might increase or decrease firm value. Enter cognition. Interest in managerial and organizational cognition slightly lagged what proved to be an explosion of interest in things cognitive in social psychology. (1995, 280)

Walsh reviews the literature on managerial and organizational psychology with the help of a general schematic, which we slightly modify in Figure 1.1. This figure can be used to summarize conclusions from a large and increasingly varied body of cognitive research, including some work referred to as "representational," "computational," and "propositional," which we discuss in greater detail in chapter 2. In overview, a deal of empirical evidence suggests that individuals are able to process only a small portion of the many stimuli their environments make accessible. To make sense of the stimuli that do come to their attention, they create organizing schema, or knowledge structures. These structures highlight some stimuli as more important than others. They also augment currently available cues on the basis of past experience. Perhaps most important for the human capacity to "act in the world," knowledge frameworks establish connections among stimuli and with other knowledge structures.

Cognitive research from an interpretive perspective emphasizes that the events attended to are related to the perceiving actor—all interpretations (including the observing social scientist's) are made from a particular point of view and are enmeshed in the actor's own activities. Furthermore, knowledge structures not only construe current context but also anticipate the future and make sense of the past. When interpretations change, understanding of this temporal context is also likely to change.

Not all codified information is put to use, of course; storage in memory and retrieval from memory are unreliable. The use of knowledge frameworks can be untrustworthy, as a great deal of research on decision bias has shown. Individuals also frequently act on "automatic pilot" without reconsidering the appropriateness of the patterns they follow. Nonetheless, most cognitive researchers would agree that many outcomes are monitored, and the interpretation of these observations becomes part of a context from which further knowledge may be created.

This generalized explanation is especially compatible with schema theories that dominated work on managerial and organizational cognition in the 1980s and 1990s but is meant to be at least partially compatible with other accounts of individual cognition now available, as further discussed in chapters 2 and 3. The schematic paradigm is itself supported by work undertaken from quite different ontological and epistemological perspectives, and different theorists emphasize very different aspects of the overall account. Positivists often rely on information-processing perspectives familiar from dy-

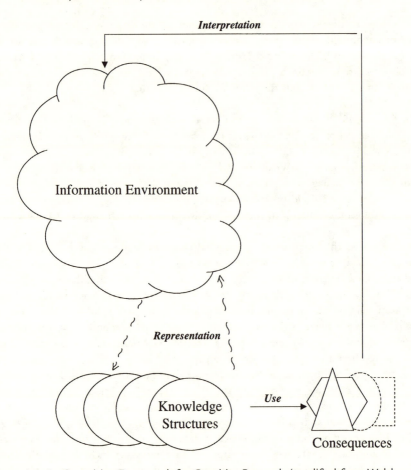

Figure 1.1 An Organizing Framework for Cognitive Research (modified from Walsh, 1995)

namic/analytic theories. Many cognitive scientists (e.g., Anderson, 1983; Schank, 1984), operating under a positivist umbrella, saw strong parallels between computer and mental processing. Corner, Kinicki, and Keats (1994) make an analogous argument that individuals and organizations have similar processes of attention, encoding, storing, and retrieving information. An extensive body of work documents bias in each of these processes (Makridakis, 1990; Tenbrunsel, Galvin, Neale & Bazerman, 1996; Das and Teng, 1999), though shortcomings are potentially remedied by collective and individual problem-solving standards.

Those who take a subjective, interpretive approach underscore the problematic nature of assumptions made by positivists—a group that includes virtually all economists and behavioralists interested in developing theories of the firm. Weick (1979, 1995), for example, highlights the difficulty of "punctuating" the stream of stimuli that surrounds individuals and organizations. He quotes Winograd and Flores (1986, 35) who insist that actors often "do not have a stable representation of the situation: patterns may be evident after the fact, but at the time the flow unfolds there is nothing but arbitrary fragments capable of being organized into a host of different patterns or possibly no pattern whatsoever" (Weick, 1995, 44).

Interpretivists thus provide very different answers to the cognitive question "How do individuals and collectives uniquely interpret complex and changing environments, and how does this knowledge inform action?" To begin with, as Mintzberg et al. report:

> For the *interpretative* or *constructionist* view, what is inside the human mind is not a reproduction of the external world. All that information flowing in through those filters, supposedly to be decoded by those cognitive maps, in fact interacts with cognition and is shaped by it. The mind, in other words, imposes some interpretation on the environment—it constructs its world. (1998, 165)

This is a distinctive epistemological perspective, akin to Feyerabend's in the philosophy of science (Huff, 1981), that has rarely been given attention by strategy researchers. It supports a view of human cognition that emphasizes the capacity "to slide, on the smallest provocation, into entirely new reaction patterns.... The only function of rational discourse may consist in increasing the mental tension that precedes *and causes* the behavioral outbursts" (Feyerabend, 1970, 217). The interpretive and other nonpositivist perspectives, including narrative theory (Czarniawska, 1997), postmodernism (Hatch, 1997), autopoiesis (vonKrogh & Roos, 1996), and structuration theory (Whittington, 1992; Tenkasi & Boland, 1993), interest us because they suggest insight-generating mechanisms critical to strategic advantage.

A second primary division in the cognitive literature has to do with its scope. Although some cognitive scientists are concerned only with neurology or with "cognitive architecture," social psychologists are united by an agreement that social context strongly affects and is affected by each aspect of Figure 1.1. Yet these researchers, including those in the organization sciences, vary in their opinion about whether the cognitive processes described for individuals can be extended to groups. The conservative position is that cognition can only be an attribute of individuals (Spender, 1998, 13). From the early days of cognitive research, however, many participants believed that social life and collective action involved a wide range of more or less shared frames of reference (Barley, 1986; Gioia & Sims, 1986a; Poole, Gioia & Gray, 1989; Louis & Sutton, 1991; Adler & Hass, 1992; Haas, 1992; Barr & Huff, 1997; Murtha, Lenway & Bagozzi, 1998). This assumption continues to be attractive, even though empirical work indicates that direct overlap in schematic representations is unlikely (Donnellon et al., 1986; Walsh, Henderson & Deighton, 1988; Langfield-Smith, 1992; Daniels, de Chernatony & Johnson, 1995; Johnson, 1999).

Weick (1995), a member of this second camp, quotes Hedberg (1981) to suggest that "theories of action" "are for organizations what cognitive structures are for individuals. They filter and interpret signals from the environment and tie stimuli to responses. They are metalevel systems that supervise the identification of stimuli and the assembling of responses" (1981, 7–8). Weick's (1995, 122) graphic depiction, based on Hedberg, is shown in Figure 1.2.

It is important to see, as with all circular models, that explanation can begin at any point. Thus, Figure 1.2 potentially unites more positivist work on managerial and organizational cognition, which focuses on the creation of knowledge structures and their

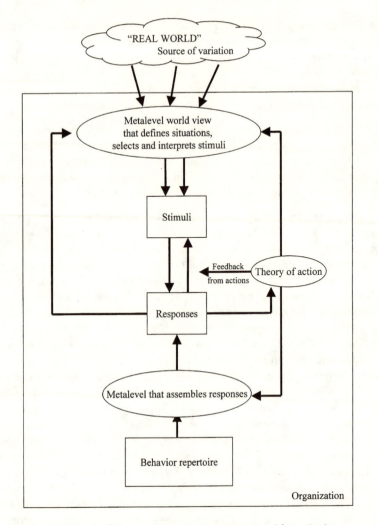

Figure 1.2 An S-R Model of How an Organization Interacts with Its Environment (modified from Weick, 1995)

potential influence on action, with Weick (1979, 1995), Starbuck (1983), and others' insistence that action leads to interpretations from which knowledge structures are formed. Figure 1.2 can also be interpreted in terms of Nelson and Winter's (1982) work on organizational routines, which are quite similar to theories of action, and to Smith et al.'s (1992) emphasis on communication, which can be more loosely linked to stimulus, response, and feedback. Furthermore, the overall form of this model is isomorphic with Walsh's discussion of the generation of knowledge structures depicted in Figure 1.1. Weick puts the formation and representation of knowledge structures into an organizational context; both individual cognition and metalevel routines, though complex in real settings, help define and are defined by context and activity.

Potential Theories of the Firm from a Cognitive Perspective

The preceding discussion suggests several approaches that can be compared with other theories of the firm, though with only one exception (Nooteboom, 1996) cognitive work has not to our knowledge been formally developed into distinct theories of the firm. Five candidates are shown in Table 1.3.

Decision Making and Choice.   The study of decision making significantly predates contemporary work on managerial and organizational cognition. Butler suggests that Chester Barnard (1938, 11) "put decision-making at the core of organization theory and the study of managerial work. At that time, there was a good reason for this since the predominant model of industrial and commercial organization was a mechanistic-bureaucratic model against which Barnard's insights represented a break from the principles of Scientific Management" (Mintzberg, Waters, Pettigraw, & Butler, 1990, 11). Cyert and March's (1963) work is one of the many responses to this reorientation included under our review of behavioral theories of the firm, but cognitive research has more recently made a number of unique and important contributions.

As Walsh (1995) observes, a great deal of attention in the first period of recent cognitive research has been given to establishing the schematic grounds of decision making (e.g., Shrivastava & Schneider, 1984; Lord & Foti, 1986; Stubbart, 1989; Lyles & Schwenk, 1992). A related idea is that subsequent decisions are likely to be "scripted" by these mental frameworks (Gioia & Mantz, 1985). The perceptions, problem definitions, and choices of decision makers are typically assumed to be strongly affected by prior experience (Beyer et al., 1997), as illustrated by Dearborn and Simon's (1958) early empirical evidence that departmental background is related to the most important problems managers identify in case studies. Prahalad and Bettis's (1986) particularly influential article suggested that firms differ because they develop different "dominant logics." Stimpert and Duhaime (1997), for example, use this idea to explain differences in the descriptions of relatedness offered by managers of diversified firms and the measures used in conventional academic research.

J.-C. Spender (Grinyer & Spender, 1979; Spender 1980, 1989) had an important impact on the study of strategic decision making from a cognitive perspective by identifying commonalities, or "recipes," in decisions made across firms. Huff (1982) pointed to interaction, common experiences, shared information sources, and other reasons that such commonalities might occur. An extensive stream of work originating at the University of Illinois added to the understanding of competitor identification and interaction (Porac, Thomas & Emme, 1987; Porac, Thomas & Baden-Fuller, 1989; Porac & Thomas, 1990; Reger, 1990; Reger & Huff, 1993; Fiegenbaum & Thomas, 1995; Fiegenbaum, Hart, & Schendel, 1996; Barr & Huff, 1997). Many others had similar interests. Baum and Mezias (1992) found hotel managers used common cues to identify the competitors they monitor most closely. Greve's (1998) data suggest that firms use information to move away from crowded market positions. Other studies, such as those conducted by Gerry Johnson and his colleagues (Hodgkinson & Johnson, 1994; Calori, Johnson & Sarnin, 1992; Daniels, deChernatony & Johnson, 1995), indicate, however, that there is considerable variation in mental models held by different individuals, even when they participate in apparently homogeneous settings.

Table 1.3 Potential Cognitive Theories of the Firm

Theory	Orientation	Process of Discovery	Central Research Problem	Theoretic Conceptualization of the Firm	Manager's Motives/Behavior	Goals of Firm	Nature of Environment
Decision making and choice	Primarily positive/ some interpretive	Inductive/ deductive	What are the characteristics of rational analysis and problem solving? What procedures can overcome bias in decision-making processes?	A boundedly rational actor	Establish reliable decision-making procedures/focus on representing the task environment, specifying goals, searching for alternative actions, choosing the best alternative to fit goals	Survival, profit	A setting that establishes temporal decision points and offers alternatives for action
Culture	Positive/ interpretive	Inductive/ deductive	Understanding the assumptions and basic vocabulary that create cohesion	A social system responding to a larger culture, creating its own culture and subcultures	Use symbols to mobilize support/subject to cultural symbols and assumptions	Grounded in and limited by culture	Source of and transmitter of symbols
Knowledge acquisition and use	Positive/ interpretive	Deductive/ inductive	What needs to be known in order to act? How can firms effectively acquire, store, update, and use knowledge?	A collection of knowledge assets and a means of extending individual learning capabilities and knowledge	Create purpose, broker information, challenge status quo/hire and train knowledge workers	Respond to changing circumstances with structures that promote learning and knowledge application	A field that can be manipulated and changed; a source of stimuli and feedback

Sensemaking	Interpretive	Deductive/inductive	How do individuals and groups recognize and interpret stimuli? How do they generate what they interpret?	Net of activities	Understand interruptions in the ongoing flow of activity/ "Author" coherent interpretations and actions	Often not central to sensemaking	Source of physical stimuli. Social setting dominated by talk, symbols, promises, lies, agreements, threats, expectations, etc.
Change	Positive/interpretive	Deductive/inductive	When, why, how much, and in what direction will firms change strategy?	A sociopolitical setting that generates satisficing outcomes diverse stakeholders	Establish "theories of action" to guide behavior in new situations/both conservative and excitable	Adapt to maintain satisficing routines; invent new routines if necessary	A setting of variation and structure influencing but enacted by human activity

21

Other research streams are more directly linked to a problem-solving focus. Winograd and Flores (1986, 14–26) do a good job of outlining how Simon's (1976) argument that human decision makers inevitably fall short of a rational ideal shaped the early agenda of cognitive science as a whole, especially work in artificial intelligence. As already noted, many cognitive scientists based their models on a computing metaphor (Rumelhart, 1989), and conversely, the computer was seen as a tool to help human decision makers more perfectly apply knowledge and make decisions (Winograd & Flores, 1986, 72). Though early confidence in the capacity of computers to mimic idealized human problem-solving capabilities has largely evaporated, a problem-solving logic continues to inform the use of computers in organizations, and a focus on decision making by boundedly rational actors continues to be an influential area of theorizing.

Behavioral decision theorists, led especially by Tversky and Kahneman (1974), have significantly elaborated on the heuristics and biases that lead individuals to depart from a rational ideal. A recent summary (Tenbrunsel et al., 1996, 320–321) of work by organization researchers points to bias associated with ease of recall, retrievability, presumed associations, insensitivity to base rates, insensitivity to sample size, misconceptions of chance, regression to the mean, anchoring, misestimation of the probabilities of conjunctive and disjunctive events, overconfidence, seeking confirmatory evidence, hindsight, and irrelevant information. Following such research findings, Duhaime and Schwenk (1985), Schwenk (1988), Bukszar and Connolly (1988), Zajac and Bazerman (1991), Markóczy and Goldberg (1998), and others have discussed why strategists may make nonrational, or apparently nonrational, decisions.

Then again, Pondy and Huff (1985) and Huff (1985) suggest that acting "as if" rational decision models are a sufficient ground for decision making may facilitate collective action. Georg vonKrogh and Johan Roos (1996, 732) outline ways in which Bettis and Prahalad's (1995) updated understanding of "domiant logic" has become much less representational, defining cognition as a creative act of bringing forth a subjective world. Starbuck and Milliken (1988) argue that accurate representation of an external world may not be possible or required, but most cognitive researchers believe that how the strategic situation is defined does make a difference. Jane Dutton's (Dutton, Fahey & Narayanan, 1983; Dutton & Jackson, 1987; Dutton, Walton & Abrahamson, 1989) work, for example, helpfully explores the implications of perceiving threats versus opportunities.

These and other theorists assume that individuals and organizations face problematic situations that can be improved, if not resolved, by identifying and choosing among alternative actions. Though their cognitive capacities are limited, managers are described as being able to develop decision-making routines, organization structures, control mechanisms, decision-support systems, and other devices to improve the processes of (1) defining a task environment, (2) setting goals, (3) identifying alternatives, and (4) making choices.

Culture

Deal and Kennedy (1982) and Schein (1985) were among the first to alert those interested in strategy and its successful implementation to the importance of organizational culture. A cultural perspective asserts that social groups, including firms, share at least some assumptions, values, and beliefs. Though they are often unexpressed, these commonalities are partially revealed in the creation and use of language and symbolic artifacts (Pondy, Frost, Morgan, & Dandridge, 1983). A cultural perspective often emphasizes the symbolic importance of managerial activities (Pondy, 1978; Pettigrew, 1979; Johnson, 1987, 1990; Pettigrew, Ferlic & McFee, 1992), but an interesting implication of this approach to understanding the firm is that managers are themselves part of and subject to organizational culture.

The cultural perspective might well have been included with behavioral theories. However, Hatch points out that "the conceptualization of organizational culture was influenced from the beginning by the symbolic-interpretive perspective ... [which] involves discovering how insiders experience and construct their world ... rather than imposing the researchers' meaning and interpretations upon them" (1997, 201):

> The symbolic-interpretive approach teaches us that symbols are inherently ambiguous; members of a culture can give different meanings to the same symbol as well as use different symbols to convey the same meaning. However, even though members may give ambiguous symbols private interpretations, their interpretations are formed under a more or less constant barrage of influence provided by other members of the culture.... Interpretations are not made in a vacuum, rather they like the culture that embeds them are socially constructed realities. (1997, 220)

Siehl and Martin's defining statement is that culture is "the glue that holds an organization together through ... values, beliefs, and expectations that members come to share" (1983. 227). Organization stories (Wilkins, 1983; Boje, 1991) have been highlighted as an important aspect of culture, particularly salient in helping newcomers understand the unique nature of a particular setting (Louis, 1980). But culture is also important for formal organization. Lou Pondy (1978) describes management as a "language game." Prasad (1993) argues that computer systems and other technologies are intrinsically symbolic. Johnson (Johnson & Scholes, 1999) uses the term "cultural web" to indicate interconnections among stories, symbols, rituals, and routines that are supported by organization structures, control systems, and power relationships to create a unique organizational "paradigm."

Hatch points out that research on culture often has a "modernist" agenda, typified by its interest in control. If the overarching concern is with the cohesion assumed necessary for collective action, the study of breakdowns in common assumptions is also of interest. Floyd and Wooldridge (1992, 2000), for example, cast considerable doubt on the extent to which strategic assumptions and agendas formulated at the top of the organization are understood or shared by middle managers. Various researchers (Pettigrew, 1985; Bartunek & Moch, 1987; Johnson, 1987; Chesley & Huff, 1998) have attributed the failure of change efforts to the difficulty of breaking down established cultures. Hatch's (1997, 213) description of a postmodernist perspective highlights the fragmented nature of human experience; in consequence, she suggests, people are likely to accept a variety of assumptions, even if they are internally inconsistent. The influence of culture is further complicated by the fact that individuals are potentially affected by cultural assumptions and values from different social systems (Sackman, 1991), including regional (Hofstede, 1980; Maruyama, 1984, 1994), national (Schneider, 1989), professional (Van Mannen & Barley, 1984), and industrial (Phillips, 1990) connections, in addition to cultural influences from the firm (Barney, 1986a;) and subgroups within the firm (Siehl & Martin, 1984).

Knowledge Acquisition and Use. Rational choice, by definition, is not possible without searching for and using knowledge. Research on culture depends in part on identifying shared knowledge and beliefs. Yet, knowledge acquisition and use is a growing area of inquiry that can be usefully distinguished as a third and separate area of cognitive theory. Nonaka and Takeuchi's (1995) report on Asian companies' experience, especially their regard for tacit knowledge, is a landmark in this literature. Crossan, Lane, and White (1999) provide a multilevel framework for understanding how individual learning is reinforced by interpretive and integrating organizational mechanisms in organizations. Indeed, *organizational* learning is typically the subject of interest in this line of research, in contrast to work on choice, which tends to be more individually oriented.

While many focus on learning explicitly (Fiol & Lyles, 1985; Huber, 1991), we prefer the broader terms of "knowledge management" or "knowledge acquisition and use" because learning often is identified with a change in mental schema or activity (Crossan, Lane & White, 1999, 523), which, in our view, is too restrictive. Knowledge may or may not be connected with change; its deployment in an organizational setting is important in its own right.

Ginsberg (1994) and Grant (1996) point out that resource-base theory needs to understand knowledge acquisition and use. Drawing on Demsetz (1991, 172), Grant emphasizes the capacity of the firm to provide directions that communicate specialist knowledge to others at low cost. Routines generalize and codify these directions. To do so, they depend upon some common knowledge and a sophisticated system of signaling. Henderson and Clark (1990) and Henderson (1993) provide details about how knowledge can be aggregated across subgroup boundaries and hierarchical levels. Cohen and Levinthal (1990) propose that the capacity to benefit from alliance and other relationships also depends on "absorptive capacity." Garud and Nayyar (1994) emphasize "transformative capacity"—the ability to maintain internally developed technology over time.

Learning is not necessarily an even process. Lant, Milliken, and Batra (1992) are among those who propose that learning is often triggered by perceptions of unsatisfactory performance. Others (Huff, 1988; Bartunek, Kolb, & Lewicki, 1992) emphasize conflict as a generative device. A critical idea, articulated by Donald Schön (e.g., 1983) and others (Brown, 1988; Hatch, 1997; Crossan & Sorrenti, 1997), is that "reflective practitioners" know much more than they can readily articulate and they use this knowledge to improvise in a flow of activity. Various authors (e.g., Cohen, 1991; Crossan, Lane & White, 1999) have cautioned, however, that intuitive and other solutions are unlikely to have a sustained impact on the organization unless the insights gained are integrated by groups of individuals and institutionalized in organizational routines, rules, and procedures. Another frequently cited risk is that past knowledge can become a liability. Hedberg (1981) was an early proponent of the importance of "unlearning" as organizational situations change. An important middle ground is articulated by March (1991), who notes that learning involves adaptively exploiting "old certainties," while also exploring new possibilities.

Bartlett and Ghoshal (1993) are among those who conclude that knowledge use will be increasingly important to firms. Their study of 19 organizations from around the world suggests that "the combined impact of... slowing market growth, accelerating technological change and transforming organizational process was to shift the focus of many firms from allocating capital to managing knowledge and learning as the key strategic task" (1993, 41). The structural result in the companies they studied was "a devolution of assets and accountability from the corporate to the division level," with a consequent reorganization of managerial roles. Top managers, they propose, create purpose and challenge the status quo, while middle managers broker information and integrate the capabilities of entrepreneurial front-line managers. Miles et al. (1997) similarly propose that the need to develop the learning capacity of organizations leads to "cellular" forms of organization.

A number of organizing frameworks have been proposed to understand these and other learning issues. Argote (1999) summarizes the extensive evidence on learning curve improvements over time. Granovetter's (1973) work on networks has been used to explore the learning implications of different kinds of associations (Mezias & Lant, 1994; Buchko, 1995). Peter Senge (1990) emphasizes systems thinking (often conceived as positivist) with action-oriented intervention techniques that are much more interpretive in tone to stress the importance of "personal mastery," and "dialogue" as a route to organizational "communities."

The unifying assumptions in most of these works is that the environment is a "field" of stimuli and feedback that is stable enough to merit the accumulation of knowledge but nonetheless can be manipulated and changed (Lant & Mezias, 1992; Rajagopalan & Spreitzer, 1996). The emphasis for managers is less on finding an optimal, or best, strategy than on identifying key components and relationships in changing environments, observing the results of experiments, and continuing to modify thoughts and behavior.

Sensemaking. Early, influential work emphasized the importance of a cognitive perspective by pointing to the equivocal nature of many situations in and around organizations (Kiesler & Sproull, 1982; Smircich & Stubbart, 1985). These situations often allow more than one plausible interpretation (Daft & Weick, 1984), which can impede action if not resolved (Westley, 1990). Though it overlaps with the learning literature, this line of thought is worth separate attention.

An active line of investigation drew on work in cognitive psychology on attribution (Fiske & Taylor, 1991, 21–56). One widely duplicated finding was that performance attribution tends to be "self-serving." Bowman (1976), for example, showed that annual reports typically blame poor returns on external events, while executives claim credit for success. Similar patterns were found by a number of researchers (Bettman & Weitz, 1983; Staw, McKechnie & Puffer, 1983), though academic research quickly replicated the equivocality of interpretation within itself. Salancik and Meindl (1984) proposed that the need to manage public opinion was an alternative explanation for what appeared to be a self-serving bias. Huff and Schwenk (1990) suggested that the need to reconsider the organization's circumstances makes it more likely and more appropriate to discuss the environment when results are disappointing. Wagner and Gooding (1997) found more relationships among internal and external attributions.

The sensemaking perspective includes a good deal of ambitious work that is less rationally oriented than this stream of research. In fact, Karl Weick, who has done the most to articulate sensemaking as a distinct point of view, claims that the sensemaking perspective goes beyond interpretation because it emphasizes not just the reading of "texts" but "the ways people generate what they interpret" (1995, 13). The point, as noted in our earlier overview, is that individuals help create the environments they are involved in interpreting (Pondy & Mitroff, 1979; Morgan, Frost, and Pondy, 1983; Ring & Rands, 1989).

Sensemaking efforts are most evident "when predictions break down" (Louis, 1980, 241; Winograd & Flores, 1986, 36–37; Weick, 1995, 5), which highlights sensemaking as an important activity for strategy theorists to understand, in that strategy often is defined in terms of "messy" or "wicked" problems that cannot be easily resolved (Eisenhardt & Zbaracki, 1992). One critical theme in the sensemaking literature is that in crisis individuals and collectives tend to move from an automatic processing mode to more conscious cognitive activity (Hastie, 1984; Louis & Sutton, 1991), though crisis can also be debilitating (Holsti, 1971), and research suggests that such sensemaking is often temporary and reversible (Goffman, 1974; Trice, 1993; Drazin, Glynn & Kazanjian, 1999; Johnson, 1999). Sensemaking also is influenced by emotion (Park, Sims & Motowidlo, 1996; Sackman, 1991, 41; Walsh, 1995, 307; Daniels, 1998) and other noncognitive phenomena that are intrinsic to the circumstances being made sense of, but these factors are just beginning to be explored as part of the sensemaking process.

Although at times "history is not generous with experience" (March, Sproull & Tamuz, 1991) and can be "a poor teacher" (Levinthal & March, 1993, 96), in general, action is seen as an important input to sensemaking (as it is in many learning theories). Starbuck (1983; Starbuck & Milliken, 1988) has already been cited for insisting on the importance of experience preceding understanding. Furthermore, he argues there are often low returns from seeking highly accurate models in a changing world. The search for payoff may be an illusion from "scientific" modes of thinking that are better abandoned in an intrinsically equivocal world (Starbuck, 1999).

Many of those interested in sensemaking would agree with this proposition; they seek to understand the development of more "organic" understanding. A key point of departure is the proposal that making sense, especially when uncertain, depends upon a "situated" understanding of self, or identity (Fiol, 1991; Fiol & Huff, 1992; Hatch, 1997, 255; Whetten & Godfrey, 1998). Weick, for example, writes:

> Depending on who I am, my definition of what is "out there" will also change. Whenever I define self, I define "it," but to define it is also to define self. Once I know who I am then I know what is out there. But the direction of causality flows just as often from the situation to a definition of self as it does the other way.... This is why the establishment and maintenance of identity is a core preoccupation in sensemaking. (1995, 20)

A compatible line of theorizing emphasizes a "narrative" perspective on cognition, typically characterized in direct opposition to computational, schematic approaches

(Tenkasi & Boland, 1993). Barbara Czarniawska (1997) is among those who have argued that individuals, groups, and organizations construct an ongoing story as they interact, which informs and is informed by identity, intent, and action. Barry and Elmes (1997) argue that strategy is itself a narrative. The power of stories has already been mentioned in the discussion of culture, and metaphors are another and perhaps more active entry into sensemaking, in that they require the user to imagine links between subjects that are not normally considered similar (Huff, 1980a; Hill & Levenhagen, 1995). One conclusion of work on identity, narrative, and metaphor is that informal interactions are often more important than formal ones. The social setting is dominated by talk from this perspective (Boyce, 1995; Taylor & Lerner, 1996)—gossip, lies, and threats, as well as expectations, promises, and agreements.

Hosking and Morley and others (Winograd & Flores, 1986; Weick, 1995) advise focusing on organizations as networks of particular tasks or projects in trying to understand talk and other contributions to sensemaking. A project can be seen "as a set of conversations which commit people to some future action. . . . The people concerned will expect to have to justify their actions, or their failures to act. Such conversations provide the process, and constitute the context, in which our most important cognitions are formed" (Hosking & Morley, 1991, 93). Though not intended as a theory of the firm, the definition of the *organization* as a "network of projects," along with the description of an equivocal environment most likely to gain attention when unexpected "disruptions" occur, is a distinctive line of argument that can be compared with other theories of the firm.

Change. We see work on change from a cognitive perspective as offering a fifth set of assumptions, though it overlaps with the other cognitive perspectives just described and often borrows from behavioral and economic theory as well. *Change* means to "substitute one thing for another," "to make (a thing) other than it was," "to become different, undergo alteration . . . vary." It also means "the act of changing" and "the different orders in which a set or series of things can be arranged" (*Oxford English Dictionary*, 1971, 267–268). Though a great deal has been written about change in static terms, the latter, more dynamic definitions are beginning to attract the attention of strategy and other organizational researchers.

We have already noted some work from economic and behavioral perspectives interested in change. Barbara Senior's (1997) detailed summary of change research distinguishes "hard" and "soft" approaches. Drawing on Flood and Jackson (1991), Senior notes that "hard" or rational procedures work best "where simple systems and unitary relationships prevail" (1997, 230). In situations of "soft complexity," characterized by complex systems and pluralist ideologies, less rational, more incremental interventions and processes are more likely to alter current patterns of activity. A prescriptive tone and focus on activism are obvious in this definition and are distinctive features of change research.

Our interest is in the second set of circumstances Senior describes. We believe that "hard" change processes are relatively easy to effect, though not as widespread as often assumed. "Soft" processes are much more difficult (Kanter, Stein & Jick, 1992) but more characteristic of strategy. Rajagopalan and Spreitzer (1996) praise the large samples and explicit operationalizations in rational studies, the dynamic approach of some authors (e.g., Ginsberg & Buchholtz, 1990; Kelly & Amburgey, 1991), and the frequent concern with antecedents and performance effects in rational studies. Nonetheless, they conclude that:

> In spite of these strengths, the rational lens perspective has provided little cumulative knowledge on strategic change because . . . the rational perspective treats the role of managerial actions and cognitions as a "black box." Such managerial processes, "namely the socio-cultural and symbolic processes which preserve current ways of doing things, the cognitive bounds of those who take and influence decisions, and the importance of political processes," are central to the strategic change process (Johnson, 1992: 34). The equivocal findings on context make us wonder about the role that managers play in shaping the need for change and reducing *resistance* to it. (1997, 55, emphasis in the original)

The quotation from Johnson (1992) specifies the primary dimensions cognitive researchers are now beginning to use as they try to answer questions about "the need for change and reducing resistance to it." They tend to use multiple theoretic lens. They pay attention to social, cultural, and political processes. Most studies are longitudinal, with strongly qualitative data collections. They are concerned with uniting thought and action by attending to content and process.

We have already noted our interest in questions of when, why, how much, and in what direction firms change strategy. An important foundation for using a cognitive perspective to help answer such questions can be found in studies motivated by discrepancies between rational models of decision making and observed firm behavior. Braybrooke and Lindbloom's (1963) influential book describes bureaucratic phenomena that slow change and make it less linear than initially intended. Allison (1971) developed multiple models to more fully understand the Cuban Missile crisis. Quinn's (1978, 1980) work on "rational" incrementalism clarifies the requirements and utility of slower change.

One result of this work and the many studies that followed these beginnings has been to make even the identification of "a decision" problematic. Minzberg and Waters (1990) suggest that a long line of people (including themselves) who thought they were studying "decision making" were, in fact, studying "actions." Eden and Ackermann draw on but extend Mintzberg and Waters's (1985) work to describe "emergent strategizing" as an ongoing process, "a stream of actions that are not random but form a pattern—a pattern which, as Mintzberg points out, usually becomes evident as such after the event rather than before" (1998, 21–22). Lundberg (1984) uses the word *decisioning* to describe the same flow.

When the world is seen in this amorphous way, the basic vocabulary of cognitive studies becomes very helpful, though, as we discuss in chapter 2, cognitive studies provide additional ambiguities. The development of knowledge structures, which can be defined in several ways, is not automatic. It involves, as Gioia and Chittipeddi (1991) point out, "sense giving" as well as "sense making." It often encounters cultural roadblocks because "the way in which members of an organization behave and decide is related to who they are and how they think within a particular organizational culture—a culture within which, to a greater or lesser extent, they have been able to presume ways of working" (Eden & Ackermann, 1998, 29). Furthermore, decisioning confronts political realities that have implications for "emergent cognizing" as well as emergent strategizing:

> Within the "everyday" process of emergent strategizing, managers talk and think about others who have a stake in the organization, in particular those who have the power to influence the future they are seeking to create. . . . Tensions derive from the extent to which adaptations to the environment and to stakeholder's expectations require resource shifts, possible restructuring . . . new products, new ways of working and so on. These shifts, in turn, inevitably mean there will be winners and losers in the organization. Anticipating such outcomes, powerful managers in the organization play up some issues, play down others and fight to retain their own power. (Eden & Ackermann, 1999, 23)

Our own work is compatible with this description of the motivated thoughts and sociopolitical processes of strategic change. It builds on descriptions of individual and group change to predict the timing, scope, and direction of significant redirection at the organization. Before outlining our work in more detail, however, it is instructive to summarize differences between the cognitive theories we have just described and the behavioral and economic theories of the firm outlined earlier.

Defining Characteristics of Cognitive Theories

Economic theories emphasize a vocabulary of cost, price, and profit; their defining interest is in "output" and "structure." Behavioral theories shift attention to interaction, influence, and exchange as the vocabulary of "process." Work in cognition, across many different fields, has focused on knowledge structures, memory, attention, attribution, and problem-solving. The defining word for cognitive theory would seem to be *understanding* or *coherence*.

Cognitive theories are an interesting addition to other theories of the firm in many different ways, in part because they mingle interpretive and positivist approaches. The economic and behavioral theories that have dominated the strategy field are almost always positivist; they tacitly assume that firms and markets are objectively, though imperfectly, knowable by managers and researchers. Some cognitive work also takes this position, as we have indicated, and a long tradition of laboratory work in the psychology field provides compelling components for deductive theory. Other cognitive researchers follow an interpretive line of theorizing that, has to date, been given less attention by the strategy field.

We believe that work on cognition from both positivist and interpretive perspectives deserves more prominence. Just as the theories we have labeled as behavioral theories of the firm shifted attention from the environment to processes within the firm, cognitive theories shift attention to the individual actor and groups of individual actors who are "logical, analytical, rational" but also "intuitive, insightful, perceptive, nonrational, and wholistic" (Gioia, 1986, 339).

The distinctiveness of a cognitive approach can be seen by comparing assertions made by theories from other perspectives with these characteristics of the cognitive perspectives just outlined.

1. *The **firm** as a social system is a unique site for sensemaking, learning, and problem-solving.* Many cognitive theorists insist that what individuals can know about the world depends not just on calculation or even interpretation of the stimuli that come to attention but on interaction with and creation of those stimuli as well. Cognition is thus the product of a unique history of experience. With the exception of rational theories of choice, most cognitive theories insist there is no neutral ground from which firms or markets can be independently described or evaluated. The coherence required to act (or purposefully not act) is a difficult, partial, and temporary objective. The firm as a unit of analysis, and a level of strategic practice, is the critical site for establishing this coherence (Pettigrew & Whipp, 1991).

2. *Managers (indeed all participants) are **motivated** to understand their own situation and the situation of the collectives that are important to them; human **behavior** is influenced by these sensemaking efforts.* Because a cognitive starting point emphasizes that people *think* about the circumstances around them and often act on these thoughts, managers in cognitive theory tend to be more powerful (though still fallible) than in most previous theories. This is a defining feature of a cognitive perspective. Descriptions of managerial behavior in economic theories of the firm have vacillated between assumed rationality (neoclassical microeconomics, traditional industrial organization, new industrial organization, and transaction cost theory) and rational self-interest (managerial economics and agency theory), though most economists now define *rationality* as bounded rationality (Simon, 1976). Behavioral theories add social and political limits but have made few changes in economic assumptions about rationality. For example, limited capacity to understand and imitate success (Lippman & Rumelt, 1982) is a central argument in resource-based theory. Cognitive theory does not just further restrict rationality when it insists upon the individual as a unique subjective site of understanding, influenced by social systems. More radical views abandon rationality as a helpful basis of theorizing in favor of more temporary, partial islands of coherence. It can be argued that this redefinition fits the changing economic landscape (Bettis & Hitt, 1995), particularly because it also focuses attention on the capacity to invent new understandings.

3. *The articulation of influential, shared **goals** is difficult; it is influenced by the interpretation, knowledge, and problem-solving abilities of individuals and by understandings shared with others.* Most cognitive theorists continue the traditional assumption of theories of the firm that leaders and other members of the organization are, in general, motivated to improve the firm's current situation. They add insight by suggesting that "improvement" is inherently equivocal, difficult to articulate, and subject to breakdown. However, to the extent coherence or cohesion exists at any level of analysis, cognitive theory suggests these frameworks are likely to affect understanding and aspirations at other levels of analysis.

4. *A firm's **environments** generate varying stimuli that tend to structure, but be structured by, cognition and action.* Organization-environment "boundaries," like "events," are seen by many cognitive theorists as an interpretive imposition. With this caveat, environments are of interest because they continue to present new stimuli, which often prompt new

interpretations and knowledge structures in individuals and the collectives that form out of their activities. The important implication is that strategy always has the raw material for transformation at hand.

We believe these are interesting and important additions to insights from the current arsenal of economic and behavioral theories. They do not supplant—but they do augment—economic and behavioral foundations for understanding strategy. This book on strategic change provides one example of how all three might work together.

INTRODUCTION TO A COGNITIVELY ANCHORED THEORY OF STRATEGIC CHANGE

We agree with Bartlett and Ghoshal (1993) that a globalizing world is changing the nature and needs of organizations by requiring them to be more quickly responsive to evolving circumstances. And we agree with Grant (1996) and others that this responsiveness relies heavily on internal resources. These and other influential authors focus on learning and knowledge deployment. Though learning is critical, we feel that the capacity to change is even more critical. Individuals and almost all organizations, even virtual ones, are not blank slates. "New" knowledge is gathered in context; it interacts with and becomes part of what is already known. An enormous amount of evidence suggests that past patterns affect and tend to dominate this process, even in those organizations that accept the need for significant renewal. We think change is a complex and problematic process—one that deserves continuing attention.

As we review the large but disparate body of work to date, it seems clear that multiple levels of analysis must be attended to. For instance, leadership, though necessary (Pondy, 1978; Greiner & Bhambri, 1989; Westley & Mintzberg, 1989; Covin & Kilmann, 1990; Isabella, 1990), is not sufficient to motivate new activities. Heroic accounts of change must be tempered with evidence about organizational readiness. One important aspect of readiness, highlighted by number of researchers (Bower, 1970; Burgelman, 1983, 1994; Floyd & Wooldridge, 2000; Balogun, 1999), involves middle managers as important sources of knowledge about the need for and possibilities of change. Their lack of involvement in imposed change programs helps account for failed programs and unanticipated outcomes (Beer, Eisenstat & Spector, 1990). More broadly, institutional theory, especially neo-institutional theory (DiMaggio & Powell, 1991; Scott, 1995; Greenwood & Hinings, 1996), makes a compelling case for considering the social canvas influencing and influenced by organizational activities.

The timing and framing of change efforts also are important and poorly understood. March's discussion of the exploitation-exploration distinction is a critical one. He points out that in many situations there is "a tendency to substitute exploitation of known alternatives for the exploration of unknown ones" (1991, 85). Weick and Westley provocatively argue that "organizing and learning are essentially antithetical processes" (1996, 440) but conclude that "learning is an ongoing and implicit feature of the organizing process. By this we mean that as organizing unfolds, it does so in ways that intermittently create a set of conditions where learning is possible" (1996, 456).

The chapters that follow focus on integrating levels of analysis and paying attention to the level and timing of change. The path we have taken, however, is also driven by a third observation, which is that anticipating and predicting the change efforts of competitors and stakeholders has received surprisingly little attention in the cognitive arena. The focus of research on change from a cognitive perspective has been on detail. It is frequently driven by case studies. It has worried about changes in "cognitive maps" (Huff, 1990). In this research effort, we wanted to acknowledge and use these insights but move on to more abstract formulations that might be used by strategists as they consider the critical competitive question of when and how competitors and other important actors might change the pattern of their activities. These strategists do not have the kind of information used to understand and design change within their own firm. Our objective is to develop cognitively *anchored* models that might be used at this necessarily more abstract level of analysis.

Key Variables and Relationships

One of the most important disciplining devices of the theory of the firm framework is that it requires specification of key variables and relationships. In the next three chapters, we attend to three paired concepts that we believe are useful vehicles for understanding when, why, where, and how much firms change. Table 1.4 provides a comparative overview of stress/inertia, first order/second order change, and position/opportunity at three levels of analysis considered in the 1st part of this book.

Each cell in this table is presumed to operate in the presence of processes described in all other cells. Collectively, they delineate three basic assumptions in the theoretic position we develop:

Assumption 1. Stress and Inertia

Intrinsically dynamic settings at all levels of analysis simultaneously engender pressures for change in current behavior and pressures for maintaining current behavior patterns.

This is a tension widely expressed in the change literature (Hedberg & Jönsson, 1978; Mintzberg, 1978; Miller & Friesen 1980, 1984; Tushman & Romanelli, 1985; Greenwood & Hinings, 1988; Fredrickson & Iaquinto, 1989; Schwenk & Tang, 1989; Fombrun & Ginsberg, 1990; Ginsberg & Buchholtz, 1990; Meyer, Brooks & Goes, 1990; March, 1991; Huff, Huff & Thomas, 1992; Amburgey, Kelly & Barnett, 1993; Baker & Cullen, 1993; Keck & Tushman, 1993; Smith, 1993; Zajac & Kraatz, 1993; Gersick, 1991, 1994; Romanelli & Tushman, 1994; Sastry, 1997). Its terms have tended to be defined by example (losing a major contract, making long-term capital investments, missing a technological window opportunity, etc.), but the definitions we develop in this book (at individual, group, organization, and industry levels) are grounded in studies of cognition from several different perspectives. *Inertia* increases as patterns of interpretation and behavior become increasingly routinized from one time period to the next, while *stress* grows out of a mismatch between expectations, interpretations, and behavior. The overarching idea is that the world has tendencies toward both order and disorder. The models we develop

Table 1.4 Key Assertions in the Cognitively Anchored Theory of the Firm

	Inertia ↔ Stress	First Order ↔ Second Order Change	Position ↔ Opportunity
Individual	Inertia arises from the reuse of schema available in the social setting and developed from the individual's own experience. Stress rises if stimuli attracting attention cannot be interpreted by established or invented schematic frameworks.	*1st*: probable because many stimuli are ignored, existing schema efficiently use past experience, and schema can be fine-tuned. *2nd*: more likely as threatening anomalies cannot be overlooked or explained—if alternative frameworks are invented.	Each individual's unique history, position within the firm, will, skill, and values provide opportunities for improving that person's own interests and the interests of others.
Group	Inertia increases as other affiliated individuals reinforce confidence in "shared" interpretations and practices. Stress increases if mavericks, newcomers, or other groups plausibly challenge shared cognition.	*1st*: probable because established coalitions have satisfied their constituents in the past. *2nd*: more likely as stakeholders doubt the benefits of current activities—if they can identify satisficing alternatives.	Each coalition's activities and network of relationships provide opportunities for generating and controlling desired information and other resources.
Firm	Inertia increases as the firm makes commitments and routinizes practices that allow individuals and groups to come and go without disrupting the status quo. Stress accumulates if the results of current strategy do not meet the performance expectations of key stakeholders.	*1st*: probable because organization outputs not only create some value but also involve activities that are costly for internal and external stakeholders to abandon or change. *2nd*: more likely as cumulative stress exceeds cumulative inertia—if an alternative strategy appears to reduce stress.	A firm's current resources and competitive position provide differential opportunities to more profitably interact with buyers, suppliers, competitors, and other actors.

go beyond simple plus-minus comparisons to pay attention to *cumulative* stress and inertia in organization contexts and how they grow and are discounted over time. This dynamic is articulated in greatest depth in chapters 4 and 8.

A second assumption questions part of the "hypercompetitive" world described by Hamel and Prahalad (1994), D'Aveni (1994), Brown and Eisenhardt (1997, 1998), and many others:

Assumption 2. First versus second order change

Dramatic change in behavior in the hope of more desirable outcomes is psychologically, socially and economically difficult; actors therefore tend to experiment with small homeostatic adaptations before attempting dramatic departures from past ways of acting. Dramatic change is more likely as unresolved stress grows relative to inertia.

Dichotomous definitions of change have been widely deployed (Watzlawick, Weakland & Fisch, 1974; Argyris, 1977; Argyris & Schön, 1978; Fiol & Lyles, 1985; Hrebiniak & Joyce, 1985; March, 1991; Meyer, Brooks & Goes, 1990). We disagree with strategy theorists who argue that first order–second order distinctions are a product of disappearing stabilities and that successful firms will have to change continuously. As already noted, we do believe that the capacity to change is increasingly a competitive necessity. Dramatic downsizing, reengineering, and changes in governance are restructuring the competitive landscape. Clearly, many organizations have changed.

However, we believe there are relatively few companies like Microsoft, the poster child of the hypercompetitive argument. More important, we believe that even aggressive actors develop recipes (Spender, 1989) that become influenced over time. That is why a hypercompetitive company like Microsoft finds it difficult to adapt to a challenger like Red Hat, as we discuss in more detail at the end of this volume. It explains why companies like USWest and Lucent Technologies continue to struggle with vestiges of Ma Bell. Significant second order change is not easy. We believe it is possible, but unlikely. What appears to be second order is often revealed to be entrenched patterns expressed in somewhat different vocabulary (Chesley, 1994; Johnson, 1999).

The first section of this book elaborates on this assertion in the following way. In chapter 2, we summarize a large body of research on the creation and adaptation of mental schema, emphasizing the stress typically involved in cognitively accounting for anomalies that go beyond experience. Schema theories are not the only accounts of cognitive activity, but we believe they continue to be a useful starting point in thinking about enduring patterns. In chapter 3, we consider the tendency of formal and informal groups to reinforce collective patterns of thinking and action but occasionally respond to and even reinforce inevitable concerns and insights that can lead to innovation and change. In chapter 4, we acknowledge the adaptive capacity of routines needed to perpetuate performance results but indicate that tensions, such as those created by competitors with higher performance, can be an externally recognizable tipping force that moves firms into considering second order change.

These chapters lead to (but were also informed by) several empirical studies. Chapter 6 investigates differential timing in response to changing regulation. Chapter 7 describes evolving definitions of alliance among biotech and established pharmaceutical firms. Chapter 8 predicts changes in strategic position and distinguishes the relatively small number of "movers" within the pharmaceutical industry from 1970 to 1990.

Table 1.4 emphasizes, and chapters 6, 7, and 8 confirm, that significant departures from current patterns of interpretation and behavior are most likely when opportunities can be identified. More formally our assumption is:

Assumption 3. Position and Opportunity

The likelihood of dramatic change attempts is contingent not only on the failure of adapting current ways of thinking and acting but also on the discovery of apparently satisfying alternative actions from relevant actors' points of view.

This distinction is less widely discussed in the change literature than the distinctions underlying assumptions 1 and 2, though it is embedded in strength/weakness, opportunity/threat analysis found in older strategic texts.[2] This logic can be extended to describe how individuals are uniquely positioned in terms of their will, skill, and values and how this "position" affects their likely actions and the likely outcomes of those actions. Often success depends upon changing (or understanding in new ways) the individual's position and opportunities for action. As groups form and coordinate with others, they, too, establish a unique position vis-à-vis other groups—opportunities that can be renegotiated or reconceptualized, though, again, the process is rarely an easy one. Industries (though this, too, is an increasingly nebulous term) also are social systems that can and do reconstitute themselves, a subject we address in the last chapter of this book.

Chapter 9 uses structuration theory (Giddens 1979, 1984) to develop the vocabulary that puts individual, group, and firm change into a broader social context. Population ecology (Aldrich, 1999) and neo-institution theory (Scott, 1995; Greenwood & Hinings, 1996) have helped strategy scholars who focus on managerial choice (Child, 1972) think about the larger context affecting decisions and their outcomes. Giddens's related perspective is particularly helpful because it brings structure and purposeful action (or "agency") into one framework. As described in further detail in chapter 9, Giddens insists that purposeful and innovative action is always possible. At the same time, actions take place in the context of rules and resources (which Giddens defines as "structure"). Structure tends to channel action but exists only to the extent that it is drawn upon by those actions. Further, actors are not omniscient. We agree with Giddens that unacknowledged conditions and unintended consequences are inevitable but assert that second order change is most likely to persist, even if it begins in a random experiment, if a logic departing from past patterns is articulated and institutionalized. This is "sensemaking" (Weick, 1995) in all its ongoing complexity, articulated in the fourth assumption informing our work.

Assumption 4. Structure and Agency

Purposeful actions are characteristic of individuals and collectives. They take place in the context of rules and resources created by past actions but in that process also create and reinterpret rules and resources.

Summary Model

Figure 1.3 provide a graphic view of key arguments found first in the theoretical chapters of this book and then elaborated in the empirical chapters that follow. The information environment at the top of the figure is familiar from Figures 1.1 and 1.2. Following dynamic/analytic models, we highlight information about competitor actions and outcomes and regulatory requirements as particularly salient aspects of the firm's environment, while recognizing that "information" is not an attribute of an "environment" independent of a situated observer. However, we believe that "external" stimuli often are routinely created and processed (which means that individuals act with little conscious cognitive processing), as Weick suggests in Figure 1.2. At the same time, some of the inevitably changing aspects of the information do attract attention, which gives latitude for creative processes and interpretivist analysis. Although automatic processing often reasserts itself, because many anomalies can be handled by adjustment in individual schemas and organizational routines, it is unlikely that all such stimuli will be resolved by adaptation, which increases the probability that more dramatic change will be sought. This is the dynamic we are interested in describing in further detail.

CONCLUSION

It will be obvious by now that in this book we draw on research from many different perspectives to construct our cognitively anchored theory of strategic change. In fact, the two of us tend to think in quite different ways, and that shows up in the chapters that follow. Jim by training and inclination is drawn to "objective" work within a positivist tradition. He is a mathematician whose work as an economic geographer has had a strong behavioral orientation. Anne chose philosophy and sociology before turning to a management doctorate. Her work in strategy and organization theory has emphasized cognition and organization politics from an interpretive perspective. Pam has been more closely focused on the management of change.

Each of these commitments has strengths and weaknesses, and focuses on some phenomena at the cost of others. Methodological choices involve further inevitable trade-offs. McGrath (1982) emphasizes that every research endeavor is thus an attempt to resolve inescapable dilemmas. Weick is much more assertive when he argues that:

> People who study sensemaking oscillate ontologically because that is what helps them understand the actions of people in everyday life who could care less about ontology. Noticing (Starbuck & Milliken, 1988), manipulation (Hedberg, Nystrom & Starbuck, 1976), interpretation (Isabella, 1990), and framing (Goffman, 1974) are all plausible events in sensemaking, even though they represent different combinations of subjective/objective as assumptions about the nature of social science and change/regulation as assumptions about the nature of society (Burrell & Morgan, 1979, 1–37). If people have multiple identities and deal with multiple realities, why should we expect them to be ontological purists? To do so is to limit their capability for sensemaking. More likely is the possibility that over time people

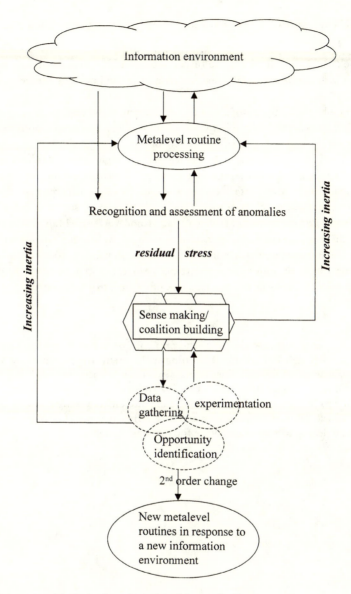

Figure 1.3 A Cognitively Anchored Model of Strategic Change

will act like interpretivists, functionalists, radical humanists, and radical structuralists. (1995, 34–35)

In this book, we have followed a multilectic logic (Huff, 1981), alternating between perspectives with the idea that each one can illuminate—and partially compensate for—the others.

Mintzberg, Ahlstrand, and Lampel feel that "the cognitive school" has a unique status as a "bridge between the more objective schools of design, planning, positioning and entrepreneur[ship], and the more subjective schools of learning, culture, power, environment, and configuration" (1998, 151). We agree, and begin with the idea that how members of an organization interpret their situation is critical to deliberate action and reaction. We believe that this interpretation is social—more particularly, that strategists are often motivated to watch competitor choices as a primary source of information about the nature of the world and what is and is not working within that world. By the end of the book, we have operationalized this subjective starting point with formal models that require parsimonious, quite "logical" expression. Such models are an anathema to many who work from an interpretive perspective, but we have been very pleased that they predict the strategic change, and lack of change, that interests us.

Notes

1. The only other cognitive theory of the firm that we know of is a working paper written by Bart Nooteboom (1996), of Groningen University, the Netherlands. We were given a copy just as we finished this manuscript. Though there are many differences, there are also many similarities. Both his theory and ours are based on schema theory, draw parallels to the philosophy of science, and are interested in using cognitive insights to develop an evolutionary theory that attends to different levels of strategic change.

2. We are indebted to Howard Thomas for this observation.

PART I

Multilevel Theoretic Accounts of Change and Stability

2

Individual Cognition, Stress, and Inertia

Charles Stubbart complains that "cognitive aspects of strategy are implied but passed over in silence" in the strategy literature. "As a consequence," he argues, "managerial cognition becomes the unnamed "missing link" in their . . . paradigm" (1989, 328). This book addresses that continuing lacuna in the strategy literature. Unfortunately, however, work on managerial and organization cognition often has its own "missing link." Theorizing about managerial and organizational cognition borrows words like *memory, attention, perceiving,* and *interpreting,* and yet the details to be found in basic cognitive research tends to be "passed over in silence."

In this chapter, we follow Jim Walsh's (1995) important review of managerial and organizational cognition by highlighting schema theory from social psychology as a basic source for research on managerial and organizational cognition. This approach, developed in the 1970s and 1980s, is frequently described (and more recently criticized) as "computational" and "representational." It is typically based on laboratory research and overly rational, focused more on the use of knowledge structures than their origins or modification (Walsh, 1995, 283). Nonetheless, basic findings about the schematic organization of human cognition are remarkably resilient. They propose that:

- Individuals need to organize and simplify the many stimuli they encounter in order to act.
- The knowledge structures developed to help interpret stimuli affect further interpretation and action in some predictable, though not totally deterministic, ways.
- Reflection and experience modify knowledge structures used in the past, but radical change in these structures is not easily accomplished.

We feel these claims have significant face validity, and in this chapter we summarize some details from basic cognitive research that support them. We then refer to a few of the many studies in managerial and organization cognition that have been influenced by schema theories, before considering the potential of more recent "connectionist" and "dynamical" models of cognition. In chapter 3, we use all three perspectives on individual cognition to consider group-level processes that affect and are affected by individual cognition.

SCHEMA

We root our cognitively anchored theory, especially the concepts of stress and inertia, in schema theories of how individual knowledge structures are developed, used, and changed. The following discussion glosses over the fact that many terms, with somewhat different meanings, have been used by different individuals and subfields interested in knowledge structures and their operation. Influential work by Kelley (1972) focuses on the "causal schema." In artificial intelligence, Minsky (1975) uses the word *frames*. Schank and Abelson (1977) identify "event schemas" or "scripts" to describe expected sequences of events in well-known situations. Rumelhardt (1980) uses "schemata." Walsh (1995) catalogs 73 different labels for schematic information process and its consequences in the organization literature alone! In this chapter, we use the generic term *schema* to generally refer to these accounts of how knowledge structures develop.

Fiske and Taylor note that work on organizing cognitive frameworks has a common debt to work done in the early 1930s:

> Schema theories first fully emerged in Bartlett's (1932) work on memory for figures, pictures and stories. His position was explicitly in opposition to the then-dominant view that knowledge was represented as a collection of isolated elements. . . . He was attempting to describe how people organize past experience and behavior into patterns that facilitate subsequent understanding and behavior. Bartlett's theory did not catch on until 40 years later, but then it received a real welcome. Taking up Bartlett's ideas, modern cognitive schema theories attempt to explain how people understand and remember complex material by drawing on abstracted general knowledge about how the world works. (1991, 103)

This chapter identifies some of the complexities involved in the work that followed Bartlett's important insights. More complete reviews can be found in many sources. See especially Fiske and Taylor (1991) from social psychology and Walsh (1995) in organization science.

Definition

Schema are units of knowledge. These units consist of the knowledge itself as well as information about how the knowledge is to be used. By imposing a structure on knowledge or information, schema allow individuals to function effectively in an otherwise vast and confusing environment.

Schema can be thought of as the routines of knowledge and understanding at the individual level. Human beings are "active sensemakers" (Kelley, 1972) who seek to understand their environments by organizing past experience and behavior into patterns.

These schema, in turn, provide the "rules" or "guidelines" for future perception and action. As suggested by Fiske and Taylor (1991, p. 97), schematically stored "prior knowledge" allows individuals to "have a sense of prediction and control [over their environment] which is essential to [individual] well being."

In these objective models of individual cognition (e.g., Rumelhardt, 1980), the structure of schema is one of variables (concepts) and relationships among variables (rules) relating to characteristics of objects and situations (Fiske & Linville, 1980; Taylor & Crocker, 1981). Each variable has a default value that serves as a "best guess" for variables that have not yet been observed. The relationships among variables are also established in a default pattern; schema, therefore, act as a prototype against which stimuli encountered by an individual are evaluated or interpreted.

Each variable and relationship pattern in a schema also has associated with it an acceptable range of variance. Situations or objects with attributes that fall within established ranges support interpretation based on the schema in use. Those that fall out of acceptable limits act against such an interpretation, a process discussed in greater detail later.

Learning: The Development of Schema from Experience

To understand how the concepts of stress and inertia are related to schema, it is important to understand how schema are widely thought to develop and change. As noted previously, schema structures are formed over time. They develop as the mind reflects on experience, constructs concepts, and imposes connections between these concepts. Connections between concepts are often arbitrary and speculative, even though they are based on experience. A particularly important conclusion is that, as a schema develops, concepts and connections become increasingly abstract and disconnected from specific experience. Increasingly, it is the connections between concepts, rather than the experiences themselves, that give meaning to the variables (Sanford & Garrod, 1981).

The process of schema development and abstraction occurs through learning and can be either an inductive or a deductive process (Rumelhardt, 1980). When an individual realizes that the new, unfamiliar stimuli he or she is encountering may be interpreted in terms of an old schema, with a few important changes, he or she may build a new schema deductively. Such a process involves copying one schema, with changes, to explain a new situation, object, or other aspect of the environment. The changes may involve changing variable concepts into constants, changing constants into variables, or substituting new concepts for old (Rumelhart & Norman, 1978; Rumelhart, 1980). If the new, unfamiliar stimuli that are encountered cannot be interpreted in terms of an old schema, a new one is formed inductively. As the individual begins to recognize a repeated pattern as meaningful, he or she forms a schema consistent with that pattern.

Once schema have been created, they must occasionally be adjusted to address changes in the environment that occur over time. Rumelhart and Norman (1978) describe two processes, accretion and tuning, to account for the process of updating or adjusting already held schema. Accretion, the most common form of learning, according to Rumelhart (1980), occurs when currently held schema are judged to be adequate in explaining new stimuli. In such cases, no real change in the schema occurs. Rather, traces of the experience are remembered and act as embellishments to an existing schema.

Alternatively, existing schema may be changed to make them more in tune with new experiences (Rumelhart & Norman, 1978; Rumelhart, 1980). Tuning may occur as a modification of variable constraints, default values, or both. This type of change is likely when the schema does an adequate job of explaining the experience but requires a small adjustment in one or more components. Because this type of change occurs only in cases where the schema as a whole is adequate, however, wide deviations from current constraint or default value definitions cannot be addressed in this way.

A more elaborate form of tuning involves replacing a part of a schema that was constant with a variable, making the schema more generally applicable. Concept generalization is most likely to occur in instances where a schema is deemed applicable, except for tight constraints on the value of one or more concepts. By relaxing those constraints, new experience may be adequately explained. The third and final form of tuning occurs when individuals tighten the constraints of one or more variables in a schema. In such cases, they may relegate to other schema experiences in which the broader schema was previously utilized.

Schema in Use

Schema are used by individuals to make sense of and act within their environments. As summarized in Figure 1.1 in the last chapter, these knowledge structures play a large role in determining what individuals notice, how what they notice is interpreted, and actions taken in response to those interpretations. As a structured form of knowledge, habits, and assumptions, schema result in expectation-driven sensemaking, meaning that sensemaking is conducted by comparing new stimuli to knowledge patterns built from past experiences.

Schema affect what is actively noticed by affecting the salience of stimuli. Cognitive research in this tradition suggests that objects or events that are important to current schema are more likely to gain the attention of the perceiver (Taylor & Crocker, 1981), while information that is only tangentially related to existing schema falls to the background and is not attended to. Individuals, therefore, tend to be highly sensitive to stimuli in schema-consistent domains but much less sensitive to stimuli and events that occur in the background (McArthur, 1981).

Schema also affect how individuals make sense of the information that is noticed. When a set of stimuli is encountered, a schema is activated (or instantiated) to identify the object or situation. Rumelhart (1980) suggests that instantiation may occur either as a "top-down" or a "bottom-up" process. In top-down instantiation, the individual starts with a schema-induced hypothesis and begins a search for various attributes or variable values related to this object. To use a common example, one might start with the expectation that the object being encountered is a face. The "face schema" would then be instantiated and the individual would begin a search for variables important to that schema (e.g., two eyes, a nose, a mouth). Once a sufficient number of variables related to the face schema have been found, the individual becomes confident that the object encountered is indeed a face. Conversely, bottom-up instantiation begins with the variables, which, in turn, activate the schema with which they are associated. So, for example, identification of the eyes, nose, and so on activates the face schema.

After considerable debate and research, a combination of bottom-up and top-down processing has been accepted to occur in practice (Fiske & Taylor, 1991, 102). Further extending the simple example already used, identification of a nose and eye might instantiate the face schema, which then leads to further evaluation based on the remaining variables in this schema (another eye, a mouth) until enough evidence has been gathered to confirm that the stimulus is a face.

The key point in this process, however, is that schema affect how stimuli are interpreted by provoking expectations about what should and should not be associated with the stimuli, and this has important implications for the process of interpretation. First, there appear to be certain central concepts in a schema that are essential to its instantiation. Noticing these central concepts will result in instantiation of the related schema. Absence of central concepts will result in a lack of instantiation or instantiation of a different schema. An example of this is provided in Fiske and Taylor's (1991) discussion of Asch's (1946) research on how people develop impressions of others:

> Asch theorized that we experience another person as a psychological unit, that we fit the person's various qualities into a single unifying theme, which in many cases resembles a schema. Asch originally made this point in an impressive series of twelve studies (Asch, 1946). The subjects' task was to form an impression of someone described by one or another list of personality traits. One group, for example, was told about someone who was "intelligent, skillful, industrious, *cold*, determined, practical, and cautious." ... Another group of subjects was told about someone who was "intelligent, skillful, industrious, *warm*, determined practical, and cautious." The simple manipulation of the traits *warm* and *cold* created large differences in people's descriptions of the target person. For example, the cold, intelligent person was seen as calculating, and the warm, intelligent person was seen as wise. (1991, 100)

In this case, the attributes "warm" and "cold" appear to be central to person perception and greatly affect the way in which the individual was perceived. It is also easy to infer from this example that the social and cultural context affects the development and use of schema, a theme of central importance in the rest of this book.

A second effect of expectation on interpretation has to do with sequence in the interpretation of stimuli. The sequence in which attributes are presented or noticed can determine how, and how fast, stimuli are interpreted. To illustrate, Galambos and Rips (1982) found that subjects could identify a situation more readily when events within that situation were given in time-ordered sequence. The expective nature of schema also has implications for action. Individuals act to confirm their expectations (Kelley, 1972). Thus, a person will act within the parameters (expectations) of the instantiated schema. In the organization literature, a currently held framework has been described as a map in novel situations (Weick, 1990, 1995), placing constraints on some behavior and encouraging others.

In sum, schema both dictate and result from the individual's experience. Significant change in environmental conditions or the individual's relationship to the environment would seem to imply significant change in the related schema. However, research indicates that schema are quite resistant to change.

THE INERTIAL CHARACTER OF SCHEMA

Given the importance of schema in helping an individual relate to his or her surroundings, combined with the ever-changing nature of the environment, it is interesting to note that research has demonstrated that there is a remarkable level of resistance to schema change. We believe this resistance at the level of individual cognitive processes is the primary source of inertia in organizations. It results not from any active external force but rather from properties inherent to the use of knowledge structures. The very properties that make schema useful sensemaking structures (i.e., efficiency, expectancy) also stand in the way of change.

Some of the most striking evidence of the resistance of schema to significant change shows that schema are resilient in the face of disconfirming evidence. For example, a series of studies by Ross and his colleagues (Ross, Lepper & Hubbard, 1975; Anderson, Lepper & Ross, 1980) suggest that people persist in maintaining theories they have formed on the basis of evidence in the research laboratory even when they are later shown that the evidence they relied on is completely false. In one experiment (Ross, Lepper & Hubbard, 1975), subjects were given pairs of suicide notes and asked to distinguish between the actual note and a fictitious note. After each comparison, they were told whether their answer was correct. However, the correct-incorrect feedback given in each case was randomly determined prior to the exercise. Subjects were informed of their overall success rate and whether it was above average or below. Next, the subjects were debriefed and given evidence that the information they had been given regarding their answers was totally invalid and that their success rate had been randomly assigned prior to the exercise. Subjects indicated that they understood and accepted this information. A subsequent survey showed, however, that despite the complete invalidation of the information provided from the first trial, subjects tended to base their evaluations of future performance on the results reported from the first study. Subjects who had earlier been told their performance was superior tended to rate their ability on future tasks as higher than did a control group, while subjects with poor performance scores in the contrived trials tended to rate future performance capabilities as lower than the control group.

Other experiments corroborated this evidence that beliefs formed in experience persist despite disconfirmation. For example, persistence was found to be greater in subjects who had provided a written explanation of a relationship as part of a lab experience. Anderson, Lepper, and Ross (1980) suggest that because schema consist mainly of relationships between concepts (such as behavior type and occupational success) and not the information that leads to its development (case studies), invalidation of the information is irrelevant to the validity of the schema itself. They further suggest that individuals believe that the very existence of a schema or belief system in and of itself suggests that some event(s) occurred that support such a system, which thus confirm its truth.

Further explanation for the effect of persistence or cognitive inertia can be found in research that suggests that memory for schema-consistent information is superior to memory for schema-inconsistent information (Rothbart, Evans & Fulero, 1979). In an early study, Bransford and Johnson (1972) performed a series of experiments in which subjects read a titled passage that contained a sentence inconsistent with the schema suggested by the title. In subsequent memory tests, in which subjects were asked to complete sentences found in the passage, most subjects could not recall the inconsistent sentence. A second group read the same passage but were given another title, which changed the context of the critical sentence to make it more schema-consistent. Recall of the critical sentence was higher for this group.

Another effect of schema on memory involves memory for schema-consistent information that was not presented. Also called "gap filling" in script theory (Schank & Abelson, 1977), this effect results in individuals who recall schema that support evidence as having been presented, even if it has not. Cantor and Mischel (1977), for example, performed a series of experiments in which selected adjectives were used to describe four fictional characters: an extrovert, an introvert, and two unclassified individuals. In a subsequent memory test where subjects were asked to identify traits that were presented as part of the description, the subjects expressed greater confidence that they had seen nonpresented but conceptually related material than they did for nonpresented, unrelated material.

The explanation offered by researchers for these memory effects rests on an efficiency assumption. Once a schema has been established, it is much easier and more efficient to slot into place new knowledge that fits the existing model than it is to handle new knowledge that cannot fit. Therefore, the tendency is to recall schema-consistent information, regardless of whether it actually occurred, and to forget or distort schema-inconsistent information, even if it is directly experienced. Disconfirming information will not be remembered because it cannot be fitted into a variable position. It becomes unessential or useless information. Unless the quantity of inconsistent or unique information is substantial, it would be inefficient to build a new schema. Sanford (1983) infers from related research that some disconfirming or "weird" information may be saved in short-term memory on a "weird list" because of its salience. However, if the information cannot be fitted into a schema, it will not be transferred to long-term memory and will, therefore, be forgotten with time.

One additional set of research findings with important implications for cognitive inertia focuses on the effects of schema or schema-related structures on interpretation. As was indicated in the discussion on schema in use, these structures are essentially expectation driven. One might expect, then, that individuals would tend to seek out schema-confirming information, not schema-disconfirming information, and this was shown in a series of important early studies.

Langer and Abelson (1974), for example, studied the effect of labels on subsequent perception. In this study, the authors tested the hypothesis that individuals would interpret relatively ambiguous information in a manner consistent with their preexisting beliefs. Subjects from differing schools of clinical psychology were asked to view a videotape of an individual talking about a recent job interview. Half the subjects were told the individual was a job applicant; the other half were told he was a patient. The authors hypothesized that, across training backgrounds, impressions of the individual by subjects who had been given the patient label would find more nonadaptive behaviors in the individual than those who had been given the interviewee label. Furthermore, the authors hypothesized that the subjects from the behavioral school, which teaches students to guard against the use of labels in diagnosis, would exhibit less label bias than those from nonbehavioral schools. The results supported both hypotheses.

In summary, the results of research on schema suggests that they are constructed and validated through experience and yet remain devoid of any detail regarding the information or experience that led to their development. The mind acts as an efficient system. There is no need to store experience, only the knowledge gained from that experience.

An unfortunate consequence is that once a schema has been developed, it is very difficult to change. The research just discussed, which is drawn from a very large body of literature, demonstrates that, because of the expective nature of schema, people attend to schema-supporting evidence, rather than evidence that challenges it. In addition, the cognitive system tends not to add new concepts or to make significant changes to old ones.

Of course, inertia in schema is not in and of itself a bad thing. Some degree of stability is required for effective interaction with the environment (Fiske & Taylor, 1991; 121–139). If individuals were required to evaluate every object or event from scratch as it occurs, very little would get accomplished. Knowledge, defined as "understanding gained through experience or study" or as "the sum or range of what has been perceived, discovered or learned" (*American Heritage Dictionary*, 1985), would be impossible without organization.

Too much resistance to reorganization, however, is counterproductive. Over time, significant changes in the environment that require a restructuring of relevant schema must be expected. Definitions, concept variables, connections between variables, and acceptable ranges of variables and connections all require periodic updating in real settings. Failure to make these changes will result in poor or ineffective interaction with the environment. Given the strong inertial qualities of schema, when does schema change occur, and under what circumstances? The answer lies in strong motivating forces or stressors.

STRESSFUL CHALLENGES TO SCHEMA

Unlike inertia, which is linked to the characteristics of a knowledge structure, stressors are active forces that result from some activity in the environment, often a change in that environment. Stress is a highly researched but problematic concept (Selye, 1956, 1974, 1976; Hamilton & Warburton, 1979; Pearlin, Meneghan, Lieberman & Mullan, 1981; Janis, 1982; Lazarus & Folkman, 1984; Monat & Lazarus, 1985) first developed by Hans Selye (1936), who noticed similar negative physiological responses among rats given various "nocuous" injections. Selye (1964) subsequently identified similar responses to cold, heat, x-rays, noise, pain, bleeding, and muscular work.

In a recent history of the widespread use of this concept, Levi (1998, vi) reports that Selye later regretted not drawing on engineering to use the word *strain,* which signifies what happens when force deforms a physical entity, like the girders of a bridge under pressure:

> Numerous attempts have been made to abandon the use of the term stress on the grounds that it is an abstraction which does not correspond to clinical reality.... Selye countered that stress is admittedly an abstraction and not easy to define, but these are faults it shares with many other terms that are none the less indispensable. ...According to Selye, stress [or what he later might have called strain] is the *lowest common denominator* in the organism's reactions to every conceivable kind of stressor exposure, challenge and demand....Another way to define and describe the phenomenon "stress" is by referring to what Seyle used to call "the rate of wear and tear in the organism." (1998, vi-vii, emphasis in the original)

In the organization sciences, stress is sometimes used to describe stimuli, rather than reaction. Particular attention has been given to job-related stress (work overload, task ambiguity, etc.) with negative outcomes such as exhaustion, depression, anxiety, illness, and burnout (Kahn & Byosiere, 1991; Zapt, Dormunn & Frese 1996). Our more macro interests include opportunities and other positive conditions, as well as pressures more likely to lead to negative outcomes. Similar thinking lies behind the Schedule of Recent Experiences (Holmes & Rahe, 1967), which correlates stress level with the number of significant experiences (job change, marriage, etc.) the individual has gone through in the past year. This book therefore generalizes from Beehr (1998, 6) to define *stress* as a general term describing stimuli that *strain* or cause "wear and tear" on an individual or larger collective without assuming that the stimuli are noxious or that the results are negative.

Though the work on occupational stress tends to emphasize harmful outcomes, this literature, too, is beginning to explore the idea that stress can be a source of innovation (Fay, Sonnentag & Frese, 1998). Furthermore, this literature consistently reveals that individuals vary in their detection of and response to stress (Cummings & Cooper, 1998, 106). Cybernetic models of occupational stress (Cummings & Cooper, 1979, 1998; Edwards, 1998) that emphasize information processing and discrepancy reduction are particularly relevant to our definition of stress, though this work continues to be problematic because it tends to assume that a "desired state" is known (Edwards, 1998, 132) or can at least be identified by each individual (Cummings & Cooper, 1998, 106). Strategists can be less sanguine.

Stress at a strategic level is interesting precisely because the desired end state and its achievement are so ambiguous. It is this social and causal ambiguity that makes individual cognition (and group feedback, as discussed in chapter 3) more important than they appear to be in Selye's original work or in most models of occupation stress.

Lazarus, a psychologist, suggests that Selye may have overlooked an important stage of the stress process; psychological effects (Lazarus, 1966; Mikhail, 1985). Because the stress responses identified by Selye do not occur if the individual is unconscious or anesthetized, Lazarus proposes that it is the mind of the individual—that is, his or her interpretation of a "demand"—that results in stress. He goes on to define two types of stress, physical and psychological. Physical stress consists of a direct assault on the body. Psychological stress results from conditions that threaten the well-established personal or social values of the individual. The distinction is made clear by the following example: "It is [physical] stress when someone's arm is plunged into icy water, and it is . . . [psychological] stress when a person is told damaging things about himself" (Lazarus, 1966, 2). Because we are concerned with stress as a motivating force for changes in mental structures, psychological stress is the focus of interest here.

The study of psychological stress can be broken down into several concepts: sources of stress, appraisal, and mediators of stress. The sources of psychological stress are many and often directly related to social context. Often referred to as life events, these are incidents that are sudden and identifiable. Such events are relative; almost everyone can recall an instance from personal experience when they either said or were told, "I don't know how you do it, I just couldn't take the stress." Also, as noted previously, stressful events are not necessarily negative. Quite the contrary, traditionally happy occasions like getting married, celebrating a major holiday, or receiving a major promotion, can be sources of great "wear and tear." What makes a situation stressful is how it is perceived.

Perception occurs in an appraisal process. Situations in which the individual has no investment may be appraised as irrelevant. Work by Lazarus (1966) and Lazarus and Folkman (1984) also identifies "benign-positive" situations, which are not stressful because the individual perceives a definite positive outcome. A stressful event, in contrast, is defined as an individual assessment that a relationship between a person and the environment is taxing, exceeding resources, or endangering well being (Lazarus, 1966).

According to Pearlin et al. (1981), the level of stress resulting from any event depends on the number of events that occur, the magnitude of change required by the events, and the quality of that eventful change. The quality of the change, in turn, is determined by the desirability of the change, the degree of control over the event, and whether the change is a scheduled life cycle transition.

Events may also cause stress by either highlighting the effects of old problems or creating new meanings about them (Brown & Harris, 1978). Similarly, stress can create new role strains or increase old role strains (Pearlin & Lieberman, 1979). In line with the negative orientation of most work in psychology and occupations, stress has been shown to increase when events result in a diminished sense of self. This diminished sense of self can occur through a loss of mastery, "the extent to which people see themselves as being in control of the forces that importantly affect their lives" (Pearlin et al., 1981, 340), or through lower self-esteem. Conversely, self-efficacy and a sense of personal control can mediate stress (Fiske & Taylor, 1991, 197–204).

Taken as a whole, these studies of the characteristics of stressful events suggest that stress occurs when the validity or usefulness of currently held schema is called into question by unanticipated events that have an important effect on the relationship between an individual and his or her environment(s). The appraisal process, essentially, is the process of comparing events with currently held schema. When current structures fail, stress is evidenced by discomfort or dissonance (Festinger, 1957), which the individual is driven to reduce. Because too much stress can have negative effects on cognitive activity (Yerkes & Dodson, 1908; Janis, 1982; Horowitz, 1986), it must be kept within tolerable levels. If it is strong enough, stress is likely to motivate change. However, if it is too strong, it can impede change (Janis & Mann, 1977).

Stress levels can be managed through controls (Horowitz, 1986) or mediators, and these can be either exterior to the individual or intrinsic. Research on social supports (Gottlieb, 1981, 1983; Cohen & Wills, 1985; Leavy, 1983) has shown that social relationships or connections with other individuals, groups, or organizations mediate stress by providing emotional support, advice, or even physical support to the individual. This context provides an external source of mediation.

Literature on internal coping mechanisms (Lazarus, 1966; Monat & Lazarus, 1977; Pearlin & Schooler, 1978; Lazarus & Folkman, 1984; Dandoy & Goldstein, 1990) discusses individual attempts to modify the situation, modify the meaning of the situation, and manage stress symptoms. Modification of the situation occurs when the individual perceives an opportunity to remove the source of the stress. Management of stress symptoms, such as depression, sleeplessness, or ulcers, is the only avenue of coping left when one cannot change the situation or modify the meaning of the situation to alleviate stress.

Individuals can modify the meaning of the situation by the way they value or devalue stimuli (Pearlin & Schooler, 1978; Pearlin et al., 1981; Horowitz, 1986). Pearlin et al. (1981) describe this coping mechanism in terms of economic achievement. They suggest that lack of economic achievement will be particularly stressful if it is a top priority in the individual's understanding of success or self-worth. By either devaluing the importance of economic success or valuing current performance that was previously considered unacceptable, the individual is able to attenuate stress levels.

A second form of modification of meaning has to do with comparative frames of reference (Pearlin & Schooler, 1978; Pearlin et al., 1981; Taylor, Wood & Lichtman, 1983). This coping mechanism involves the comparison of oneself with others who are worse off in an effort to make one's own situation appear better. Taylor et al. (1983) place comparative frames of reference in a category of coping mechanisms they refer to as selective evaluation. In a study of cancer victims, they identified four additional types of selective evaluation: selectively focusing on attributes that make one appear advantaged, creating hypothetical worse worlds, construing benefit from the victimizing event, and manufacturing normal standards of adjustment that make one's own adjustment appear exceptional.

These are but a few of the coping mechanisms that have been identified by researchers (Hamilton & Warburton, 1979; Horowitz, 1979; Monat & Lazarus, 1985). Despite a vast amount of research, however, there is still debate regarding the extent to which mediators have a buffering effect on stress or a more direct effect. Research aimed at elucidating this relationship (Pearlin et al., 1981; Cohen & Wills, 1985; Zeidner & Hammer, 1990) found that the effect depends on the nature of the event, the perceived locus of causality, and the degree of integration into a social network. The overall desirable effect, however, is to bring stress levels to the point where cognitive change can occur.

COPING MECHANISMS AND SCHEMA CHANGE

The process of change in schema incorporates all the aspects of stress previously discussed—its source, appraisal, and mediators. As already noted, schema store knowledge and guide action. Because of their importance in helping the individual to understand

and operate within his or her world, it would be inefficient to rebuild schema following every small change in the environment. Therefore, schema are a source of inertia over time, which acts to prevent change. Basic cognitive research suggests schema will not change without a significant motivator. When an event occurs in the environment that appears to contradict currently held schema, that event becomes a potentially stressful motivator. An appraisal process is expected to follow. Using Lazarus's (1966) definition of such an event, the individual can be described as making a determination as to whether the discrepancy caused by the event exceeds his or her explanatory ability. In other words, do the implications of the event seriously contradict currently held schema? If yes, the event is appraised as being stressful, and the discrepancy results in dissonance, an uncomfortable state the individual is motivated to relieve.

At this point, coping mechanisms come into play. Coping mechanisms serve two purposes. First, they prevent premature change in schema. Because individuals are motivated to reduce all dissonance or stress, some mechanism is required to attenuate stress caused by what may be, over time, relatively isolated stimuli that should not be addressed through significant change in schema. Coping mechanisms help to alleviate stress levels and prevent change until evidence builds, either through a series of stimuli or through the occurrence of a major stimulus, to the point that, despite coping mechanisms, the level of stress surpasses the level of inertia and the change process begins. Even at this point, coping mechanisms are important to counteract limiting effects of extreme stress.

The process of cognitive change in response to high stress levels is described well by Horowitz as the completion of a process that resolves mental structures with external stimuli:

> Until completion occurs, the new information and reactions to it are stored in active memory.... News and immediate responses to serious life events remain stored in active memory because, on first encounter, the meaning seem to have great personal importance.... Because the contents are strongly coded in active memory they tend to be represented intensely and frequently.... Inner models will eventually conform to the new reality, as in the process of completion of mourning. When this happens, information storage in active memory will terminate. (1979, 249)

Horowitz's description of cognitive change in response to stressful events highlights an important aspect of the process: change takes time. While important stimuli or events are stored in short-term memory, their image is likely to recur. This allows the individual the time necessary to develop new meanings and to identify the changes in schema that are required. New information that becomes available over time may be added in ways that help construct new understandings. Changes in long-term memory, in "inner models" or schema, do not occur until after this process of understanding has been accomplished.

SCHEMA AND MANAGEMENT THEORY

Walsh (1995) notes the implicit recognition of managerial cognition and schema-based information processing that appears in many early classic works (e.g., March & Simon,

1958; Cyert & March, 1963). More explicit treatment of cognitive processes in management and organizational studies began in the early 1980s. For example, Shrivastava and Mitroff published a paper titled "Frames of Reference Managers Use: A Study in the Applied Sociology of Knowledge" in 1983. Other work identified the social sources of schemas used in organizations (Huff, 1982) and worried about biases and heuristics resulting from the expective nature of schema-based processing (Kiesler & Sproull, 1982; Schwenk, 1984). *The Thinking Organization*, by Sims and Gioia (1986), provided a particularly influential collection of theoretical and empirical papers that highlighted the usefulness of schema theory for understanding many organizational processes.

Since the mid-1980s, both theoretical and empirical work relating theories of cognition to organizations increased exponentially. Much of this work sought to identify the structure and content of management schema and to relate schema to organizational action. Huff (1990) arrayed the tools for examining managerial and organizational cognition in terms of increasingly ambitious concerns (attention, categorization, causal relationships, argument, and underlying structures) that also required increasing interpretation on the part of the researcher. Empirical work supported theoretical expectations that managers' experiences lead to the development of schema that, in turn, affect what is noticed (Dearborn & Simon, 1958; Walsh, 1988; Bowman & Daniels, 1995; Beyer et al., 1997), how what is noticed is interpreted (Lord, Foti, & DeVader, 1984; Lurigio & Carroll, 1985; Steinberg, 1985), and what actions are taken (Day & Lord, 1992; Ginsberg & Venkatraman, 1992). Our understanding of performance appraisals (DeNisi, Cafferty, & Meglino, 1984; Northcraft, Neale, & Huber, 1988), problem and issue identification (Walsh, 1988; Beyer, et al., 1997; Jackson & Dutton, 1991), strategic choice (Duhaime & Schwenk, 1985; Day & Lord, 1992; Thomas, Clark, & Gioia, 1997; Lowstedt, 1993), and industry structure (Porac, Thomas, & Baden-Fuller, 1989; Reger & Huff, 1993), among many other managerially relevant topics, has been greatly enhanced by insights from schema theory.

Of particular interest for the theory developed here is work that links cognition to strategic change. Several authors have related organizational and strategic change to the belief systems, or schema, held by managers. Bartunek (1984), for example, provided a detailed look at how shifts in the primary activities of a religious order coincided with changes in the belief systems (schema) of its members. Similarly, in a study of differences in the responses of several hospitals to a physicians' strike, Meyer (1982a) concluded that differences in action were consistent with differences in the belief systems of the organizations. Dutton and Dukerich (1991), in a study of the New York Port Authority's response to an increase in the number of homeless persons in their facilities, discovered that organizational response was constrained by management's beliefs about the organization and its role in the community.

Consistent with evidence regarding the inertial properties of schema, several studies have linked delays in changing strategy to the schema held by management. Nystrom and Starbuck (1984), for example, attributed the failure of several companies to successfully adjust to changing environments to a lack of learning—or an inability to change schema. The link between strategic change and schema was explored further by studies that linked the cause maps in organizations (often but not always interpreted in schema terms) to the capacity to respond to shifts in the environment (Hall, 1984; Fahey &

Narayanan, 1989; Barr, Stimpert & Huff, 1992). These studies show that schema remain steadfast even in the face of declining organization performance, a finding we explore further in chapter 6.

BEYOND SCHEMA THEORY

While schema theory was strongly influencing studies of managerial and organizational cognition, and work in many other fields as well, it is not surprising that exploration of schema theory began to generate decreasing returns in psychology, and the attention of many cognitive scientists moved to other theoretic frameworks. The first challenges, according to Bechtel and Abrahamsen (1991, 149–151), were from those who felt some knowledge could be better represented as "images" than as propositional relationships among categories.

Imagistic Accounts of Cognitive Processing

Research reviewed by Kosslyn (1980) and J. R. Anderson (1987) that involved observing reaction times to questions comparing size or other physical relationships suggested that individuals sometimes rely on mental images rather than sentence like, verbal knowledge structures. Though there is debate about the extent to which mental images resemble photographs (Glasgow & Papadias, 1992), Johnson-Laird's *Mental Models* lists four points on which "imagist" psychologists agree:

1. The mental process underlying the experience of an image is similar to those underlying the perception of an object or picture.
2. An image is a coherent and integrated representation of a scene or object from a particular viewpoint in which each perceptible element occurs only once, with all such elements being simultaneously available and open to a perception-like process of scanning.
3. An image is amenable to apparently continuous mental transformation, such as rotations or expansions. . . .
4. Images *represent* objects. They are analogical in that structural relations between their parts correspond to the perceptible relations between the parts of the objects represented. . . . (1983, 147)

A somewhat analogous development in organization theory is the investigation of stories (Boje, 1991; Wilkins, 1983) and rumors (March & Sevon, 1984) as the repository of organizational memories and the grounds for developing new explanations as organizational situations change. Here, too, the emphasis is on "complete" representational systems, rather than more formal and linear systems.

Of course, stories and rules are not necessarily antithetical. Johnson-Laird's book suggests ways in which imagist and propositional theories of cognition might be related but quotes Einstein and Infeld to observe that there can be no definitive resolution of differences among theoretic explanations:

Physical concepts are free creations of the human mind, and are not, however it may seem, uniquely determined by the external world. In our endeavour to understand reality we are somewhat like a man trying to understand the mechanism of a closed watch. He sees the face and the moving hands, even hears its ticking, but he has no way of opening the case. If he is ingenious he may form some picture of a mechanism which could be responsible for all the things he observes, but he may never be quite sure his picture is the only one which could explain his observations. He will never be able to compare his picture with the real mechanism and he cannot even imagine the possibility of the meaning of such a comparison. (Einstein & Infeld, 1938, p 152, cited by Zukav, 1979) (Johnson-Laird, 1983, 148)

The image of looking for an adequate description for mechanisms behind the observable is a wonderful metaphor for the quest of cognitive science, and the impossibility of opening the watch case to verify suppositions illustrates the dilemma of those who are interested in rooting their research in models of human cognition. Two other ultimately unreconcilable explanations for human cognition, in addition to the imagists', have been especially important in the last decade.

Connectionist Networks

David Rumelhart, whose work has already been cited in this chapter in support of schema theory (though he used the word *schemata*), was among those who developed the first of these challengers. Closely intertwined with the move from serial computers to parallel processing, "the basic strategy of the connectionist approach is to take as its fundamental processing unit something close to an abstract neuron. We imagine that computation is carried out through simple interactions among such processing units" (Rumelhart, 1989, reprinted in Thagard, 1998, 209).

Connectivism requires

- a set of *processing units*;
- a *state of activation* defined over the processing units;
- an *output function* for each unit that maps its state of activation into an output;
- a *pattern of connectivity* among units;
- an *activation rule* for combing the inputs impinging on a unit with the current state to produce a new level of activation for the unit;
- a *learning rule* whereby patterns of connectivity are modified by experience;
- an *environment* within which the system must operate. (Rumelhart in Thagard, 1998, 211-212)

Bechtel and Abrahamsen define "connectionist networks [as] intricate systems of simple units which dynamically adapt to their environments. Some have thousands of units, but even those with only a few units can behave with surprising complexity and subtlety" (1991, 21). They are especially enthusiastic about connectionist systems' capacity to recognize and learn patterns, including complicated patterns such as the correct past tense of verbs in an irregular language like English. The emphasis is on analogy rather than rules, on "knowing how" over "knowing that." While procedural or propositional rules are often offered for helping someone learn or know how to do something like ride a bicycle, Bechtel and Abrahamsen suggest that

> such instruction alone typically is inadequate to establish skilled performance of the activity; our interlocutor must actually practice *doing* the activity (or at least mentally rehearse doing it; see Neisser, 1983). Thus, something more than simply committing verbal rules to memory seems to be required. . . .
>
> Connectionism is an intriguing and promising contender. Unlike rule systems, connectionist networks bear little explicit resemblance to propositional formats. They are composed of units that are interconnected rather than ordered in strings, and often these units are not even symbols in the ordinary sense. When some of the these units are activated, the unit *knows how* to respond by propagating activation along weighted connections. (1991, 154)

Though proposed as a theory that operates at a more micro level than traditional schema theory (Bechtel & Abrahamsen, 1991, 19), connectionist networks are particularly interesting to us as a potential basis for defining organizational cognition. Members of collectives exhibit often startling similarities (Haas, 1992), and many organizational researchers (e.g., Barr et al., 1992; Dutton & Dukerich, 1991; Isabella, 1990; Gioia, Donnellon & Sims, 1989; Porac et al., 1989) have assumed shared schematic frameworks as a basis for collective behavior. Nonetheless, careful investigation of individual schemas reveals problematic differences among individual constituents of such groups (Johnson, 1999; Johnson, Daniels & Asch, 1998; Hodgkinson & Johnson, 1995; Daniels et al., 1994; Langfield-Smith, 1992; Walsh, Henderson & Deighton, 1988). Klimoski and Mohammed (1994) and Johnson (1999) are among those who advise that assumptions about shared schematic frames underlying group cognition must be critically examined.

A connectionist definition of cognition hints that not all units need to have the same characteristics, an observation that fits Weick and Roberts (1993) account of "heedful interaction" perfectly. The distinctions drawn by connectionists between different kinds of knowledge also have attractive applications. Ragu Garud (1997) is among those who have explored these differences in an organizational context. He suggests, along with Dutton and Thomas (1985), that to "know why" involves "learning by studying," a process that is close to computational models of individual cognition. "Know how," however, is "learning by doing" (Argote & Epple, 1990). It is often partially articulated but partially tacit; in organizations "know how" often resides in routines. "Know what" is a third category generated by customers when they use the products and services generated by an organization (Glynn, Milliken & Lant, 1994). Garud's emphasis is on the competitive importance of bringing these three different kinds of knowledge together in flexible ways. Nichols-Nixon (1997) points out that competitive situations also generate the need to "know where" and "know when" to employ such knowledge.

Dynamical Alternatives

Cognitive scientists have more recently been interested in developing "dynamical" theories of cognition. Dynamic accounts are of increasing interest in many different branches of science and social science, including management theory. Eliasmith (1996) summarizes cognitive work in this area as a rejection of both symbolicism and connectionism in favor of cognition "explained as a multidimensional space of all possible thoughts and behaviors that is traversed by a path of thinking followed by an agent under certain environmental and internal pressures, all of which is captured by sets of differential equations" (1996, in Thagard, 1998, 305).

This definition is attributed to van Gelder and Port (1995). In a particularly interesting essay, van Gelder (1966) describes a "noncomputational" regulator that was critical to the harnessing of steam power. Though a computation regulator directly linked to the production of the engine can be imagined, the invention of Watt's generator operated on a different principle. The arms of this device are influenced by the speed of the engine:

> yet the arms are directly connected to the throttle value which controls the flow of steam to the engine. Thus, at all times, the angle of the arms is also influencing the speed of the engine.... In order to describe the relationship between arm angle and engine speed, we need a framework that is *more powerful*... than talk of representations. That framework is the mathematical language of dynamics. (van Gelder, 1996, 427)

Van Gelder compares the dynamic approach to other cognitive theories in a table, which we expand in Table 2.1. Eliasmith (1996) expands on this description by emphasizing the potential capacity of dynamical descriptions to provide "a natural account for be-

Table 2.1 Differences among Theories of Individual Cognition

	Schematic, computational	Imagist	Connectionist	Dynamical
General description	Propositional relationships	Representations of a visual or spatial character	Networks of (neural) units	Sets of coupled magnitudes
Variables	Abstract, discrete categories	Analogic images	Quantitative—activation levels	Quantitative—states and rates
Changes in states	Discrete, sequential fine-tuning	Comparison and rotation of images	Propagated interaction	Independent, in real time
Metaphoric examples	Serial computer	Height comparisons	Parallel computer	Watt's governor
Tools for description	Scripts, programs	Gestalt figure-ground distinctions	Weighted-sum equations	Differential equations
Organizational applications	Strategic arguments	Stories, rumors, competitor identification?	Know-how developed from experience	Industry evolution

Adapted from van Gelder, 1996.

havioral continuity," to model (in contrast to connectionist accounts) "very complex behavior with low-dimensional descriptions," to couple components in multiple equations so that it is not necessary to account for representations "passing" between components, and to embed cognitive systems in a larger environment. He finds each of these attributes appealing, though he concludes that dynamical systems have not yet been able to identify and quantify parameters that adequately describe complex cognitive phenomena.

There has been a similar burst of energy around developing dynamic theories in the management sciences (e.g., Porter, 1991; Garud & Kumarswamy, 1993; Amburgey & Dacin, 1994; Stacey, 1995; Teece et al., 1997) and a compatible concern for understanding the embeddedness of organizational activity (e.g., Lam, 1997; Uzzi, 1997). Our own formal models outlined in chapters 4 and 8 fit the description of dynamic models, and the multilevel account we offer is a move toward a more complete account of the embeddedness of strategic change. However, we, too, feel that dynamical accounts are insufficient, though the capacity to account for nondeterministic continuity is an important contemporary agenda.

CONCLUSION

In this chapter, we have discussed several different approaches to understanding individual cognition. Recent "connectionist" and "dynamical" models are very helpful in considering cognition at more aggregate levels of analysis, as the next two chapters will show. They are less useful, however, in the search for explanations of persistence.

We therefore continue to draw upon schema theory as an approach with considerable face validity. Schema theory suggests that the roots of inertia and stress can be found in the way individuals seem to make sense of their unique information environments. Although other definitions of cognition are available, we find it still plausible to assume that individuals store a great deal of knowledge of their environments in schema that are built and changed through various learning processes. Given the nature of schema development and use, commitment to existing schema, or inertia, is described as intrinsic to cognition. As a result, only a strong motivating force can lead to a change in schematic frameworks that can generate changes in understanding and purposeful action. We propose stress as that motivating force.

Research on psychological stress, including recent work in organizations, suggests that it is indeed a powerful force, but one that is subject to perception and mediation. This chapter focuses on the fact that an event must first be perceived as stressful (that is, conflicting with beliefs that are perceived to have important consequnces). Second, the event must overcome mediating factors that act to attenuate stress by preventing change in schema. If schema change does occur, it does so through a process of learning where the information gained through interaction with the environment is stored and worked on in active memory until new understandings are developed and become schema-based knowledge.

Often, schema persist because they use previous experience to process new stimuli relatively efficiently and because evidence that might be incongruent with existing

Table 2.2 Three Critical Aspects of the Individual's Contributions to Strategic Change

	Inertia ↔ Stress	First Order ↔ Second Order Change	Position ↔ Opportunity
Individual	Inertia arises from the re-use of schema available in the social setting and developed from the individual's own experience. Stress rises if stimuli attracting attention cannot be interpreted by established or invented schematic frameworks.	*1st*: probable because many stimuli are ignored, existing schema efficiently use past experience, and schema can be fine-tuned. *2nd*: more likely as threatening anomalies cannot be overlooked or explained—if alternative frameworks are invented.	Each individual's unique history, position within the firm, will, skill and values provide opportunities for improving that person's interests and the interests of others.

schema is ignored or discounted. Modest, first order change takes place when individuals fine-tune their existing schema to account for information that cannot be easily ignored or discounted. More dramatic, second order change in individual cognition occurs when previously held schema are repudiated or new schema are developed. In subsequent chapters, we will emphasize individual goals and self-interest in this process.

These ideas are summarized in Table 2.2. We have not yet addressed, however, the strong effect of social context on schema formation and change. Almost all work on cognition recognizes that the social setting, from the time of infancy, significantly affects the formation and use of knowledge structures. Fiske and Taylor review some of this research and conclude: "Situationally induced salience can put relevant attitudes or norms in the mental foreground, making them more available as guides to action.... What is salient defines the situation for the individual, reducing ambiguity and inconsistency ... it tells you what should be relevant to your behavior if you are uncertain of what to do" (1991, 532). We consider these and other effects in much greater detail in the next chapter.

3

Group Effects That Make Second Order Change Less and More Likely

This chapter examines how individual inertia and perceptions of stress are affected by group context but can also affect that context. Our basic argument is that organizational subgroups, both formal and informal, tend to support the status quo and strongly suppress individually perceived stress, as long as the group is producing generally satisfactory outcomes for its members. However, conversations about unsatisfactory aspects of the current way of doing things are inevitable to some degree in a changing world. If those who raise such issues find a significant audience, we believe the group is increasingly likely to explore and reframe stressors identified by individuals. The shared (or at least group-informed) ideas that emerge are an important source of strategic change, or lack of change. The outcome of sharing questions about the current way of operating may or may not lead to changes in the triggering individual's assessment, changes in group activities, or impacts on the larger organization. Whatever the outcomes, just considering significant change within a group is of critical importance because conversation about change adds to and alters more widely shared cognitions.

The impact of social and political settings on individual cognition is a largely neglected topic that is just beginning to surface in the strategy literature (cf. Pettigrew, 1991; Eden & Ackermann, 1998), even though Cyert and March (1963) expanded the theory of the firm some time ago by emphasizing the difficulties individuals have in establishing mutually satisficing relationships and the inevitability, once a group with similar interests is formed, that other groups will not share all their priorities.

At the end of the chapter, we pay particular attention to those who attempt to manage social, political, and cognitive processes to achieve desirable group or organization outcomes. Our observations highlight the need to avoid two possible extremes of the changing dynamic we outline in this chapter: undue conservatism in collective interpretation and action on the one hand and overreaction to new events and possible events on the other. Chapter 4 then uses this discussion to develop a more formal model of strategic change as a firm-level phenomenon.

THE NEED FOR A BRIDGE BETWEEN INDIVIDUAL AND
AGGREGATE LEVELS OF ANALYSIS

As noted in chapter 1, our objective in this book is to present a compatible account of individual, group, firm, and industry change. Bringing different levels of analysis and theory together has always attracted social scientists (Schelling, 1978; Alexander, Gieesen, Munch & Smelser, 1987) but been difficult to achieve. Nowhere are the problems more starkly revealed than in organizations—collectives that are quite remarkable for the fact they are able to at least partially coordinate individual activities. A great deal of work on strategic change has avoided the problems of aggregation and disaggregation by focusing either on individual processes (e.g., Hambrick, 1981) *or* on organizational processes (e.g., Mintzberg, Raisinghani & Théorêt, 1976). Group-level analysis is often overlooked altogether. Clearly, the organization context influences individual behavior, and vice versa, yet it is difficult to bring multiple levels of analysis into accord (House, Rousseau & Thomas-Hunt, 1995). We believe that a missing link in the strategy field has been the careful consideration of frequently communicating work groups at all levels, from industry associations on down.

In this chapter, we develop an account of group change that reflects what Giddens calls "the dialogue of structure" (1981, 27). As Pettigrew notes, "Context is not just a stimulus environment but a nested arrangement of structures and processes where the subjective interpretations of actors perceiving, comprehending, learning and remembering help shape process" (1990, 6). Understanding the interface is particularly important when change is the subject of analysis (Schneider & Angelmar, 1993). If groups and organizations exist as mechanisms to coordinate individual action, as Chester Barnard (1938) and others argue, then understanding how coordination is achieved and then *reachieved* is of central importance.

The work presented in chapter 2, though often done by social psychologists, is of little help. It typically assumes social context but rarely finds it problematic. Even the discovery of explanatory schema typically is found less interesting than schema's effect on subsequent interpretation. As already noted, many organization theorists and strategy researchers interested in cognition, especially in the United States, have been strongly influenced by this line of work. They, too, have tended to overlook the importance of sensemaking in context.

Work done outside the United States often has taken organization context more seriously and found it more problematic (Spender & Eden, 1998). Hosking and Morley's (1991) *A Social Psychology of Organizing*, provides a particularly good synthesis of the connections among cognitive, social, and political processes that need to be explored.

Hosking and Morley speak against "entitive" definitions (in which it is assumed that groups and organizations are formally bounded, easily characterized by shared purpose, and separated from their environments) in favor of conceptualizing collectives that "define themselves as members . . . organizing through their relations with one another" (1991, 56). This insistence on "negotiated order" (Strauss et al., 1963) makes it more difficult to specify group effects but even more likely that the group will have an influence on cognition through interacting self-definitions and ongoing negotiation. Hosking and Morley observe that the strong social aspects of Bartlett's (1932, 1958) foundational work, previously mentioned in chapter 2, are too often overlooked: "He made it plain that many . . . [cognitive] constructions were conventional . . . meaning they were current in some group to which the person belonged (see Bartlett, 1932, p. 118). He also recognized that groups were important because they provided 'a persistent framework of institutions and customs' which acted 'as a schematic basis for constructive memory' (p. 255)" (Hosking & Morley, 1991, 94).

An important influence of social context, from our point of view, is exactly this reinforcement of conservative aspects of individual cognition described in chapter 2. For example, Bartlett's "general conclusion was that people's memories were 'rationalizations' designed to reduce the material to 'any form which an ordinary member of a given social group will accept with a minimum of questioning'" (Hosking & Morley, 1991, 94). By extension, to be part of a group is to give more attention to some referents than others (Sherif & Sherif, 1969; Fiegenbaum & Thomas, 1995). "Common language and everyday social interactions" (Walsh & Ungson, 1991, 60) create and renew interrelated meanings. In short, organization (whether formal or informal) requires prioritizing some things, and de-emphasizing others.

While people within a group constantly provide each other with clues about the meaning and consequences of events (Armenakis, Harris & Mossholder 1993), these interactions can be quite problematic from a larger organizational point of view:

> As groups become more cohesive (whether in interpersonal or task terms) they may become more inward looking, and increasingly isolated from other groups in the enterprise, even though members may be drawn from each of the main functional areas of the business. . . . Some groups are composed of people who have lost touch with those networks of people who could provide them with organizational intelligence. (Hosking & Morley, 1991, 107)

Janis's (1982) work on "group think" among advisors of President Johnson outlines some of the ways organization structure and the personal needs of individuals can further reduce the ideas available from group interaction.

The conservative requirements and tendencies of organizing would make change quite unlikely if the stressors felt at the individual level were not also reinforced at the level of the group. These stressors are rooted in the inevitable individual differences in interpretation and valuation of the environment around them. They are reinforced by inevitable differences between groups. As Pettigrew (1990) observes, organizations of any size are a nested in a set of more or less loosely coupled groups. In these days of increasingly unified supplier-buyer networks, competitor-collaborator alliances, virtual organizations, and other arrangements, almost all individuals have connections that are likely to suggest interpretations that depart from locally shared understanding.

When we speak of relationships between "the group" and "the organization" in this chapter, we mean to include formal and informal links of many different kinds, within and across the boundaries of legal entities. Thinking of many collectives makes it easier to see that completely shared, homogeneous interpretations are unlikely (Walsh, Henderson & Deighton, 1988; Langfield-Smith, 1992; Johnson, 1999). At the same time, individual interpretations are moderated by interaction with others, and consensus on advantageous activities is often the desired outcome of group argument, negotiation, and exchange. This interesting tension is at the heart of our cognitively anchored theory of the firm.

FIRST AND SECOND ORDER CHANGE

The introductory chapter of this book pointed to the frequently drawn distinction between first and second order change. If we take a discontinuity between these two kinds of change seriously, though of course we are "punctuating" in Weick's (1979) terms, it becomes important to identify two very different group settings as a starting point for investigating individual-group interaction. The first kind of setting must support incremental first order changes in thinking and behavior, the kind of changes that facilitate maintenance of existing schema. The second setting must be qualitatively different— allowing and even facilitating challenges to the status quo. The characteristics of this second context must tolerate or even encourage individuals who search for and adopt new ways of thinking and acting that, when coordinated with others, can create significant breaks with the past.

In the rest of this chapter, we simplify the complexity of this problem by defining four rather distinct group states: one quite stable state facilitates incremental change, thereby reaffirming current ways of interacting. The other three states are inherently unstable and thus expected to be shorter in duration, but they create the possibility of more dramatic, disruptive second order change. These states include periods in which key individuals are deciding whether to seriously consider a significant change in group activities, periods in which an alternative to current operations is being actively discussed, and the important period in which group members and "outside" stakeholders (Freeman, 1984) begin to act in accord with new formulations of what should be done.

Our agenda is to try to explain how individuals within a group context might think and behave in each of these distinct states, how the group context affects this behavior, and the likely conditions under which the move from one state to another might be accomplished. However, we do not suppose that there is a unidirectional progression through the abstracted states we identify—they are "states," not "stages." Furthermore, individuals can (and often do) vary the effort they put into trying to change others' activities, and they can pull back from actively considering change to refocus on day-to-day task performance. Nonetheless, the four states identified have interesting differences, which correspond to our observations of many different groups and organizations.

The "Stable" State: Incremental Adaptation within a Largely Accepted Framework

Propositions

• *Most individuals, most of the time, do not think about changing the mental frameworks that inform their activities, even in hypercompetitive environments.*

- *Formal organizational procedures and informal interactions reinforce this tendency.*
- *The initial response to stressful anomalies, at both the individual and the group level, tend to be ignored or avoided.*
- *Stress from anomalies that cannot be ignored is often reduced by small homeostatic, or state-maintaining, alterations in procedures.*

Our starting point is the "group" operating in a relatively satisfactory way to meet the demands of internal and external stakeholders. By putting *group* in quotes, we mean to emphasize a nonentitive concept. Formal organizations establish formal working groups, specifying, controlling, and evaluating their procedures and outputs. Informal groups exist within and across this structure on the basis of task relationships, friendship, outside connections, demographic similarities, and many other connections. Although performance requirements may or may not be specified, they fill some needs or they dissipate.

These groups, even the informal ones, develop patterns of interaction over time. In formal organizations, it is important to see that formal, task group demands are likely to occupy most members most of the time. When one adds involvement in multiple groups, few people have the energy to generate or consider complaints and new ideas about the way things are. This is an important aspect of organizing. As Pred notes (in a study of urban context) "institutional projects are dominant in terms of the demands they make upon the limited time resources of the resident population and the influence they can therefore make upon what can be done and known" (1985, 341).

Typical organizing arrangements not only occupy their members but also help establish the unexceptionable nature of their activities. When the outcomes of various jobs and the projects they entail generate tangible and intangible rewards, current arrangements are further institutionalized, and their mechanisms tend to become less visible (Reger & Palmer, 1996). One helpful reinforcement is that work groups tend to be relatively homogeneous (when compared with the diversity of the larger organization); in the course of day-to-day activities, individuals therefore encounter people who are likely to see things the same way they do. The anomalies and concerns that do rise out of specialized tasks also will be of relatively little interest to groups with other assignments, and thus the stress that is shared within a particular working group is unlikely to be transferred to other units.

Formal procedures also dampen the transmission of unhappiness and support the status quo. Reports and budgets keep attention and interpretation focused on current strategy. Reporting requirements specify not only who talks to whom but also the categories within which they speak. When categories are given, other inconsistencies and bits of disconfirming information are less likely to be transferred. In other words, current group activities under relatively "stable" conditions (defined in terms of past group experience and expectation) are so well entrenched in day-to-day formal and informal interactions that most individuals will not think about change as long as the group is meeting the demands placed upon it.

Even under these conditions, of course, a few individuals at various levels within the organization will not only feel but also voice dissatisfaction, and some individuals will come up with ideas for carrying out tasks in better ways. If these ideas appear promising and require relatively small adjustments, the resilient group will find ways to accommodate them within the bounds of current cognitive, social, and political frameworks. In fact, insightful political players find ways to present new ideas in exactly this unexceptional way (Pondy & Huff, 1985).

Theorists identify resilience as the capacity for homeostatic adaptation "within a stable system that itself remains unchanged" (Meyer, Brooks & Goes, 1990, 98). Homeostatic adaptation is a critical capacity for rapidly responding to new conditions. Adaption is important even in dynamic, rapidly changing settings, although the framework that supports homeostatic change in these settings can lead to actions that many other organizations would find extremely disruptive.

The description of the stable state is reinforced by noting that even ideas for homeostatic change often are isolated (along with their human carriers) via special task forces or work assignments. The result is often quite similar to the avoidance procedures documented in studies of individual cognition. Just as the individual often ignores, considers irrelevant, or "forgets" data that do not fit with existing schema, so, too, groups lose many suggestions and projects by sequestering them; the transfer from short-term to long-term memory is far from automatic at either the individual or group level.

If new ideas are not easily isolated, a good deal of previous work (e.g., Cyert & March, 1963; Hannan & Freeman, 1984; Tushman & Romanelli, 1985; Schwenk & Tang, 1989) suggests they, too, will fall on unreceptive ground. In a stable system, most group members have more to gain from supporting the status quo than they do from exploring alternatives to the status quo, and they will resist potentially disruptive thoughts and actions among their fellows. As Pfeffer says, "attacks on the dominant beliefs or paradigm of the organization are likely to be met with counter argument and efforts to reinforce the paradigm" (1981b, 325).

In short, as outlined in Figure 1.2 from chapter 1, largely unexamined beliefs and practices become tacit "theories of action" that lead individuals to recognize and attend to problems they can solve. Formal and informal arrangements encourage the individual to think in ways that support current operations within the group and the larger organization of which they are a part. These settings make quiescent behavior more likely by ensuring that individuals are fully occupied by well-specified tasks that are consonant with current arrangements and the shared interpretations that support them. Group interactions among similarly situated individuals tend to quell the relatively small number of deviant thoughts that do emerge. These ideas are summarized in Table 3.1.

Though mavericks or "wild ducks" almost always exist within a group, the major threats to group stability under this scenario of business as usual are not internal; they are invasive and external. New recruits bring new ideas and are often less easily repressed by their fellow workers or by established routines, in part because they less clearly realize they are being repressed (Clark, 1970). Even though boundaries are increasingly blurred, events that are largely beyond group influence also can change on a scale that overwhelms the many individual, group, and organizational practices that channel and soften the impact of disruptive ideas. Insiders as well as outsiders are then more likely to doubt the wisdom of the current way of doing things. Their concerns, when shared, begin to move the group out of its normal pattern of homeostatic adjustment and into

Table 3.1 "Business as Usual"

Individuals	"Groups" / "Organizations"
• Focus on task performance	• Limit what can be done and known through: Strong task demands Homogeneous work groups Structured communication channels
• Recognize individual benefits from the status quo	• Recognize and celebrate individual and group success • Put informal peer group pressure on those who rock the boat
• Experience some dissatisfactions	• Often isolate new ideas for evaluation before presentation to others
• Generate some creative ideas	• Incorporate meritorious ideas that can be made compatible with the current strategy

a very different situation in which dramatic change is possible. The nature of the individual-group interface shifts as a key feature of this transition.

"Deciding to Decide" Whether to Pay Attention to Unanswerable Questions

Propositions

- *As individuals who verbalize concerns about current strategy encounter other individuals with similar concerns, questioning behavior is reinforced, and the informal organization begins to amplify rather than repress troublesome evidence about the inadequacy of current ways of operating.*
- *Individuals are not likely to be convinced by new ideas from others who are relatively similar to themselves and by individuals whom they view as more powerful than themselves.*
- *Ongoing conversation will edit individual interpretations of the group's situation. Some concerns will be highlighted; others will be dampened. The ideas that survive as a basis of shared conversation will tend to become more compelling within the group and more likely to be repeated in subsequent conversation.*
- *Unanswered questions require new data, which often must be sought from people not encountered in day-to-day task performance. The information added by new data interpreted by less familiar sources will yield some homeostatic resolutions but also increase the possibility of more radical change.*

The dynamic between the individual and the group changes once the relatively stable conditions we've just described are disrupted. What will constitute a "disruption" depends upon the flexibility of the group in question, which, in turn, depends upon the variations normally encountered in day-to-day task performance. Sooner or later, however, most groups will encounter conditions that go beyond the bounds of their normal experience, beyond relatively easy adaptation of their activities and the schematic frameworks that support them, and thus beyond their homeostatic capabilities. This situation leads to less stabilizing interactions between the individual and the group.

The trigger for a new kind of interaction is corroborated evidence that the group is not satisfactorily meeting the needs of its internal and external stakeholders, and vice versa. As the remedial "fixes" Braybrooke and Lindblom (1963) describe as central to incremental decision making seem unsatisfactory to a growing number of people, it is more likely that any individual who begins to question whether current activities are adequate will happen to voice his or her dissatisfactions to another individual who shares somewhat similar concerns. These individuals have moved into a more conscious mode of cognitive processing and are more likely to find innate differences in the group a helpful sensemaking tool (Isabella, 1990). As a result, the probability that dissatisfactions escape the dampening social and political factors just described also go up. In fact, the group context can begin to amplify rather than suppress individual concerns.

Active processing at the group level is an intrinsically political form of sensemaking. Concerns and complaints among a few create broader conditions of equivocality. As individuals interact, some may attempt to be "sensegiving" (Gioia & Chittipeddi, 1991); more are likely to be "sense-contesting." This involves more than rational processing. It is likely that new stories are invented for what the group has been doing, and might do. Weick's (1995, 127–131) discussion of literature in this area suggests that such stories invent new causal orders and suggest rationales for action that fall outside current organizational routines to address emergency situations. Stories also may "help in the prevention of emergencies. Suppose that imagined threats are less stressful than are actual threats. If that is plausible, then imagined threats should induce less 'perceptual' narrowing than actual threats. This should mean that imagined threats can be 'examined' more thoroughly and comprehended more fully than can actual threats" (Weick, 1995, 131).

A particularly important destabilizing dynamic begins with the search for new data. As described in chapter 2, individual stress increases as dissatisfactions that cannot be easily fixed or ignored. If existing schema cannot be fine-tuned, the individual and his or her fellow travelers are more and more likely to trigger a search for resolution. The search for new, thus unfamiliar data will often require turning to contacts within the broader organization who know about things questioners do not encounter in their day-to-day activities. The modern organization is especially helpful in this regard, providing everything from intranet connections to databases that can be manipulated in new ways by those who are allowed access. Informal contacts and persuasive argument, particularly among those who feel they have some commonality of interest, can reach deeply into even the largest organization.

If the new data collected can be used to reconcile the apparent discrepancies that triggered the search for data, an easy return to the stable state may be achieved. At times, however, new data about new conditions, or previously known data interpreted in new ways with the help of a new perspective, will not fit current beliefs and expectations. The gossip and other informal interactions that always go on in organizations (March & Sevon, 1984; Isabella, 1990) are likely to increase, a natural occurrence of what Hedberg and Jönsson (1978) suggest as a purposeful intervention. "Semiconfusing information" from the group in a more activated state will further challenge individuals to look at accepted stabilities in new ways, and seek yet more information. In Weick's (1979) terms, variation in stimuli makes new interpretation more likely. This phenomenon is quite similar at the group level to evidence that psychological stress can generate innovations in individual interpretation and behavior.

Another important result of new questions with semiconfusing answers is that they are likely to attract the attention of individuals who were not at first concerned about the adequacy of group operations or broader organization strategy. If the number of concerned individuals grows, the contagious capacity of the group also grows. Furthermore, shared concerns can spread to other groups with which the dissatisfied are connected. The individuals thus encountered have had different experiences and have different concerns and needs. Their voices will almost certainly bring new (and often disharmonious) ideas into discussion.

The new but confusing information generated from expanded, more conscious processing often requires looking backward as well as forward (Evered, 1979; Das, 1986), and this, too, can be destabilizing. Previously unexamined assumptions underlying current activities are likely to be more specifically stated, and means-ends chains may be more formally articulated. If greater attention and more encompassing analysis do not resolve the dilemmas that led to reassessment, the nature of new information is likely to continue to stimulate curiosity and provide the impetus for further data collection and further contacts outside established connections. Even though they connect relative strangers, the expanding network is likely to bring together some people who find themselves to be more similar that they realized. This is a basic condition for the effective dissemination of new ideas (Rogers, 1995) and for the reorganization of group membership.

There is no guarantee that the results of more, somewhat like-minded people thinking about threatening data will be positive from an organizational point of view. In fact, group-level activities at this point can be quite similar to those observed by psychologists considering the effect of established schema on individual cognition. Janis and Mann (1977) amply illustrated that groups under stress evade responsibility, develop fatalistic explanations, vacillate, try to "pass the buck," and engage in other apparently pathological responses observed among individuals. Nonetheless, the activities summarized in Table 3.1 no longer hold. Individuals continue to "infect" each other with their concerns in ways that increase emotion and energy (Hedberg & Jönsson, 1977), which is itself a contagious condition.

It should still be observed that the group setting continues to channel individual thinking about strategic change. Conversation with others will underscore and amplify the importance of some questions, while generating little interest in others. Powerful actors will be able to have considerable influence on this editing process by channeling the attention of those who work for and around them, often with little conscious awareness by either party. The overall dynamic, at the level of the idea, can be expressed in portfolio terms. The dissatisfied speaker begins with a certain portfolio of concerns. In the process of voicing these concerns, some ideas will be added, while unappreciated ideas will tend to be abandoned (Huff & Chappell, 1993). In short, through social interaction, the individual's original thoughts about the positives and negatives of a situation are homogenized into a smaller set of ideas that are much more "actionable" because they more closely coincide with the interpretations of others.

In our view, this early period of "shopping ideas" (Quinn, 1980) is an important one to identify as a distinct period in the process of group change, even though it may not last for a long time and is not separately discussed in most models of individual decision making (e.g., Mintzberg, Raisinghani & Théorêt, 1976). Alternatively, the state we have just described can last a long time in situations that are difficult to make sense of. Situations that are more difficult to interpret evoke at least four quite different responses: (1) behavior that continues to follow established routines, even if the individuals involved are aware their activity does not fit changing the situation very well; (2) experimentation, or "shooting from the hip," in response to novel circumstances; (3) following the lead of other actors; or, in the most stressful situations, (4) inability to act at all.

We believe that confusing situations often evoke all four responses at once—and, in fact, all four are quite sensible. Ritualistic behavior can be a helpful stabilizer even if the behavior it produces is not that well suited to the situation. People "know more than they think they know" (Weick, 1979), and happy accidents are always possible; thus ad hoc responses also are advisable. Mimetic behavior is often institutionally reinforced (DiMaggio & Powell, 1991). Responding to others' actions more broadly construed is critical to coordinating in a "theatric" sense (Czarniawska, 1997), which in itself is an appealing form of sensemaking. Even inaction can be a sensible response to a situation that does not yield clues for action. In all four cases, the potentially contagious interaction between individual sensemaking and the social and political context just described is expected to hold. Until some collective sense of purpose begins to emerge, it is unlikely that there will be a move toward articulating a new rationale for action.

This is a period of *deciding to decide* whether it is worthwhile to undertake the arduous and disruptive task of more systematically examining the utility of current operations and searching for a better alternative. As people interact, formal and informal leaders are able to assess the breadth of initial concern and therefore whether a change effort is likely to find a minimum level of cooperation. The difference in individual, group, and broader organization interaction while this assessment is being made can be seen in Table 3.2.

Although the result of these complex interactions obviously can move in many different directions, two generic results are of interest. Interaction with others may yield innovative ideas for adjustment that allow the group (formal or informal) to make satisficing incremental modifications and return to business as usual. If these solutions do not adequately deal with the rising tide of emotion, more and more individuals will begin seeking and experimenting with more dramatic alternatives. The individuals involved may or may not be close enough to the "dominant coalition" (Cyert & March, 1963; Thompson, 1967) to easily attract attention or new resources from the broader organization. We will lay aside the complicating case of renegade groups, however, and turn to the situation in which there is an increasingly formal move to consider second order changes.

Table 3.2 Conditions of "Deciding to Decide" about New Strategy

Individuals	"Groups" / "Organization"
A significant number of influential players: • Lose confidence in current strategy and begin to question group and organization capacity and thus move from automatic to conscious processing	• Support contagion via established networks as compelling questions find a reception
• Need new data to consider unanswered questions	• Usually have directories and databases that facilitate collecting data beyond immediate task requirements
• Are more likely to creatively respond to new data	
• Retrospectively assess the pluses and minuses of current activity within the group and within larger collectives	• Generate new networks with new problem-solving skills as different individuals assess unfamiliar data
• Begin to identify new alignments of concern among individuals and groups	• Homogenize individual problem definitions through communication and debate and diffuse them to a larger group

Envisioning Second Order Change Alternatives

Propositions

- *Political behavior (rather than rational analysis) often dominates the search for new ways of acting even though politics contributes to rational analysis by clarifying the issues that concern key individuals and groups, and analysis helps specify political issues.*
- *Both the standards of rational analysis and the difficulties of achieving satisficing coalitions will limit the generation of alternative ways of doing things.*
- *Discomfort with ambiguity and the need to deliver output will speed the development and analysis of alternative approaches.*
- *The redefinition of opportunities and threats is likely to require the reorganization of group boundaries.*

As noted in chapter 1, Cyert & March (1963) and many others have pointed out the inevitability of individual and group differences in organizations, differences that mean any given outcome will affect various individuals and groups in different ways. Foreshadowing current interests in organization inertia, these authors also note that strategic change will always be destabilizing, because it jeopardizes the negotiated order that satisficed disparate interests in the past. Some individuals and groups are likely to gain with a new way of doing things, while the position of others will deteriorate. The capacity to assess the political landscape is therefore an important source of power (Krackhardt, 1990). In our view, even the *contemplation* of reallocating benefits destabilizes current task performance in the group, though it is also a critical goad for innovation.

Similarly, change by drift, once it is recognized, is likely to generate active processing by individuals and groups who rightly worry that new ways of doing things might change their position and benefits. In short, the political context becomes increasingly important as significant departures from past ways of action are made or contemplated.

Social processes do ameliorate the disruptive effects of considering changes in individual and group behavior. As more dramatic second order change seems possible, almost all individuals become much more serious about the way they voice their concerns and ideas. If they are to influence events, they must forsake idiosyncratic ideas that do not excite others in favor of an agenda that will gather support. Because the "window of opportunity" for developing new shared ideas cannot be expected to last (for reasons we discuss later), the collapse of individual concerns into an agenda that echoes the concerns of the largest possible number of groups is often quite dramatic.

The structural complexities of large organizations and the difficulties of communicating new ideas introduce further simplifying forces into the more serious and more public discussion of change we now want to discuss. As groups begin to convey their views on action alternatives to other units with a different history and different task requirements—units that are perhaps further from or less informed by the disturbances that are generating concern—it is necessary to highlight a very small number of ideas about the need for change and its resolution. Problems begin to be labeled and ordered in ways that can be communicated to diverse and distant recipients, especially those in the dominant coalition. Preferred solutions must be packaged with an eye toward political and analytical success. The result is the emergence of a small number of possible alternatives to the status quo; in fact, many observers have noticed that groups often focus on a single alternative in change situations (e.g., Cyert & March, 1963).

It is important to see that the group is now the key unit of analysis for understanding change processes, because individual actors without group backing are less and less effective in more public debate. Those whose interpretation of the group's situation cannot find a quorum of like-minded individuals are more likely to remain silent rather than risk being labeled an outsider. They also are more likely to leave the organization altogether (Hirschman, 1970), a situation with important consequences that we consider at the end of the chapter. Those who stay grapple with issues of legitimacy. As Pettigrew notes, "change requires creat[ing] legitimacy for one's own ideas, actions and demands and . . . delegitimat[ing] the demands of one's opponents. If one sees major change processes at least partially as a contest about ideas and rationalities between individual and groups, then the mechanisms used to legitimate and delegitimate particular ideas or broader ideologies are crucial" (1992, 9). Recharting group boundaries is often the result of this process.

The socially and politically motivated collapse of individual concerns into more broadly legitimated ones is often less disturbing than it might seem. For example, the focus of group discussions is often on means, or fairly immediate means-ends chains. Public discussion often avoids articulating mid-distant goals that different individuals and groups can continue to envision and value idiosyncratically (Simon, 1947; Hambrick, 1981; Donnelon et al., 1986; Daniels, de Chernatony & Johnson, 1995) while emphasizing very general long-range futures that allow a variety of interpretations. Further, if there is a rising tide of support for a new way of acting, infectious enthusiasm can capture support for this alternative, even though it does not address all concerns that sparked doubts about the status quo.

The form and content of public analysis are thus very important. A particularly interesting issue involves analysis. Formal organization procedures often require rational analysis. Internal and external stakeholders (employees, stockholders, suppliers, financial institutions, the media, etc.) also expect rational analysis and sometimes need (or think they need) the output of such analysis to make their own assessments. Often, the less these stakeholders understand the complexities of a group's situation, the more rational analysis will be expected.

Western society widely disperses the script for this kind of analysis. It begins with careful problem specification, moves to extensive data gathering, generates and compares several alternatives against a common set of evaluative criteria, and selects the most promising alternative. While problems with these procedures are amply cataloged (e.g., Johnson, 1988), more organic assessments are inherently difficult to control (Huff, 1985) and perhaps more open to political maneuvers (Pfeffer, 1981a). In an anxiety-producing setting, many individuals therefore not only expect but also desire analysis that follows a rational script and act in ways that generate such analysis. Even if the motives are political, this is an example of Weickian (1979) "enactment."

Simplification of ideas is very helpful to the performance of rational analysis. If social and political processes facilitate consensus among subgroups, the number of variables is reduced to a more manageable level. More generally, social processes will have defined the kind of analysis that will be judged acceptable. In addition to direct contributions to task performance, there is an interesting reciprocal effect. Just as interest group building simplifies issues and makes rational analysis possible, so, too, skillful rational analysis can simplify issues and facilitate creative solutions in the political arena (Thomas, 1984).

Nonetheless, as many theorists interested in real settings have long pointed out, it is almost always impossible to meet the idealized standards of rational expectations. Rational analysis cannot be pursued to its logical conclusion because of limited human rationality (Simon, 1947) and because of inherent inconsistencies among individual and group values (Cyert & March, 1963). Often individual discomfort with the possibility of change leads the retreat from full rationality before either of these natural limits are reached (Daft & Steers, 1986, 575).

At the same time, ongoing pressure for task performance also limits full-fledged rational analysis. Members and other stakeholders anticipate certain outputs, and something must be delivered if the group is to survive. The excitement of new possibilities and the discouragement of those who do not anticipate benefiting from the way the debate is coalescing, make normal task performance to provide needed outputs increasingly difficult. The small fixes that maintained vitality in more stable states are much less likely to work as a group begins to consider radically changing the way it does things. Not only do an increasing number of individuals have a decreasing amount of energy for implementing doubted routines but also unsatisfactory performance is accentuated by the probable exit of individuals who were most supportive of the now doubted strategy.

Table 3.3 The Search for New Shared Understanding

Individuals	"Groups" / "Organizations"
• Find task performance increasingly difficult as the old framework is questioned	• Are increasingly politicized and unstable as new coalitions are considered
• Become excited if new ideas are attractive	• Encourage the collapse of ideas for change into a small number of issues that can be widely communicated and discussed
• Attempt to influence others to coalesce around new ideas and repudiate alternative interpretations	
• Are more likely to exit if disenfranchised by new ideas	• Give less attention to recalibration of old routines
• Begin to act in ways that are compatible with new ways of understanding	• Are less and less likely to generate satisfactory task output
	• Early adopters begin to act in new ways, and others are drawn into facilitating them

As individuals and groups convince themselves that new behavior is appropriate, they will begin operating in ways that do not mesh well with others (Quinn, 1980), and this, too, subverts the completion of rational analysis. As groups develop and demonstrate a new logic for action, they illustrate it to others. If things go well, early movers are likely to press other units to alter their activities to fit. The basic dynamic is summarized in Table 3.3.

It is difficult to predict the outcome of the increasingly public search for new alternatives and new logics to understand them. In some cases, early experiments will not generate a satisfactory alternative to current routines. Given the stress of continued uncertainty, the dominant coalition may try to return to the past way of acting. If some homeostatic improvements have been discovered, one possibility is that the organization will move back to "better business as usual." Exhaustion or lack of faith also can lead back to established patterns of action.

Alternatively, ready-made solutions for mimetic adoption are available from airport books and consultants-with-a-recipe, and they are frequently rewarded in the marketplace. More formal groups are often subject to dictates from above, a common situation we discuss in more detail at the end of this chapter. The second and more likely possibility is thus that the group will adopt externally available logic structures, collectively "tuning" them as described in chapter 2, In fact, the availability of such solutions may have been a critical contribution to destabilizing dissatisfaction in the first place. Their adaption can be satisficing, especially if they can be connected to other agendas within the group. A third possibility is that inspiration and experimentation will craft a new way of acting that will support new coalitions. In both the second and the third cases, the dynamics between individuals" thinking about what the organization should do and the organization setting take on yet another character.

Honeymoon in a New Framework

Propositions

- *The latitude individuals and groups allow before negatively evaluating a new framework for action, even though concrete evidence of its success is not available, plays a significant role in successfully implementing a second order change in activity.*
- *Standardizing new procedures will speed the group back to business as usual, if inevitable problems with the new ways of acting can be satisfactorily resolved.*
- *Bridges from the old strategy to the new can facilitate understanding and build support.*

Groups that begin to significantly change the way they act will once again alter the context for individual cognition and action. If there is a formal or semiformal adoption of a new logic, or frame, for activity, we anticipate a "honeymoon," when the doubts and complaints that are almost certain to remain in many individual minds will not be widely expressed. (In an era of rapid change, patience may be short. One weary participant in many change efforts describes herself as suffering from "banner fatigue.")

The honeymoon is the joint product of reduced energy for continued debate, individual good manners, uncertainty, and social norms to "give new ideas, or new leaders, a fair chance." During this period, the dissatisfied who find it difficult to grant a honeymoon are more likely than before to exit rather than attempt to voice their complaints (Hirschman, 1970). Meanwhile, the more positive find enough overlap in new interpretations to increasingly coordinate their actions (Klimoski & Mohammad, 1994), and new cultures based on new paradigms (Pfeffer, 1981b; Bartunek & Moch, 1987; Johnson, 1987) can begin to form.

Some delay in evaluating the results of this emerging framework is critical, because new ways of acting cannot be articulated and put into effort instantaneously. We suggested in Table 3.3 that even before a new framework is widely accepted some individuals and subunits are likely to have begun acting in ways that are consistent with it, as Quinn (1980), Burgelman (1994, 1996), and others both describe and prescribe. Nevertheless, full operation will almost certainly generate unanticipated problems. The time required for testing, problem-solving, and coordination means that for a period the group will almost certainly be operating in ways that are consistent both with the old "logic" and the new (Pondy & Huff, 1988). This continues some of the frustrations and disappointments of the period before the new way of working achieved sufficient consensus among key players to prompt second order change.

Counteracting these difficulties is the enthusiasm and energy of those who believe in the importance and ultimate efficacy of new activities. Their capacity to voice as yet unrealized benefits is critical and is facilitated by creating, publicizing, and learning from "small wins" (Weick & Westley, 1996). Because astute supporters also recognize that exit, negative voice and underperformance by the dissatisfied can increase, it is wise to quickly devise new structures, routines, and control procedures. The energy available for this task is increased by the contrast between "doing something constructive" and the doubt, uncertainty, and poor task performance that initiated the search for new direction. These complexities are summarized in Table 3.4.

Table 3.4 Affirming a New Strategy

Individuals	"Groups" / "Organizations"
• Grant a "honeymoon" period due to • Good manners • Uncertainty • Exhaustion • Political expedience	• Reinforce the honeymoon via social norms of politeness and fair play • Temporarily operate within two incompatible frameworks
• If committed, devote extraordinary energy to task and related sensemaking activities	• Experiment and make adjustments in new procedures
• If disenfranchised, initially tend to exit or underperform rather than voice complaints institutionalize new structures and administrative mechanisms	• Institutionalize new structures and administrative mechanisms

Because any new arrangement is likely to decrease some valued benefits of past associations, and outcomes of new activities are often uneven, the period of affirming a new strategy continues to be unstable. If the framework around which agreement is coalescing cannot meet demands rather quickly, it is likely that group dialogue will move back either to the search for other alternatives or to the more general discussion of whether change is desirable. In fact, it is interesting that in many different social settings, including families making household relocation decisions (Huff & Clark, 1978), the probability of change is highest directly after a change has been made.

Groups may try to return to old activities, but this option is often foreclosed by changed composition and understanding of key internal and external players. Thus, the more likely move is back to the search for a desirable alternative. To the extent the mechanisms put into place to realize new ideas are successful, however, and to the extent they enable the group to execute tasks that satisfy internal and external constituents, it is more and more likely that the group will re-create the state of business as usual and the dynamics described in Table 3.1.

IMPLICATIONS FOR LEADERS

Up to this point, we have described individuals, groups, and their organizations as both highly conservative and quite "excitable." Managing these two extremes is a critical task for leaders, because both extreme conservatism and unfocused activity hamper effective task performance.

There are four related issues here. On the one hand, effective leaders must keep groups from casting out all those who deviate from shared perceptions. They must think about ways to encourage individual creativity and dissatisfaction because these ideas and their carriers are the gene pool from which responses to new situations can be devised (Huff, 1988). Using another metaphor, in environments perceived to be changing and perplexing, the ability to "camp on seesaws" (Hedberg, Nystrom & Starbuck, 1976) must be actively encouraged. Even in placid environments that require little radical innovation, new ideas and feelings of dynamism are needed to address the concerns of unsatisfied (or bored) members. Unrelieved, these emotions are likely to reduce involvement or be translated into game playing that diverts individual attention from current work.

On the other hand, we have characterized individuals, groups, and organizations as potentially "excitable" under stressful conditions, once the options for evasion begin to be exhausted. Now the leadership question is how to help channel initially idiosyncratic energy into a more collective response. New attention and energy can move toward too many, perhaps inappropriate (from the leader's perspective) issues for cooperative action. The limited rationality and shortage of "air time" in collective forums, along with the need to find allies in the broader organization, are helpful aspects of the group context we have already described. But leaders must worry that these forces will not be sufficient, and thus the group's ability to work as a collective will be undermined. If contagion uncovers new problems, splinter groups can come to very incompatible conclusions about what should be done to address very different issues.

Thus, there are pitfalls on both sides: problems of individual inattention and group conservatism at one extreme and of idiosyncratic enthusiasm and incompatible solutions on the other. Searching for "coherent" (Pettigrew & Whipp, 1991) cognitive frameworks, introducing formal procedures, and supporting group culture become critical. The ideal organizational setting is commodious enough to allow homeostatic adaptation to many of the stressors encountered, without being so flexible that convergence is not possible as stress increases.

A particularly important issue for managerial attention has to do with the individual's exit-voice option. As already noted, both exit and voice have positive and negative implications for the organization. Hirschman (1970), Clark (1970), and Hedberg (1990), among others, have already described the basic dynamic. Early exit by those who disagree with the apparent trend of collective sensemaking can leave the organization without the divergent perceptions needed to create viable new ways of acting. In addition, exit of the most able can leave the organization without the human resources to carry out many task alternatives that would otherwise be attractive, including the tasks required to return to the status quo. But exit also holds the promise of balancing individual opinions and talents within the organization so that coordinated, task-focused performance can be carried out while new ideas can be generated.

Leaders thus must give a great deal of attention to the question of loyalty. As Bo Hedberg (1990) notes, the correct amount is neither too little nor too much. It is important to create a setting that will bind individuals to the group even when stress rises, but this force cannot be so strong that the exit of heterogeneous and dissatisfied elements is foreclosed entirely. The latter point is especially important in these times of enthusiasm for mission, vision, worker participation, and the rest. Too strong a culture— too much individual identification with established ways of doing things—is as bad as

Table 3.5 Managing Exit, Voice, and Loyalty

	Implication		
Option	Too Much	Ideal Middle	Too Little
Exit	jeopardizes the resource base needed to carry out key tasks over time	balances homogeneity and heterogeneity in group membership	reduces opportunities to import new ideas and experiences
Voice	distracts attention from problem solving and task performance	provides a "gene pool" of requisite variety for maintaining and renewing group activity	minimizes early warning signs of potential problems
Loyalty	may excuse unsatisfactory performance or ignore opportunities for enrichment	tolerates experimentation but pushes for performance improvements	depletes commitment to problem solving and change

too little. Leaders must encourage voice and support loyalty but also allow exit. Table 3.5 summarizes these final ideas.

Managing exit, voice, and loyalty is particularly important when change is imposed from outside the group. This attempt to begin the change process in our fourth state is increasingly common in a change-oriented world, yet we believe that truly establishing new forms of activity within groups requires allowing and supporting interactions of individuals and groups we have described as "deciding to decide" and "seeking a new framework for action." This is because it is impossible to dictate behavior under all circumstances. As many who have attempted to impose change know, desired results are often not achieved. It is impossible to anticipate and prescribe all needed behaviors. Change requires cognitive and behavioral realignment (Beer et al., 1990). In emphasizing the way in which "individual" dissatisfactions interact with the social and political behavior of groups, we also mean to describe interactions that must take place between formal authority and the groups over which they preside if second order change is likely to succeed.

Those who attempt dramatic, second order change know that exit is a key lever, and they often make quite significant adjustments in the workforce, not only through invited and enforced exit but also through radical reorganization of existing task groups. Yet the conditions described in Table 3.5 still seem to hold. Disbanding too many groups can leave the organization without needed memory and experience; too little reorganization can leave too many collectives adhering to past repudiated strategies. Similarly, insufficient voice will subvert the fine-tuning needed to move the organization into workable longer term routines; giving subgroups too much voice can easily subvert the new strategy by overemphasizing its inevitable problems. Too little loyalty can lead (directly and through contagion) not only to further exit but also to internal sabotage. Too much loyalty is less likely in forced change situations, but loyal followers can weaken the questioning needed to objectively assess imposed arrangements.

Table 3.6 Three Critical Aspects of the Group's Contributions to Strategic Change

	Inertia↔ Stress	First Order ↔ Second Order Change	Position ↔ Opportunity
Group	Inertia increases as other affiliated individuals reinforce confidence in "shared" interpretations and practices. Stress increases if mavericks, newcomers, or other groups plausibly challenge shared cognition.	*1st*: probable because established coalitions have satisfied their constituents in the past. *2nd*: more likely as stakeholders doubt the benefits of current activities—if they can identify satisficing alternatives.	Each coalition's activities and network of relationships provide opportunities for generating and controlling desired information and other resources.

CONCLUSION

In this chapter, we have drawn attention to the group as an important middle ground often overlooked by those interested in strategic change. Most academics interested in organization change have focused on either individual or organization dynamics, either on the resistance to change or on the need to embrace change. We have sacrificed detail to draw these four themes into one account, even though we have had to dichotomize and treat as relatively static behaviors that are more fluid and dynamic in practice.

The intent of the chapter is to provide a portrayal that is consistent with previous discussions of individual, schema-based cognition but is much more specific about social and political context. In this, we move toward *connectionist* views of cognition. While connectionist theories were developed in response to evolving agendas in neuroscience, artificial intelligence, and other fields, the account of individual-group interactions found in this chapter falls at least metaphorically within Rumelhart's (1989) work in the late 1980s that locates cognition in patterned networks of processing units activated by stimuli and capable of producing new activities through rule-based patterns of connectivity. More broadly, the discussion of cognition in a group context incorporates arguments that intelligence is multifaceted and may be described as developing from both internal and external sources (Sternberg, 1990).

Our account within an organizational context emphasizes the idea that the groups with which an individual associates can be very conservative settings, facilitating fine-tuning of schematic frameworks and behavior but resisting more dynamic change in either. We have also argued that as individuals (particularly those with credibility) begin to publicly doubt the current way of doing things, the group setting can magnify and help elaborate individual concerns, allowing and even facilitating contagion of stressful dissatisfaction among those who would not otherwise interact. Individuals are capable of a similar range of response from conservatism to excitement about new ideas, and their interpretation of the group's situation may lead them to voice opinions and new ideas or to exit from this association. In aggregate, such changes in participation and membership can either dilute the strength of the group or contribute to its coalescence around significantly different activities.

The contributions of these ideas to a cognitively anchored theory of the firm were summarized in Table 1.5, the group portion of which appears in Table 3.6.

In the next chapter, we consider change as a more aggregate, firm-level phenomenon in each of the three categories covered in this table.

4

A Formal Model of Strategic Transformation

with Howard Thomas

This chapter moves from considering interactions within and among formal and informal groups to considering the probability of change in formal organizations.[1] While an organization can be defined as a "group of groups" and thus is subject to the observations made in chapter 3, in this chapter we introduce additional aspects of stress and inertia, first and second order change, position and opportunity derived from the legal status of firms, and the more explicit performance demands placed upon them. These characteristics justify a more abstract consideration of the probability of strategic change. The insights available from the model we develop in this chapter are illustrated in a series of simulations of first and second order change. The results support the viability of the cognitively anchored theory developed in the last two chapters and introduce the empirical studies reported in the second part of the book.

KEY CONSIDERATIONS FOR FIRM-LEVEL ANALYSIS

Chapter 3 deliberately considered a variety of formal and informal groups, including those potentially crossing formal organizational boundaries. The argument so far is thus applicable at the firm level of analysis. To offer just one example, social and political processes affect how the insights of middle managers are incorporated into corporate directives (Bower, 1970b; Burgelman, 1994, 1996; Balogun, 1999; Floyd & Wooldridge, 2000).

We have already suggested that certain aspects of the group setting have interesting isomorphisms with phenomena described for individual cognitive schema in chapter 2. Just as schema are critical structures for reducing the complexity of stimuli from the environment into a smaller, more manageable set for the individual, interactions among middle managers that support organizational change will tend to highlight and intensify a few of the many concerns and interests found among these inevitably disparate individuals. This distillation is critical for moving insights from operations to corporate actors because cohesive arguments can be more clearly related to corporate strategy (a cognitive argument) and because unity is more likely to influence other decision makers (a political argument). Interaction among those in the middle of the organization will also bring conflicting interests and concerns to the attention of top executives, which can be an important impetus for developing new strategy (Floyd & Wooldridge, 2000). The potential for innovation inherent in conflict among managers might be compared with the impact of stressful life events that often spur individual creativity.

The organizational setting has other attributes, however, that merit analysis beyond what we have already offered. As legal entities, organizations tend to persist over time, often far beyond the attention span of individuals and their specific associations. Nelson and Winter's (1982) evolutionary theory of the firm made a major contribution to the literature by clarifying how routines allow organizations to transcend the insights and talents of individuals. They describe routines in terms of " 'organizational genetics'—the processes by which traits of organizations, including those traits underlying the ability to produce output and make profits, are transmitted through time" (1982, 9). The organization is thus a distinct level of analysis, but organizational routines suggest a further isomorphism with individual and group cognitive processes: all three abstract general knowledge from specific experience.

There are other interesting aspects of formal organization that also justify separate analysis. For example, although social settings subject all actors to performance expectations, institutionalized processes allow firms to be compared across quite different domains on very specific performance criteria (Chakravarthy, 1986; Cool & Dierickx, 1993) and make possible quite abstract assessments of risk associated with patterns of activity (Thomas, 1984; Jemison, 1989; Cool, Dierickx, & Jemison, 1989). These and other structures justify a move toward more dynamic models (Greenwood & Hinings, 1988; Keats & Hitt, 1988; Hoskisson & Johnson, 1992; Amburgey & Dacin, 1994), in which specific representations are replaced by more abstract regulatory mechanisms.

More explicitly, the two characteristics of the firm just identified—the tendency to generalize and routinize past experience and the capacity to enter into long-term legal arrangements that are routinely assessed by outsiders who have relatively little information about the operational knowledge available within the firm—justify a more abstract consideration of strategic persistence and change. To move in that direction we begin by expanding previous definitions of *inertia* and *stress* but keep them consistent with previous discussions of cognitive processes at individual and group levels of analysis.

Cumulative Inertia

In an organizational context, inertia continues to be defined as commitment. A number of researchers (e.g., Hannan & Freeman, 1984; Tushman & Romanelli, 1985; Schwenk & Tang, 1989) have suggested why organizational inertia will tend to grow over time. First, putting strategy into place presupposes some initial level of commitment (Barnard, 1938). If basic task demands are met, more detailed and routinized policies and procedures are developed to increase reliability, and the organization begins the process of institutionalization (Selznick, 1957). Capital expenditures for buildings, equipment, and training cause commitment to grow; less tangible but often equally important contributions to inertia are accumulating goodwill assets with suppliers, buyers, and others that cannot be completely transferred to any other strategy (Williamson, 1979).

The "framework" of assumptions that comprise an organization's strategy (Huff, 1982) needs less and less attention under conditions of satisfactory performance. In fact, as already outlined in chapter 3, a smoothly functioning strategy channels managerial and other stakeholder perceptions such that the question of changing strategy is unlikely to arise. Resistance to second order change also can be attributed to the fact that it would be time consuming to abandon increasingly complex current activities and to discover alternative procedures for meeting internal and external demands. Frame-changing efforts would subject the organization to the inefficiencies and uncertainties of new innovation and require new contracts among important agents (Cyert & March, 1963; Eisenhardt, 1989). As current commitments become less easy to change and riskier to change, as administrative mechanisms are put into place and satisfactory results are more predictable, members are motivated to work with what they have inherited. More broadly, institutional and economic commitments also begin to take on lives of their own, independent of the comings and goings of specific individuals. These commitments are channeled and reinforced by expectations outside the organization, largely embodied in institutions that again operate at a level above individual decision making (Crozier, 1964; Powell & DiMaggio, 1991; Scott, 1995).

The implication of this discussion is that organization inertia can be usefully seen as a diffusion process (Lave & March, 1975; Abrahamson, 1991) with a tendency toward a predictable life cycle. In the period immediately following adoption of a new strategy, organizational inertia is relatively low, but as time goes on, inertia and the associated resistance to changing a satisfactory strategy will tend to follow a classic "s-shape" adoption curve (Rogers, 1995, 106) with interesting parallels to the process Kuhn (1970) describes for the adoption of a new scientific paradigm (Sheldon, 1980; Huff, 1982; Rumelt, 1984; Pitt & Johnson, 1987).

Figure 4.1 provides a stylized illustration of the expected change in inertia following the adoption of a new strategy. While growth in inertia can be expected to be relatively smooth, reflecting the incremental, homeostatic adjustments and improvements described in chapter 3, certain events or reinterpretations may more unevenly increase the apparent advantages of a given strategy. The unexpected exit of a competitor might suddenly increase commitment to current strategy in this way. A new ad campaign that both exemplifies current strategy and immediately achieves a dramatic increase in sales provides a second example of organizational activity that might lead to a step-level change in inertia.

Growth in inertia also may be dampened, and may even decline, if confidence in the current strategy begins to erode. Chapter 3 suggested that new hires can dilute the ranks of the committed (Clark, 1970). Similarly, champions (Schön, 1967) can retire or leave the organization. Institutional repositories of organizational memory can be eliminated (Walsh & Ungson, 1991). But most important, commitment to the current strategy can begin to falter under conditions of escalating organization stress associated with relative performance inadequacies. This suggests the need to model inertia and stress as interdependent processes.

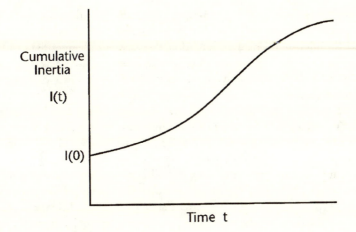

Figure 4.1 Cumulative Inertia

Cumulative Stress

While the forces of inertia in general gain strength, often binding organizations to one strategy for long periods of time, the grounds for significant, strategic, second order change are always present as well. The business policy and strategy literature has long focused on the many events (including poor performance, technological advances, changes in the number and activity of competitors, demographic and social shifts, internal reorganization, and new leadership) that make past strategic positions less viable (e.g., Learned, Christensen, Andrews, & Guth, 1965; Andrews, 1971; Rumelt, 1984). "Organization stress" is a summarizing concept that expresses ways in which current strategy is not satisfactory; it reflects stakeholder dissatisfactions with current performance.

Stress as an organization-level phenomenon is always present because no strategy is perfect. It will increase if implementation falls short of expectations (March & Simon, 1958; Sproull & Hofmeister, 1986), a fairly frequent occurrence because abstract plans almost always incorporate inconsistencies that become obvious only in operation. Stress also increases because the environment is dynamic. As opportunities develop, as new technologies and new ideas become available, the inadequacies of current strategy are underscored (Van de Ven, 1986). Not all of these stressors have negative connotations. "Opportunities"—new inventions, new resources, new leaders, deregulation, and so on—are important contributors to discomfort with the current way of doing things. Other stressors (performance decline, lawsuits, lost contracts, and the like) are of the type more frequently associated with negative constructions of stress. New strategies of other firms, including new entrants to the industry, may increase "wear and tear" on the organization. If old or new competitors achieve results that the focal organization does not, stress is almost certain to increase (Grinyer & McKiernan, 1990).

Competitive assessment is an organization-level issue, but increasing dissatisfaction at the personal and group levels is equally likely. Over time, members of the organization experience the limits of their current situation; they compare their positions with others; they experience changes in their personal lives that alter their needs and desires (Becker, 1964). Groups make similar comparisons; and differences in observed treatment can escalate dissatisfaction.

Some individuals and groups learn to be satisfied with conditions that others would label as unacceptably stressful. Nevertheless, cumulative stress appears to be inevitable in almost all organizations, the result of living in a dynamic world, the logical limitations of any given strategy, and changes in human aspirations.

Stress accumulating over time is likely to lead more and more people in an organization to perceive the benefits of strategic second order change, in contrast to the processes that increase commitment to current strategy. Because this stress tends to be associated with specific events (inventions, executive succession, poor performance reports, etc.), its upward course can be thought of as a series of uneven steps.

Organizations are designed, however, as problem-solving entities. Many dissatisfactions can be quickly addressed by small changes in operations, personnel reassignment, product improvements, and the like (Cyert & March, 1963; Nelson & Winter, 1982). Stress also tends to dissipate as attention to and memory of specific stressful events fades. In addition to internal adjustments in perception and current practice, fortuitous changes in circumstance can also reduce stress.

These adjustment processes are all aspects of the important form of renewal described in chapter 3. *Homeostasis* is "the tendency of a system . . . to maintain internal stability owing to the coordinated response of its parts to any situation tending to disturb its normal condition or function" (Stein, 1966, 679). But all problems cannot be satisfactorily resolved within one strategic framework (Rumelt, 1984), and thus it is unlikely, over time, that homeostatic efforts can completely counteract dissatisfaction (Mintzberg, 1978). The anticipated result is the generalized path of gradually accumulating stress shown in Figure 4.2)

A comparison of Figures 4.1 and 4.2 is of some importance. While a number of authors discuss stress and inertia as theoretic complements (Bigelow, 1982; Lundberg, 1984; Tushman, Newman & Romanelli, 1986; Olivia, Day & MacMillan, 1988), we have suggested reasons not to treat them as reverse images. The cumulative resistance to significant strategic change grows primarily out of gradually accumulating resource commitments and institutional routines, many of which receive little ongoing attention. Cumulative stress, which makes renewal more likely to be sought and accepted, is more often associated with specific events that directly capture individual and group attention.

There is little guidance from the literature on stress and inertia to suggest *when* response to stress will focus on incremental, homeostatic adjustments and when the more dramatic 2nd order change in direction traditionally of interest to strategy researchers is likely to occur. A number of researchers suggest that larger stressors (and short time horizons) will generate synoptic (Hrebiniak & Joyce, 1985) or quantum (Miller & Friesen, 1984) strategic change, while smaller inconveniences lead to more incremental efforts. This answer is not completely satisfactory in that many organizations do not attempt renewal even when larger changes occur in their environments (Barr, 1991).

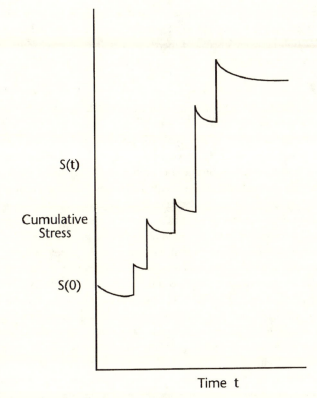

Figure 4.2 Cumulative Stress with Homeostasis

Nor is there much guidance as to the nature of the interdependence between the evolutionary paths of stress and inertia. Some authors have associated the size of the gap between stress and inertia with the probability of a jump from first to second order change and have modeled this transition via catastrophe theory (Bigelow, 1982; Tushman et al., 1986; Olivia et al., 1988). Our account is compatible with this general line of thinking but emphasizes the idea that the history of renewal efforts in any firm generally includes episodes in which major change is considered, or even initiated, without ultimately being brought to fruition. This history is important because it often affects future renewal efforts.

Although renewal in our view must be seen as an ongoing process, it is theoretically useful to describe distinct organization activities that arise out of and subsequently generate different relationships between stress and inertia. The purpose of this chapter is to explore how the interaction between stress and inertia can change over the history of renewal efforts. We are also interested in how the transition from one strategic initiative to another will have an impact on subsequent levels of stress and inertia and thus on the likely path of further renewal efforts. The four states of activity we describe in chapter 3 offer theoretically appealing break points for a more formal investigation of stress and inertia as driving forces capable of generating many different renewal paths. Our intent is to develop a formal model of strategic second order change that uses the changing interaction between stress and inertia as a source of insight into the timing, level, and success of change efforts.

A FOUR-STATE MODEL OF SECOND ORDER STRATEGIC CHANGE

A formal model must fall short of conveying the potential richness and texture of previous theoretic statements, but it has several advantages for understanding a complex process. First, a formal model requires the identification of key forces from among the many variables typically included in broader, but less specific, theoretical accounts. In our formulation we use the demands of this methodology to pinpoint how second order change evolves from unique initial conditions of stress and inertia and from the idiosyncratic ability of the organization to respond to these circumstances.

Second, a formal model can more specifically distinguish different change processes. Though increasingly dynamic environments make it appropriate to describe second order change as an ongoing activity, there is often an empirically observable distinction between dramatic, state-changing efforts and other equally important, though less dramatic, first order change efforts that maintain the current trajectory of the organization. The crux of the model developed in this chapter is the difference between interpretations of and response to stress and inertia in "day-to-day" activity and in more dramatic strategic reconceptualizations.

The third advantage of a formal model is that we can generate concrete strategic change scenarios that illustrate key elements of the stress-inertia interdependencies encompassed within the frame of the general theory we are developing. The model also can be used to explore the implications of different organization histories for subsequent strategic responses. The simulation reported at the end of the chapter clarifies these implications by simulating three theoretically plausible scenarios through 10 different histories of second order change efforts.

The stress-inertia dynamics associated with first and second order change, as outlined in the theoretical arguments in chapter 3 and in the foregoing discussion of stress and inertia, is formalized as a four-state model of strategic change involving:

State I: Business as usual—incremental adaptation within the framework of current strategy

State II: "Deciding to decide" to consider second order change

State III: Envisioning second order change alternatives

State IV: Honeymoon for a new strategic framework

State I: Business as Usual—Incremental Adaptation within the Framework of Current Strategy

The most likely state of organization activity in relatively mature and stable industries involves incremental homeostatic first order change processes within the framework of current strategy.

Only if stress significantly exceeds the ability of the organization to adjust will questions arise about whether a significant second order change effort should be considered, disrupting this stable state.

Mintzberg's (1973b) early research on managerial work provides the archetypal empirical description of activity within a relatively satisfactory strategic framework. As described in chapters 2 and 3, the individual in a reasonably complex task environment can be expected to focus on immediate demands, making small adjustments in his or her work and the work of others to accomplish assigned tasks as necessary. Though in some organizations "small" homeostatic adjustments can include innovative and entrepreneurial responses, the key idea is that day-to-day activity does not engender basic existential questions. This mode of activity thus has an orderly core even when innovation is the norm. Just as Kuhn (1970) describes rules, instrumentation, and experimental standards as the component parts of a scientific paradigm, so, too, the details of administrative structure and day-to-day organizational activity constitute the reality of an accepted organization strategy.

As long as the tasks to be accomplished are demanding enough to occupy most people's time, and as long as they can be carried out with reasonable success, there is little incentive to question the principles that organize activities. Of course, some individuals and groups will be inclined to question whether the larger endeavor is a reasonable one, but they will get little support from their fellows. Those who complain can expect negative consequences from verbalizing an interest in the larger patterns that frame daily activity to the extent that such ruminations interfere with immediate task demands.

In this mode of "normal" activity (adopting the adjective Kuhn [1970] uses to describe "normal" science), the researcher interested in working with the concepts of inertia and stress to understand change can observe only atomistic components of satisfaction-dissatisfaction that evolve as separate and largely unconscious entities. The formal articulation of cumulative inertia in State I, $I_1(t + 1)$, is expressed as a simple contagion process linked to t, the length of time that the current strategy has been in place, such that

$$I_1(t + 1) = I(t) + bI(t)[1 - I(t)], 0 \leq b \leq 1, 0 \leq I(t) \leq 1. \qquad (4.1)$$

This expression specifies that the level of commitment to strategy in the next time period will be directly related to the current level of commitment, an assumption at the organization level that is quite consistent with descriptions of inertia associated with the operation of schema in chapter 2. The second part of the expression describes growth in inertia as a function of the interaction between $I(t)$—which can be thought of as the percent of people committed to the current strategy and/or the percent of all possible actions that have currently been taken to implement the current strategy—and $[1 - I(t)]$, the potential for further additions to inertia (convincing those not yet committed or taking actions left to be done), scaled by a rate parameter, b, which can be thought of as an expression of how compelling the current strategy is, or how well represented by championing individuals or groups.

Cumulative stress, $S_1(t + 1)$, is similarly assumed to be governed by the stress accumulated in the previous time period, $S(t)$. Increases in stress are also dependent upon z(t), the incremental amount of "new" stress experienced by the organization during the time interval (t, t + 1) and homeostatic reduction in stress, $H_1(t)$, such that

$$S_1(t + 1) = S(t) + z(t) - H_1(t) \tag{4.2}$$

$$H_1(t) = aS(t); O \leq a \leq 1. \tag{4.3}$$

When calibrating the model against observed behavior, the values of the "new" stress function, z(t), are assumed to be exogenous to the model, and z(t) is defined as a random variable whose values reflect industry volatility. The constant, a, is assumed to reflect the *effectiveness* of stress-reducing internal adjustments.

The implication of equations 4.1 through 4.3 is that an organization in the incremental adaptation mode (State I) will experience steadily increasing commitment to the current strategy, while incrementally renewing that strategy in response to new stress. We assume that the organization is likely to remain in State I so long as homeostatic first order change mechanisms are adequate to the task of maintaining a stress level *below* some critical threshold, $\bar{S}$, an assumption that is again consistent with arguments developed in chapters 2 and 3. This threshold varies from organization to organization and reflects norms, set by long-term experience, relating to the expected stress levels within the organization and the industry under normal (State I) conditions.

When stress accumulates rapidly and the gap between S(t) and $\bar{S}$ widens, the probability of considering more significant second order change increases. For modeling purposes, this observation is made explicit by assuming that the probability of leaving State I and entering State II of the second order change process, $P_{12}(t)$, is equal to the positive difference between organization stress, S(t), and the critical threshold, $\bar{S}$, such that

$$P_{12}(t) = \begin{cases} S(t) - \bar{S} \text{ if } S(t) > \bar{S} \\ 0, \text{ otherwise} \end{cases} \tag{4.4}$$

where both organization stress and the critical threshold are appropriately scaled to ensure that $0 < P_{12}(t) < 1$.

Expressions 4.1 through 4.4 thus endow the organization with memory. The organization and its members have a history of responding to stress and accumulating inertia. Predicting strategic change requires a knowledge of that history.

The model also puts the notion of a "triggering event" in context. The impact of triggering events has been frequently noted in the literature (e.g., Lyles & Mitroff, 1980), but the nature of these events is usually assumed to be context specific. The preceding formulation suggests that the stressful events associated with more dramatic second order change efforts are similar in kind to an ongoing stream of events experienced by the organization. The event that has been called the triggering event is temporally closest to the time when homeostatic 1st order change seems inadequate. (In our description, it is closest to the transition to State II.) However, the event that has been called triggering accounts for only part of the stress leading to a conscious consideration of a more discontinuous second order change effort; it is often symbolically useful to change agents, but its force almost always depends upon the accumulation of other stressors.

Figure 4.3 illustrates a typical cumulative stress function and the critical threshold $\bar{S}$ for an organization that is moving through several periods with positive probabilities

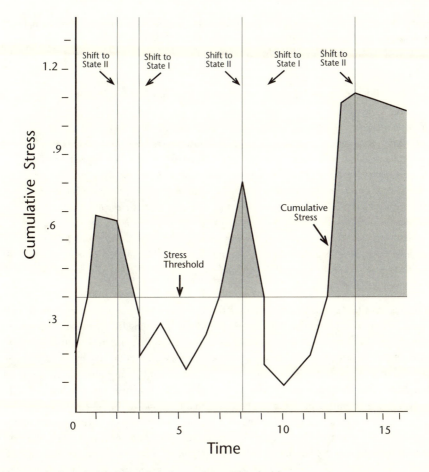

Figure 4.3 Cumulative Stress Relative to Stress Threshold

of consciously considering more dramatic second order change. These periods are shown as shaded regions between the two curves. The shaded areas thus represent the magnitude and the duration of potential instability.

The stress function illustrated in Figure 4.3 provides an example of the homeostatic response to stressors impinging on the organization. In this particular example, homeostatic first order change is governed by the parameter a = .4. New stress was generated by a Poisson process with the parameter, λ = .8, representing the expected frequency of stressful events per unit time period such that

$$\Pr\,[z(t) = nz] = \lambda^n e^{-\lambda}/n! \tag{4.5}$$

where n is the number of stress inducing events occurring during time t. Each stressful event is assumed to result in a fixed amount of new stress, z, which is set at .25. The figure and model reflect our view that in most organizations, most of the time, strategic renewal is not a topic of sustained consideration. Instead, it is accomplished as part of the ongoing problem-solving activity that Lundberg (1984) describes as "decisioning," as opposed to "decision making."

State II: "Deciding to Decide" to Consider Second Order Change

If the homeostatic capability of the organization inadequately reduces new stress, serious questioning of day-to-day decision-making activity becomes more likely. In the face of increasing but unresolved stress, individuals and their supporters within the organization begin to ask whether the current situation could be better dealt with in some other way. The key characteristic of this organization state is that important actors within the organization are forced by unresolved stress to consider the pluses and minuses of current strategy in an abstract and holistic way that is quite different from the unquestioning problem-solving characteristic of day-to-day organizational activity. Broader consideration of pro and con forces, especially in an organizational context and especially when the stakes are high, is also likely to bring to the forefront more "rational" modes of thought and communication. Both support a more direct comparison of stress and inertia.

Questions about the viability of current strategy cannot be answered solely within the context of day-to-day activity (Watzlawick, Weakland & Fisch, 1974). Events and activities that have been seen in isolation must be abstracted and brought into juxtaposition (Kelly, 1955; Maybury-Lewis & Almajor, 1989). The relevant mental schema must change from one that emphasizes the *execution* of tasks to a much broader one that brings into question the *desirability* of carrying out the activities that have been consuming so much energy. From a cognitive perspective, the individual is checking the schematic categories that were previously assumed to be self-evident and potentially constructing new categories that can encompass more extensive data, including data generated by the current uncomfortable situation (Smircich & Stubbart, 1985). The increasing importance of group contexts on such deliberations is expected to homogenize thought and make it more relevant to the organizational setting.

Huber (1991) reviews some of the rich empirical evidence indicating that organizations often fail to learn as much as they might from these circumstances. Cohen, March, and Olsen (1972), Schwenk (1984) and Nutt (1984), similarly argue that decision makers do not in fact follow the full precepts of the more rational decision-making models based on cost-benefit and similar forms of analysis. While we concurred with these arguments in chapter 3, we nevertheless believe that it is almost impossible to escape the general organization of such models. In fact, the "objective" and "rational" form of argument and analysis is so intrinsic to Western culture that it permeates "problem" conceptualization at all levels of concern. In large organizations with complex interconnections, abstraction becomes critical, even though that abstraction is often supported by compelling specific examples. As the issues under question become more strategic, as they reach out to have more significant effect on a larger number of people over a longer time span, it is also more and more likely that the basic structure of rational argument will come into play and provide useful analysis (Thomas, 1984).

In addition to the influence of largely unexamined assumptions about "good" decision making, pro and con arguments that can often be translated into stress-inertia constructs are highly likely because they facilitate organization communication. Widespread formal training in rational forms of analysis provides a commonality that facilitates understanding. The value placed on rationality in our society also improves the chances that arguments made in a familiar, rational, pro-con framework will be trusted. Finding a basis for communication and trust is particularly important in strategic decision processes that require connecting different hierarchical levels and communicating with people who are relatively unaware of the specific circumstances that motivate the need for strategic second order change (Bower, 1970b). Hence, "rational" argument is likely to be used as a symbolic as well as an analytic tool.

Retrospective construction of the pros and cons of the current strategy, which we believe map theoretically onto the concepts of inertia and stress, is likely to reveal associations among events that were previously dealt with in isolation. In accord with the group process described in chapter 3 but not raised to an organization level, more conscious consideration of problems is quite likely to unearth potential indicators of trouble that were not recognized previously and to reveal connections between problems that were previously separate, further increasing organization stress. Then again it is possible that standing back from day-to-day decision making will lead key decision makers and groups to discount previous difficulties or suggest more inclusive ways of addressing problems that will then add to the commitment surrounding current strategy.

The overall result of retrospective rationality is likely to be considerable fluctuation in inertia, as well as stress. The key question is whether the situation is grave enough to risk jeopardizing current coalitions (Cyert & March, 1963), grave enough to justify committing resources that could otherwise be used directly to reduce stress within the context of current strategy, and grave enough to deflect organizational energies along new paths, many of which are likely to be dead ends. The dominant coalition makes this "decision," and in formal settings we argue that the attributes of "decisioning" are likely to give room for more formal processes.

The formal model of this process highlights the gap between stress and inertia as the critical factor guiding the behavior of the organization in this and subsequent states of the change process. It is assumed that the effectiveness of the homeostatic response to stress in State II, $H_2(t)$, is affected by the level of commitment to the current strategy, $I(t)$, such that

$$S_2(t + 1) = S(t) + z(t) - H_2(t) \qquad (4.6)$$

$$H_2(t) = a\, I(t)\, S(t),\ 0 \le a \le 1,\ 0 \le I(t) \le 1. \qquad (4.7)$$

Greater consciousness of the forces of inertia—and the more explicit comparison of stress and inertia that characterizes a move away from "business as usual"—also necessitates the introduction of stress into the inertia function. Inertia now is assumed to change in proportion to the *difference* between inertia and stress in the previous time period such that

$$I_2(t + 1) = I(t) + b [I(t) - S(t)][1 - I(t)], 0 \leq b \leq 1, 0 \leq I(t) \leq 1. \qquad (4.8)$$

If stress exceeds inertia, commitment to the current strategy begins to decline and the organization is motivated to focus more explicitly on major second order change efforts, thus shifting to State III. The probability of shifting from State II to State III at time t, $P_{23}(t)$, is assumed to be related to the positive difference between stress and inertia such that

$$P_{23}(t) = \begin{cases} S(t) - I(t), & S(t) > I(t) \\ 0, & \text{otherwise.} \end{cases} \qquad (4.9)$$

If upon comparison inertia exceeds stress, however, then the organization is motivated to *reaffirm* the current strategy and return to State I. The probability of returning to State I, $P_{21}(t)$, will increase if inertia dominates stress such that

$$P_{21}(t) = \begin{cases} I(t) - S(t), & I(t) > S(t) \\ 0, & \text{otherwise.} \end{cases} \qquad (4.10)$$

Finally, the probability of remaining in State II, $P_{22}(t)$, is the residual

$$P_{22}(t) = 1 - [P_{23}(t) + P_{21}(t)] \qquad (4.11)$$

where stress and inertia are appropriately scaled to ensure that all transition probabilities are positive.

Reaffirmation of the current strategy occasioned by a return to State I at time t is also assumed to lead to a reduction in cumulative stress and an increase in inertia such that

$$S_{21}(t) = S(t) - a\, S(t) \qquad (4.12)$$

and

$$I_{21}(t) = I(t) + bI(t)[1 - I(t)]. \qquad (4.13)$$

These expressions reflect the likelihood that more broadly considering the organization's strategy and finding it strong enough to return to business as usual will have the beneficial effect of renewing that strategy's homeostatic capability for dealing with stress, as well as increasing commitment to current strategy.

In summary, more dramatic second order renewal efforts begin with the overt recognition of tension between voices for change and more conservative voices that typically argue for a renewed commitment to find adaptive solutions within the framework of current strategy. The effectiveness of further homeostatic renewal efforts increasingly comes to depend upon the level of organization commitment to the current strategy. The overt evaluation of current strategy signals the *possibility* of a major change. If stress levels continue to increase, current stress and the possibility of change retard continued growth in commitment to the current strategy, making a major renewal effort more and more likely.

State III: Envisioning Second Order Change Alternatives

Second-order change depends upon the construction of an attractive alternative to the current strategy. Problem solving often collapses as conversation moves to consider a few, or even one, alternative approach. The process of framing this alternative is a distinct phase of second order change activity that can be very divisive, as proponents of the current and emerging strategy vie for attention and resources.

Cyert and March (1963) offer an early description of the difficulties of finding mutually acceptable ways of organizing and the reluctance of decision makers to abandon past solutions. The difficulties of coalition formation are likely to be felt with particular strength as the organization actually begins to formulate second order change alternatives, because each alternative will require somewhat different contributions from the members of the organization and thus different coalitions, different "deals." The key idea is that there are many more unsatisfactory combinations of benefits than satisfactory ones (Bateson, 1972), at both group and organization levels. The difficulties of finding a satisfactory alternative, along with the difficulties of operating without explicit and tacit contracts, pushes the organization to satisfice in searching for an alternative strategic direction rather than more rationally construct and compare many alternatives.

The strain of considering alternative ways of acting is considerably heightened by the fact that the costs and benefits of various second order change alternatives are rarely commensurate. One redirection makes certain issues important and offers an approach to dealing with them successfully. Any other idea for second order change will highlight a somewhat different set of stressors and offer a different approach to their resolution. In fact, each strategic frame by definition makes different assumptions, highlights different data, and suggests different problems as the most important ones to solve (Huff, 1982; Rumelt, 1984).

The result of considering such alternatives is more volatility in stress and inertia throughout the organization. Given high stress and the increasing probability of significant change, it is not surprising that some units will begin acting in ways that are consistent with a new strategic direction even before it is formally adopted. Quinn (1980) and Burgelman (1994, 1996) go so far as to suggest that those interested in second order change might be well advised to foster some of these "early movers" as a deliberate change strategy.

Before considering the process in more detail, it is possible to predict two general outcomes from this difficult interaction. One possibility is that no viable second order change alternative presents itself (perhaps due to lack of internal ingenuity, perhaps due to lack of external opportunity). In this case, the organization's return to State I is abetted by an interpretive process that will tend to push inertia and stress apart—discounting current stress and underscoring commitment (Fiske & Taylor, 1991). If, however, at least some components of a viable contender are articulated within a relatively short time, interpretive processes can be expected to further reduce commitment to the old strategy by underscoring its many problems, hastening the day in which the organization puts into place significantly different strategic ideas.

The key idea behind this description of strategic second order change is that the process of *selecting* a direction for second order change is better described as *developing* a direction for second order change (Daft & Weick, 1984). Quinn's (1980) description of rational incrementalism helps explain why this process takes time and a significant transformation in the organization even as the substantive details of second order change are still being worked out. He argues that complex organizations, even in the face of crisis, cannot move immediately into a new way of acting. Initially, key issues in the environment (including the very forces that helped initiate the process of dramatic redirection by increasing stress) take time to unfold. Then, the details of complex strategy cannot be outlined instantaneously. Even if a few people have a very detailed view of what must be done, just preparing marching orders takes time in large and complex organizations. It is more likely that the details have to be discovered by interaction among many different people who have the knowledge necessary to construct the total picture. It is also important that people who have not been as close to stress-causing events be convinced that dramatic second order change efforts are necessary. Finally, true second order change will be more likely if people across the organization gain ownership in the new strategy by putting together pieces of it for themselves (Hampton-Turner, 1994), and this again is time consuming. All of these activities change the balance between stress and inertia. Borrowing again from Kuhn (1970), if the alternative being developed appears to be able to reduce stress that the old strategic frame was not capable of addressing, the inertia supporting the old way of acting can quickly erode.

Formally expressing the exploration of second order change alternatives begins by defining *, potential new strategy. With the transition from State II to State III, the initial level of commitment to the development of this new strategy, $I^*(t)$, is assumed to be some baseline value, $\bar{I}$, with a corresponding reduction in commitment to the current strategy such that

$$I^*(t) = \bar{I}, \tag{4.14}$$

$$I_{23}(t) = I(t) - \bar{I} \tag{4.15}$$

Commitment to the new strategy grows as supporters begin to coalesce such that inertia surrounding the new strategy in Stage III, $I^*_3(t + 1)$, is

$$I^*_3(t + 1) = I^*(t) + bI^*(t)[1 - I^*(t)]. \tag{4.16}$$

As long as State III continues, the organization will tend to divert energy and resources away from supporting the old strategy since inertia surrounding the old strategy in Stage III is

$$I_3(t + 1) = I(t) + b[I(t) - S(t)][1 - I(t)] \tag{4.17}$$

which implies that inertia is declining so long as stress exceeds inertia.

If the old strategy is not robust enough to terminate the more dramatic process of second order change, the business of "minding the store" becomes increasingly difficult under State III conditions, as attention and allegiance is redirected. As things begin to fall apart within the frame of the old strategy, one important negative consequence is that there is a corresponding reduction in the efficiency of homeostatic controls on stress surrounding the strategy now in jeopardy, because internal adjustment mechanisms are closely linked to commitment. Stress, $S_3(t)$, which continues to be described as in equations (4.6) and (4.7), will increase quickly as inertia declines since

$$S_3(t + 1) = S(t) + z(t) - H_3(t), \tag{4.18}$$

$$H_3(t) = a\ I(t)\ S(t). \tag{4.19}$$

The probability of deciding to affirm the new strategy * at time t (and thus move to State IV) is assumed to be proportional to the difference between the commitment to the newly emerging alternative, $I^*_3(t)$, and the commitment to the current strategy $I_3(t)$ such that

$$P_{34}(t) = \begin{cases} I^*_3(t) - I_3(t), I^*_3(t) > I_3(t) \\ 0, \text{otherwise.} \end{cases} \tag{4.20}$$

It is also possible that commitment to the old strategy will reassert itself if cumulative stress falls below inertia. Following the logic of equation (4.10), the probability of terminating State III 2nd order change efforts and reaffirming the current strategy (return to State I) again is assumed to be proportional to the positive difference between inertia and stress such that

$$P_{31}(t) = I_3(t) - S_3(t), I(t) > s(t). \tag{4.21}$$

The associated changes in stress and inertia are as described in equations (4.12) and (4.13). The probability that the search for a new alternative continues is

$$P_{33}(t) = 1 - [P_{31}(t) + P_{34}(t)] \tag{4.22}$$

where stress and inertia are scaled to ensure that all transition probabilities are non-negative.

State IV: Honeymoon for a New Strategic Framework

Evidence from a number of different sources suggests that there is a relatively long period after a synoptic second order change effort has been formally put into place before the organization returns to "business as usual." In the interim, those who are most enthusiastic about the new strategy act as if the strategy were achieving its potential, while even those who are not convinced often allow a period for evidence to accumulate. In effect, this is a "honeymoon" period that quickly becomes a period of trial and evaluation as the relatively incomplete strategy begins to generate observable results.

The shift between States III and IV can be very dramatic. Especially if a formal announcement is made that the organization will follow a new direction, the uncertainties and reinterpretations called for in comparing different paths for second order change significantly decrease. As noted in chapter 3, organization participants are often tired of the uncertainty and debate that major second order change involves. New assignments also divert attention to new issues. These factors, in conjunction with social norms about fair trial (and fear of reprisal for undercutting new commitments), help generate a "honeymoon" period following formal adoption of a new strategy.

Wise promoters of the new strategy will be as visible and convincing as possible during this period (Bibeault, 1982). Consistent with Schön's (1967) description of product champions and Kuhn's (1970) description of early efforts by promoters of a new theoretic paradigm, these key individuals will promote redirection even though compelling evidence of the new strategy's success has not yet been generated.

At the same time, the organization now must come to grips with implementation. This phase of the second order change process involves trial and error. There is still a substantial risk of reverting back to State III in search of yet another strategic alternative because expectations are high, while the actual effectiveness of the newly formulated strategy is likely to be relatively low (Sproull & Hofmeister, 1986).

The countermanding forces of stress and inertia are thus immediately in evidence, but consciously considering further dramatic change is time consuming and distracting at this critical point in the organization's history. If the initial indicators are positive, the efficiencies of operating without questioning the basic underlying logic of action are great. The organizational context will therefore help move people back to a "business as usual" mode if positive results begin to accumulate. More elements of the old strategy will be phased out. More people will be directed to tasks associated with the new strategy (Pondy & Huff, 1988). If satisfactory performance can be sustained, the organization will move on to State I activity, in which needed adaptations are achieved through less costly homeostatic adjustments.

In the formal model, the affirmation of the new strategy * is assumed to be accompanied by a reduction in stress, such that

$$S_{34}^*(t) = S(t) - aS(t). \tag{4.23}$$

This phase of the second order change process is called a honeymoon state because the initial reduction in stress tends to be *anticipatory*; stress falls *before* the new strategy takes effect. Thereafter, stress changes in a fashion described by equations (4.6) and (4.7):

$$S_4^*(t + 1) = S_4^*(t) + z(t) - aI_4^*(t) S_4^*(t). \tag{4.24}$$

On the inertia side, it is assumed that the initial commitment to the newly affirmed strategy, $I_{34}^*(t)$, is

$$I_{34}^*(t) = I^*(t) + bI^*(t)[1 - I^*(t)]. \tag{4.25}$$

Thereafter, inertia grows steadily, such that

$$I_4^*(t + 1) = I^*(t) + bI^*(t)[1 - I^*(t)]. \tag{4.26}$$

The organization is still very much in an evaluative mode in State IV. Consequently, the transitions out of State IV under the new strategy are assumed to mirror the transitions out of State II under the old strategy. If the commitment to the new strategy, $I^*(t)$, exceeds stress, $S^*(t)$, the probability of entering State I with the new strategy is assumed to be

$$P_{41}(t) = \begin{cases} I^*(t) - S^*(t), & I^*(t) > S^*(t) \\ 0, & \text{otherwise.} \end{cases} \quad (4.27)$$

If stress exceeds inertia, however, the probability of initiating a search for yet another alternative (a return to State III) is assumed to be

$$P_{43}(t) = \begin{cases} S^*(t) - I^*(t), & S^*(t) > I^*(t) \\ 0, & \text{otherwise} \end{cases} \quad (4.28)$$

The probability that the implementation of the new strategy, *, continues is

$$P_{44}(t) = 1 - [P_{41}(t) + P_{43}(t)] \quad (4.29)$$

where stress and inertia are scaled to ensure that all transition probabilities are non-negative. The changes in stress and inertia associated with transitions to State I or State III are as described in equations (4.12), (4.13), (4.15), and (4.18).

A SIMULATED HISTORY OF STRATEGIC CHANGE

The model just outlined has several attractive features, one of which is that it is able to generate quite interesting results with just two key variables: cumulative stress and cumulative inertia. The stress-inertia interdependencies described in equations 4.6, 4.7, and 4.8 represent the core relationships driving the nonlinear dynamics of the second order strategic change process. For the purposes of illustration, stress and inertia can be viewed as deterministic processes if the expected value, **z,** is substituted for the new stress function, **z(t),** in equation 4.6 such that

$$S(t + 1) = S(t) + z - H(t) \quad (4.30)$$

$$H(t) = a\,I(t)\,S(t), \quad (4.31)$$

$$I(t + 1) = I(t) + b[I(t) - S(t)][1 - I(t)]. \quad (4.32)$$

As in equation 4.10, the probability of movement is

$$P(t) = \begin{cases} S(t) - I(t), & S(t) > I(t) \\ 0, & \text{otherwise.} \end{cases} \quad (4.33)$$

As expected, when the model is run as a simulation, the resulting histories of strategic change are quite sensitive to the values of the three parameters in the model: a, z, and b. The probability of deciding to seriously consider a significant change in strategy (i.e., shifting into active search mode in State III):

(a) decreases with reductions in the magnitude of new stress, **z,** impinging on the organization;

(b) decreases with increases in a, as a measure of the efficiency of the organization's homeostatic response to rising stress levels; and

(c) decreases with increases in b if inertia exceeds stress, where b is a measure of the rate at which the organization creates commitment to the current strategy; or

(c′) increases with increases in b if stress exceeds inertia, where b is a measure of the rate at which the organization loses commitment to the current strategy.

In addition to the general relationships between the parameter values and the probability of deciding to seriously consider a second order change in strategy, the preceding equations describe a very simple but quite interesting nonlinear system. Under the assumptions of this model, organizations tend to evolve toward either a high inertia and low to moderate stress condition that is associated with "stayer" firms (or "business as usual" firms), or they tend toward a high stress, low inertia condition that precipitates a second order change decision. Low stress, low inertia and high stress, high inertia conditions tend to be quite unstable conditions in this model; there is a marked tendency to orbit back into a high stress, low inertia "mover" state or to settle into a low stress, high inertia "stayer" state.

Figures 4.4 and 4.5 describe the orbits of firms under identical values for the parameters, a, b, and z but with differing initial conditions, **S(0)** and **I(0)**. As suggested in the simulations shown in Figures 4.4 and 4.5, small changes in initial stress and inertia levels clearly can lead to very different patterns of behavior. In fact, the configuration of the orbits illustrates the existence of a negative attractor in the neighborhood of $S(t) = I(t) = \sqrt{z}/a$ that supports the qualitative observation that the system tends to produce a set of movers associated with the upper left-hand orbit and a set of stayers associated with the lower right-hand orbit. These results are very important because they begin to explain how and why firms with similar strategies and subject to similar environmental conditions might come to very different conclusions concerning the need to make significant changes in strategy.

To explore the heuristic power of the fully specified four state model, we performed a series of simulations. Figure 4.6 illustrates one such simulated history of strategic second order change. The figure shows that the model produces a smooth inertia function, rapidly rising in the early stages of strategy and then tapering off as the strategy reaches maturity. Stress, by contrast, follows a much more erratic course, reflecting the impact of external shocks and the homeostatic ability of the organization to respond to these shocks. In this particular simulation, the new stress impinging on the organization, z(t), is a random variable whose values are generated by a Poisson process with $\lambda = 1.0$ and $z = .20$.

The simulation begins with the organization experiencing moderately high stress, $S(0) = .5$, and low inertia, $I(0) = .2$, as initial conditions. Rapidly increasing stress in year 4 results in a shift to State II, in which the organization begins to critically evaluate the effectiveness of the current strategy. The shift to State II signals the end of growth in inertia and less effective homeostatic responses to new stress impinging on the organization. The search for and the construction of an alternative strategy begins in year 5.5 with the shift to State III. As commitment shifts from the old strategy to the newly

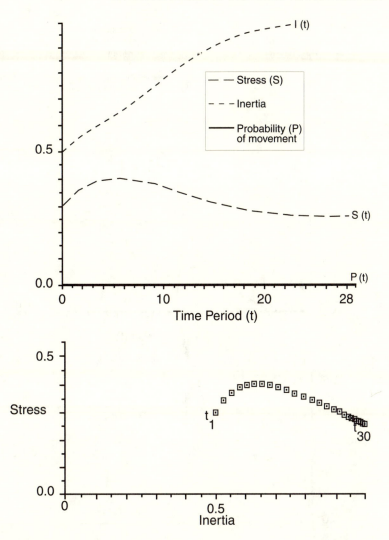

Figure 4.4 Strategic Renewal Simulation 1

emerging strategy, the probability of replacing the old strategy with the new alternative increases until the decision to adopt the new strategy is made in year 7.5.

The shift to the new strategy results in a rapid reduction in cumulative stress. As commitment to the new strategy grows, the effectiveness of the homeostatic response to new stress increases during State IV. The honeymoon-trial state ends in year 10, when the organization returns to State I with the new strategy firmly established. In the remaining 5 years of the simulated history, the organization exhibits a non-zero probability of critically reevaluating its current strategy, but no action is taken and the

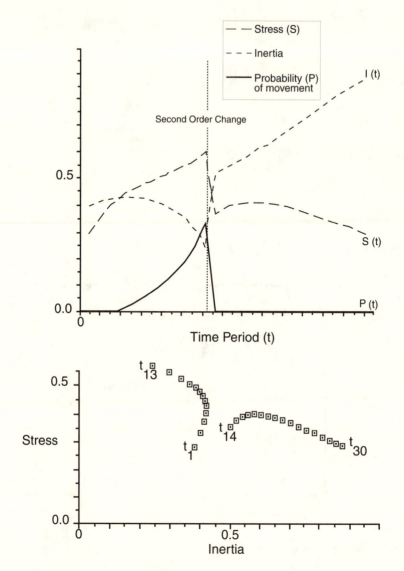

Figure 4.5 Strategic Renewal Simulation 2

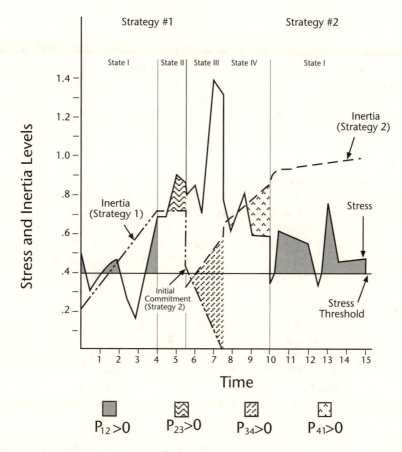

Figure 4.6 A Simulated History of Strategic Renewal

organization continues to operate in a "business as usual" mode. The simulation thus is consistent with evidence of "punctuated equilibrium" (Tushman & Romanelli, 1985), described by several authors (Hedberg & Jauonsson, 1977; Mintzberg, 1978; Miller & Friesen, 1980, 1984; Gersick, 1991) as typically consisting of periods of experimentation and redirection (often accomplished after several false starts and reversals—symptomatic of high stress, low inertia conditions), followed by periods of much more quiescent consolidation, a condition that is symptomatic of a shift to low stress, high inertia.

Of course, it is possible that the achievement of a second period of relative equilibrium shown in Figure 4.6 might not have occurred. Poor performance is a major element in our definition of stress at the organization level, and the basic model is compatible with empirical research on organization decline. Studies indicate that firms in trouble often are involved in a "downward spiral" (Hambrick & D'Aveni, 1988), the first indicators of which generally can be traced back well before direct indicators of failure become publicly available. Bibeault's (1982) observation of turnaround failures indicates that internal organizational factors, most of which could be thought of as factors of inertia, appear to be more responsible for lack of success in reversing a pattern of decline than factors from the external environment. Whetten (1980) notes that poor performance and other indicators of organizational decline exacerbate stress. A particular problem is that stress can lead to inflexible behaviors (McCaskey, 1982), which helps explain why small incremental changes almost always are the first responses to indicators of trouble (Schendel, Patton, & Riggs, 1976; Grinyer & Spender, 1979; Nystrom & Starbuck, 1984; Barker, 1991). Patterns compatible with these observations can be seen in other simulation runs.

Successful turnarounds of serious performance decline, though sometimes based on first order change at the operational level, often require major reorientation. The new perspective implicit in such a second order change frequently involves changes in the CEO, the top management team, or the board of directors (Schendel et. al., 1976; Bibeault, 1982; Slatter, 1984; Grinyer et. al, 1988). Ford and Baucus (1987) suggest that these new leaders not only bring new causal knowledge into the firm but also are unconnected to previous commitments of the firm. In other words, new leaders are a mediating force (Barker, 1991) between the forces of inertia and the forces for change in the organization.

To further explore the ability of the model to generate various patterns of strategic change, we next set up a series of simulations in which industry level conditions are established through common λ and z parameters that define the incidence and magnitude of new stress impinging on organizations in a single industry. As a further simplification for comparative analysis, three other parameters in the model are held constant over all simulations: $\bar{S}$ is set at .4 and $\bar{I}$ is set at .3. Firm differences are explored by varying a, b, I(0), and S(0). As indicated earlier, the parameters a and b can be thought of as the organization's ability to resolve stress through internal adjustment and 1st order change (a) and the rate at which the current strategy is being institutionalized (b). A less effective strategy could be explored by decreasing a. A more rapidly implemented strategy, which would increase the impact of inertia on the probabilities of transition from one state of the model to another, would be expressed in a higher value for b.

Table 4.1 shows the three different scenarios investigated via these simulations. In the first scenario, inertia is initially high, stress is low, and the company's homeostatic capacity, a, is high, as is its ability to incorporate new changes in current strategy, b. This is the kind of company that has a successful strategy in place. Among retailers, for example, Wal-Mart would fit this profile. The second scenario might be thought of as

Table 4.1 Model Parameters for Three Strategic Change Scenarios

Model Parameters and Initial Conditions	Scenario 1	Scenario 2	Scenario 3
I(0)	.5	.2	.5
S(0)	.2	.5	.5
a	.4	.4	.4
b	.3	.3	.1

describing companies like Benetton or the Body Shop in their early days as new entrants in the industry. (Figure 4.6 provides an example of strategic change under this scenario.) Stress is high as such companies deal with entry, and cumulative commitment to a new strategy is relatively low. However, the company in this scenario is assumed to respond well to stress, as shown by a high **a**, and to do a good job of incorporating new people and ideas in its strategic vision, shown by a high value for **b**. The situation is somewhat different in the third scenario, which might be thought of as a well-entrenched competitor like Sears in the 1980s. While many aspects of an old strategy are firmly entrenched [high I(0)], and experience helps the company deal with new stressors, perceived inadequacy of current strategy [S(0)] is also high, and relatively little is being done to refurbish that strategy (low value for b).

Table 4.2 shows the results of 10 runs under each of the three archetypal scenarios. None of the runs under Scenarios 1, 2, 3 resulted in a major strategic second order change over the 15-year period simulated, while 5 of the 10 runs yielded major strategic change in Scenarios 2 and 3. These results have rather startling implications for researchers attempting to correlate strategic change with industry-wide changes in the competitive environment or with different attributes or qualities of the organization. Recall that the distribution of stressors, z(t), is identical for all simulations and yet the firms react very differently to the same set of stressors, depending upon their levels of cumulative inertia and cumulative stress at the beginning of the simulation and differences in the parameter b governing the growth of inertia.

The differences between the three scenarios become even more apparent when the simulated histories are summarized in terms of the observed transition rates between the four states for each scenario. Table 4.3 summarizes the observed patterns of strategic change under Scenario 1. Under this scenario, companies are likely to spend most of their time in State I and there is a low probability (.12) that they will leave State I once they have entered that state. Although some cycling between Scenario I and Scenario II does occur, none of the 10 simulations ever exhibit a shift to State III. The strategic second order change processes in the form of internal adjustments to the current strategy are sufficient to cope with the new stressors impinging on the organization.

The observed patterns of strategic change under Scenarios 2 and 3 are summarized in Tables 4.4 and 4.5. These firms also have a low probability of leaving State I (.11 and

Table 4.2 Observed Changes in Strategy under Three Scenarios (10 simulations per scenario)

Number of Changes in Strategy per Simulation	Scenario 1	Scenario 2	Scenario 3	Total
No Changes	10	5	5	20
1 Change	0	2	0	2
2 Changes	0	3	1	4
3 Changes	0	0	4	4

Table 4.3 Observed Transition Rates for Scenario 1

To:	State I	State II	State III	State IV
From				
State I	.88	.12	.00	.00
State II	.39	.61	.00	.00
State III	.00	.00	.00	.00
State IV	.00	.00	.00	.00

Table 4.4 Observed Transition Rates for Scenario 2

To:	State I	State II	State III	State IV
From				
State I	.89	.11	.00	.00
State II	.25	.65	.10	.00
State III	.00	.00	.71	.29
State IV	.22	.00	.17	.61

Table 4.5 Observed Transition Rates for Scenario 3

To:	State I	State II	State III	State IV
From				
State I	.90	.10	.00	.00
State II	.07	.86	.07	.00
State III	.00	.00	.72	.28
State IV	.00	.00	.41	.59

.10 respectively). If they do enter State II, there is a high probability that they will either remain in State II or return to State I. However, the transition rates from State II to State III are non-zero (albeit small) under both Scenario 2 and Scenario 3, and the transition rates between States III and IV also are non-zero. By implication, firms under Scenarios 2 and 3 have a low probability of initiating the search for a new strategy, but once search begins, it is quite likely that a new strategy will be adopted. Scenario 2 differs from Scenario 3 in that there is a substantial possibility that the Scenario 2 firm will find a viable strategy and reestablish "business as usual" (the transition rate from State IV to State I is non-zero), whereas the adoption of a new strategy by Scenario 3 firms tends to create the basis for further strategic change.

CONCLUSION

We began this chapter with the observation that many things conspire against organizational second order change, and these factors should be expected to gain strength over time. Nevertheless, 2nd order change tends to become more necessary and more likely over time, as individuals, work groups, and interorganizational relationships change and past patterns of organizational activity become less appropriate. Our description of how these forces interact is consistent with the work on individual cognition in chapter 2 and the behavioral issues explored in chapter 3: across levels of analysis there is a tendency to give little attention to knowledge frameworks, including strategy, as long as outputs are relatively satisfactory. We also discuss at a more abstract level than provided in chapter 3 the relationship between stress and inertia that we expect to generate more conscious consideration of pro and con arguments for significant renewal. We consider the way this relationship might change as the strengths and weaknesses of alternatives to past strategy are more formally considered, and describe changing levels of stress and inertia that accompany newly adopted strategy.

The focus of this chapter is on weaving these ideas into a more abstract consideration of changes in aggregate stress and inertia. Our formal model is expressed in a form widely used in the literature on the diffusion of innovation, which is also theoretically appropriate for expressing the aggregation of individual cognitive interpretations into more collective forms of organizational activity. It is based on the idea that radical renewal efforts are more likely as the stress individuals encounter in day-to-day tasks exceeds their individual or collective abilities to make state-maintaining adjustments. However, unlike previous models that used catastrophe theory to model an unexplained shift between one organization strategy and another, the logit model developed in this chapter focuses on likely shifts in the balance between stress and inertia and the consequent impact of this balance on the course of renewal efforts. The link between these considerations and the performance demands placed on formal organizations is more fully explored in chapter 8.

The simulations reported at the end of the chapter behave in ways that are compatible with theoretic descriptions found throughout part I of this book, and with previous empirical work as well. The performance of the model in these simulations suggests that it might be a useful tool for comparing archetypal change experiences, such as the difference between renewal efforts in more and less turbulent environments. It also serves to clarify the relationship between past experience and the adoption or nonadoption of new strategic initiatives.

Taken together, this chapter and chapter 8 explore the relationships found in Table 4.6. Three generalizations are particularly compatible with our general theoretic observations:

- The organization's history of strategic change has an important bearing on subsequent tendencies to change strategy
- Initial levels of stress and inertia have long-term effects upon the organization's history of strategic change

Table 4.6 Three Critical Aspects of the Firm's Contributions to Strategic Change

	Inertia ↔ Stress	First Order ↔ Second Order Change	Position ↔ Opportunity
Firm	Inertia increases as the firm makes commitments and routinizes practices that allow individuals and groups to come and go without disrupting the status quo.	1st: probable because organization outputs not only create some value but also involve activities that are costly for internal and external stakeholders to abandon or change.	A firm's current resources and competitive position provide differential opportunities to more profitably interact with buyers, suppliers, competitors, and other actors.
	Stress accumulates if the results of current strategy do not meet the performance expectations of key stakeholders.	2nd: more likely as cumulative stress exceeds cumulative inertia—if an alternative strategy appears to reduce stress.	

• A bifurcation emerges between "stayers," firms that stay within one strategic framework for long periods of time, and "movers," firms that tend to make major changes in strategy.

In stress-inertia terms, the distinction between "movers" and "stayers" is between firms characterized by high stress and low inertia (second order change candidates) and firms characterized by low stress and high inertia (first order change candidates). These ideas are further developed in the second half of this book, which outlines empirical work in the pharmaceutical industry.

Note

1. This chapter is based on an article by James O. Huff, Anne S. Huff, and Howard Thomas that appeared in the Summer 1992 special issue of the *Strategic Management Journal*, which, in turn, was based on a paper by J. O. Huff and W. A. V. Clark (1978) on the role of cumulative stress and inertia in residential mobility decisions.

PART II

Empirical Studies of Change and Stability in the Pharmaceutical Industry

5

The Pharmaceutical Industry
1970–1995

Kurt A. Heppard and Jim Blasick

All those who drink this remedy recover quickly, except for those whom it does not help, all of whom die. It is, therefore, obvious that it fails only in incurable cases.

Galen, second century C.E.

STRATEGIC ISSUES FACING THE INDUSTRY

Several factors distinguish the pharmaceutical industry from others:

- The long period of time required to develop and market a newly discovered medicine or drug;
- The high degree of financial risk and uncertainty of a medicine's future, even after it is launched;
- The large number of highly restrictive regulations that govern all aspects of a medicine's development, production, and marketing;
- The inability to predict when the next important medicine discovery will occur. (Spilker, 1994, 17)

The industry remained relatively stable over the period examined in this book, though by the end of the period the industry was beginning to respond to the cumulative effect of changes in the environment. Until the late 1980s, the industry maintained a strong product orientation, selling to an increasingly global market that was generally inelastic with regard to price (James, 1994, 49). Companies within the industry competed largely on the basis of their R&D efforts, marketing their patented products at a premium price in a growing market. Due to the cumulative changes in the environment, that stance is being challenged. By the early 1990s, James observes:

The simple model of pharmaceutical industry competition anchored in the ability to develop a stream of patent-protected new products is beginning to degrade in the face of a decline in exclusivity, a reduction in differentiation, increasing consumer sophistication, rising operating costs, the blurring of the market, and sharply increased levels of competition. (1994, 56)

In common with other industries, the industry became much more concentrated because of "larger and more frequent acquisitions and mergers," with the number of firms in the industry decreasing substantially while the remaining firms became much larger (PMA, 1996f, 3). At the same time, competitive pressures between firms increased. Biotechnology firms, which did not exist in the pre-1970 period, proliferated. Regulatory requirements and the costs of research increased dramatically, while the time to develop a new medicine increased from 2 or 3 years to between 8 and 12 years (Spilker, 1994, 32). In addition, there were more regulatory controls over marketing and advertising at the same time that generic medicines rapidly eroded the positions of medicines whose patents had expired.

Bogner and Thomas (1992) identified three strategic issues that affected the industry between 1970 and 1990. In 1977, rules governing price advertising were eliminated as the result of a Supreme Court decision, and laws regarding substituting prescribed drugs with lower priced drugs that were biologically equivalent were repealed. Then, in 1980, the industry was confronted with the emergence of and potential competition from new biotechnology firms using recombinant DNA techniques. Larger established firms reacted by broadening their research and by entering into numerous strategic alliances with the biotechnology start-ups. Finally, in 1985, the Drug Price Competition and Patent Restoration Act of 1984 was enacted. The effect of this legislation was twofold: research-oriented firms gained some extension of their patent protection, but generic firms gained almost immediate access to the market after patents expired. McCutcheon (1993), in a study of research activities before and after the 1981 R&D tax credit, suggests that research intensity is another critical strategic issue driving the industry.

Our selection of these strategic issues is supported by work on strategic groups in the pharmaceutical industry. Cool and Schendel (1987, 1988) examine the industry after the enactment of the 1962 Food and Drug Act amendments and find four stable time periods: 1963–1969, 1970–1974, 1975–1979, and 1980–1982 (when their study ended). The break between 1974 and 1975 roughly corresponds with the change in rules governing price advertising, and the break between 1979 and 1980 corresponds both with the emergence of biotechnology firms involved in recombinant DNA technology and with the passage of the R&D tax credit. Fiegenbaum, Sunharshan, and Thomas (1990), investigating the period 1974–1981, found three stable strategic time periods (SSTPs)[1]: 1974–1975, 1976–1980, and 1981. These breaks also correspond with the strategic issues affecting the industry, which are presented here and in the work of Cool and Schendel (1988; 1987).

We add a fifth strategic issue, "industry reconfiguration," which includes strategic alliances, globalization, and the consolidation of the pharmaceutical industry. This industry reconfiguration was occurring at a macro level during the 1970–1990 period and continues today. Thus, five strategic issues facing the pharmaceutical industry during this time period can be identified: pricing and health care costs, regulation and patent protection, research and development, marketing and advertising, and industry reconfiguration (see also PMA, 1996c). These issues are detailed separately in the following sections.

PRICING AND HEALTH CARE COSTS

During the 1970–1995 time period, the debate continued regarding whether drug pricing decisions should reflect the cost of the drug in question or whether prices should also take into account the cost of drugs that failed to make it to the market and the costs of future development (Comanor, 1986, 1180). Significant costs in marketing and in research and development must be borne by pharmaceutical manufacturers before a new product is introduced. In the industry, "high rates of product introduction and obsolescence are found regardless of the magnitude of price-cost margins" (Comanor, 1986, 1186).

The prices of pharmaceutical products came under ethical scrutiny as well. Spinello (1992) explores the obligation of companies in the industry to charge fair prices for essential medicines, drawing on Rawls's notion of distributive justice as a potentially important factor in the pricing decision. Yet, given the future benefits of new medicine discovery and development, justice with regard to current prices might not be the only concern; the future viability of the company and the benefits its future products might provide can also be considered.

Compliance with government regulations increased the cost of discovering and developing new medicines over the 1970–1990 time frame. The regulations are discussed in detail later in this chapter, but in addition to direct regulation, the U.S. government passed maximum allowable price restrictions and encouraged generic competition by "providing bonuses to pharmacists who dispense generic medicines" (Spilker, 1994, 18). In addition, in many other parts of the world, competitive market forces are much more restricted than they are in the United States. The PMA observed that "in most European countries and [in] Japan, the government is the largest purchaser of pharmaceuticals [and uses its] power to negotiate or set prices, [distorting] the market for pharmaceuticals and undermining the vitality of the ... pharmaceutical industries" (1996g, 1).

At the same time, the analysis of medical treatment became increasingly focused on cost effectiveness. The choice between competing medications and the choice between medication and surgery were evaluated in terms of cost considerations as well as clinical effectiveness (Seigleman, 1992). Even so, Grabowski and Vernon (1992), studying the impact of the entry of generic drugs on nongeneric market share, noted that the typical response of the previously patented drug's manufacturer was to maintain price increases at the same rate as before the entry of the generic.

It is significant that companies spent hundreds of millions of dollars to develop new medicines, and it is possible that they are willing to do so only because of the significant profits they are able to enjoy on those few products that are medically and commercially successful (Spilker, 1994). Comanor points out the basic conflict "between consumer interests in (1) low priced pharmaceuticals and (2) the development of new drugs that are both safe and effective" (1986, 1211). These two interests are somewhat exclusive of one another: pharmaceutical manufacturers that reduce prices will have fewer resources with which to develop new drugs, and companies that spend greater percentages of their revenues in R&D must recoup those costs on products that are successful in the market.

REGULATION AND PATENT PROTECTION

During the 1970–1990 period, regulators of the pharmaceutical industry appeared to recognize the potentially detrimental effects of earlier legislation on the long-term viability of the industry. With the exception of the Maximum Allowable Cost Program (MAC) in 1977, which limited drug reimbursement under Medicare and Medicaid (described more fully in the section on pricing), additional legislation was directed toward removing needless or unnecessary regulation from the industry.

The R&D tax credit passed in 1981 affected all industries but particularly pharmaceutical manufacturers because of their slow and costly programs of new drug discovery and development. Comanor cites earlier research to show that federal regulation had little or no effect on R&D spending in the 1960s but had, by the period in question here, a significant impact on increased research expenditures (1986, 1205). McCutcheon notes that "research intensity is an important strategic dimension and driving force in the [pharmaceutical] industry." He found a significant increase in research intensity (research as a percentage of sales) following the passage and implementation of the tax credit (1993, 575). The tax credit has been extended six times, for shorter periods, since its original expiration in 1985; it has not yet been implemented on a permanent basis.

While R&D expenditures increased dramatically over the past decade, the time required for approval (notably less than the 44–month average in 1969) consistently decreased, as indicated in Figure 5.1. This reduction in approval time came about after the passage of seminal legislation. The Drug Price Competition and Patent Term Restoration Act (1984), Title I, loosened restrictions on testing new drugs, allowing an abbreviated new drug approval (NDA) process. It requires only that companies prove bioequivalence in "me-too" drugs and in generics in order to promote price competition by shortening the time and costs of approving these not-really-new drugs. Additionally, a streamlining of the FDA approval process, driven by the AIDS "epidemic," reduced the number of steps required for regulatory approval and allowed some drugs to be

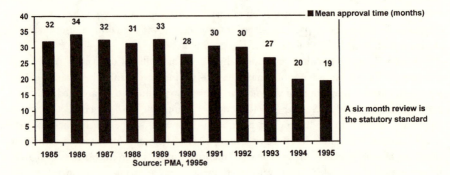

Figure 5.1 FDA Processing Time from NDA Submission to Approval, 1985–1995

made available during or even before regulatory scrutiny (Foreman, 1991). This, of course, coincides with the decrease in approval times that is apparent in Figure 5.1. However, the legislation requires the pharmaceutical companies to take on a greater role in educating patients and doctors about the medications they sell (Lewin, 1993).

Title II of the Drug Price Competition and Patent Term Restoration Act (1984) extended patent protection for up to 14 years after Food and Drug Administration (FDA) approval. Because the time from patent application to the completion of the approval process took as much as 8 to 12 years from the life of a patent, this represents a significant improvement. Comanor cites studies by Stetler (1991) and by Grabowski & Vernon (1992) that show effective patent life declining from around 15 years in the 1960s to less than 10 years by the end of the 1970s (1986, 1201–1202). The restoration of effective patent life to 14 years represents a regulatory change welcomed by the industry.

In the international arena, patent infringements are a major issue facing the industry. The PMA names Argentina, Brazil, India, and Turkey as countries that are particularly problematic for "condon[ing] pharmaceutical patent piracy" (1996h, 1). There is an increasing call for international standards in patent protection, which is largely viewed as a potential benefit to the U.S. pharmaceutical companies, both for the protection it offers and because of the generally longer terms of patents in other countries.

However, in spite of the general fine-tuning of industry regulations by legislators, the increasingly regulated environment can be associated with several negative impacts on the pharmaceutical industry:

- Fewer medicines are brought to the market each year;
- The costs of medicine development have increased;
- Some physicians suggest that their ability to choose a medicine to prescribe has been limited compared to the past;
- There is a greater delay for introducing most medicines in the United States than in several European countries. (Spilker, 1994, 24)

The pharmaceutical industry has consistently lobbied for changes favorable to producers.

MARKETING AND ADVERTISING

"Most pharmaceutical companies' decisions are dominated by the thinking of senior managers in either marketing or research and development. . . . The trend during the last 20 years or so in the industry has clearly moved toward increased domination by marketing interests" (Spilker, 1994, 423). Hill and Hansen (1991, 189) noted that by 1990, advertising budgets were equal to approximately 7% of sales revenue in the pharmaceutical industry.[2]

The gradual decrease of regulatory review requirements suggests that "drug makers and distributors will have to assume more responsibility for educating patients about the medications they dispense" (Lewin, 1993). Spilker suggests that medical staff should play a role in the development or approval of all advertising but notes that the degree to which it is critiqued by medical staff prior to release varies widely among companies

(1994, 453–454). He also notes, somewhat counterintuitively, that there is a significant potential for marketing information to enhance the medical value of a product:

- Marketing groups may target a medicine for use by a more broad (or narrow) patient population than originally conceptualized by the medical group. As a result, the medicine may eventually be used more widely, or at least more appropriately;
- Marketing may create a new means of packaging a medicine that enables it to be used more easily and correctly;
- Marketing might suggest and promote a more convenient form for a medicine that improves patient compliance and, hence, medical value. (Spilker, 1994, 443)

The question of advertising was brought up early in the Kefauver hearings and has remained a significant issue to the industry ever since. At that time (1962) the focus was on sales agents or "detail men" and the effect they were having on physicians' prescribing behavior. Since then, and in spite of financial, legal, and ethical questions, patients themselves became a significant new target for the pharmaceutical companies' marketing efforts over the course of the 1970–1990 time frame (Festervand & Tucker, 1990). Advertisements for prescription pharmaceutical drugs that reduce gastrointestinal distress, reduce cholesterol, and increase hair growth are regularly seen on television and in print.

This has been driven by the increasing availability of generic and "me too" products, which has increased customers' sensitivity to price as they have come to perceive drugs as increasingly standardized products (James, 1994, 57). A reevaluation of marketing strategy and practices is necessary if branded medicines are to compete against equivalent generics. The increased flow of information, to include patients as well as physicians and other medical professionals, has the potential to benefit all. However, the level of customer understanding can not be directly inferred from a literal reading of marketing efforts (Scheffet & Kopp, 1990).

"Customers are no longer buying new technologies in the form of new products; instead, they are buying solutions to problems that meet their therapeutic value and economic considerations" (James, 1994, 54). The knowledge gap between producers and customers has decreased dramatically over the period 1970–1990 (James, 1994, 57).

Competitors' ability to adopt new technology has improved, with the effect that they are able to successfully imitate a new product in much less time than was required for the initial breakthrough. This "significantly reduces the exclusivity of innovators and the premiums they are able to charge." In the United Kingdom, the "time elapsed between pioneer product launches and their first follow-on market entry" has been decreased by a factor of slightly more than half, from 52 months in the 1970–1974 period to 25 months in the 1985–1989 period (James, 1994, 55).

RESEARCH AND DEVELOPMENT

The cost of product innovation in the pharmaceutical industry has risen dramatically (e.g., Teitelman, Siwolop & Baldo, 1989; Hill & Hansen, 1991; PMA, 1995a). Siegelman (1989) observed that the 17 companies originally involved in penicillin research spent approximately $25 million perfecting the drug; by 1988, the industry spent more than

$6 billion on drug discovery and development. The Pharmaceutical Manufacturers' Association estimated 1995 R&D expenditures at over $14 billion (PMA, 1996a). Redwood (1989, 25) shows that from the early 1960s to the middle 1980s, measured in 5 year intervals (e.g., 1961–1965, 1966–1970), the amount spent on R&D as a percent of production nearly doubled (from 4.8 to 8.7%) while the number of new chemical entities (NCEs) introduced was nearly halved (from 431 to 278). James (1994, 54) notes that "moving up the technology evolution curve is incurring exponential cost increases." The increase in the cost of developing a new drug is illustrated in Figure 5.2.

Comanor (1986, 1195) shows that the return on research has fallen by more than half since the peak returns of 21 to 23% in the 1960s. Omta, Bouter, and Engelen (1994) suggest that a minimum of $150 to $250 million is necessary merely to maintain an innovative position and that economies of scale in research and development appear above $750 million. Bartholini (1983) estimates that the critical mass for the discovery and development of a new medicine is in the range of 600 to 800 people.

Yet, for many companies in the industry, the most critical issue affecting their growth and sometimes survival is the creation of a stream of efficacious new products that can be marketed successfully (Spilker, 1994, 15). McCutcheon (1993), in a study of research activities before and after the 1981 R&D tax credit, suggests that research intensity is a critical strategic issue driving the industry. This is true particularly as the profits from old products decline with the introduction of generic competition at patent expiration. Comanor observed that "changes in overall market share were closely tied to the number of new chemical entities (NCE) introduced" (1986, 1186).

Grabowski and Vernon (1992) analyzed 18 drugs that experienced generic competition after the 1984 Drug Price Competition and Patent Term Restoration Act had been implemented. They found that all of the drugs had lost significant market share to the lower priced generics, typically losing half of their market within 2 years of the generic drug's entry. In 1992 and 1993, 18 different drugs, with a total market value of approximately $6 billion, came out from under patent protection (Loesel, 1993), further driving the need for additional successful research and development projects in the industry. The impact of generic competition is illustrated in Figure 5.3.

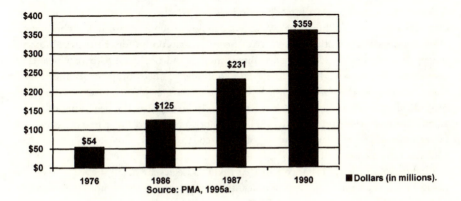

Figure 5.2 R&D Costs for a New Drug

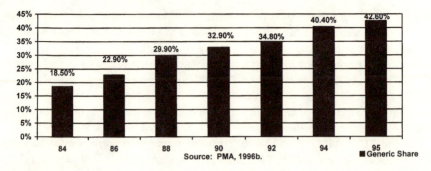

Figure 5.3 Generic Portion of the U.S. Drug Market

Spilker (1994, 230) identifies the following continuum of research activities in a pharmaceutical company:

- Purely targeted "applied research"
- Work conducted solely for medicine discovery or development
- Screening or evaluating compounds as potential medicines
- Developing improved biological or analytical methodologies to test compounds
- Evaluating potential targets to use for future screening and/or evaluation of compounds
- Evaluating hypotheses that probably will help in medicine discovery activities
- Conducting research or evaluating hypotheses that probably will not help in medicine discovery activities
- Research without connections to medicine discovery or development
- Purely exploratory "basic research"

A major point here is that as costs for research are increased, and short-term cost-benefit analysis is employed, the potential for serendipitous discovery based further from specifically targeted applied research is diminished. Spilker (1994, 21) estimates that for every 10,000 compounds that are synthesized for potential use, only 10 are ever tested in humans and, of those 10, only 1 will ever be marketed.

Some have argued that within the period 1970–1995 there was a decline in new drug discovery caused by the limits of available technology. However, two new technological areas, developed late in the period, have shown great promise for the future: biotechnology and combinatorial chemistry. Biotechnology did not live up to the hype that surrounded the early work in the field and continues to focus on proteins and monoclonal antibodies. However, it is likely to prove to have a major impact on the pharmaceutical industry and its structure. Sapienza (1989) suggests the beginning of a paradigm shift at the end of the 1970–1990 period, caused by the emergence of biotechnology and the large number of R&D collaborations and alliances associated with the field, as seen in Figure 5.4.

Tarabusi and Vickery (1994) concur that R&D strategies are being shaped by biotechnology. Combinatorial chemistry significantly increases the types of molecules available and can broaden the pool from which medical discoveries can be made. Relying on

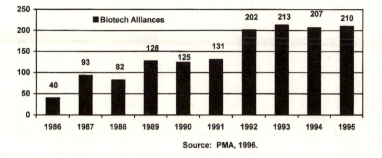

Figure 5.4 Biotech Alliances (Source: PMA, 1996)

randomness, combinatorial chemistry techniques create very large numbers of chemical compounds simultaneously. The process holds great potential for the pharmaceutical industry in the future, as these compounds can be tested for use as or in new drugs (Baum, 1998).

INDUSTRY RECONFIGURATION

From the 1960s until the late 1980s, the pharmaceutical industry was relatively stable and had a producer orientation characterized by a low level of product knowledge and little relative power from buyers. Companies in the industry were able to charge premium prices and worry little about costs because of a lack of competitive pressure (James, 1994). In the late 1980s, buyers began to exert power and demand lower prices, while still expecting new drugs to be developed.

The innovation behind the development of new drugs was seen as the key to financial success and a critical asset of firms in the industry. The importance of innovation is evident in a review of pharmaceutical company annual reports or in the study of R&D budgets (approximately 15% of sales) at pharmaceutical companies (Whittaker & Bower, 1994). By the end of the 1980s, the development of a new drug took more than 12 years and cost more than $230 million (Vagelos, 1991).

In the early 1990s, the pharmaceutical industry began fundamental restructuring through consolidation and strategic alliances. The primary reason for industry consolidation and strategic alliances has been the need to contain the ever increasing costs and risks associated with developing new drugs (Whittaker & Bower, 1994). One particularly important area of industry evolution has revolved around developments in biotechnology.

The basic discoveries that led to the development of a biotechnology industry took place primarily in the 1960s and 1970s at U.S. and European academic institutions (Fildes, 1990). However, during that period, the large and financially successful chemical and pharmaceutical firms were not willing to accept the risks associated with biotechnology; therefore, small entrepreneurial firms led the formation of the new industry (Fildes, 1990). Biotechnology caught the attention of more established industries in what some researchers have referred to as a "technological discontinuity" in the early 1980s (Hamilton & Singh, 1991, 215). A technological discontinuity is a major technological change resulting in the creation of a substitute technology for products or processes. Typically, firms established after this discontinuity adopt the new technology and have a competitive advantage over established firms. Scientific discoveries and advances over the last 20 years in biotechnology clearly represent technical discontinuities (Hamilton & Singh, 1991). These discontinuities forced firms in other industries to recognize the biotechnology industry and become involved in it to a limited extent.

Hundreds of firms in the United States became involved in biotechnology research, product development, and commercialization efforts (Hamilton & Singh, 1991). Several of the original firms in the industry have become fully integrated in the pharmaceutical industry (e.g., Genentech, Cetus, and Amgen; Fildes, 1990). Most of these biotechnology firms have been focused primarily on research and development rather than the commercialization and distribution of products.

From the inception of the industry in the mid-1970s until the mid-1990s, much of the financing needed to fund biotechnology companies came from stock market investors and venture capitalists, who were eager to cash in on the high levels of potential earnings that were characteristic of the industry. However, in late 1980s and again in 1992 and early 1993, earnings decreased, investors lost interest in the industry, and financing from capital markets dropped approximately 50% (Thayer, 1993).

At the same time, the industry became increasingly capital intensive. In order to fill the financial void, biotechnology companies have begun to form strategic alliances with other biotechnology and pharmaceutical companies (Thayer, 1993). By 1994, these strategic alliances accounted for over 27% of biotechnology equity financing (*Standard & Poors*, 1/5/1995).

Developments in both the pharmaceutical industry and biotechnology forced the industries to consolidate and adopt alternative structures (James, 1994). As discussed previously, the pharmaceutical industry faced more powerful buyers, the increasing cost of technological development, competition, and a new market structure that demanded cost containment and could quickly erode profit margin. Firms in the biotechnology industry needed financing for research and development.

In addition to providing financial support for biotechnology companies, alliances with or acquisitions by pharmaceutical firms typically provide the biotechnology firm with much needed expertise in marketing, manufacturing, and regulatory affairs (Dibner, 1993). In return, the biotechnology firms provide the critical new product innovation needed by the pharmaceutical companies. In fact, of the approximate 300 biotechnology-related drugs in clinical trial in the early 1990s, most were the result of collaboration between companies in the biotechnology and pharmaceutical industries (Dibner, 1993).

The Institute for Biotechnology Information (IBI) reports that U.S. biotechnology firms formed approximately 700 alliances (including acquisitions) in 1992 (Thayer, 1993). About 58% of these alliances were between domestic partners, and about 38% of the alliances involved foreign companies (20% with companies in Japan, 19% with U.K. companies, and 13% with Swiss companies; Thayer, 1993). In the 18 months through June 1994, European pharmaceutical firms were involved in more than 25% of approximately 300 biotechnology alliances (*Standard & Poors*, 1/5/1995). These European firms were attracted by the technological leadership of U.S. companies and stock prices that were believed to be depressed (*Standard & Poors*, 1/5/1995).

IBI conducted a research study of alliances between 1981 and 1992 that had at least one U.S. biotechnology partner, one pharmaceutical partner, a therapeutic product, and the pharmaceutical company paying the biotechnology firm for access to a product, technology, or research. Most of the alliances were licensing-marketing agreements (46%); the remainder were for R&D contracts (21%) and multiple types or reasons (33%) (Dibner, 1993). Some examples of leading pharmaceutical firms and their biotechnology partners include (Thayer, 1993):

American Cyanamid: Cambridge Biotech, Immunex, RedImmune, and Regeneron

Eli Lilly: Athena Neurosciences, Centocor, Enzon, GenPharm International, Glycomed, NeXagen, Repligen, and Sibia

Marion Merrell Dow: Affymax, Cortech, Oncogene Science, and Scios Nova

Rhone-Poulenc Rorer: Applied Immune Sciences and Immune Response

Sandoz: Affymax, Bio-Technology General, Cytel, Repligen, and SyStemix

Schering-Plough: Celltech, Cephalon, and U.S. Bioscience

SmithKline Beecham: Cambridge Biotech, Cephalon, Genelabs Technologies, Human Genome Sciences, and Oxford Glycosystems

In typical pharmaceutical and biotechnology alliances (primarily acquisitions), the pharmaceutical companies have preferred to enter the alliance by paying a premium price for technology or products that are already developed rather than sharing the costs for development as they are incurred (Thayer, 1993). Once a biotechnology company has developed a potentially successful drug, it typically can find pharmaceutical firms willing to buy or license the new product and, in turn, provide the biotechnology company with the funds necessary for future R&D work (*Standard & Poors*, 1/5/1995).

Consolidation

In 1995, there were more than 7,000 firms in the global pharmaceutical industry, but about 70% of all new product development and 60% of all direct and indirect sales came from only 50 companies. These 50 firms were expected to be cut by more than half as the industry moves toward other industry models such as aerospace, automobiles, and consumer electronics, where a handful of very large companies dominate the industry. A number of factors point toward this industry consolidation:

Access to new technology and products

Access to global markets

More aggressive competition

Industry consolidation is typically attained through mergers and acquisitions. In a merger, two firms combine their resources to form a new and integrated organization.

In an acquisition, one firm purchases another and absorbs it into its current organization or a modified organizational structure. The following significant mergers and acquisitions that were completed in 1994 are indicative of the industry trend toward consolidation (*Standard & Poors*, 10/6/1994):

American Home Products's $9.7 billion purchase of American Cyanamid

Roche Holdings's $5.3 billion acquisition of Syntex Corp

Eli Lilly's $4 billion acquisition of McKesson Corp's PCS Health Systems

Integration

Prescription and over-the-counter segment marketing efforts are converging because of buyer and government efforts to limit the profitability of patent drugs. Buyers became more concentrated at the wholesale level and include health maintenance organizations (HMOs), preferred provider networks (PPOs), and pharmacy benefit management firms (PBMs). PBMs serve essentially as middlemen between pharmaceutical companies and large drug buyers such as HMOs, hospital and pharmacy chains, large employers, and insurance companies, as well as organized buyers such as the AARP. Merck & Company, Inc. (a leader in the pharmaceutical industry) recognized the value of PBM connections to the markets and their vast databases of patient information and purchased Medco Containment Services (the second largest PBM in the nation) for $6.6 billion. This purchase provided a huge captive market for Merck products, as well as access to Medco information databases. SmithKline Beecham made a similar strategic integration move when it purchased Diversified Pharmaceutical Services for $2.3 billion (*Standard & Poors*, 5/4/1995).

Throughout the period, the U.S. pharmaceutical industry saw the global distribution of its activities continue to increase in absolute terms. However, the trend toward increasing percentages of sales in foreign markets that started in the 1960s was reversed starting in 1980 (Table 5.1). By the end of the period covered in this book, the industry stabilized at approximately a 2:1 ratio between domestic and foreign sales, though in the next few years there was dramatic change.

In addition to globalization in distribution, U.S. firms saw Japanese pharmaceutical companies emerge as international competitors during the 1970–1990 period, particularly from 1980 onward (Reich, 1990). While the United States still leads the world in pharmaceutical R&D, accounting for almost one third of worldwide expenditures, Japan follows in second place, with 20% of expenditures (PMA, 1996c); the result of these expenditures is shown in Figure 5.5, indicating the country of origin for major global medicines, those that are sold in six or more of the world's leading markets.

The size of Japan's pharmaceutical market, as well, was second in the world after the United States by the end of the period (Yoshikawa, 1989), having achieved tremendous growth in the postwar years. Gaeta (1991) reports that by the end of the 1970–1990 period, of the 30 top marketed pharmaceutical products in the United States, 12% of the personal selling time was associated with products licensed from Japanese firms.

Japanese pharmaceutical firms were also adopting global strategies for production and for conducting clinical studies, with the goal of establishing a global network with

Table 5.1 Domestic and Foreign Sales of Drug Firms Headquartered in the United States, 1970–1995

Year	Domestic U.S. Sales $ Million	% Change	Foreign Sales $ Million	% Change	Annual Total $ Million	% Change	Foreign Sales as a Percentage of Total
1970	4552.5	N/A	2084	N/A	6636.5	N/A	31.4
1971	5144.9	13.0	2459.7	18.0	7604.6	14.6	32.3
1972	5210.1	1.3	2720.2	10.6	7930.3	4.3	34.3
1973	5686.5	9.1	3152.5	15.9	8839.0	11.5	35.7
1974	6470.4	13.8	3891.0	23.4	10361.4	17.2	37.6
1975	7135.7	10.3	4633.3	19.1	11769.0	13.6	39.4
1976	7951.0	11.4	5084.3	9.7	13035.3	10.8	39.0
1977	8550.4	7.5	5605.0	10.2	14155.4	8.6	39.6
1978	9580.5	12.0	6850.4	22.2	16430.9	16.1	41.7
1979	10651.3	11.2	8287.8	21.0	18939.1	15.3	43.8
1980	11997.6	12.6	10515.4	26.9	22513.0	18.9	46.7
1981	12872.0	7.3	10658.3	1.4	23530.3	4.5	45.3
1982	14986.9	16.4	10667.4	0.1	25654.3	9.0	41.6
1983	17095.0	14.1	10411.2	-2.4	27506.2	7.2	37.9
1984	19403.1	13.5	10450.9	0.4	29854.0	8.5	35.0
1985	21153.5	9.0	10872.3	4.0	32025.8	7.3	33.9
1986	24106.8	14.0	13030.5	19.9	37137.3	16.0	35.1
1987	26566.1	10.2	15068.4	15.6	41634.5	12.1	36.2
1988	29324.6	10.4	17649.3	17.1	46973.9	12.8	37.6
1989	33321.6	13.6	16817.9	-4.7	50139.5	6.7	33.5
1990	39229.3	17.7	19838.3	18.0	59067.6	17.8	33.6
1991	45264.1	15.4	22231.1	12.1	67495.2	14.3	32.9
1992	49901.8	10.2	25744.2	15.8	75646.0	12.1	34.0
1993	52911.3	6.0	26467.3	2.8	79378.6	4.9	33.3
1994	55996.2	5.8	26870.7	1.5	82866.9	4.4	32.4
1995	58046.5	3.7	29567.1	10.0	87613.6	5.7	33.7

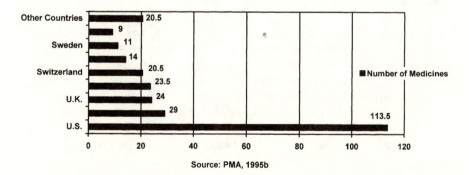

Source: PMA, 1995b

Figure 5.5 Major Global Medicines by Country of Development, 1970–1992

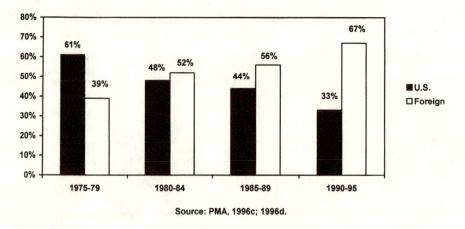

Source: PMA, 1996c; 1996d.

Figure 5.6 Location of First Human Studies of New Chemical Entities, 1975–1995

centers in Japan, Europe, and the United States (Takahashi, 1994). However, similar strategies had been adopted by firms of other countries, including the United States. The increasing percentage of new chemical entities (NCEs) developed by U.S. firms for which the first clinical tests were performed in a foreign location was indicative of this trend (Figure 5.6).

Nonetheless, during the time period we studied, U.S. biotechnology enjoyed a strong lead in the global marketplace. The Pharmaceutical Manufacturers" Association (PMA) observed that "of the 150 genetic engineering healthcare patents issued by the U.S. Patent and Trademark Office in 1995, 122 went to U.S. applicants" (1996c, 2). A similar situation existed with major global drugs: "Of the 265 . . . developed between 1970 and 1992, almost half were of U.S. origin" (PMA, 1996g).

CONCLUSION

The years from 1970 to 1995 were a period of largely undramatic but nevertheless important change in the pharmaceutical industry. The cumulative effect of the environmental changes that occurred changed the structure of the industry and intensified competition. In addition, increasingly specialized laboratory equipment and personnel added to the pharmaceutical companies" costs. This was particularly salient as the profit stream from old products was jeopardized by the introduction of generic competition at patent expiration.

The following chapters explore only a portion of this complex picture.

Notes

1. For an interesting discussion for determining SSTPs, see Fiegenbaum et al., 1987.
2. By comparison, R&D expenditures for the same year were 15.9% of sales (PMA, 1995d).

6

Understanding Diversity in the Timing of Strategic Response

This chapter[1] draws on the concepts of cognitive schema found in chapter 2 to understand timing differences in U.S. pharmaceutical company responses to significant changes in the Food and Drug Cosmetic Act. While the amendment passed in 1962, our data trace strategic responses throughout the decade—changes that inaugurate the study period more intensely covered in chapter 8.

Detailed content analysis suggests some of the differences in firm understanding of environmental change associated with strategic change. Importantly, we show that multiple concepts associated with environmental change must be directly linked to organizational performance before new strategies are initiated. These results emphasize the importance of stress as a precursor to strategic response. Content analysis also allowed us to distinguish strategic change in anticipation of environmental stress from change after the stressful event occurred.

SHARED SCHEMATIC FRAMEWORKS WITHIN THE FIRM

Many researchers interested in associating firm response to the environment with cognitive processes treat "the firm" as a unitary actor noticing changes in its situation. This practical simplification is problematic, of course, because cognition is an attribute of individuals. One way out of the conundrum is to consider the absolute necessity of *common* schematic frameworks for achieving coordinated action. Several interesting lines of inquiry outside the management field emphasize the necessity of shared belief and interpretation as the basis for social behavior. These streams of research augment the discussion found in chapter 3 to suggest how commonalities that support collective activity come about. For example, an interest in the sources of scientific discovery led Kuhn (1970) to define scientific communities on the basis of a shared paradigmatic framework. This work emphasizes the importance of shared understanding for defining the most important scientific work to be pursued. Kuhn points to professional training, established procedures, compelling experiments, accepted tools and instrumentation, and formal and informal interaction among scientists as the means of establishing and solidifying common assumptions.

An analogous line of reasoning in political science investigates the development of "epistemic communities" (Haas, 1992). This work is driven by an interest in understanding how new policies (e.g., monetary reform or environmental protection) are developed by government agencies. Peter Haas suggests that such groups have:

1. a shared set of normative and principled beliefs, that provide a value-based rationale for the social action of community members;
2. shared causal beliefs, that are derived from their analysis of practices leading or contributing to a central set of problems in their domain and which then serve as the basis for elucidating the multiple linkages between possible policy actions and desired outcomes;
3. shared notions of validity, that is, intersubjective, internally defined criteria for weighing and validating knowledge in the domain of their expertise; and
4. a common policy enterprise, that is, a set of common practices associated with a set of problems to which their professional competence is directed, presumably out of the conviction that human welfare will be enhanced as a consequence. (1992, 3)

These and other works are convincing testimony for the necessity of shared understanding to accomplish coordinated social tasks. The possibility of coordination is what leads to social organization in the first place (Barnard, 1938), and there are strong philosophical arguments that extensive commonalities are necessary for *any* kind of social exchange (Gilbert, 1989; Kelly, 1955). The consequence for the organization is that "organizational cognition cannot be seen as an individualized act, but rather as an 'inseparable aspect' (Lave & Wenger, 1991) of the continual, local negotiation and re-negotiation of meanings between actors" (Wood, 1996, 1). Thus, organization cognition is a reciprocal concept, in which the individual's interpretation is shaped by the organization and other social contexts, but that cognition is simultaneously creating context (Weick, 1979). There is room for individual differences, but patterns emerge from the whole (Allard Poesi, 1994; Ehlinger, 1994; Fiol, 1994; Stjernberg & Ullstad, 1994).

The underlying assumption of this chapter is that organizations, and especially the top management team of organizations, must be "epistemic communities" of some strength in order to be viable economic units. While individuals continue to have unique beliefs and interpretations, they share many beliefs and understanding with others (Bougon, Weick, & Binkhorst, 1977; Hodgkinson & Johnson, 1994). To the extent that beliefs are shared by key actors, the resulting shared schematic frameworks simplify a complex world and provide the basis for coordinated activity. Similar structures have been labeled "shared understanding" (March, 1991), "cognitive consensuality" (Gioia & Sims, 1986b), "dominant logic" (Prahalad & Bettis, 1986), or shared "strategic frames" (Huff, 1982) within the organization.

Chapter 2 outlines research from social psychology suggesting that the processes of noticing and interpreting stimuli are directed by cognitive structures called *schema*. We extend this concept to the organizational level by recognizing the necessity of some level of shared understanding to conduct coordinated activity, and call these shared belief systems "shared schematic frameworks."

Figure 6.1 provides a general model for understanding the timing of change in such frameworks. The model incorporates work on stress and inertia with ideas of schema-based interpretive processes as developed in the theoretic section of this book.

As initially discussed in chapter 1, organizations are assumed to have various formal and informal mechanisms in place to scan their environments. These mechanisms are more or less sensitive to bits of information that might be used to reconsider firm well-being. Failure to notice potentially anomalous stimuli results in continued routine scanning. Even if an anomaly-producing event is given attention, it must be interpreted or given meaning (Daft & Weick, 1984). Any given event is likely to be imbued with many types of meaning. Of particular relevance to the idea of stress-inertia and strategic change is interpretation of the likely impact (if any) of the event on the firm. Such an interpretation may result in one of two basic outcomes. First, the stimuli may collectively be interpreted as not having a significant impact on the firm. In this case, current routines and procedures are not questioned, and, thus, the event is not considered stress-

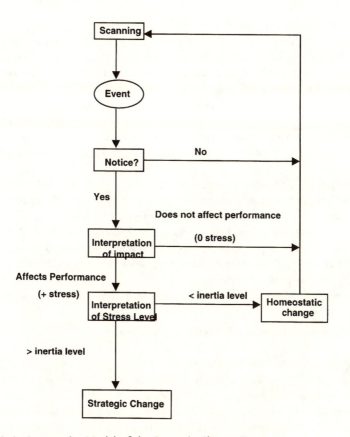

Figure 6.1 An Interpretive Model of the Strategic Change Process

ful. The level of organizational stress is not increased, and scanning continues, although future events (or input from other scanning mechanisms) may result in a reinterpretation at a later time.

When an event is interpreted as having an impact on the firm, the pressure to make some change in activity will increase. At this point, a second determination must be made: is the pressure to change (level of stress) greater than the pressure to maintain the status quo (level of inertia)? As outlined in chapter 4, if stress is less than inertia, it is probable that discomfort will be addressed through homeostatic adjustments in current strategy. However, as stress exceeds inertia, second order strategic change is more and more likely to occur.

We used this model as an organizing device in designing an empirical study of timing issues. Linking interpretation to action required solving a number of methodological issues, which will be discussed before returning to the model and our analysis.

STUDY OF PHARMACEUTICAL RESPONSE TO REGULARY CHANGE IN 1962

To assess the relative capacity of firms as "epistemic communities" to recognize and respond to stimuli potentially indicating a need for a change, we needed to identify a relatively homogeneous set of firms and isolate a strong, unconfounded change in the competitive arena shared by these firms. Data had to be available from the time period in which the event took place, and similar data had to be available for all companies studied. Furthermore, the firms had to be homogeneous enough to be expected to be similarly affected by the environmental change. In addition to these issues of data selection, we needed to establish methods for separately identifying strategic actions and the shared schematic framework or "strategic frame" that might be expected to direct these activities.

The challenges of identifying environmental changes with relatively homogeneous effects are typically solved by looking at key events in the relatively small number of industries dominated by single-business firms (Meyer, 1982a; Smith & Grimm, 1987a; Scheid-Cook, 1992). We followed this tradition by choosing to study the U.S. pharmaceutical industry. A long period of sustained growth and profitability after the Second World War is evidence of a relatively stress-free environment. However, it is a regulated industry, and we were particularly drawn to the 1962 amendments to the Food, Drug, and Cosmetic Act of 1938 as an interesting example of significant environmental change.

The Exogenous Shock of 1962 Regulatory Change

The 1962 amendments were preceded by years of government hearings and the introduction of several proposed regulatory changes in both the House and Senate. The powerful Pharmaceutical Manufacturers's Association was able to influence the content of these amendments, and many observers felt they might even defeat the congressional proposals made in the early 1960s. However, the unexpected thalidomide disaster in Europe and Canada came to light in early 1962, and public concern about birth defects caused by prescription sleeping pills (and, by extension, negative side effects of other prescription drugs) added new dimensions to the bill being considered in Congress, considerably strengthening the provisions the drug companies had anticipated, and hastened the bill's approval.

The bill contained many provisions, but its major impact was to add several new phases to the drug approval process. The time the Food and Drug Administration (FDA) had to approve a new drug was doubled, with automatic extensions granted to the FDA if the deadline was not met. The FDA was also given the power to withdraw without notice approval from existing drugs if they were found to be unsafe, lacked "substantial" evidence of effectiveness (evidence of effectiveness was a new requirement in itself), or contained misstated applications. The 17-year legislated life of a drug patent begins at the time the patent is awarded. To protect prospective new drugs from competition, patents commonly are applied for at the time of discovery and prior to testing. The new, more stringent testing requirements resulting from the amendments thus increased the time and expense associated with introducing a new drug and decreased the time available for profiting from patent protection. In fact, the time elapsing from FDA processing time from submission of a new drug application to approval increased from 17 months in 1962 to 44 months by 1969 (Temin, 1980), significantly reducing the effective life of the patent.

Several subsequent trends in the industry have been attributed to these changes in the environment. First, there was a significant decline in the number of new drugs introduced in the United States. Between 1950 and 1961, 564 new chemical entities (NCEs), the basis of the FDA approval and patent protection process, were introduced. In the next 8 years, only 159 went through the system. While a portion of this decrease is due to a "knowledge plateau," comparative studies of U.S. and U.K. new drug introductions suggest the amendments also contributed significantly to the decline in new drug introductions (Grabowski, Vernon & Thompson., 1978; Wardell, 1971).

Second, U.S. pharmaceutical manufacturers became increasingly active overseas. Foreign sales as a percent of total for all U.S. manufacturers increased steadily during the 1960s (Temin, 1980), and U.S. firms increased their investments in overseas activities. For example, the percentage of NCEs first studied and tested in the United States by U.S. firms decreased from 100% at the time the amendments were enacted to less than 80% by 1970 to 50% by 1974 (Lasagna & Wardell, 1975).

A third major trend in the industry following enactment of the 1962 amendments was growth through diversification. Most of this activity occurred through acquisitions, both inside and outside the pharmaceutical industry. Of particular significance, U.S. pharmaceutical companies diversified into nonprescription medicines, consumer products such as cosmetics and sundries, and medical equipment and diagnostic aids. Cool (1985) attributes these moves to the pharmaceutical companies' ability to transfer technical knowledge and take advantage of established distribution channels, as well as the hefty profit margins and growth rates available in these markets.

To summarize, the 1962 changes in FDA regulation are seen by analysts as leading to significant changes in the industry, including a significant increase in the time and expense associated with bringing a new product to market and a shorter effective patent life. These changes in the environment were reflected in strategic change across the industry, including an increase in overseas expansion and diversification into related businesses. Our questions were (1) Could we identify significant changes in the *timing* of such responses to the 1962 legislation? and (2) Could these changes be explained in terms of the theoretic ideas summarized in Figure 6.1?

Sample Selection

Selection of a homogeneous sample for the study was based on four criteria. First, because the stimulus event was significant change in U.S. regulation, we decided candidate firms had to be U.S.-owned, with over 50% of their business conducted in the USA at the start of the study period. Second, all firms in the sample had to have significant commitment (which we defined as over 50% of U.S. sales) to pharmaceutical manufacturing in 1962. Third, all sample firms were required to have at least 10 years of history in the pharmaceutical industry prior to the beginning of the study period, to assure the formation of relatively well-developed schema, which at the organizational level we call "strategic frames," prior to the change in legislation. Fourth, sample firms were also required to be financially healthy at the time of the regulatory change, to avoid confounding changes in strategic frames due to regulatory change with responses to other performance concerns. Our criterion was that changes in profitability should not differ significantly from the experience of the industry as a whole; it was not necessary to be more specific because financial performance in the study period was not a discounting factor for any of the firms considered. Fifth, sufficient financial and textual data had to be available for analysis.

Because of the extensive coding requirements of the cause mapping methodology described later, which we use to identify the strategic frames of each firm over a minimum of 7 years, the sample size had to be restricted to a relatively small number of firms. For that reason, the sample was drawn from *Forbes*'s 1962 list of the top 10 U.S. pharmaceutical companies. Of those 10, 6 manufacturers met the four criteria and thus make up the final study sample: Abbott Laboratories (Abbott), Merck and Company (Merck), Parke, Davis and Company (Parke-Davis), Smith Kline and French (SKF), Charles Pfizer (Pfizer), and Schering. Once the sample was identified, the next steps were to identify the points in time in which significant changes in strategic action occurred in each firm during the period of interest and to identify the strategic frames of each firm for each year during the same time period. We then used the outcomes of both processes to categorize firms as fast or slow responders and to link the content of strategic frames to the timing of strategic change.

Points of Change in Strategic Action

Two preliminary analyses were required before the core questions of the study could be addressed. The first involved identifying the timing of strategic change in each sample firm. Following the definition of strategy proposed by Mintzberg and Waters (1982), change in strategy was defined as a significant break in the pattern of resource allocations made by the firm. Four variables associated with industry trends following the

1962 amendments were selected as important indicators of potential strategic change that could be tied to the effects of the amendments: percentage of foreign assets to total assets, research and development (R&D) expenditures as a percentage of sales, selling expense as a percentage of sales, and liquid to total assets.[2] Percentage of foreign assets to total assets was assumed to directly reflect strategic orientation toward geographic expansion. Research and development as a percentage of sales was used as an indication of commitment to the development of new ethical pharmaceuticals; as an increase in this measure is a likely indicator of increased investment due to the new testing requirements, a more diversified focus might be reflected in a decline in R&D as a percentage of total sales. Selling expense as a percentage of sales is also a measure of product emphasis; the marketing of pharmaceuticals required sales visits to physicians and was typically more expensive than marketing over-the-counter remedies or other consumer products. Last, liquid to total assets reflects significant changes in capital expenditure. Historically, pharmaceutical manufacturers had been fiscally conservative, funding capital expansion through internal funds. Shifts in this measure following 1962 are primarily attributed by industry observers to the significant increase in diversification via acquisition.

Data were collected from published financial reports of each firm from the period 1950 to 1970—the 20 years surrounding the change in regulation chosen for study. Break points indicating change in strategy along key dimensions were identified through the use of cluster analysis, a procedure frequently used by strategy researchers to identify strategic change (Hambrick, 1984; Harrigan, 1985; Smith & Grimm, 1987a). Firms were analyzed individually with Ward's method of cluster analysis. This clustering method was considered the most appropriate of the several that might have been used (SAS, 1990) because it offers a straightforward translation of the idea of patterns in resource allocation. Ward's method clusters data by minimizing variance within clusters and maximizing variance across clusters. The algorithm involved initially separates the four measures for each year; it then joins clusters, beginning with those that explain the least variance by existing separately. The procedure continues until all cases are joined in a single cluster. The researcher must decide when the program begins to join clusters with inappropriately high variance, using the semipartial R^2 of each clustering iteration as an initial indicator of the appropriate clustering solution (number of clusters) (Hartigan, 1976). A review of the output indicated that a semipartial R^2 of greater than .1 represented a significant loss of explained variance in the next iteration of the program. The final determination of the number of clusters was made much easier because of the easy interpretability of the clusters themselves (Evritt, 1980). No restrictions were placed on the algorithm to force sequential clusters. With one exception, however, when the procedure was terminated, the break points between clusters allowed them to be placed in longitudinal sequence; which suggests that the selected variables do capture cohesive strategic decisions made over time.

The one exception involved Parke-Davis. For this company, a significant drop in sales, coinciding with an increase in asset expenditures, led to a significant dip in liquid assets as a percentage of total assets from 1960 to 1963. This dip caused the clustering algorithm to identify the 1957–1959 cluster as much more similar to the 1964–1969 cluster than to the 1960–1963 cluster. Analysis of the remaining three variables suggested, how-

Table 6.1 Initial Categorization of Firm Responsiveness Based on Cluster Analysis

Firm	First Strategy	Second Strategy	Third Strategy	Fourth Strategy
Merck	1952–1957 [.582][2]	1958–1963 [.115]	***1964**–1970	
			1960–1963 [.101]	***1964**–1969
Parke Davis[1]	1952–1956 [.413]	1957–1959 [.210]		
SKF	1952–1956 [.540]	1957–1964 [.207]	***1965**–1970	
Pfizer	1952–1956 [.442]	1957–1960 [.211]	1961–1964 [.121]	***1965**–1970
Schering	1952–1954 [.251]	1955–1958 [.373]	1959–1965 [.146]	***1966**–1970
				*1967–1970
Abbott	1952–1956 [.231]			
		1957–1960 [.439]	1961–1966 [.129]	

[1]Cluster solution after adjusting for liquid assets as a percent of total. Parke Davis was purchased by Warner-Lambert in 1970; therefore, the last cluster terminates in 1969.
[2]Numbers in brackets are the semipartial R^2s. This is the loss in explained variance that occurs if the cluster is combined with the cluster to the right.

ever, that it was reasonable to maintain the three break points involved, and thus the ultimate decision was that significant changes in strategy occurred in 1957, 1960, and 1964.

Table 6.1 summarizes the breaks identified in the pattern of each firm's strategic decisions, along with the descriptive statistics used to guide our decisions. As shown, the 1962 regulatory change coincided with the third or fourth strategic change made by the sample firms during the 1952–1970 study period. Based on the starred dates, we identified Merck and Parke-Davis as the fastest responders to legislative changes in 1962, with new strategic actions initiated in 1964. SKF and Pfizer, firms that show evidence of significant strategic change in 1965, were identified as midgroup responders. Schering and Abbott, with changes in 1966 and 1967, respectively, were identified as the slowest two firms to respond.

Identifying Strategic Frames

The second stage of preliminary analysis involved identifying the strategic frames used by the top management team of each firm. This task posed its own methodological challenges. Questionnaires can be used to ask about environmental and strategic changes (e.g., Smith & Grimm, 1987a; Milliken, 1990), but the very act of asking an individual to reflect on an issue may cause his or her a priori interpretations to be reevaluated, a problem that becomes more acute as the events of interest fall out of active memory (Golden, 1992). Real-time interviews avoid the retrospective nature of questionnaires but also suffer from intervention effects. In fact, face-to-face contact heightens the distorting human tendency to impress the observer (Eden, Ackermann & Tait, 1993). Ethnographic approaches to the study of changing interpretations provide a less obtrusive method of study (Meyer, 1982a; Scheid-Cook, 1992; Bartunek, 1984), though impression management cannot be discounted. In addition, these studies are even more time consuming than interviews and rely more heavily on subjective interpretations by the researcher.

We were attracted to studying a stressful event that occurred more than 30 years ago because the impact of the focal event and possible confounding effects were easier to identify after the passage of time. None of the methods just described is very practical in this circumstance, however, and thus we were drawn to a fourth methodological alternative, content analysis of documents written during the period of interest. Documents are a real-time, nonintrusive indicator of the interpretations of top managers that are especially useful when, as in this case, other data sources (interviews, questionnaires, direct observations, etc.) are not available. The basic assumption is that the subjects that decision makers discuss in communications such as letters to shareholders reflect concerns of importance to the speaker. This assumption dates back to the first recorded use of content analysis, an investigation of the heretical content of new hymns in eighteenth-century Sweden (Woodrum, 1984).

Annual reports are the most obvious documentary data source for longitudinal studies. They are produced by many companies at the same time of the year, and they are readily available. In addition, we believe that annual reports and other public documents are an important forum in which strategic frames are articulated. They both reflect and help create needed commonalities in the interpretation of events. Furthermore, they have been used in past research to assess and explain corporate strategies (Bowman, 1984; Fahey & Narayanan, 1989; Fiol, 1989; Lant et al., 1992), to identify key arenas of competition (Birnbaum-More & Weiss, 1990) and to explore causal reasoning within firms (Bettman & Weitz, 1983; Clapham & Schwenk, 1991).

To expand the data set available from annual reports, we also tried to locate public speeches made by representatives of the study firms in our study period. None of the six firms was able to provide transcripts of speeches from the time period studied.[3] There were, however, a total of 19 speeches from this time period published in *Wall Street Transcripts,* a publication that provides a full record of many executive speeches to securities analysts and similar audiences. At least two speeches were available for each of the six firms in the sample, with the exception of Schering, for which we found only one.

The exact authorship of both letters to shareholders and speeches is open to question, but when a shared strategic frame is the unit of analysis, ambiguity about authorship of such documents is not particularly problematic. The notion of epistemic community discussed earlier, as well as an increased emphasis on the fact that the leadership of larger organizations is dispersed among many individuals (Hambrick & Mason, 1984), makes it plausible to use such documents as an indicator of shared understanding.

Annual reports and speeches to analysts are more problematic because they are persuasive documents and subject to deliberate distortion, but persuasion and distortion accompany all possible data sources. We have noted already that biased recall and impression management can have contaminating effects on data drawn from questionnaires, interviews, and participant observations. Even accounting data and financial information can be slanted to present the firm in the best possible light. While we recognize that annual reports and speeches are explicitly persuasive, we echo Giere's (1988) argument that unrealistic theoretic statements in science are constrained by a broad body of "common observation." Securities analysts, institutional investors, the business press, and the Securities and Exchange Commission all constrain errors of commission and omission. Salancik and Meindl (1984) present evidence that firms are rewarded for being truthful in these circumstances. The bottom line is that we chose to study a set of documents that are not the ideal indicator of shared belief, but no ideal data source exists.

Despite their limitations, these documents provided a very interesting source of data for study. Even before beginning detailed coding, initial analysis of statements made in the documents for Pfizer, Abbott, and Parke-Davis provided insights that required a change in the original categorization of faster versus slower responders. (That is, we found we had an error rate of 50% using a method commonly used in strategy research to identify strategic change.) Beginning with the general premise that topics covered in the letters to shareholders and speech transcripts reflect issues of importance to top managers, we looked for statements concerning the legislation and related events (hearings, introductions of earlier versions of the legislation, etc.) in the documents of each firm. Letters and speeches for Pfizer and Abbott during 1959–1961 contained several statements concerning Senate investigations of the industry and the introduction of the Kefauver bill in early 1961.[4] Pfizer letters and speeches following the 1962 change in legislation make no mention of it. Abbott continued to mention the legislation but only as a side issue; statements concerning the potential change in legislation during the 1959–1961 time period were much more frequent and substantial than statements made after 1961. In short, the 1965 change in action for Pfizer and 1967 change for Abbott appear not to be directly related to the new legislation that provided the stimulus event for this study. Content analysis indicates that both firms made a *proactive* response to initial legislative moves rather than wait for the actual enactment of the legislation in 1962. This conclusion was corroborated by a systematic study of business press and industry articles about each firm during this same time period. Both companies therefore were recategorized as faster responders.

A review of the content of Parke-Davis documents was even more interesting. The data reveal *no* references to regulatory issues over the entire study period. This company's statements were focused on relative lack of R&D productivity and declining sales of chloromycetin, its primary product. Complete lack of attention to legislative events, combined with numerous statements regarding R&D, suggests that their 1964 change in strategy was not strongly motivated by the legislative change that interested us as a stressful event. This firm was therefore excluded from comparative assessment of response to stressful legislation. Of course, Parke-Davis did compete in an environment almost all other observers felt was significantly restricted by new legislation. This environment presumably had an impact on the outcome, if not the formulation, of their strategy. It is well to remember, however, that even "major" changes in the environment do not have a homogeneous effect on all firms.

Given the cross-check of quantitative measures of change in allocation of strategic resources with qualitative content pertaining to government actions, our final classification is shown in Table 6.2. Pfizer and Abbott are identified as fast responders to new regulation with 1961 changes in strategic action anticipating 1962 legislation. Merck, SKF, and Schering are classified as slower responders with changes in action occurring

Table 6.2 Reassignment of Firms Based on Content
Analysis

Response Time	Name of Firm	Years
Faster Response	Pfizer	1961–1964
	Abbott	1961–1966
Slower Response	Merck	1964–1970
	SKF	1965–1970
	Schering	1966–1970
No Response	Parke-Davis	

in 1964, 1965 and 1966, respectively. Parke-Davis must be analyzed separately and is addressed in the discussion section of this chapter.

EMPIRICAL EVIDENCE OF THE INTERPRETIVE PRECURSORS TO STRATEGIC CHANGE

Once it was clear that there were significant differences in the timing of response to 1962 regulatory changes among pharmaceutical firms, we wanted to determine if these responses could be explained in terms of the theoretic ideas summarized in Figure 6.1. The figure suggested three points at which the interpretive processes of faster responding firms might be significantly different from slower firms. Faster firms might (1) more rapidly notice changes in the environment, (2) more quickly interpret changes as significant, or (3) more quickly determine that the stress associated with the new event merited action. Differences at even one of these points might explain differences in the timing of strategic action; alternatively, faster firms might be distinguished from slower firms by multiple indicators of difference. To address these issues, we looked more closely at statements made in annual reports and the *Wall Street Transcripts*.

Causal Mapping Methodology

Of the several procedures available to systematically content-analyze written documents (Huff, 1990), we chose to focus on causal reasoning under the assumption that firms typically initiate strategic actions based on the shared belief that they will cause desirable changes; many other organization researchers have made the same assumption (e.g., Bougon et al., 1977; Salancik & Meindl, 1984; Shrivastava & Lin, 1984; Narayanan & Fahey, 1990; Barr et al., 1992; Eden, 1993; Allard Poesi, 1994; Ehlinger, 1994; Jenkins, 1994; Laukkanen, 1994; Markóczy & Goldberg, 1995). The method of "cause mapping" we used was initially developed by Axelrod (1976) and elaborated by Huff, Narapareddy, and Fletcher (1990). The process is time consuming, but the resulting maps provide a parsimonious synthesis of a great deal of material.

The procedure requires that all statements of relationship in the document analyzed be identified by the coder. The nature of the relationship is placed into one of the nine categories identified in Table 6.3. After all relational statements have been identified, the linked concepts are examined. Those judged to be equivalent are given the same code. A cause map is then constructed by connecting coded concepts with arrows and labeling the arrows with the appropriate symbol for the type of relationship. As a simple example, the sentence "Substantial construction was undertaken in 1961 for the manufacture of new products as well as increased capacity to meet rising demands for established ones," would be coded as follows:

Substantial construction undertaken in + [ability to] manufacture new products
1961 (l.a) (1.b)

Substantial construction undertaken in + [ability to] meet rising demand for es-
1961(1.a) tablished products (1.c)

and then represented in graphical form:

[ability to] manufacture new products
(1.b)

Substantial construction undertaken in
1961 (l.a)

[ability to] meet rising demand for established products (1.c)

The coding manual also makes provisions for linkages that are not directly stated but are implied by context. These coder decisions are distinguished on the map by use of a dotted, rather than a solid arrow. In addition, sometimes the ultimate effect of a chain of reasoning is implied rather than explicit. The coding procedure therefore allows the coder to specify a positive or negative impact on the "utility" of some actor or entity. All inferences, even linking words such as "ability to" in the example, are indicated by brackets, which signify a departure from the source material.

The documents utilized for coding in this study were the 42 letters to shareholders (LTS) from the annual reports for each firm from 1960 to 1966 (1 year prior to the earliest response among the firms and 1 year after the latest response) and transcripts of the eight speeches recorded in the *Wall Street Transcript (WST)* (out of 19) that included references to government legislation. Letters to shareholders averaged two 8.5" x II" typed pages of text, and the *WST*s averaged six 8.5" x 11" typed pages. In total, approximately 132 pages of text were coded. Comparisons of maps from both data sources show consistency in causal assertions for all six firms studied, a consistency in causal reasoning also found by Axelrod (1976) and his associates. Material from the *WST* speeches was therefore added to LTS of the same year.

Document coding was performed by two independent research assistants unaware of the research questions. Each coder was trained separately in the coding process. Two *WST* speeches from sample firms were coded by both coders to ascertain intercoder reliability. These texts were among the longest and most complicated documents to be coded, consisting of 122 total statements. Based on Robinson's (1957) measure of agree-

Table 6.3 Coding Categories

Symbol	Definition
/+/	Positively affects
/−/	Negatively affects
/⊖/	Will not hurt, does not prevent, is not harmful to
/⊕/	Will not help, does not promote, is of no benefit to
/a/	May or may not be related to, affects indeterminably
/m/	Affects in some non-zero way
/0/	Does not matter for, has no affect on, has no relation
/=/	Is an equivalent to, is defined as*
/e/	Is an example of, is one member of*

*Categories not used by Axelrod.

ment, which is also used by Axelrod (1976), intercoder agreement on the number of codable assertions was 82%. This is a reasonable degree of reliability, though not outstanding; the differences between coders, however, were primarily due to two sentences with particularly subtle causal assertions. Had the coders agreed on these two statements, reliability would have been 89%, well within the range of acceptability. Agreement on which part of the statement contained the causal concept was 98%. Identification of the part of the statement containing the effect was 97%. Agreement as to the sign of the causal relationship was 88%, with most differences involving subtle signs such as "no effect on" and "no negative effect on."

Once training was satisfactorily established, the remaining documents were divided between the coders, who completed all coding independently. In analyzing the results, we were guided by the three questions drawn from Figure 6.1:

1. Do firms that quickly take action more rapidly identify changes in their environments?
2. Do they more quickly interpret unfamiliar stimuli as important?
3. Do they more rapidly identify stressful consequences of new stimuli?

Finding 1: Faster firms could not be distinguished from other firms in our data set by their attention to legislation change.

The most straightforward link between the interpretation of an event and new strategic action is direct stimulus-response. That is, the most basic hypothesis relevant to our interest in the length of time it takes firms to respond to environment change would be that the strategic frame used by faster responding firms will contain references to a precipitating environmental event prior to slower responding firms. Figure 6.1 proposes, however, that the simple process of noticing significant changes in the environment is not in and of itself a sufficient trigger for adaptive changes in strategy.

In analyzing the maps in the data set, any and all concepts dealing with proposed or actual legislation were identified, regardless of how they were connected to other concepts. Because the faster responders changed in 1961, both the 1960 and 1961 maps for all sample firms were analyzed. The maps of both early and late responders make references to the proposed legislation as early as 1960. Only Parke-Davis, as previously noted, failed to attend to either the pending legislation or to its enactment.

Finding 2: A necessary condition for strategic actions in our sample is that firms perceive their welfare is directly affected by environmental change.

As indicated in Table 6.3, the faster firms (Pfizer and Abbott) actually responded in 1961, prior to the 1962 change in legislation. Therefore, the 1961 cause maps of each firm were examined. These maps show that the proposed change in legislation is directly linked to concepts affecting firm performance and well-being in the faster responding firms. In analyzing the maps, strength of association was determined by the type of linkage (a direct, stated association versus an indirect, implied association), the strength of the linkage code, and the number of linkages between the concepts surrounding the new legislation and concepts about performance and well-being (the greater the number of linkages, the stronger the association).

The 1961 cause map of Pfizer (excerpted in Fig. 6.2) can be used to illustrate the type of associations displayed. The bill itself (concept 47e) has a total of nine linkages to Pfizer utility (1b) and Pfizer's growth (2g). In addition to the seven direct linkages to Pfizer utility (47m.1–47m.3; 47n.1–47n.4), the bill is seen as an example of government actions which, in turn, are causing both problems and opportunities for the firm, of which Pfizer is "aware" (47h and 47j) and is "preparing for" (47i and 47k). These preparations are seen as having a direct and positive effect on Pfizer's growth (a performance measure). Abbott's maps reflect similar causal associations between the proposed legislation and firm performance. In this company's 1961 map, the proposed legislation is directly linked to firm utility and to R&D, a concept that is, in turn, linked directly and strongly to measures of firm performance.

The 1961 maps of the three slower responding firms do not exhibit this type of association. The cause map of Schering does not contain any concepts related to the legislation. Merck's map contains concepts related to the Senate subcommittee investigation of the pharmaceutical industry that preceded the introduction of the legislation, but not to the legislation itself. While this map does demonstrate an understanding of the implications of the investigation, the implications are all linked to *industry* utility. There is no connection between the investigation and concepts related to firm-specific performance. Finally, SKF's map also contains legislation concepts, but, like Merck, this understanding is not related to firm-specific performance or well-being.

We then looked at the 1962 maps of the slower responding firms. If significant connections between legislation concepts and measures of firm performance existed as soon as the bill was adopted, the assertion would be undermined that a distinguishing characteristic of rapidly responding firms is a strategic frame with strong and direct links between the 1962 legislation and measures of firm performance. However, once again firms that were slower to respond did not relate aspects of change in their environment to concepts concerning organization performance or well-being, even after the stressful event had taken place. The relevant portion of the 1962 map of SKF (Fig. 6.3) illustrates this finding.

In this map, SKF is "prepared to speak out against any such legislation" (25o) that it equates with being "unnecessary or restrictive..." (25q), but these concepts are not

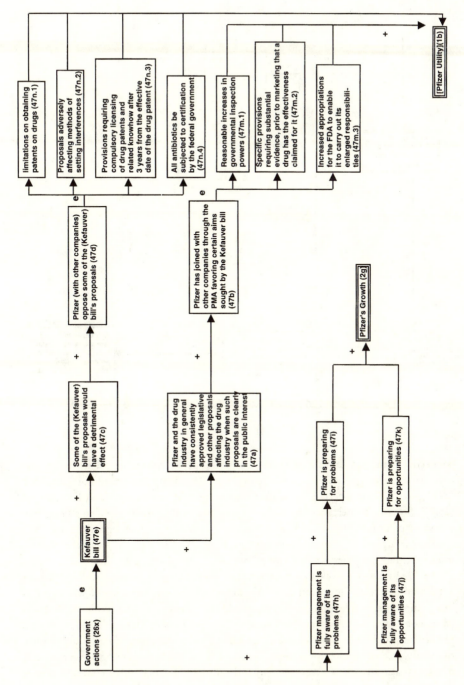

Figure 6.2 Portion of Pfizer 1961 Cause Map

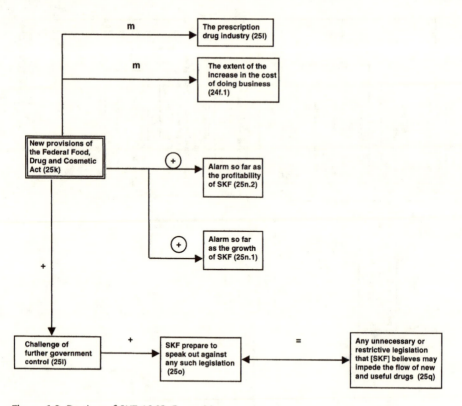

Figure 6.3 Portion of SKF 1962 Cause Map

connected in any way to firm utility or measures of performance. The event (25k) is also expected to have some effect (m) on the industry (25n.1) and the cost of doing business (24f.1), yet it is not expected to increase alarm over SKF profitability (25n.2) or growth (25n.1). Schering's interpretation of the new amendments is also unrelated to firm performance or utility. In 1961, this firm did not address impending legislation; by 1962, concepts related to the new amendments are seen as having a negative association with industry utility, but they are not interpreted as directly affecting the firm itself.

The 1962 map of Merck differs somewhat from the two just described. In Merck's 1962 map (Fig. 6.4), legislation is weakly linked to firm performance or well-being at two points. First, the legislation "if properly administered" (18a.1) is weakly linked by a "does not have a negative effect on" code to "the progress of Merck" (18b), an implied performance indicator. This weak causal link is a more peripheral connection between the stimulus event and firm performance than links found in the rapidly responding firms. It is also weak when compared with the stronger linkages other concepts have to performance measures in the complete map. A second relevant link comes from the expectation that legislation will increase company expenses (4c), a concept that is, in turn, directly linked to firm utility (3g). However, given that the regulation itself is not interpreted as significantly affecting the progress of the firm, this single link does not suggest that the legislation is interpreted as significantly affecting this measure of performance.

In sum, the maps, taken as an indicator of strategic frames, indicate that attention was being paid to the 1962 change in legislation by all five responding firms. However, slower responding firms do not initially interpret new regulation as affecting *firm*-level performance or well-being in any significant way, while firms responding more quickly do interpret those changes as having a direct impact on firm performance and well-being. To use Milliken's (1987, 1990) term, there was no "state uncertainty" for pharmaceutical firms in the early 1960s. It appears from the data that the slower firms were well aware of new legislation but did not understand or believe its implications until much later than their competitors.

An empirical study by Barr et al. (1992) provides empirical support for the importance of this additional interpretive step. This study of two railroad companies facing increasing competition found that both companies quickly noticed changes in the transportation industry in the period following World War II. However, only the firm that survived into the 1970s linked changing conditions to a need to change its own strategy. The second firm noticed and discussed changes in the environment but failed to interpret them as requiring action. This company delayed changing its strategy, suffered financial decline, and eventually went bankrupt. Taken together, it appears reasonable to conclude that it is interpretation rather than noticing that plays the most important role in triggering strategic adaptation; noticing appears to be a necessary but not sufficient precursor to change. Firms must not only recognize a new event in the environ-

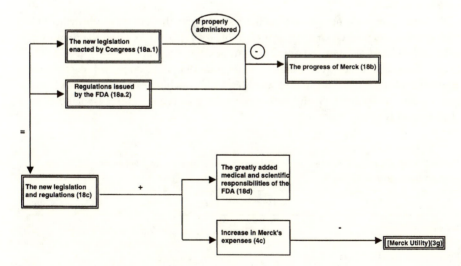

Figure 6.4 Portion of Merck 1962 Cause Map

ment but also understand its connection to their own activities. In fact, our data suggest that even more significant connections must be made before action is likely.

Finding 3: Firms do not act until they identify multiple effects of environmental change and these effects are supported by other indicators of the need for strategic change.

The third focus of attention in this study is the amount of stress created by an external event before strategic change occurs. Two scenarios are suggested by research on the causes of continuing inertia. First, it may be that a single perceived consequence of an external event is not sufficient to significantly change performance expectations for the firm. At the individual level, chapter 2 summarized a considerable body of literature suggesting that generalized schemas persist despite disconfirming evidence. Other literature (Anderson et al., 1980; Ross et al., 1975) argues that there must be significant modification in understanding before adjustments in activity are made. Analogous reasoning at the organization level suggests that a change in the environment may have to be interpreted as having *many* significant connections to concepts of firm performance or well-being.

Our data support the idea, formalized in Figure 6.1, that attention to multiple direct effects of the environment must precede strategic change. To investigate this idea, the maps from the 3 years up to and including the year of change in strategic action were examined for each of the five responding firms. The 1962 legislation was considered to have multiple, direct effects if there was more than one direct linkage to concepts about firm performance or well-being. All five firms exhibited such linkages. Once again, the 1961 map of Pfizer (Fig. 6.2) is illustrative. The Kefauver bill (47e) contains proposals that Pfizer opposes (47d), as well as some that Pfizer supports (47b). Leading from these concepts are seven aspects of the bill that are interpreted as having strong direct effects on Pfizer's utility (1b).

The remaining maps provide less dramatic support for the idea that identifying multiple impacts will precede strategic change. Table 6.4 lists each firm and the number of linkages between legislative concepts and firm performance and well-being in each year analyzed. As shown, Abbott's change in strategy in 1961 is accompanied by two links between legislation and the firm. SKF and Merck each establish two links the year before new actions take place. Schering makes two such connections in 1964 but does not change strategy until 1966.

Table 6.4 Number of Linkages between Legislative Concepts and Measures of Performance and Well-Being

	1960	1961	1962	1963	1964	1965	1966
Merck			0	1	0		
SKF				0	2	0	
Pfizer	0	7					
Schering					2	0	0
Abbott	0	2					

Table 6.5 Related Events by Firm

Firm	Events
Merck	1962 Amendment, Medicare
SKF	1962 Amendment, withdrawal of Parnate, changes in HEW regulations.
Pfizer	1958 Amendment, 1962 Amendment, tetracycline sales contract
Schering	1962 Amendment, overseas regulatory changes, Medicare
Abbott	1962 Amendment, Delany Amendment, taxation of overseas earnings
Parke-Davis	Decline in NPD, decline in sales of chloromycetin

A second scenario about the type of stress that must precede strategic change involves the linkage between a stressful event and other events that are also perceived to have an impact on performance. If one event is perceived to have relatively few direct connections to firm performance, it may have to be seen in association with other events that also affect performance measures before strategic change occurs. In examining this idea, the maps for the 3 years up to and including the year of change in strategic action were again analyzed. *All* concepts with a strong, direct link to measures of firm performance or well-being were traced back to their concept of origin, and these concepts were examined for connections to the new legislation.

The results of this analysis are that *multiple maps exhibit the presence of more than one triggering event before a change in strategic action occurs.* This is a finding that strongly supports the idea developed in the first part of this book that stress must accumulate before strategic change occurs. The 1964 map of SKF (Fig. 6.5) illustrates the kind of reasoning involved. The map shows three events interpreted by firm management as affecting SKF utility (lg). First, as discussed earlier, the 1962 amendments (25k) affect utility through a decline in new medicines (26i) brought on by increased paperwork (26h.2) and approval times (26k). A second, related event is the withdrawal, by the FDA, of SKF's drug Parnate (28i). This is related to the new regulations by a common relationship to the FDA because all paperwork for drug approval is submitted to the FDA. Also related to the FDA and SKF utility is "new regulations of the Department of Health, Education, and Welfare" (25o), which increase the administrative problems "now harassing the FDA and the industry" (29a). In short, as the firm changes its strategy, three different events, all related to FDA activities, are interpreted as having strong negative links to the utility of the firm.

As a summary of the other data supporting this finding, Table 6.5 lists each sample firm and the related events found in the maps immediately prior to that firm's change in strategic action. All concepts were related through some form of government institution or action. It must be noted that it was not until 1965, a year after the change in strategy we identified through examining the pattern of resource allocation, that Merck's maps indicate concern with any other issues. However, the maps do reveal that those issues are connected to a long-standing concern over "continuing government intervention" in the industry that may indicate some unstated concern with these other events prior to 1965.

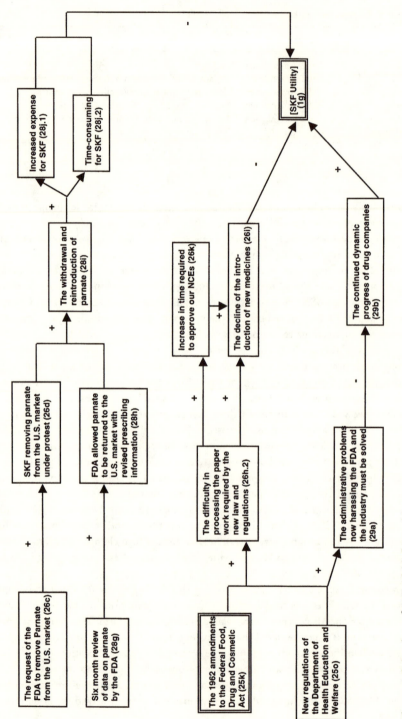

Figure 6.5 Portion of SKF 1964 Cause Map

DISCUSSION

The purpose of this study was to use the ideas of strategic frames and stress and inertia to explore the temporal relationship between firm-level interpretation of an important environmental event and significant changes in strategy. We began by referring to the basic tenet of strategic management that firms should alter their strategies to adapt to new conditions but noted wide variation in the timing of such an adjustment across firms in the same industry (Ginsberg & Buchholtz, 1990; Haveman, 1992; Smith & Grimm, 1987a). Many models of strategic change and problem formulation include a trigger that sets the process of change in motion (Mintzberg et al., 1976; Lyles, 1981; Ginsberg, 1988). However, the nature of the triggering process has not been well defined. This study significantly expands our understanding of the triggering or timing of strategic response by suggesting that response is closely linked to changes in interpretation that appear in the strategic frames of the organization. How a newly recognized event is incorporated into the strategic frame—in particular, how it relates to the performance of the firm and to other events that affect performance—is more closely associated with variations in the timing of strategic response across firms than noticing the event. In other words, the old strategic frames, which are unlikely to hold concepts corresponding to a new environmental event, must change in quite specific ways before new action is initiated. Furthermore, the types of changes in interpretation identified through the maps are consistent with the theories of stress and inertia developed in this book.

Several studies have sought to investigate the potential of cognitive maps to both provide insights for theory development and to aid management practice. Use of cognitive mapping for theory development has, for example, revealed correlations between industry structure and managers' understanding of the environment (Porac et al., 1989; Reger & Huff, 1993; Calori, Johnson, & Sarnin, 1994) and between cognitive maps and firm performance (Hall, 1984; Barr et al., 1992). Mapping techniques have also been used to aid managers in problem resolution and strategic planning by highlighting previously unstated, or unrecognized, beliefs (e.g., Eden, 1990b, 1993).

In this study, we utilize mapping techniques to identify organization-level beliefs (strategic frames) and then identify patterns of change in these maps that reflect changes in noticing and interpretation. Our results reveal a temporal relationship between these patterns of change in maps and changes in strategic action and thus represent an important step forward in our understanding of the link between interpretation and action.

The changes in strategic frames associated with the timing of strategic change identified in this study support the idea that cumulative inertial forces build in firms over time and tend to prevent second order change until they are surpassed by higher levels of stress (Ginsberg, 1988; Huff et al., 1992). The data indicate that stress may follow from either or both of two types of strategic frame characteristics. First, the interpreted strength of the impacts of the event on the firm appears to be moderately important to the timing of response. The maps of all of the five responding firms exhibited multiple links between amendment concepts and firm performance prior to strategic change, suggesting that the event was interpreted as having a very strong impact on the firm.

Furthermore, while the maps of faster responding firms did not exhibit stronger links between the event and firm performance than slower responding firms, they did exhibit multiple links prior to the slower firms. This suggests that strength of impact, represented in this study by the number of perceived impacts on the firm, is an important trigger to change.

Another observation related to stress involves the effect of multiple events. The five firms in our sample related the change in legislation to several other events, all of which exhibited direct links to firm performance or well-being prior to changing strategy. The immediate implication of these results is that these multiple linkages reflect increased levels of stress that are likely to surpass existing levels of inertia and trigger change. Because change did not occur until after these links appeared in the maps, it adds to the argument that cumulative stress is necessary to trigger change.

A broader implication of these results is that strategy researchers must look more closely at what we mean by the term *response*. First, we found a very large discrepancy between quantitative and qualitative indicators of strategic change. Second, more detailed analysis of the maps suggested that strategic actions that might easily be attributed to widely recognized changes in the industry were not necessarily made in response to legislation alone. Rather, change in strategy can be linked to the effects of numerous, related events. For example, early responders undertook a change in strategy prior to actual enactment of the 1962 version of the bill. It was the introduction of an earlier version of the bill that, combined with the perceived impacts of other *prior* government events, increased the pressure for change beyond the level of inertia. Late responders, whose maps indicated no prior concern regarding government actions prior to the change in legislation, did not change strategy until the occurrence of additional governmental actions that were linked, in the maps, to firm performance.

The "nonresponse" of Parke-Davis also highlights the importance of related events and trends to organizational response. As noted earlier, the maps of Parke-Davis suggest that their 1964 change in strategy was not strongly motivated by legislative change. Rather, concepts related to performance and well-being during the time were concerned with R&D, a lack of new product development (NPD), and declining sales of their primary product.

Parke-Davis's' R&D efforts had not resulted in a significant new product since the late 1950s. Furthermore, 43% of sales in 1960 came from a single product, chloromycetin, which was due to come off patent in 1966 and was already suffering declines in sales overseas, where patent protection was less strictly enforced. Certainly, the lack of NPD could have been exacerbated by the change in legislation. However, because the lack of NPD began prior to 1962, the effect from legislation was, perhaps, made less salient. In fact, the 1964 change in strategy undertaken by this firm, an increase in diversification, is not accompanied by changes in map concepts related to the external environment. This suggests that the change in strategy was less a response to a change in the external environment than it was a response to trends in the internal environment: the continued lack of NPD, coupled with the impending loss of patent protection on, and declining sales of, their primary product. While Parke-Davis may not have "responded" to the change in legislation, it is interesting that its maps are consistent with the theory of interpretation and change suggested by the maps of the other five firms.

Before strategic change, three concepts (R&D, NPD, and patents) in the maps are strongly and directly linked to Parke-Davis's performance and well-being. Furthermore, concepts related to both R&D and concerns about chloromycetin can be traced back to lack of NPD—different issues with a common root.

In general, the results of analysis of the maps from all firms suggest that actions undertaken following a significant event in the environment are not just a response to that event. Rather, strategic change responds to a perceived *trend* in the environment, in this case increased governmental action in the external environment and a lack of NPD in the internal environment, that affects firm performance. Although beyond the scope of this study, action may also reflect the constellation of external stakeholders who are making their own interpretation of these events. The experience of early responders may also play a role, though this influence is not explicit in the data set we used. These complexities are consistent not only with stress-inertia theories of strategic change but also with other theories that suggest significant changes in strategy are undertaken in response to shifts in the environment in general, while response to specific events is limited to activities of a more tactical nature (Meyer, 1982a).

Several questions raised by this study can serve as directions for continued research on the link between strategic frames and strategic response. First, why the strategic frames of some firms quickly associated environmental change with performance concepts while others did not is unclear from our analysis. We purposely selected an event for study that was specifically designed to have an impact on the manner in which *all* members of the industry operated. Thus, one would expect a greater consistency across firms in their realization that this event would affect their firm than, perhaps, would be expected in response to less overarching events, such as moves made by competitors (Porac et al., 1989). Because of their history, the prior experiences of top management, or the information-processing capacity of the top management team (Thompson & McDaniel, 1990), it may be that some organizations have more complex strategic frames with more linkages to performance issues. This complexity should increase the likelihood that a major event will be conceptually linked to performance and well-being. It may also be that frequent, though minor, changes in strategic behavior enhance the complexity of strategic frames and make it more likely that new stimuli can be interpreted in terms of strategic action (Hedberg et al., 1976).

A second question raised by the study is related to the type of data we used to construct the maps. Clearly, the firms in our sample differ in the way in which they interpret the new legislation, especially the aspects of the legislation that are highlighted as onerous or stressful. But it also is interesting to step back and consider these differences in light of the data sources used. Because the source documents are speeches and annual reports designed to communicate with multiple audiences, diversity in response may also reflect this diversity in audience, or firm stakeholders. In other words, our finding that multiple indicators of pressure on the firm precede action could be as much an effort to persuade multiple stakeholders of the need for change (or respond to multiple demands for change) as it is an indication of internal sensemaking alone. These observations are beyond the scope of the study but well worth further investigation. Complicated conditions of sensemaking only add to our interest in the problem of timing and underscore the potential significance of the patterns we found.

Finally, another interesting sensemaking complication lies in the observation that the slower responding firms may be learning from the faster responding firms. Because only the largest firms in the industry were selected for study, all the firms had the resources to wait and observe the experiences of others prior to forming their own strategies. Such an explanation for timing differences is consistent with the notion of industry recipes and industry influences proposed by Spender (1989) and Huff (1982), but it is not inconsistent with the premise that interpretation affects the timing of response. It is certainly possible—in fact, likely—that the "borrowed experiences" (Huff, 1982) of faster responding firms might aid managers of the slower firms in forming their own interpretations, though there is no explicit reference to such influences in the data sources we used. Mimetic behavior is of interest to institution theorists (e.g., DiMaggio & Powell, 1983), but we also need further enquiry into the conditions that encourage some firms to relate environmental change to their welfare without such examples.

CONCLUSION

Establishing the links between interpretation and action is frequently called for (Walsh, 1995) but only recently tackled by research on managerial and organization cognition. Previous research has suggested that the *type* of strategic change made by a firm is linked to managerial interpretation of the environment (Bateman & Zeithaml, 1989; Dutton & Jackson, 1987; Thomas, Clark & Gioia, 1993). This study addresses the issue of the timing of strategic response to environmental change. Our results suggest that the timing of change involves more than just assigning meaning to a particular event. Consistent with work on individual cognition summarized in chapter 2, this study shows that data that is not interpreted as affecting central concepts (performance or well-being) in the firm's strategic frame do not lead to a change in action. Furthermore, change appears to be triggered by interpretations that link a given event to other concurrent or prior events, consistent with stress-inertia theories of change.

It may appear that our analysis counters suggestions by Weick (1979), Starbuck and Milliken (1988), and others that managers act first and interpret their actions later. However, we suggest the results of this study point to an important middle ground between researchers who are interested in the purposeful, deliberate development of strategy and those who feel that strategy is more often an outcome of action. The changes in interpretation we identify here focus on an important interpretive step before change can take place: the realization that *something* needs to be done. Theories of institutional inertia and evolutionary theories of organization change provide needed insight into why this interpretive step is not taken without significant pressure to do so. Additional study of strategic frames and their relationship to the content of strategic response may provide a clearer picture of enactment processes and pose an interesting avenue for future research. The study reported in this chapter suggests that firms need a map in which they have confidence before they undertake a major journey (Weick, 1990); they must "know something" before they act. With this confidence, they then "see what they do," and develop more detailed knowledge of new terrain in the way that Weick, Starbuck, and others have been describing.

The next chapter in this book uses a very similar logic to explore interpretation as an industry wide process as biotech firms entered the pharmaceutical industry in the late 1980s. The focus is more explicitly on the way in which a collective "recipe" for "what to do" emerges within industry subgroups.

Notes

1. This chapter is based on an article by Pamela S. Barr and Ann S. Huff titled "Seeing Isn't Believing" in the May 1997 *Journal of Management Studies*. An earlier version was presented at the 1992 Strategic Management Society meeting, London, October 14–17. The research reported draws on the first author's dissertation. Suport from the Richard D. Irwin Foundation and the input of the dissertation committee are gratefully acknowledged.

2. A fifth variable, R&D emphasis on specific therapeutic categories of drugs, was also identified as a significant strategic variable. However, relevant firm-level information is not publicly available, and therefore this dimension of strategy could not be investigated.

3. All six companies were contacted about the availability of historical documents, but only two have promising repositories. To ensure an equal level of documentation for each firm, documents from these two firms were not used in this analysis.

4. The Kefauver bill referred to in this text is the original bill submitted to committee early in 1961. The two main provisions of this early version were compulsory licensing of new drugs after 3 years and the requirement that new drugs be efficacious in use, as well as safe. This bill died in committee in 1962.

7

Industry-Level Learning and the Social Construction of Recipes

Gail E. James

This chapter[1] relates to the arguments about group influences on cognition found in chapter 3 to make sense of the rapid transformations in strategic thinking concerning biotech firms over a 10-year period beginning in 1984. The biotech story that unfolds through the analysis of industry documents traces the sensemaking efforts of key actors within different subgroups of the biotech community. The study traces the evolving understanding of the benefits and disadvantages of interfirm collaborations or strategic alliances involving biotechnology firms from the first published beginnings of alliances in 1984, through a sequence of industry-wide shifts in "industry recipes" (Spender, 1989), as firms observe and learn from direct experiences and from the experiences of other firms within the industry.

Changing understandings about interfirm agreements are tracked longitudinally via consecutive composite cognitive maps, extending the mapping techniques used in chapter 6. The maps identify homogeneous assumptions of individual biotech leaders and show how shared beliefs evolve into different generic understandings about how best to create and orchestrate interfirm alliances. A more complete summary of the maps created can be found in James (1996); in this chapter, illustrative maps show how an assumption is often first articulated by one industry expert or epistemic community leader, then later by another, and eventually by several other experts, all reporting common causal assumptions. This consensus-building process appears related to both (1) direct firm experience and (2) vicarious social learning from another firm's experience, as well as (3) the influence of industry analysts who disseminate best practice knowledge.

STUDY OF RECIPES FOR BIOTECH/PHARMACEUTICAL ALLIANCES 1984–1994

In this study, substantially different strategic ideas were documented for each of three industry groups: (1) dedicated-biotech-company (DBC) key executives, (2) pharmaceu-

148

tical (pharma) company managers, and (3) biotech analysts and observers. These biotech groups are assumed to be separate epistemic communities because of their specific interests and different bases of resources. As evidenced by the following examples, each of these three interdependent communities held some unique perceptions about alliances as well as some overlapping or shared assumptions about how and when interfirm contracts and collaborations should be used. The overlaps among communities help exhibit their interdependence in learning about contracts, collaborations and strategic alliances, while their unique, more specific assumptions support the idea that each group has an independent objective (Haas, 1992) or resource base (Pfeffer & Salancik, 1978).

Four propositions guide a systematic investigation of what level of support exists for biotech social learning regarding different approaches to interfirm alliances. These propositions are general statements intended to explore the process of learning and the possibility of subsequent industry-level shared understandings and are not meant to be read as specific hypotheses that can be "tested" or "supported" by the data presented. While the interrelatedness of process and content issues is recognized, this chapter initially focuses on the industry-level learning process, leaving the presentation of the more substantive content issues for later in the chapter. Propositions 1 and 3 focus on the social learning process, and propositions 2 and 4 refer to the specific content of the recipes observed.

THE EXISTENCE OF INDUSTRY RECIPES

According to Spender (1980, 1989) "recipes" are industry-level, supra-individual cognitive structures. The interrelated sets of causal assumptions held in common by interacting "experts" within an industry community evolve through both direct and indirect social interaction into rather homogeneous generic abstract common conceptualizations.

The social context that fosters the emergence of industry recipes can best be viewed as an "epistemic community," as originally posited by political scientists (Haas, 1992; Adler & Haas, 1992). It refers to a group of influential professionals united by their shared causal beliefs about their uncertain environment where the resultant consensus understanding of these knowledgeable leaders is legitimized by their collective reputations. As theorized (Haas, 1992; Adler & Haas, 1992), consensus within a knowledge or epistemic community is enhanced, thereby influencing beliefs and action within a wider community, by the following conditions:

- significant reputations of the epistemic leaders,
- very similar educational backgrounds,
- common business experience, and/or
- great opportunity, due to their close ties, for intense and frequent intercommunication of experiences and/or learning.

The existence and development of industry recipes anticipated in the literature leads to the following proposition:

Proposition 1. A base of common understanding among industry participants grows, through social interaction, into industry recipes for responding to shared circumstances. In the biotech industry, these recipes are likely to include observations about the benefits and problems of strategic alliances.

Evidence of an Emerging Industry Recipe: Contract / Collaboration (C/C)

The first comprehensive report focusing on the biotechnology industry—*Commercial Biotechnology*—was published by the Office of Technology Assessment (OTA) for the U.S. Congress in 1984. This report gives early evidence that industry-level thinking regarding the use of interfirm contracts and collaboration was in place and that a common understanding about the impact of interfirm collaborations was developing. Six pages of the OTA report are devoted to describing the effective role of collaborative ventures between new biotechnology firms and established companies in financing biotech R&D (OTA, 1984, 103–109). In essence, the 1984 OTA report presents a general model for interfirm contract relationships between new biotechnology firms and established pharmaceutical companies. The OTA interfirm cooperation model is referred to in 1984 as "contract/collaboration" (C/C). Three generalizations summarize the 1984 OTA C/C model:

1. A new biotechnology firm or NBF is reliant on an established company for working capital which is either in the form of research contract revenue or equity investment (OTA, 1984,106).
2. Interfirm contract relationships, and their associated revenues, are very likely to be transitory (OTA, 1984,107) or interim (OTA, 1984,109).
3. Contracts between new biotechnology firms and established companies are usually tightly written, making it difficult for most new biotechnology firms to capitalize on interesting new research findings which occur in the course of their contracted work (OTA, 1984,111).

One sign that a belief has emerged as a recipe is the close resemblance among the terms, names, or acronyms referred to as "family resemblance." Rather than using the multiple terms "contract," "collaboration," or "collaborative," separately or independently, the combined term "contract/collaboration" was used consistently to articulate the concept of using interfirm cooperation to finance biotech R&D. Starting in the 1984 OTA report, contract/collaboration was frequently abbreviated as "C/C." The combined term was also used 36 times in Ernst & Young's *Biotech 86*, which contrasts with only three mentions of "contract," two mentions of "collaboration," and two of "collaborative" alone (Burrill, 1987). Two full-page charts in *Biotech 86* use C/C to portray the importance of interfirm collaborative research revenue. The first chart illustrates the use of C/C by company size, and the second compares the use of C/C with various levels of R&D expenses.

From a cognitive perspective, we are interested in the contract/collaboration recipe as a concept that is distinct and unique to the biotechnology industry. To be considered categorically distinct at the document level, one or more of the following criteria must be fulfilled (Barr, Stimpert, & Huff, 1992). A term must

1. contradict an existing understanding,
2. delete a previous causal association, or
3. change a previous causal association.

Similarly, these criteria need to be fulfilled within an industry. When assumptions in one industry sector contradict, delete, or change understandings held in another industry, they are categorically distinct at the industry level. Furthermore, these criteria need to be substantiated across an industry's documents and transcripts instead of within a single document.

The 1986 biotech concept "contract/collaboration" is categorically distinct from the understandings of other industries by these criteria, further supporting C/C's recipe status. In 1986, the practice of biotech companies' financing their R&D costs through entering into C/Cs was widespread, yet this practice was actually unique to the biotech industry. For example, at the same early stage of development of the semiconductor industry, the use of interfirm contracts was unusual (OTA, 1984, 531–541; Burrill, 1987, 24). Instead of contract/collaboration agreements, most other new high-technology industries, including the semiconductor industry, financed their R&D costs through product sales (OTA, 1984, 531–541). Thus, the C/C recipe articulated in the biotech industry changed a previous causal association, because it changed previously accepted models that were used in other industries to finance high technology R&D. This evidence further supports Proposition 1 and C/C's unique recipe status.

Industry Group Recipes

Although widely adopted assertions may develop into recipe status and become influential, subindustry groups with different resource bases may develop more specific understandings that may also be very influential among like subgroup participants. Because they respond to more particular circumstances, they do not gain the status of an industry-wide recipe. Thus:

Proposition 2. Multiple group recipes are expected in an emerging industry like biotechnology. Some components of these different recipes will overlap, yet others will contain divergent assumptions, reflecting different experiences and unique perspectives.

What follows is preliminary evidence that several group biotech alliance recipes developed, reflecting the different experiences of group participants. To preserve focus, only content from the year 1986 of multiple recipes and different epistemic communities is reported; James (1996) has additional supporting data from the subsequent 7 years of this study. The content of three separate 1986 epistemic community understandings will be considered here.

The causal assumptions of the 1986 C/C recipe were most relevant to top-tier DBC executives, and the C/C recipe first originated as the composite recipe of DBC executives. Figure 7.1 depicts a composite cognitive map derived from the sensemaking of eight key biotech executives, including the CEOs of Genentech and Cetus, who participated in 1986 roundtable discussions that included the biotech industry practice of using contract/collaboration agreements. The structure of the cognitive map shown in Figure

7.1 was inferred from the content of the roundtable discussions following strict coding rules. These rules expand the protocols used in previous cognitive mapping studies to this new setting (Axelrod, 1976; Huff, Narapareddy, & Fletcher, 1990; Barr et al., 1992) and can be found in James (1996, 71–77).

Evidence that the map shown in Figure 7.1 represents a generic industry group recipe for DBCs comes from confirming assertions published in other data sources: the Arthur Young 1986 survey of biotech executives and later articles in *BioVenture View* (1989, 15–18) and *BioPharm* (1988, 43–46).

The DBC executives are a close-knit group, as evidenced by the familiarity expressed within the published roundtable discussions facilitated by Ernst and Young (Burrill, 1987, 1988a, 1989, 1990; Burrill & Lee, 1991, 1992, 1993, 1994). They clearly know each other on a first name basis and communicate informally, as well as more formally within their industry associations (originally IBA, Industrial Biotechnology Organization, and ABC, the Association of Biotechnology Companies, which merged in 1993 to become BIO, the Biotechnology Industry Organization). United in their common intent to educate the public of the value of biotech, DBC executives support an industry grassroots advocacy program (Burrill & Lee, 1993). "SWAT teams" of DBC CEOs are often organized ad hoc to address common policy issues and lobby Congress. The close ties and common perceptions of DBC executives have also been noted by others. For example, a *Wall Street Journal* article remarks on how closely knit the biotech community is in 1994 and how united biotech CEOs are in their outlook for their industry (*WSJ*, October 16, 1994). The leaders are especially important. Industry analysts follow only the largest, most prominent biotech companies, because, as Jeff Casdin, well-known Oppenheimer biotech analyst, noted: "This consequential minority represents companies with the most potential of surviving and making long-term profits".[2]

The understanding regarding the use of the contract/collaboration recipe, found in a 1986 biotech survey report, *Biotech 86*[3] (Burrill, 1987), is very similar to that first presented in the 1984 OTA biotech report. *Biotech 86* contains 34 pages of discussion of the first industry-wide survey of biotech CEOs. Eighteen pages mention the use of contract/collaboration as a common means by which biotechnology R&D was financed (Burrill, 1987). Contract/collaboration projects were reported as a very important means of acquiring revenues to finance R&D operating costs because total industry revenues in 1986 from C/Cs were three times greater than revenues from product sales, the next largest revenue source. In fact, of the 137 executive respondents in 1986, 82% reported that most of their company's revenues came from contract/collaboration agreements. The exception was larger diagnostic biotech firms, who were generating revenue from product sales. The 1986 Young survey questionnaire specifically queried the use of contract/collaboration research projects between larger established companies and smaller entrepreneurial biotech firms, referred to as dedicated biotech companies, or DBCs. According to the findings, the majority of DBC respondents reported that contract/collaboration agreements were used primarily as an expedient source of revenue until profitable products could be developed. Of note is that survey respondents did not link C/Cs with long-term business strategies but, instead, identified C/Cs as interim or short-term arrangements used to finance working capital (Burrill 1987, 2, 9, 18, 25). Key DBC

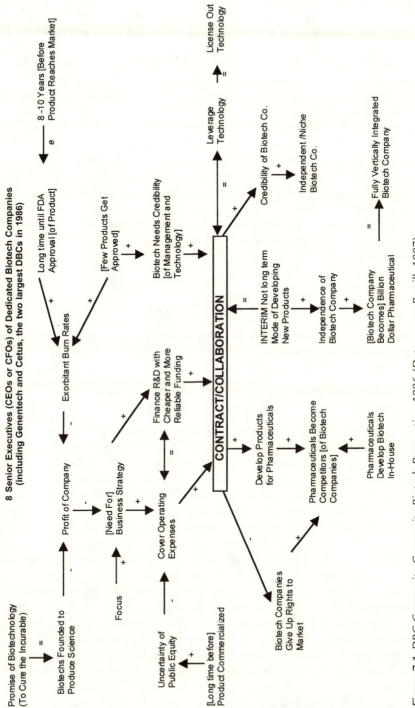

Figure 7.1 DBC Composite Composite Biotech Perspective, 1986 (Datasource: Burrill, 1987)

executives, in 1986 roundtable discussions (also facilitated by the Arthur Young Company), reported that interfirm C/Cs were "transitional financing vehicles" providing "cheaper" and "more reliable funding than public equity" (Burrill 1987, 26, 58, 75, 82, 88).

A recipe is a reservoir of industry-level learning. The introduction of new or different causal relationships to an understanding signals that learning has occurred. New inclusions may be significant enough to create a consistent shared understanding with the prescriptive assumptions defined as a recipe. The "pattern of inclusion" refers to the introduction of new, different causal relationships to the core concept. (In this study, the core concept is interfirm biotech alliances.) Within a recipe, new causal relationships reflect learning and the status of the industry-level causal understanding. Examining the relationships surrounding the core concept permits systematic analysis of the status of industry-level understanding and helps determine whether new relationships are distinct enough to reflect significant learning, thereby creating a new recipe. As one examines the C/C understanding in 1986 (Figure 7.1), one observes the following five key assumptions. The last three represent causal relationships surrounding the core concept—contract/collaboration:

1. **interim**
2. **tightly written** contracts
3. established primarily to **finance** operating expenses.

Beyond linking the use of contract/collaboration agreements to financing, two other expectations for C/Cs apparently evolved among DBC executives after 1984. Contract/collaboration agreements were additionally assumed to provide biotech companies:

4. **cheaper, more reliable** funding than public equity, as well as
5. **legitimacy** for new, unproven technology and/or management.

The first three elements of the recipe initially appeared in the 1984 OTA report. Elements 4 and 5 were added over the next 2 years. The evidence from industry publications indicates that by 1986 DBC executives "learned" that funding their working capital needs through revenue from collaborative interfirm contracts was easier than acquiring public equity, which was unreliable because of the vagaries of the stock market (Burrill, 1987). These executives also learned that by establishing C/Cs, particularly with a large, established firm, their company would gain credibility on Wall Street, increasing the likelihood that the price of their stock would rise (Burrill, 1987, 34). When a C/C was established, Wall Street observers assumed that either the technology or the management of the DBC had commercial potential; otherwise, the established firm would not have entered into a contract to pay up front for rights to market an unapproved product or drug. Figure 7.1 illustrates the consistent consensus industry-level understanding surrounding the C/C concept with the generic prescriptive qualities defined to be a recipe. As illustrated in this map, DBC executives assumed that if they established a C/C they would gain cheaper, more reliable financing than that available from Wall Street, as well as legitimacy for their unproven technology and credibility for their management.

A change in concept linkages in cognitive maps can also signal learning. In this case, we propose that learning should show up as different linkages in the form of distinct causal chains or clusters connected to the core concept—biotech interfirm alliances. In 1986, support for this idea largely overlaps with the support given for categorical distinctiveness. The two new causal relationships introduced after 1984 also represent new linkages to the C/C core concept. The new links are the connections among "cheaper," "more reliable funding," and "legitimacy" and the C/C concept. Because these connections did not exist in 1984, their emergence by 1986 signals that learning occurred.

A pharma recipe also existed as a separate pharmaceutical community alliance recipe in 1986. Key causal assumptions articulated in 1986 by Schering-Plough's executive vice president, Hugh D'Andrade, were reiterated in other publications (Burrill, 1987, 1988b; *InVivo*, 1990 18–19) and thus are representative of the consensual understanding of other pharma executives in 1986. Because this study investigated learning and recipes only with regard to the core concept—biotechnology interfirm alliances—there are fewer observations of analysts and consultants articulating what pharmas were experiencing. Five of the six publications, which were cognitively mapped with regard to interfirm alliances, focus almost entirely on the biotech industry. Only one of the sources, *InVivo*, actually targets pharmaceutical executives. The more limited number of pharmaceutical-focused sources probably accounts for the lower incidence of pharma recipe articulation by both pharma executives and analysts. It could also be hypothesized that pharma executives actually communicate directly with each other less frequently than DBC executives to avoid any appearance of collusion, given greater antitrust concerns for established firms.

The pharma recipe of 1986 is cognitively mapped as shown in Figure 7.2. In contrast with the DBC cognitive map (Fig. 7.1), pharma executives do not refer to contract/collaborations as alliances or link them to any long-term strategy. Instead, the pharma map contains these important assertions and causal assumptions:

Pharmas:

- have world-class, **superior R&D capabilities,**
- **need new products,**
- have **deep pockets,**
- have enough **capital to buy the whole biotech industry**, and thus
- can **dominate** their less established, needy biotech company partners.
- Collaborations are an **interim** step to acquiring biotech companies with promising technology.

From a pharma manager's perspective, contract/collaborations:

- create new products,
- gain time,
- acquire excellent technology,
- determine which technologies are successful, and
- screen biotech companies with successful technologies before acquisition.

From a pharma manager's perspective, biotech companies:

- have more of an academic culture than pharmas,
- have competence in genetic engineering,
- have competence developing new technology, and
- are a good potential source for new products, but
- need financing to develop their technology.

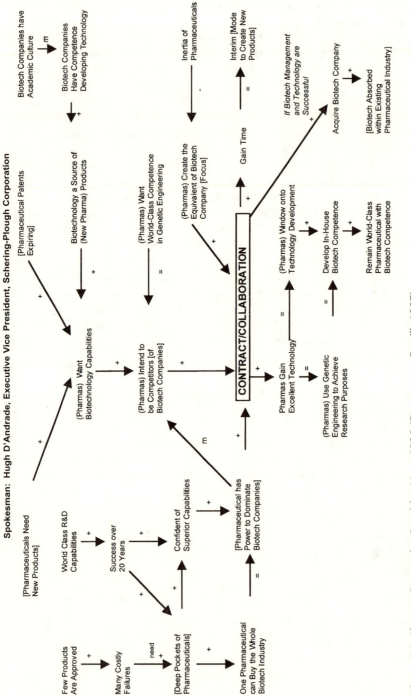

Spokesman: Hugh D'Andrade, Executive Vice President, Schering-Plough Corporation

Figure 7.2 Pharma Composite Cognitive Map, 1986 (Datasource: Burrill, 1987)

Additionally, in 1986, pharma executives believed that the biotech industry:

- would eventually consolidate, and
- be absorbed within the existing pharmaceutical industry.

1986 Consultant/Analyst's assumptions

Steven Burrill, a leading biotech consultant, first articulated his alliance assumptions in *Biotech 86* (Burrill, 1987). Later, his assertions were widely accepted and rearticulated by other consultants and industry observers, such as George Wirtlin (Wirtlin, 1989) and Mark Edwards (Burrill, 1989), and subsequently published in other biotech publications, thereby establishing subgroup recipe status. These widely circulated consultant-analyst assumptions became the foundation for an enduring composite understanding of DBC CEOs and the 1989 industry-wide SA recipe.

The cognitive map depicted in Figure 7.3 summarizes the observer-analyst recipe as it existed in 1986. The observer-analyst recipe contains the following key assertions:

- The number-one concern of DBCs is to finance the exorbitant cost of R&D.
- The application of biotechnology is growing, but it is not yet profitable.
- DBCs need to let their business strategies direct their financial strategies, not vice versa.
- Biotech alliances are crucial business strategies for three important reasons: (1) to fund R&D off the balance sheet; therefore, they do not directly affect profit and loss; (2) to provide credibility for a DBC's management and its technology; and (3) to provide public benefits, assuring that a bioproduct gets manufactured and marketed.
- Neither public equity nor venture capital investors are long-term funding sources for biotechnology because they are impatient for profits.
- Interfirm alliances are appropriate interim structures for companies before they are acquired or become independent, fully vertically integrated pharmas.
- Pharmas finance interfirm contract-collaborations to acquire rights to promising technology, product, and/or an entire DBC with proven technology and good management.
- Observers-analysts expect that the biotech industry will consolidate, fewer biotech companies will survive, and surviving biotech companies will be fully vertically integrated.

The Basis for an Industry-Wide Recipe

Several of the 1986 identified group recipe assertions, listed previously, overlap two epistemic communities and qualify as an industry-wide understanding. Although evidence of overlap is presented here from just the three identified 1986 epistemic community recipes, partial overlap is frequent and easily documented with content from subsequent years" cognitive maps (James, 1996).

Overlap between Observer-Analyst and DBC Understandings. Both the composite DBC 1986 recipe and the 1986 analyst-observer recipe contained the following assertion: Alliances provide legitimacy for not-yet-proven technology and management.

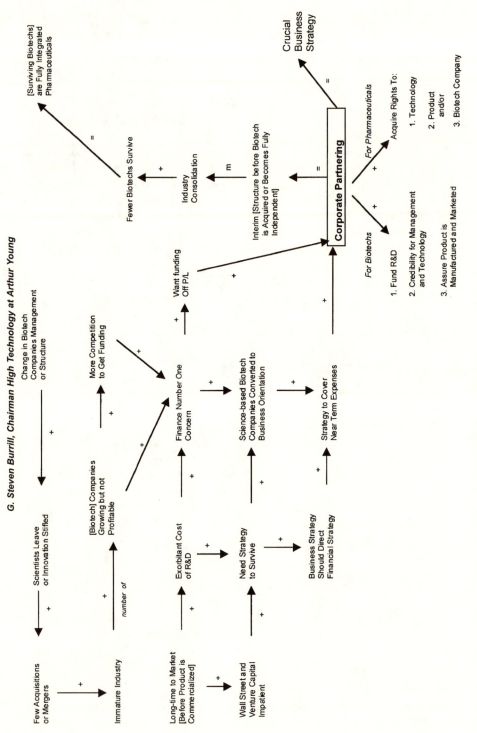

Figure 7.3 Analyst/Observer Composite Cognitive Map, 1986 (Datasource: Burrill, 1987)

Overlap between DBC and Pharma understandings. In 1986, DBC executives and pharma executives agreed on the following assumptions about interfirm alliances:

- C/Cs are primarily financial arrangements for biotech firms.
- Pharmas gain access to excellent technology through alliances.

Overlap between Pharma and Observer Understandings. In 1986, pharmaceutical executives and analyst-observers held the following common alliance assumptions:

- Pharmas finance interfirm C/Cs to acquire technology and products.
- Pharmas intend to acquire the majority equity of DBCs if their technology proves commercially viable.
- The biotech industry will consolidate, small DBCs will merge or be acquired by pharmas and thus biopharmaceuticals will become pharmas.

When assertions span multiple epistemic communities, they are considered components of an industry-wide recipe. A key causal assumption of the industry-wide C/C recipe of 1986 is that alliances bring cash and credibility. In 1986, all three epistemic communities held the following nine common assumptions, which have already been described as key understandings of the 1986 industry-wide C/C recipe:

1. The number-one reason to establish a C/C is to bring in cash or capital to finance a DBC's operating expenses.
2. C/Cs are interim, short-term relationships.
3. C/Cs are tightly written contracts.
4. C/Cs provide credibility and legitimacy for new, unproven technology or management.
5. C/Cs help DBCs remain independent in the short run.
6. A DBC that survives in the long run will have become a FIPCO (fully vertically integrated pharmaceutical company).
7. Pharmas need new products; many blockbuster drugs are coming off patent.
8. Biotechnology is a promising source for new blockbuster drug products.
9. Because of past success, pharmas have deep pockets to finance R&D.

LEARNING AND THE EVOLUTION OF NEW RECIPES

An individual firm's singular experience may cause it to question an existing recipe's assumptions. Similarly, firms with particular interests and resources may develop specific understandings uniquely related to their circumstances When experiences are dissonant, they can modify an existing recipe's acceptance and potentially change that recipe to reflect new experience and circumstance. Industry participants with similar objectives and resources often communicate their unique experiences among themselves, either directly or through the conduit of industry analysts or publications; as a result of their close interaction, they are likely to develop group understandings. If a new insight is specific and pertinent to only a certain industry group, it may stay closely shared within that particular community, becoming a group recipe without wide appeal. Some such group understandings, however, may eventually modify or replace previously accepted recipes with broader appeal.

Learning by individuals that contradicts expectations and past experience is often the impetus to new social learning (Walsh, 1995). Consistent with social learning theory, as one company's experience shows promise of benefiting other firms, it is exchanged either directly within intraindustry relational exchanges or indirectly through the recounting of a situational experience by an industry observer or analyst (Oliver, 1990; DiMaggio, 1988). Once learning occurs, it may remain the understanding of just the firm that experienced the learning; otherwise, if it has broader appeal, it may be adopted as a prescriptive understanding or recipe by other intraindustry subgroups. Occasionally, its usefulness may span most industry participants, thereby making it an industry-wide recipe. In summary:

Proposition 3. Although significant persistence in an industry recipe is expected, recipes can and do change as firms learn from the borrowed experience of successful competitors.

The social learning process is usually postulated to originate endogenously (Walsh, 1994); a single firm's experience is articulated within its closely knit community of interacting firms, stimulating recipe development or recipe change. However, the social learning process observed within the biotechnology industry does not appear to originate as endogenously as has been postulated. In this research, many DBC executives communicate *publicly*, outside their epistemic community. DBC CEOs routinely speak with Wall Street analysts and other biotech observers, for example. This communication pattern is probably due to the competitive nature of U.S. business and the need of young companies in an entrepreneurial industry to improve the firm's reputation for providing competitive products and services.

In addition, many key links in biotech industry recipes were frequently articulated by biotech industry consultants-analysts, who are identified as outside the DBC epistemic community because of their different resource base. Yet, these biotech analysts appear to be the conduits for strategic learning within the DBC epistemic community, and key links in shared learning and the social construction of a prescriptive enduring alliance understanding have been documented. Biotech analysts disseminate new experience, assumptions, and learning, which they observe or hear about from DBC executives. The basic claim is that analysts help create DBC recipes, which then function as the mental templates that give meaning to the industry's information and serve as the cognitive foundation for individual biotech firm action. It should be noted that observing more private direct communication between DBC executives was beyond the methodology of this study. However, biotech analysts like Mark Edwards have reported how DBC CEOs have ample opportunity to communicate directly and privately as they work together on various industry association committees and programs (Edwards, 1994).

Genentech and the Strategic Alliance Recipe. There is significant evidence in the data that the pioneering alliance experience of Genentech was largely responsible, by 1989, for a new composite, industry-wide recipe, the strategic alliance (SA) recipe. Genentech publicly valued its interfirm collaborations for the important knowledge it was gaining from its established pharma partners. During the bull market of 1986–1987 (which preceded the stock market crash in October 1987), Genentech continued to use C/Cs, even though public equity was very accessible and cheaper than the financing secured with C/Cs (Burrill, 1988a). Thus, Genentech was using its partnerships to learn strategically from its partners and less to finance its R&D. The community of DBC executives observed that Genentech was learning effective scale-up procedures required to conduct successful clinical trials from its pharma partner, Eli Lilly (Burrill, 1988a). As late as January 1989, Genentech's publicly state goal was to become an independent, fully integrated pharmaceutical company, but to continue to use cooperative interfirm arrangements for strategic purposes to accelerate its products' commercialization (Burrill & Lee, 1991). In other words, Genentech's interfirm contract collaborations did not follow the prominent industry-wide consensus recipe, C/C.

It is widely reported that, up until 1990, Genentech was influenced by Syntex's experience in the 1960s and 1970s. Genentech also wanted to establish itself as an essentially one-product, fully integrated pharmaceutical company (Burrill, 1990; Wirtlin, 1989, *Bioventure View*, 1990, 12, 27). Through the 1970s, Syntex's model of vertical integration was in keeping with the extensive belief of strategists that a *critical mass*, or minimal organizational size, was needed for a firm to compete profitably in a maturing market, such as pharmaceuticals were becoming. According to theory (Porter, 1980; Pisano, 1990), critical mass could be attained either through merger or acquisition or through vertical integration. Without critical mass, a company would not have the necessary economies of scale and scope to successfully compete in a competitive global market.

Syntex had vertically integrated around its billion dollar patented blockbuster birth control pill. Genentech initially chose to also achieve critical mass by mimicking Syntex's strategy and become fully vertically integrated (Burrill & Lee, 1991). But unlike Syntex, Genentech used extensive interfirm partnering to accelerate the commercialization of its planned-for blockbuster biopharmaceutical drugs (Burrill, 1989). Through partnering Genentech accelerated its learning and focused its internal resources more strategically, all with anticipation of more quickly becoming an independent, fully integrated pharmaceutical company (Burrill & Lee, 1991). The vehicle intended to parlay Genentech from entrepreneurial biotech status into full standing with recognized, profitable pharmaceutical companies was a potential blockbuster therapeutic biotech drug, tPA.

Other biotech companies, not as far along the learning curve as Genentech, were still largely applying the prominent 1986 C/C recipe without new caveats. Whenever possible, during the years 1986 through 1988, the majority of DBCs were attempting to leverage their technology to finance working capital; they were forming alliances well before their products reached the clinical trial stage of commercial development (Burrill, 1989). For example, in the report *Biotech 88*, C/C was described as providing cheaper, more reliable financing than any other alternative financial source, "with no strings attached" (Burrill 1988a, 32). Contracts with established pharmaceutical firms provided off-balance sheet financing. Contracts were seen by Wall Street analysts as giving credibility to those biotechnologies financially supported in a collaboration with an established pharmaceutical company (Wirtlin, 1989).

A key point is that, until close to 1989, financing R&D was given far more weight than was long-term business strategy by most DBC executives. (See Table 7.2, later in this chapter, which displays the number of individuals using the business strategy concept from 1986 through 1994.) Because there were no profits from product sales, the valuation model used until the early 1990s by Wall Street analysts to evaluate the stock price of a biotech company was based not on its profits but on its R&D expenditures. These R&D expenses became known as a company's "burn rate" (Burrill, 1990, 34; Wirtlin, 1989, 4). With an emphasis on R&D spending as evidence of this commercial promise, most DBC executives focused on financing "burn" (Burrill, 1989; Wirtlin, 1989). Survey responses of DBC CEOs from 1986 through 1989 further support the content of the C/C recipe. DBC executives considered their contract/collaborations as essential for financing their "burn," particularly after the 1987 market crash, when public equity all but dried up (Burrill, 1987, 1988a, 1989, 1990).

Important common perceptions about strategic alliances (SAs) apparently developed inductively from a single biotechnology firm's (Genentech's) experiences and then evolved over time through social learning, creating a more generic industry understanding and thereby fulfilling important recipe protocol criteria (Spender, 1980; Barr et al., 1992; Reger & Huff, 1993). Biotech analysts encouraged DBC executives to mimic Genentech's SA practices. Through the interaction of biotech analysts and DBC executives, a new industry-wide recipe developed—the 1989 SA recipe. (Refer to Figure 7.4.) This description of the creation of the 1989 SA recipe is consistent with theoretic accounts of the social construction of an industry recipe (DiMaggio & Powell, 1983, 1991; DiMaggio, 1988; Scott & Meyer, 1983), as well as recent strategy literature (Pettigrew, 1992; Powell & Brantley, 1992; Galaskiewicz & Wasserman, 1989; Oliver, 1990).

Empirical Analysis of the Transition to the Strategic Alliance Recipe. Interaction effects among biotech leaders are observed in the several roundtable discussions published in the yearly Young biotech reports and corroborated in the consensus findings of the annual surveys of DBC executives (Burrill, 1987, 1988a, 1989, 1990). These documents show analyst observations that appear to have preceded and hastened new social learning among DBC executives. The following assertions, although only representative snippets of understandings from the more complete mapped recipes, give examples of the social interaction effects among analysts and DBC executives.

Making contracts and doing collaborative research with larger established pharmaceutical firms was a widely accepted DBC practice to finance working capital and the cornerstone of the DBC 1986 C/C recipe (Fig. 7.1). But in the 1986 analyst understanding, "corporate partnering," not "contract/collaboration," was the usual term articulated by analysts-observers to convey their understanding of the appropriate use of interfirm collaboration (Fig. 7.3). Using this different term to identify the core concept is symbolic and significant. Although analysts knew that DBCs were using C/Cs primarily to fund R&D expenses, prominent analysts encouraged DBC executives to first establish long-term business objectives before entering into an interfirm contract. Steven Burrill, an influential consultant from Ernst and Young, was most notable in emphasizing the inherent potential for alliance partners to develop win-win relationships in which both partners would gain something valuable by collaborating.

The link that exists between corporate partnering and business strategy in the 1986 analyst map shown in Figure 7.3 illustrates the importance analysts put on having a DBC's long-term business strategy direct its financial strategy, not vice versa. Also of interest, the term "strategic alliance" is not used per se in the 1986 source documents summarized up to this point, but Burrill explicitly links corporate partnering to both "alliance" and to "business strategy" (Burrill, 1987, 3). Other biotech analysts similarly described the use of interfirm contracts as partnering and explicitly referred to the contract relationships established by Genentech as partnerships. Genentech was still an independent, prominent DBC until 1989 and was using interfirm partnerships for strategic purposes rather than just as a source of working capital to finance R&D (Burrill, 1987, 23). Several biotech observers (i.e., Steven Burrill, Kenneth Lee, and Mark Edwards) grew concerned that short-term expectations for interfirm contracts would doom alliances to be used as transactional contracts to secure working capital. This concern was eventually publicly voiced by key DBC executives (Burrill, 1987, 3; Burrill, 1988a, 7, 22).

It is our belief that strategic considerations for interfirm contracts grew first within the analyst epistemic community (Haas, 1992) and then spread to the DBC community. Two DBC executives referred to their use of interfirm contracts as "partnering" in 1987 (Burrill, 1988a). One of these executives directly linked partnering to access to markets (Burrill, 1988a, 37); the other linked partnering to speed in commercialization (p. 39). Both executives, by referencing market access and commercialization of products, were considering longer term business objectives. Yet, based on the data reviewed, DBC executives did not use the term "strategy" per se in 1986 or link the concept of interfirm collaboration with business strategy.

As discussed previously, in 1986 Burrill first directly linked partnering to business strategy. He was the first to articulate the benefits to DBCs of becoming more strategic and developing business objectives rather than continuing to focus all their resources on developing their science and technology. Burrill observed in 1987 that "Genentech had moved beyond allying for cash" (Burrill, 1987, 6). Later other prominent analysts similarly articulated the need to make alliances strategic. Figure 7.4 illustrates the consensus 1987 analyst understanding (Burrill, 1988a). By 1987, analysts were using the terms "alliance" and "partnering" interchangeably and increasingly stating that strategy was more important than a DBC's financial or scientific objectives.

According to the data sources reviewed, Burrill was also the first to use the term "strategic alliance" (SA). In *Biotech 88: Into the Marketplace*, Burrill used the terms "strategic partnering" and "strategic alliance" interchangeably; then he and the editor apparently settled on "strategic alliance" (Burrill, 1988a). Later that same year, George Wirtlin, another prominent biotech analyst, also urged DBCs to use alliances to further their long-term business strategies rather than continue to use them to cover their short-term working capital needs (*BioPharm*, 1988, 32). Genentech's strategic actions, particularly its use of strategic alliances, were cited as "the model" for a successful biotech company (Burrill, 1987; *BioPharm*, 1987). In 1988, Burrill stated:

> The high cost and extended duration of R&D in the therapeutic group led, some years ago, to the development of strategic alliance with large pharmaceutical firms. These alliances have become the *de facto* model, in other segments of the biotech industry for alliances with corporate partners. These agreements may be relatively straightforward transfers of certain marketing rights to the larger partner in return for R&D funding in a focus area and sharing of the commercial risks and rewards. They may also be quite elaborate structures involving finely sliced market rights, joint or sole responsibility for clinical trials in the United States or abroad, etc. (Burrill, 1988a, 28)

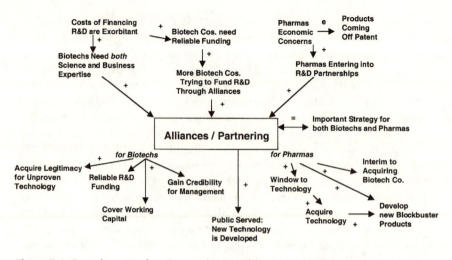

Figure 7.4 Consultant/Analyst Composite Cognitive Map, 1987 (Datasource: Burrill, 1988a)

After 1987, the use of the term "strategic alliance" grew, and eventually it largely replaced all other terms referencing interfirm collaborative agreements. SAs were directly linked to long-term business strategies, as just noted in the quote by Burrill. The analyst-observer understanding initiated in 1986 by Burrill (and shown in Figure 7.3) became increasingly accepted by other industry analysts, and eventually it developed into the consistent prescriptive understanding of a recipe.

Figure 7.4 illustrates the composite analyst understanding of 1987. Although analysts in 1987 still considered vertical integration the best model for a DBC's success and survival, they were noticing that some biotech companies were operating as niche players or R&D boutiques, "surviving on royalties from their pharma partners" (Burrill, 1987, 32). As shown in Figure 7.4, analysts causally linked strategic alliance to "niche" strategy in 1987. DBCs were said to be using a niche strategy whenever they targeted a specific market niche for their product and then partnered with an established (usually pharmaceutical) firm that could more effectively assume the marketing of the new product, rather than have the DBC itself establish marketing and distribution of its product (Burrill, 1988a). A niche strategy was assumed by analysts to allow DBC adopters faster commercialization of their new technology and thus the ability to secure greater financial rewards than could be achieved by independently marketing their bioproducts.

According to survey findings for 1987, becoming a vertically integrated pharma was the consensus goal of the vast majority (87%) of DBC executives (Burrill, 1987); but, in 1987 most DBC executives did not yet believe that using interfirm partnerships could facilitate or accelerate their firm's independence as a vertically integrated biopharmaceutical firm. According to the data set analyzed, the causal linkage of SA to the concept of an independent vertically integrated biopharmaceutical company was not articulated by DBC executives until after 1987.

Acquiring cash via C/C was the essence of the 1986 DBC recipe (as illustrated in Figure 7.1). Later this recipe gradually evolved, incorporating the analyst's strategic understanding. The analyst understanding also grew more complete after 1987. Initially it did not include the following two important concepts, which, according to data used in this study, were first publicly articulated in 1988:

1. Strategic alliances allow a DBC to become an independent firm by learning skills from its partners. These partnerships were expected to enhance a DBC's ability to eventually become a vertically integrated company by "operationally achieving vertical integration before investing in downstream functions" (*BioPharm*, 1988, 19).
2. SAs are as important to a DBC for establishing faster manufacturing of a bioproduct as they are for implementing the marketing and distribution of the manufactured product (*BioPharm*, 1988, 22).

Changing Cognitive Maps. We take different examples used to explain the C/C concept after 1986 as an indication that a new understanding regarding interfirm partnership had developed. When one compares the composite cognitive map of key DBC executives in 1986 (Figure 7.1) with the DBC understandings of subsequent years, particularly as illustrated by Figure 7.5, one can observe that new, different examples were offered for C/Cs after 1986. For example, in 1988 DBC executives were considering two ways to achieve success as an independent company. The best way to secure independence in 1988 was still believed to become a fully vertically integrated pharmaceutical

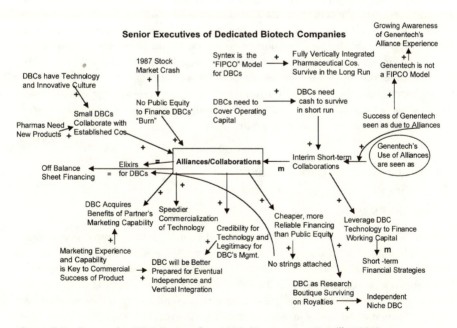

Figure 7.5   Composite DBC Perspective, 1988 (Datasource: Burrill, 1989)

company per the Syntex model (Burrill, 1988a), but the alternative of becoming a niche company or "boutique" with a specific R&D focus was given serious consideration. According to this model, a DBC received royalties for the use of its technology to develop a bioproduct with an established company, usually a pharmaceutical, with the capability of commercializing (gaining FDA approval, marketing, and distributing) the product (Burrill, 1988a). Later, this practice became so common that it was referred to as RIPCO, an acronym meaning "royalty income from a pharmaceutical company." This additional example for securing independence as a stand-alone is evidence of a new understanding about alliance use.

The operative word for the 1989 strategic alliance (SA) recipe is *strategic*. When an alliance is strategic, objectives are long term and more than financially motivated. The SA recipe is depicted most completely in the 1989 DBC executive composite understanding, Figure 7.6. The key SA recipe assumptions and their incidence are displayed in Table 7.1. The foundation assumption of the 1989 SA recipe is that SAs are formed by DBCs to accomplish their long-term strategic objectives. Its incidence of articulation was tracked from 1986 through 1994. That incidence is displayed in Table 7.2. Note that articulating the influence of a recipe is actually stronger support for that influence, because firms should be expected to implement many widely held assumptions without articulating any motivation for their actions.

Table 7.3 shows the aforementioned nine 1986 C/C industry-wide recipe assumptions (see p. 158) and the incidence of their articulation by DBC executives from 1986 through 1994. As Table 7.3 illustrates, the highest incidence of articulation was found for assumption 1 (the purpose of an alliance is cash or capital) and assumption 2 (alliances are interim, short-term relationships used to fund R&D); their peak support was in 1986 and dwindled over the following years of this research tracking. In the publications reviewed, by 1994 there is no longer any evidence that alliances are being formed with the assumption that they will be short-term interim relationships, per assumption 2. This change in assumption 2, as well as the fewer articulations of many other key 1986 recipe assumptions by 1993, provides support for a changing industry-wide alliance recipe. Importantly, the support for assumption 4 (alliances provide legitimacy or credibility) actually increases over the span of this study, signaling its growing acceptance and durability in subsequent biotech alliance recipes.

THE DEVELOPMENT OF GROUP RECIPES

Evidence of Social Learning

Through social learning, some understandings that are unique to just one epistemic community evolve into quite specific one-community or group recipes. These recipes represent a particular community's independent perspective, versus understandings with broad appeal in overlapping epistemic communities with more potential to evolve into industry-wide recipes. While some group recipes may eventually grow beyond their epistemic community borders and became industry-wide recipes, others may grow only more complex and specific, remaining less applicable to other resource bases beyond their epistemic community. Following Spender (1980),

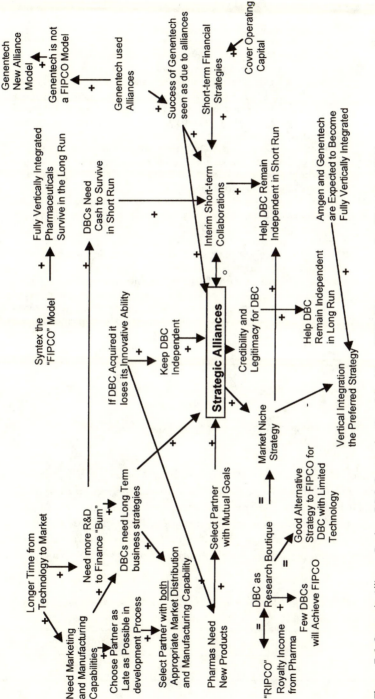

Figure 7.6 Strategic Alliance Recipe: DBC Composite Cognitive Map, 1989 (Data source: Burrill & Lee, 1990)

Table 7.1 Incidence of Articulation of SA Recipe Assumptions in 1989

Number of Separate Articulations[1]	Causal Assumption
17 (14)	1. Alliances are formed with long-term/strategic objectives.
7 (5)	2. Alliance contracts should serve the mutual goals of partners.
8 (6)	3. SAs permit a DBC to remain independent with a choice of two models.
5 (3)	4. The best model allows the DBC to rapidly commercialize its technology by accessing needed manufacturing, marketing, and regulatory capabilities without owning them, thereby postponing yet facilitating eventual full vertical integration.
6 (5)	5. The other model permits a DBC to operate as a research boutique focused on a specific market niche, using royalty payments from its partner with the necessary deep pockets and skills required to rapidly bring its technology to market.
6 (4)	6. A DBC's eventual goal is to become an independent biopharmaceutical in contrast to a pharma or, more specifically, a FIPCO, a fully vertically integrated pharmaceutical company.
5 (4)	7. Neither acquisition nor merger is an acceptable goal for a DBC.
6 (6)	8. A key element of vertical integration is manufacturing capability where previously just marketing capabilities were considered.
4 (4)	9. Strategic alliances are usually more than science projects.
4 (2)	10. SA contracts need to have milestone payments and termination or exit clauses that protect both partners but particularly the DBC's technology.
3 (3)	11. SAs should be made as late as possible, preferably during human trials.

[1]The number of individuals who made a statement is in parentheses.

Proposition 4. Group recipes are justified by their apparent relevance to a specific set of uncertain situations critical to the interests of the industry group.

The "poison pill" was just such a group recipe that became widely adopted by the DBC executive community in 1990.

Poison Pill Group Recipe. In early 1989, one influential biotech analyst, Sarah Good of Hambrecht and Quist, voiced concerns that interfirm contracts for research were actually "poison pills." These concerns were later articulated by DBC executives. She observed: "It's not that difficult to give away too much of what makes you [DBC] special," and "once a biotech company gives up its marketing rights to its core technology it's given up what makes it valuable" (*BioVenture View*, 1989, 157). Good's obser-

Table 7.2 Number of Individuals Asserting That DBCs Form SAs to Accomplish Long-term Strategic Objectives

	1986	1987	1988	1989	1990	1991	1992	1993	1994
Assertion 1	—	3	9	14	12	13	9	13	11

Table 7.3 Number of Individuals Making Key 1986 C/C Recipe Assertions

Assertion	1986	1987	1988	1989	1990	1991	1992	1993	1994
1	20	16	15	8	7	3	4	1	2
2	17	12	10	4	1	2	—	—	—
3	11	12	7	8	3	3	1	—	—
4	9	8	8	12	7	9	9	9	10
5	7	5	5	7	4	3	4	4	6
6	8	8	8	6	4	4	3	1	1
7	6	5	5	7	4	5	4	6	8
8	11	12	11	13	10	9	10	9	10
9	6	4	6	5	5	6	2	5	4

vations increasingly became the concern of many DBC executives. A consensual under-standing evolved among biotech executives and by 1990 achieved recipe status (Fig. 7.7). In 1990, DBC executives like Gensia's CEO, David Hale, articulated the vicarious learn-ing that had developed: terms of contract agreements are critical. "Do partnering in light of a strategic plan; don't let circumstances decide. Do lots of planning and nego-tiating, considering how your partnerships will be reviewed and terminated if necessary. ... Don't let your contract become a poison pill" (Burrill, 1990, 167).

Similarly, DBC executive Frank Kung, CEO of Genelabs, cautioned: "Projects may be delayed or bumped by a pharmaceutical company ... retain control over the process. Set up [contract] terms [so that] if your Pharma partner doesn't continue to fund the pro-ject, make sure that it [the technology] reverts to you. Partnering is not a sure thing; there are delays and 'divorces.' ... An inappropriate contract can later become a 'poison pill' " (Burrill, 1990, 158). Still another DBC executive, Stephen Duzan, CEO of Immunex stated: "Create and control products not only in the lab but through the regulatory process. ... Don't give away the company through partnering" (Burrill, 1990, 193).

These concerns about alliances voiced by DBC executives in 1990 were the first real negative assertions about the use of alliances and were in clear contrast to the "elixir" descriptions used from 1986 through 1988 and cognitively mapped as the consensus understanding of DBC executives (James, 1995, Appendices B1–B3). The 1990 recipe openly considered the impact of an alliance's eventual termination. Its new negative considerations defined a new recipe with new causal links satisfying several important recipe protocols discussed in this chapter, including categorical distinctiveness, gener-alization, pattern of inclusion, linkage to other concepts, and different examples, as well as interaction effects. Most important, the resulting dissemination of concern among DBC executives quickly translated into action. Different interfirm contracts were nego-tiated and written. Starting in 1990, new contracts were more focused (Burrill & Lee, 1991, 1992; InVivo, 1991, 1992; Edwards, 1994). Alliance contracts carefully described the specific research and technology covered, thereby freeing a DBC to retain control of any breakthrough technology not specifically licensed by contract to the partner but developed coincident to a contract project (Edwards, 1994). From 1990 on, almost all alliance contracts included milestone payments and termination clauses (InVivo, 1992,

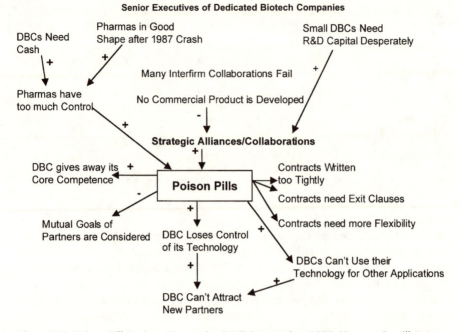

Figure 7.7 Poison Pill Recipe: Composite DBC Perspective, 1990 (Source: Burrill & Lee, 1991)

26), whereas previously they did not usually exist. Additionally, after 1990, several ideal contracts negotiated true mutuality of partner interests and included licensing in a pharma's already established technology to be further developed and then marketed by the DBC partner (*BioPharm*, 1991, 54).

It should be noted, however, that although carefully written new contracts were the model prescription for successful alliances following 1990, many small lower-tier DBCs were still without leverage, desperately needing to structure any possible contract with an established company that would secure enough revenue to stay afloat. These small lower-tier private DBCs were observed to have no option but to negotiate whatever alliance contract possible in order to survive. This meant that they were often in essence swallowing a poison pill (Burrill & Lee, 1991, 183) and "giving up their birthright" (Edwards, 1994).

The key assertions of the poison pill (PP) group recipe include:

1. An alliance contract can become a "poison pill" if a DBC gives up what makes it valuable.
2. Terms of alliance contracts are critical, particularly exit clauses.
3. Many collaborations don't work out.
4. If a DBC gives up the rights to its patented technology via contract, it has no potential to remain independent or subsequently ally with other partners to commercialize its technology.

The PP recipe, like the SA recipe, appears to have originated with the exhortation of a prominent biotech industry observer, but, unlike SA, its greater importance to the survival of DBCs more specifically affected the wording of new alliance contracts and changed the perception of DBC executives about alliances. Instead of seeing alliances as "elixir" financial remedies (per the earlier 1986 C/C recipe), after 1990, DBC executives often viewed alliances as "necessary evils" (Burrill & Lee, 1991). The 1990 PP DBC group recipe thus exhibits significant learning beyond the 1989 industry-wide SA recipe. The content of PP reflects how DBCs learned that interfirm collaborations with established pharmaceutical companies could lead to their demise. DBCs learned that if an alliance contract was too tightly written and assigns all rights to its technology to the contract project, without exit provisions or caveats, it is unlikely that the DBC can subsequently ally successfully with other partners to commercialize other applications using its technology. Like the 1989 SA recipe, PP considered the strategic importance of alliances but focused on the negative considerations.

The PP recipe, in contrast to both the SA recipe and the recent virtual integration understanding, appears to have been quickly integrated into firm-level action (Edwards, 1994). As soon as poison pill concerns were voiced, DBC executives, whenever possible, changed contract wording to avoid the possibility that their alliances would become poison pills. However, this research didn't find evidence that PP, with its negative expectations for alliances, was widely articulated beyond the DBC executive community. Because PP appears to have remained essentially a one-community or group recipe, yet very influential in the subsequent actions of DBCs, it gives preliminary support to proposition 4.

Virtual integration. Virtual integration (VI) is a newly emerging alliance understanding articulated in 1994 by several analysts, and illustrated comprehensively in Figure 7.8. VI asserts that strategic alliances are in the process of establishing "virtual integration." Virtual integration, as defined by Steven Burrill,[4] appears to let a DBC achieve the benefits of full vertical integration. However, VI is better than the reality of full vertical integration for DBCs because it requires considerably less commitment of time and financial resources. VI's central assumptions follow:

1. Emerging VI strategic alliances allow a DBC to be *virtually* integrated to achieve the benefits of vertical integration without spending valuable time and finances in purchasing necessary resources such as marketing, distribution, manufacturing, or clinical trial capabilities.
2. Virtual integration is better than the reality of full vertical integration for a DBC, because allying with resourceful partners requires considerably less time, allowing a DBC quicker commercialization of new technology.
3. VI enhances a DBC's ability to survive and become totally independent.

The content of VI presents strategic alliances as the preferred strategic choice of many successful independent DBCs. Analysts observe that DBCs that were strategically partnered achieved faster commercialization of their technology than those that invested their scarce time and finances in vertical integration; therefore, they expect allied DBCs to be more successful. Eventually, DBC and pharma executives may affirm VI and pub-

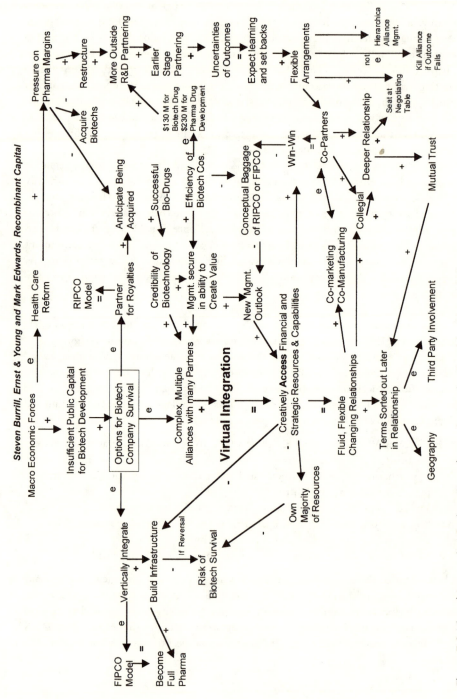

Steven Burrill, Ernst & Young and Mark Edwards, Recombinant Capital

Figure 7.8 Virtual Integration Recipe: Consultants Composite Cognitive Map, 1993

licly state that their motivation for forming strategic alliances is to achieve vertical integration without owning additional resources. Then this analyst group recipe would achieve industry-wide recipe status via the institutional influence of industry analysts and consultants.

By allying with resourceful partners, a DBC attains quicker commercialization of its new technology and thus actually enhances its ability to survive and ultimately become totally independent as a fully vertically integrated company in the model of Syntex, but more likely as a biopharma company instead of a pharmaceutical company without biotechnology capabilities. At the time this study ended, VI was largely the understanding of industry analysts-consultants. Through 1995, no evidence of the specific articulation of VI by a DBC executive was found. Only analysts like Edwards, Burrill, and Wirtlin had their VI assumptions published. Yet, these industry observers state that DBC firms are widely adopting strategic alliances as a means of achieving virtual integration. The VI understanding may be evolving into another industry-wide recipe because of the influence of its biotech analyst mentors. At the time this study ended, it was too early to know whether DBCs could survive in the long term, per the VI analyst group recipe, by which they remain smaller independent niche firms contractually linked to the resources and capabilities of several other firms. Learning how to best structure long-term successful strategic alliances is still evolving in biotechnology and in all other industries. At the end of the study, the only DBC that appeared relatively secure as an independent company was Amgen (Edwards, 1994; *InVivo*, 1994). Amgen is a fully integrated biopharmaceutical company. It has many alliances with smaller niche DBCs, as well as larger established pharmas. At this point, Amgen's success with multiple strategic alliances appears to be the model for other smaller DBCs who want to avoid acquisition or merger (Edwards, 1994; *BioPharm*, 1994), replacing the earlier Syntex model of the early 1980s. Nonetheless, unlike the 1986 C/C recipe and the 1989 SA recipe, whose assumptions were publicly stated within all three biotech communities, to date there is no clear evidence that VI is becoming an industry-wide recipe.

CONCLUSION

The main theoretic insights from the present study are summarized in a series of propositions that describe the cognitive basis for the formation of industry recipes. It is assumed that an industry involves groups of firms that become epistemic communities. Epistemic communities are the basis for creating a shared understanding of how best to respond to an uncertain environment. Particularly within an emerging industry such as biotechnology, different group recipes are expected to develop, each reflecting different experiences and perspectives associated with the epistemic community in question. Over time, industry recipes emerge as generalizations from group recipes, reflecting growing consensus among industry participants. Once established, industry recipes tend to be quite persistent; however, recipes can and do change as industry participants are exposed to potential flaws in the current recipe and learn from the experiences of other actors in the industry.

These theoretic arguments are supported by an empirical study of alliance formation within the biotechnology industry from 1984 through 1994, which focuses attention on the links between industry learning and the social construction of recipes within the industry. The observed changes in the content of understandings about the use of bio-tech alliances signal that learning about biotech alliances did occur and almost certainly continues to occur, suggesting that recipes are dynamic. One good example is what originated in 1986 as a unique analyst assumption: business strategy should direct in-terfirm collaboration, not vice versa. By 1989, this assumption became the foundation of the industry-wide recipe. The data reviewed suggest that the social construction of the 1989 SA recipe replaced the industry-wide C/C recipe of 1986. The 1989 SA recipe, like the earlier 1986 C/C, was widely articulated across all three epistemic communities studied, evidence of its industry-wide status.

These two industry-wide recipes were given extensive lip service, as noted earlier, yet specific changes in firm-level actions were not observed during either recipe's tenure, at least not the convincing evidence of firm-level adoption, such as the specific changes made in the way contracts were written after the adoption of the 1990 DBC poison pill recipe. The poison pill recipe was a group recipe that quickly spread through the DBC community. After the adoption of the poison pill recipe, alliance contracts were struc-tured to prevent future new biotech discoveries from being subject to partner dictates (*BioPharm*, 1991, 56). It has been hypothesized that recipes become justified by their apparent relevance to a specific set of uncertain situations (Spender, 1980, 95–96). The poison pill's more immediate influence on contract structure helps illustrate its relevance to the DBC executive community and their vested interest in the survival of biotech companies.

Biotech alliances continue to proliferate, and strategic alliances still appear to signal institutional legitimacy, even though many interfirm contracts (particularly agreements adopted by smaller, unprofitable DBCs) cast a shadow on the future independence of these companies. Specific firm-level decisions, such as whether to form an interfirm collaboration, may be overwhelmed by the pressures of an overriding industry recipe that dictates strategic alliance adoption, despite increasingly obvious negative effects of partnering. For example, complexities often arise when DBCs form alliances with mul-tiple competing pharmas because multiple alliances with various competitors contradict one industry-wide heuristic—RIPCO (royalty-based alliance with a potential pharma par-ent)—which assumes that the partnered DBC will ultimately be acquired or merged with its more established pharma partner. Firms may find existing recipes useful in dispelling the need for new learning and recipe revision, or, industry-level cognitive blocks may exist, prohibiting new learning and adoption of new recipes like the VI recipe articulated in 1993 (Burrill & Lee, 1993).

Do Institutionalized Recipes Limit a Firm's Strategic Options?

Industry consensus doesn't mean that an articulated industry-wide recipe is correct or has adequate empirical support. Evidence from this research suggests that biotech lead-ers probably overemphasized the benefits of strategic alliances in the 1980s, encouraging DBCs to form alliances without caution per an "elixir" recipe, because prior to 1990 no clear evidence that strategic alliances could become poison pills existed (Burrill & Lee,

1991). But, rather than detract from the evolving intelligence of biotech community leaders by noting excessive application of lessons still being learned, this study reviews the recent explosion of biotech strategic alliances in light of the influence of institutional pressures of widely accepted industry strategic alliance recipes. For example, C/C recipe assumption 4, "alliances provide credibility and legitimacy for new, unproven technology and/or management," was found to remain fairly constant in articulation over the 8 years its articulation was documented. This causal concept, which directly links the formation of an interfirm alliance with the outcome of legitimacy for new unproven technology or management, has the obvious potential of encouraging new entrepreneurial DBCs to establish an alliance with the strategic purpose of gaining credibility.

Future firm-level research will be needed to establish whether adopted institutionalized recipes significantly influence a DBC's success. For example, future firm-level research can systematically explore whether biotech firms that announced having structured a strategic alliance (per the industry-wide recipe whose content has been described in this research) subsequently enjoyed stock price escalation or some other institutional benefit. Such evidence would support the institutional influence of a recipe and support the assertions of biotech analysts like Mark Edwards, George Wirtlin, and Jeff Casdin, who believe that alliances have had a positive impact on performance.

Notes

1. This chapter is from the author's doctoral dissertation (James, 1996).
2. Jeff Casdin was interviewed by telephone June 12, 1993, by Gail James.
3. *Biotech 86: At the Crossroads*, published in 1987 by the Arthur Young Company, focused on the status of the biotechnology industry by using transcribed discussions among biotech industry leaders, plus survey data based on 137 biotech company respondents (96 public companies and 41 private companies). See appendices B and C in James (1996) for detail.
4. In most contexts, "virtual" means beyond present reality, a reality that doesn't yet exist but appears to exist. Burrill indicated to me (interview, June 5, 1994) that he derived the term "virtual integration" from Davidow and Malone's concept of the "virtual corporation." However, further investigation showed that "virtual integration" had been used in the computer industry about 1985 by Scott Flaig and others to refer to the integration of various computer telecommunication systems. Flaig used "virtual integration strategies" to refer to advanced manufacturing processes that use sophisticated computer systems. Flaig joined Arthur Young's Management Consulting Group from Digital Equipment and became an associate of Burrill in 1989.

8

Predicting the Magnitude and Direction of Strategic Change

As noted in chapter 5, an array of strategic issues helped to reshape the pharmaceutical industry from the 1970s through the mid-1990s. These industry-wide trends reflect changes in the strategic environment that triggered adaptive strategic responses from individual firms within the industry. If all or even most firms within the industry responded similarly to these changes in the strategic environment, then a causal analysis at the industry level would suffice, and firms could be treated as identical actors in the strategic change process. However, as will be seen in the subsequent empirical analysis, individual firms within the pharmaceutical industry respond quite differently to industry-wide changes in their strategic environment; furthermore, these differences in strategic response are predictable.

A good deal has been written about why firms change strategies—to respond to new regulation, new technology, and other threats and opportunities in the environment; to carry out the vision of a new leader; or to erect or solidify barriers to entry or otherwise gain competitive advantage. While these and other descriptions have theoretic appeal, several problems make them difficult to apply to actual case histories. Firms almost always feel buffeted by their environments and thus almost always have reason to make a strategic move, even in eras that in retrospect seem minimally stressful in comparison with current pressures. Conversely, not all firms change strategy, even when simultaneously faced with several factors that might be expected to induce a significant strategic response. Moreover, it is not always easy to transform vague and contradictory signals from the firms' environments into messages about threats, opportunities, rents, barriers, or competitive advantages.

Attention to the forces that bind firms to one strategy has done a great deal to summarize the micro and macro factors that reduce the likelihood that a given firm will be able to respond (or quickly respond) to indicators that strategic change might be desirable. Firms that have had the same general strategy for some time are likely to view the prospect of strategic change very differently than firms that have recently changed strategy. Firms "see" the same set of potentially destabilizing events through different interpretive lenses, thus triggering qualitatively different strategic responses. The firm draws upon past experience, as well as the borrowed knowledge of the successes and failures of its competitors, to craft a strategy that capitalizes on the firm's resources, embodied in its current strategic position, while responding to emerging competitive opportunities.

Although this general approach appears promising, more needs to be done in the empirical domain to evaluate theoretic arguments pertaining to the dynamic interplay between stress and inertia and how this interplay affects the timing of strategic change. The analysis in this chapter draws on chapter 4 to explore these issues.

In the discussion that follows, the goal is to empirically validate earlier theoretic arguments pertaining to the strategic change process, while also contributing to an evolutionary perspective on organization and industry change that has received considerable attention in organizational sociology, industrial economics, and management-centered disciplines, as outlined in chapter 1.

Following earlier theoretical arguments, the decision to make second order changes in strategy is framed in terms of the interdependence between organization stress and inertia. In support of these theoretical arguments, second order changes in strategy are shown to be associated with high stress, low inertia conditions. Particular attention is paid to the *history* of accumulating stress and inertia, and the "mover-stayer" distinction that was hypothesized in chapter 4 is strongly supported.

The empirical analysis concludes with the prediction of the magnitude and direction of strategic change along three strategic dimensions that are particularly salient to success in the pharmaceutical industry: R&D effort, advertising effort, and the scope of the firm's product portfolio. A stress-inertia model is used to predict the set of firms making second order changes in strategy along each strategic dimension from 1970 to 1990. In the second stage of the model, the direction of change is predicted based on the competitive positioning of the firm vis-à-vis the distribution of attractive strategic opportunities. The significance of the modeling effort is further confirmed by a regression analysis successfully predicting strategic change for the sample as a whole. The results of these analyses provide strong evidence in support of our theoretic arguments, while also providing insight into the dynamics of strategic change within the pharmaceutical industry over the 20-year period studied.

COGNITIVE FOUNDATIONS

The cognitively anchored theory of the firm outlined in the preceding chapters establishes the theoretic foundations for an empirical investigation of strategic change and industry evolution. The cognitive aspects of stress and inertia have been discussed extensively in earlier chapters; only the key arguments necessary to motivate the empirical analysis will be outlined here. The discussion then turns to an investigation of the competitive context and its role in strategic change decisions from a cognitive perspective.

Stress and Inertia

The inertia surrounding the current strategy arises from growing institutional commitment and routinization, as well as the associated costs accompanying major changes in strategy, whereas organization stress arises from perceived inadequacies in the current strategy vis-à-vis the demands of the firm's competitive environment. In the absence of compensating adjustments in strategy, stress is cumulative and will ultimately undermine commitment to the current strategy, thereby precipitating a second order change in strategy.

The literature in this area suggests that, as the world changes, increased stress over time is also almost inevitable (Huff, Huff & Thomas, 1992; Schwenk & Tang, 1989; Tushman & Romanelli, 1985) because the fit between the organization and macro environmental forces and between the organization and individual stakeholders deteriorates (Christensen, Andrews, Bower, Hamermesh & Porter, 1985, 94).

Although firms may not expect to achieve the benefits of industry leaders in very different circumstances, firms are expected to compare themselves with similar firms in assessing their performance. Furthermore, stockholders, lending institutions, industry analysts, and other outsiders will make similar comparisons. Thus, below-par performance over the preceding time period is expected to create stress and make a change in strategy more likely.

Many authors conceptualize stress only in terms of poor performance or other negative terms. Such conceptualizations of stress are not useful, however, for explaining above-average rates of strategic change for high-performance firms. Increasing stress associated with both high performance and low performance suggests a U-shaped relationship between performance and organization stress. In the empirical analysis that follows, it is assumed that stress is associated with very high performance conditions as well as very low performance conditions. High performance conditions are stressful in the sense that they generate resources and they tend to be associated with high-risk, high-return strategies. High performance conditions also raise expectations that are difficult to sustain.

Variation in organization stress is not a sufficient explanation for observed variation in the incidence of second order change. An equally important concept, as a number of authors have recently observed, involves the level of inertia within the organization. Organization inertia is a measure of both economic and psychological commitment to the current way of acting (Williamson, 1975, 121; Schwenk & Tang, 1989). Most observers suggest that, as with stress, on balance inertia will increase as the time since the last change in strategy increases as outlined in chapter 4. As time passes, individuals find ways to accommodate their interests within the confines of a given strategy (Hannon & Freeman, 1984). At the organizational level, more efficient operation follows increasing experience. Also important are an increasing number of capital expenditures, accumulating R&D and other knowledge, and growing goodwill assets with suppliers, buyers, and others (Bower, 1970b; Williamson, 1975). Policies and procedures are developed to solidify these gains (Selznick, 1957). Not only would it be time consuming to abandon these activities and discover new procedures but also it would resubject the organization to the inefficiencies and uncertainties of new innovation (Dierickx & Cool, 1987; Cooper & Schendel, 1976).

A fundamental assertion that will be directly evaluated in the empirical analysis that follows is that firms experiencing high stress are more likely to make second order changes in strategy and that firms exhibiting high inertia are more likely to resist second order changes in strategy.

A key premise in this section and in the earlier theoretic arguments is that first and second order change arise out of fundamentally different decision-making processes, with first order change involving incremental adjustments to current strategy that occur as part of day-to-day operations of the firm and second order change associated with major shifts in strategy that precipitate fundamental changes within the structure and function of the organization. For most organizations, most of the time, strategic renewal involving second order change is not a topic of sustained consideration consuming significant amounts of the organization's resources. Instead, incremental adjustments to strategy are accomplished within an ongoing, problem-solving, "business as usual," mode of operation. The shift to an active mode of strategic evaluation and the consideration of strategic alternatives signals a shift into a second order change decisioning process triggered by the accumulation of unresolved stress surrounding the current strategy and supplanting arguments in favor of continuing with business as usual.

An important implication of the cognitively anchored model of strategic change outlined in chapter 4 is that the firms within a given industry are likely to exhibit two very different strategic responses to a changing competitive environment. On the one hand, there will be the set of "stayers" characterized by incremental change and "business as usual" and, on the other hand, a set of "movers" accounting for a disproportionate number of second order changes in strategy in a nearly perpetual high stress, low inertia state.

The discussion of strategic change along specific strategic dimensions suggests the possibility that organization stress and inertia may also vary, depending upon the dimension in question. For example, a pharmaceutical firm may make significant changes in R&D activity while making no major changes in its advertising strategy. As a consequence, the organizational commitment to the new R&D strategy might be relatively low following the change, whereas the inertia surrounding the current advertising strategy could remain relatively high. An interesting corollary of the preceding observations when applied to high-stress firms is that "prospector" firms (Miles & Snow, 1978) with strategies on the competitive frontier with respect to a given dimension (e.g., firms with very high R&D commitments) are following high-risk strategies and consequently high-stress strategies, which have a greater likelihood of precipitating second order change along that particular dimension.

Industry Context

An important consequence of a cognitive perspective is the need to reframe the concept of "industry." While the concept of an "industry" is becoming increasingly problematic as firms grow and reconfigure themselves and as products move away from aging SIC code definitions, this level of analysis remains important as an intermediate step in understanding both changes in the world economy and changes in firm-level opportunities. In many situations, it still seems true, as Porter observes, that "the industry is the arena in which competitive advantage is won or lost" (1990, 34).

The traditional definition of an "industry" is a set of interacting firms with roughly substitutable products or producers (Grant, 1991a). An attractive alternative is to focus on the defining aspects of the firm rather than on product characteristics. In particular, in a world of faster product cycles, firm strategy will dominate product as a useful area of industry analysis. A key assumption in the analysis that follows is that firm strategies define the industry. Consequently, the analysis begins with a conceptualization of the pharmaceutical industry as the joint product of firm strategies and an assumption that firms within the same industry are operating within the same "strategic space." Their strategies are similar in that they are formulated in terms of the same set of key strategic dimensions (Fiegenbaum, 1987; Reger, 1988). The range of choices made by individual firms along these critical dimensions is assumed to define the industry. Firms change competitive position within the industry via changes in strategy, and the content of a newly constructed strategy necessarily builds upon the resources and the knowledge embodied in previous strategies identified by both the firm in question and others responding to similar conditions.

The cognitively anchored definition of "industry" is an essential element of our characterization of the strategic change process, in that the industry as defined in terms of the strategic positions of firms also serves as the basis for defining the domain of strategic decision making. The basic notion is that the domain of decisions considered is not the full logical range of each strategic dimension but a smaller set of alternatives defined by the current strategies of members of the industry.

The identification of the strategic search domain ultimately comes down to an attempt to formalize the observation that strategic positions too far from the current positions of other firms in the industry should not be included within the choice set because, perceptually, industries are defined by their participants. If a firm were to move to a "remote" location, it would be considered to have moved outside the industry; furthermore, the activities of the firms in the industry tend to enact the industry environment, thereby increasing the likelihood that remote positions will be nonviable positions.

MAPPING STRATEGIC CHANGE

The strategic positioning and repositioning of firms within an industry context suggests an immediate visual analogue in the form of a strategic map. As noted earlier, firms within the same industry are assumed to be operating in the same strategic space, defined in terms of a limited set of strategic dimensions critical to firms in the industry; these dimensions serve as the axes of the strategic map. Figures 8.1, 8.2, and 8.3 illustrate the competitive positions of a sample of pharmaceuticals firms at three points in time, 1970, 1978, and 1986.[1] (Full names for abbreviations can be found in appendix 1.)

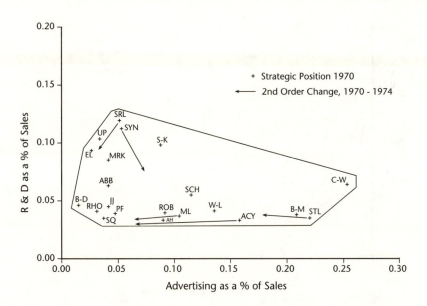

Figure 8.1 Strategic Positions and Second Order Changes, Pharmaceutical Firms, 1970–1974

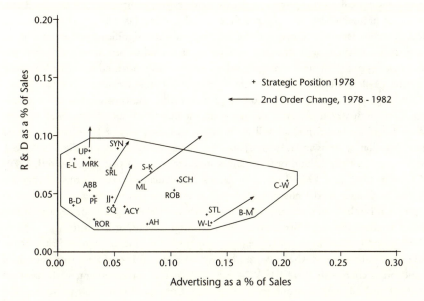

Figure 8.2 Strategic Positions and Second Order Changes, Pharmaceutical Firms, 1978–1982

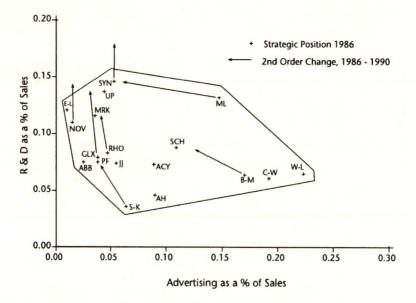

Figure 8.3 Strategic Positions and Second Order Changes, Pharmaceutical Firms, 1986–1990

The strategic maps illustrate the strategic positioning of the firms along two strategic dimensions critical to the pharmaceuticals industry: expenditures on R&D (as a percentage of annual sales) and expenditures on advertising (as a percentage of annual sales). A comparison of the maps of the industry indicates significant differences in the strategies across the sample of firms—differences that tend to persist over time. Certain firms have research oriented strategies, others are primarily oriented toward advertising, and others follow mixed strategies with more or less intensive resource commitments.

Given a graphic means of "positioning" a firm within the constellation of strategies defining the industry, it is possible to represent the magnitude and direction of strategic change for individual firms, as well as industry evolution arising from the associated reconfiguration of firms in strategic space . For example, the arrows in Figures 8.1, 8.2, and 8.3 represent the second order changes in strategy over 4-year time periods, 1970–1974, 1978–1982, and 1986–1990. The details of calculating second order change are deferred until later in the chapter. However, as expected from theoretic arguments in chapter 4, it can be seen that most firms make incremental changes in strategic position, while a smaller number of firms make relatively large, second order shifts.

The second order changes in strategy are responsible for major changes in the structure of the industry as a whole. As can be seen in Figure 8.1, the dominant pattern of second order change in the 1970–1974 period is that of retrenchment, with firms on the R&D and advertising frontiers pulling back from the higher risk positions. The resulting impact on the structure of the industry is shown in Figure 8.4, which compares the industry boundary in 1970 with the boundary in 1978.

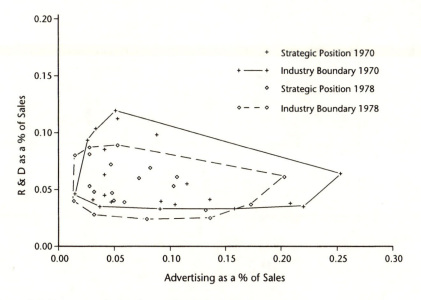

Figure 8.4 Pharmaceutical Industry Boundaries, 1970 and 1978

The pattern of second order change in the 1978–1982 period represents a clear reversal in the 1970–1974 trend and contributes to a marked expansion in the industry's strategic boundaries, as shown in Figure 8.5.

Finally, the pattern of second order change in the 1986–1990 period differs from the two previous patterns, with a tendency toward retrenchment in advertising coupled with a marked pattern of continued expansion in R&D.

What is particularly interesting about these maps is a general absence of support for those who would argue that firms within the same industry are following the same or very similar strategies (a common assumption in neoclassical theories of the firm). Nor do we find evidence that firms are converging toward a single optimal strategy (i.e., moves pointing toward a single focal point).Then again, the observed strategic changes are not all pointing in the same direction either; which suggests that a simple structural shift model driven by an exogenously determined change in the industry's environment (e.g., changes in the interest rate) is inadequate to the task of explaining observed changes in strategy across firms within the industry.

These strategic maps provide a very different way of thinking about and visualizing strategic change and industry evolution. The maps provide a much clearer image of how firms are positioned with respect to other firms in the industry and how their strategic positions are changing over time. The strategic maps also provide a clearer sense of the industry boundaries and how the strategic frontiers of the industry are changing over time as firms on or near the boundaries shift their strategic positions. A final comment on these maps is that they are an excellent heuristic device for exploring possible patterns in the data and associated explanations for the observed patterns in the timing and the direction of second order strategic change.

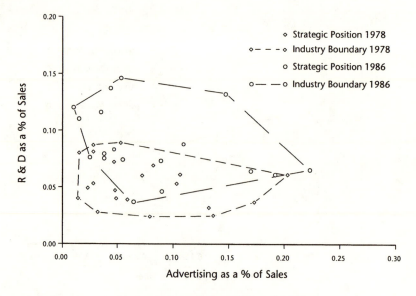

Figure 8.5 Pharmaceutical Industry Boundaries, 1978 and 1986

Our intent in the remainder of the chapter is to show that industry evolution is a cause and consequence of changing strategic positions among competitors within the industry, in which a firm's strategic decisions are influenced by and subsequently influence the strategic decisions of other firms in the industry.

Competitive Position and Strategic Opportunity

In the analysis that follows, the attractiveness of possible alternatives is identified and calibrated by comparing firm strategy and outcomes with those of similar firms (Huff, 1982). More specifically, we suggest that, when evaluating strategic alternatives, decision makers endeavor to predict the firm's potential performance under different strategic scenarios by extrapolating from the performances of competitors who are employing a range of strategies. All else being equal, a firm will tend to move toward a strategic position that has a high performance potential and away from a strategic position with a low performance potential. Furthermore, firms are assumed to be inherently conservative in the sense that the attractiveness of a strategic opportunity for a specific firm decreases with increasing distance from the firm's current strategic position. That is, locations that are associated with demonstrably superior performance are nonetheless decreasingly attractive as they are associated with strategies that depart significantly from the firm's current strategy. Strategic renewal is achieved through the *re*construction of the firm's existing strategy. The current strategy defines and is defined within the constellation of resources, assets, and expertise constituting the firm. Consequently, the decision to "move" (or make a second order change in strategy) represents a trade-off between the performance potential of a competing alternative to the present strategy and the match between the capacities of the firm and the implied requirements of the alternative strategy.

For the purpose of analysis, it is assumed that firms employ an interpolation procedure to predict the performance potential associated with a strategic alternative, based upon the observed strategies of the other firms in the industry and the performance levels associated with those strategies. The resulting performance potential surfaces are shown in Figures 8.6 through 8.11. The x and y axes of this space are defined by key dimensions of strategic decision making in the industry, advertising as a percentage of sales and R&D as a percentage of sales. The interpolated surface of the figure adds a third axis based on known performance information for firms in the industry. Figures 8.6, 8.7 and 8.8 use annual sales growth figures for 1970, 1978 and 1986, respectively, as the key performance measure, whereas Figures 8.9, 8.10 and 8.11 use return on sales (ROS) for 1974, 1982, and 1990 as the key performance measure. (The process used to construct the map is discussed in greater detail in appendix 2 at the end of the chapter.) The sales growth and the ROS performance potential surfaces appear to capture similar general patterns, with low performance potential attached to very high commitments of resources to advertising and relatively high performance potential associated with mixed stategies emphasizing high R&D commitments and moderately high resource commitments to advertising.

In summary, a visual comparison of the performance surfaces indicates significant variation in performance potential across the strategic space, supporting the basic premise that a firm's performance is related to its strategic position. A comparison of the strategic change maps shown earlier and the performance potential maps also supports our strategic opportunity argument in that firms do appear to respond to perceived performance differentials by moving away from low performance positions and toward high performance positions.

EMPIRICAL ANALYSIS, 1976–1990

Before proceeding to more sophisticated analyses of the strategic change process, it is instructive to demonstrate that pharmaceutical firms experiencing high levels of stress and low levels of inertia are, indeed, the firms that tend to make major changes in strategy as reflected in significant reallocations of resources for R&D and advertising.

A precise operational definition of second order change is required in the empirical analysis that follows. The operational definition of strategic change involves (a) the selection of a unit time interval over which change is defined, (b) the strategic dimensions defining the structure of the industry, and (c) the minimum amount of change along each strategic dimension that is assumed to constitute a major or second order change in strategy.

Throughout the analysis, changes in strategy for the pharmaceutical firms included in the study are defined in terms of observed differences in R&D expenditures as a percentage of sales and advertising expenditures as a percentage of sales at the beginning and end of each 4-year period. The strategic position for each firm was recorded at the

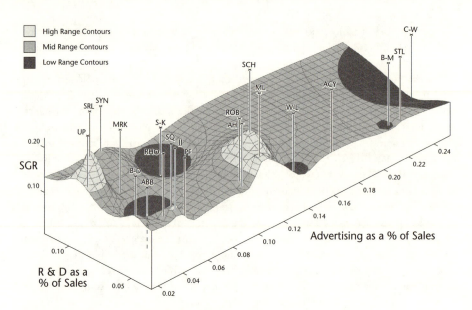

Figure 8.6 Sales Growth Performance Surface, 1970

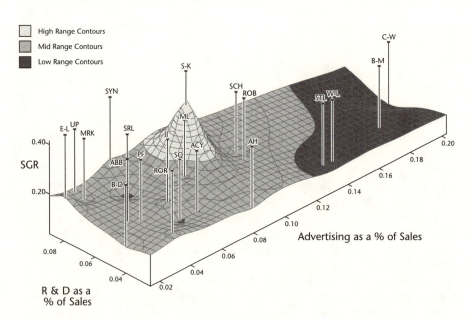

Figure 8.7 Sales Growth Performance Surface, 1978

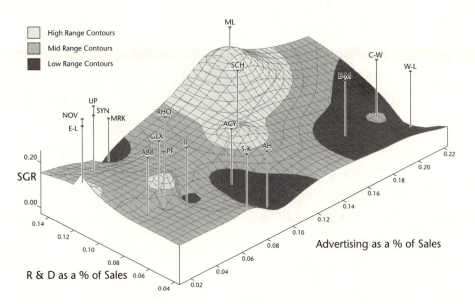

Figure 8.8 Sales Growth Performance Surface, 1986

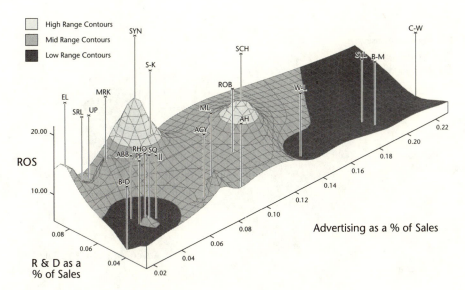

Figure 8.9 Return on Sales (ROS) Performance Surface, 1978

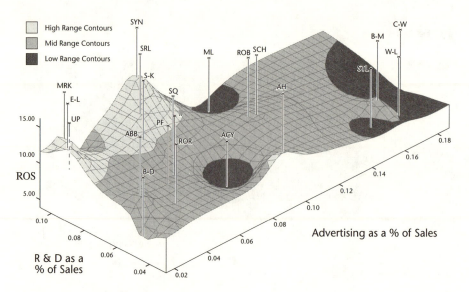

Figure 8.10 Return on Sales (ROS) Performance Surface, 1982

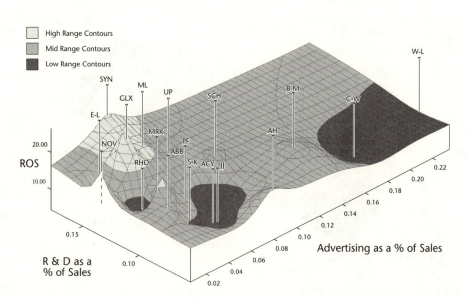

Figure 8.11 Return on Sales (ROS) Performance Surface, 1990

beginning and end of each 4-year period from 1966 to 1990. Relatively long time intervals were chosen in an effort to capture longer term changes in strategy and to minimize the effects of short-term fluctuations in strategic variables. Furthermore, the time intervals closely parallel the stable strategic time periods identified by Cool and Dierickx (1993) in their analysis of the pharmaceutical industry. Because the firm's prior strategic change experience is expected to influence subsequent decisions to make second order changes in strategy, only strategic change events during the last five time intervals are included as observations on the dependent variable (i.e., the firm's decision to make a second order change in strategy) in the following analysis; second order strategic change during the 1966–1970 period enters the analysis only as baseline data.

The empirical problem of defining the threshold between incremental changes in strategy and second order changes in strategy is not so easily resolved because there are no clearly discernible break points in the distribution of observed changes along the key strategic dimensions. In the present analysis, the threshold values are defined as 15% of the average range for each dimension. We have experimented with other threshold values in this general range, and the results are not significantly different from those presented.

Given these operational definitions, there are 52 second order changes in strategy and 80 instances in which firms retain the same strategy over the 4-year periods in question. Approximately 40% of the firms make second order changes during a given 4-year period.

As noted earlier, organization stress arises from a mismatch between the changing demands placed upon the organization and the capacity of the current strategy to respond to those changes. In the present analysis, organization stress and the associated pressure for second order change in strategy are measured in terms of a firm's performance relative to industry norms. Performance levels near the industry average are assumed to be associated with low levels of organization stress and correspondingly low propensities to make second order changes in strategy. Consequently, firms experiencing moderate performance levels are expected to engage in incremental modifications to the firm's current strategy, strategy-sustaining mechanisms to keep organization stress within manageable bounds. By contrast, firms following strategies associated with *either* high performance *or* low performance relative to industry norms are assumed to be experiencing high organization stress and are expected to exhibit relatively high propensities to make second order changes in strategy.

The hypothesized U-shaped relationship between stress and performance differs from standard practice in the strategy field, wherein stress is generally assumed to be associated only with poor performance. However, high performance conditions are likely to be stressful because they tend to raise expectations beyond the firm's capacity to consistently perform at that level, thereby pushing the firm into a search for yet higher return strategies. A further source of stress is that higher return strategies are likely to be higher risk and inherently unstable strategies.

Table 8.1 provides direct empirical support for:

Hypothesis 1. *Both high and low performance are likely to be high stress conditions that are associated with a firm's decision to make a second order change in strategy.*

The sample was split into quartiles based on each firm's reported rate of sales growth, SALG (during each of the five time intervals, 1970–1974, 1974–1978, 1978–1982, 1982–

Table 8.1 Relationship Between Stress and Strategic Change

| | High Stress Firms | | Low Stress Firms |
	High Performance	Low Performance	Moderate Performance
Change strategy	20	21	11
Retain strategy	11	10	59

1986, and 1986–1990). The high stress group consists of firms in the top quartile ("high performance" firms) and firms in the bottom quartile ("low performance" firms). The low stress group consisted of the firms in the second and third quartiles.

As expected, high stress firms (high performance and low performance firms combined) were much more likely to change strategy than were low stress firms ($\chi^2 = 35.10$, 1 df), and there is no significant difference in the propensity to change strategy between high and low performance firms ($\chi^2 = .07$, 1 df).

A stress-inertia perspective on strategic change recognizes that organizations are very resistant to change. Significant changes in strategy are not without cost and are not undertaken lightly, even under high stress conditions. Furthermore, organization inertia associated with a particular strategy tends to increase over time as the strategy becomes institutionalized.

Hypothesis 2. *High inertia conditions are positively associated with a firm's decision to retain its current strategy and not make significant changes in that strategy.*

The distinction between firms experiencing high inertia and firms experiencing low inertia is defined in terms of the time since the firm's last major change in strategy. If the firm changed strategy during the previous 4-year period, the firm is assigned to a low inertia state. If no major changes occurred in the last time period, the firm is assigned to a high inertia state.

The importance of strategic inertia in the strategic change decision is illustrated in Table 8.2. The data from the sample of pharmaceutical firms indicate a clear relationship between the decision to retain the current strategy and the retention of the strategy in the previous time interval ($\chi^2 = 14.37$, 1 df).

Before moving into a discussion of more sophisticated strategic change models, it is instructive to summarize the joint effects of stress and inertia on the strategic change

Table 8.2 Relationship Between Inertia and Strategic Change

	Low Inertia	High Inertia
Change strategy	26	26
Retain strategy	15	65

Table 8.3 The Joint Effects of Stress and Inertia on the Strategic Change Decision

	High Stress, Low Inertia	Low Stress, Low Inertia	High Stress, High Inertia	Low Stress, High Inertia
Change strategy	22	4	19	7
Retain strategy	6	9	15	50

decision, as shown in Table 8.3. When firms are partitioned on the basis of both stress and inertia, it is evident that the probability of changing strategy is quite sensitive to the combined effects of stress and inertia ($\chi^2 = 39.8$, 3 df).

The overall message from the foregoing analysis is that firms experiencing high levels of stress (as indicated by performance levels significantly above as well as significantly below industry norms) are more likely to make major changes in strategy than are low-stress firms. Our findings also support the cumulative inertia hypothesis outlined in chapter 4. When taken together, organization stress and organization inertia clearly can be used to differentiate between perspective movers and stayers within the pharmaceutical industry, as shown in Table 8.3.

Strategic Change and Performance Improvement

In our preoccupation with understanding the strategic change process, it is important to remember that firms decide to make major changes in strategy because they anticipate that these changes will result in improved performance.

Hypothesis 3. *Firms making second order changes in strategy have a greater chance of either improving their performance or retaining their high performance position than do firms that do not make second order changes in strategy.*

To analyze performance levels before and after a major change in strategy, as compared with changes in performance levels for firms making no major change in strategy, annual return on sales measures were used. The performance categories were: high, the top quartile in sales growth; medium, the two middle quartiles; and low, the bottom quartile. A change in strategy was assumed to be successful if high performers remained high, medium performers became high performers, or low performers became medium or high performers. The results of the analysis are shown in Table 8.4.

Of the firms making a change in strategy, 53% were successful in relative performance terms. Of the firms retaining the current strategy, only 20% maintained a high performance level or improved their performance from one period to the next.

A more detailed analysis of performance changes following a significant change in strategy suggests that high performance firms have the most to gain from major changes in strategy. For high performers, there is a 67% chance of remaining in the high-performance category after a major change in strategy, whereas high performers that do not make significant changes in strategy have only an 18% chance of retaining their

Table 8.4 Changes in Performance for Movers and Stayers

Before\After		High	Medium	Low
Movers				
N = 18	High	12	3	3
N = 11	Medium	4	6	1
N = 20	Low	3	7	10
Stayers				
N = 11	High	2	8	1
N = 58	Medium	12	35	11
N = 13	Low	2	5	6

high performance status, suggesting that high performers can't follow a "stayer" strategy for very long and hope to maintain their high performance position within the industry. Even though the large majority of middle-performance firms are "stayers" and vice versa, a comparison of performance changes for movers and stayers for this group suggests that movers have a greater chance of improving their competitive position than do stayers because middle-performance movers become high-performance firms 36% of the time, whereas middle-performance stayers achieve high-performance status 12% of the time. Low-performance firms have about the same chance of improving their performance position irrespective of their decision to "move" or "stay."

Movers and Stayers: The Dynamics of Strategic Change

This section focuses attention on the changes occurring over time in organization stress and inertia and the associated changes in the firm's propensity to make second order changes in strategy. Theoretical arguments in chapter 4 point to a behavioral distinction between firms with a marked tendency to retain the same strategy while making incremental adjustments over time (the "stayers") and firms making a series of major changes in strategy over time (the "movers").

An important hypothesis suggested by the mover-stayer model in chapter 4 is:

Hypothesis 4. Firms achieving a high inertia, low stress "stayer" state will tend to remain in that state, and firms experiencing high stress and low inertia will tend to remain in a high stress, low inertia "mover" condition over time.

By implication, firms tend to move along certain predictable and distinctive orbits, suggesting a topology of "movers" and "stayers"; that is, once firms begin making strategic changes, they tend to continue to do so, and once they have been at rest, they are more likely to continue following the same strategy.

A four-state Markov chain will be employed to explore these strategic orbits, the four states being the four stress-inertia categories used in the previous analysis. In this instance, however, the focus will be on the time paths (through these four states) followed by individual firms over the 20-year period 1970–1990. Two relatively distinct patterns emerge. Firms either tend to orbit around the high stress, low inertia state (movers) or to orbit around the low stress, high inertia state (stayers), with the low stress, low inertia state and the high stress, high inertia state representing transient or unstable strategic conditions.

The existence of these two strategic orbits is best illustrated by a transition matrix, T, summarizing the conditional probabilities of shifting from state i to state j during a given time interval. Table 8.5 presents the transition matrix summarizing the experiences of the pharmaceutical firms in our sample.

This table shows a total of 34 instances (in one of five time periods) in which firms originate in a high stress, high inertia state. Given that a firm begins a 4-year period in a high stress, high inertia state, there is a .382 probability that the firm will end the 4-year period in a high stress, low inertia state and a .235 probability that the firm will end the period in a low stress, high inertia state.

From the matrix T of transition probabilities shown in Table 8.5, it is evident that firms tend to follow a rather limited set of evolutionary paths. The critical distinction is between movers and stayers. A firm with high stress and low inertia not only is very likely to change strategy (move) but also is likely to remain in that same high mobility state in the next time period ($t11 = .643$), whereas firms in the low stress, high inertia state are likely to retain the current strategy and to remain in that low stress, high inertia state from one time period to the next ($t44 = .649$). The low stress, low inertia state is clearly unstable ($t22 = .077$), with a marked tendency to shift into a high stress state. The high stress, high inertia state isn't stable either. Only 20% of the firms remain in that state from one time period to the next; ultimately, they spin off along a stayer orbit ($t34 = .235$), or they change strategy ($t31 + t32 = .558$) and enter the mover orbit.

The structure of the transition matrix thus suggests a pattern of strategic change in which a limited set of firms do most of the changing while the majority of the firms in the industry retain the same strategy for relatively long periods of time. Some volatile firms exist. They can and apparently do reduce stress through changes in strategy, thereby moving the firm toward a more stable strategic position; once stabilized, the firm tends to remain so. By contrast, rising stress levels may precipitate a change in a

Table 8.5 Transition Probabilities between Stress and Inertia States

From\To	HS/LI	LS/LI	HS/HI	LS/HI
HS/LI N = 28	.643	.143	.107	.107
LS/LI N = 13	.231	.077	.462	.231
HS/HI N = 34	.382	.176	.205	.235
LS/HI N = 57	.035	.088	.228	.649

The transition probabilities are estimated from the 132 observed transitions between the four stress-inertia states made by the sample of firms over 5 time periods (each period is 4 years in duration).

long-established strategy, which, in reducing inertia, may stimulate further change thereby transforming a stayer into a mover.

SIOP: A TWO-STAGE MODEL OF STRATEGIC CHANGE

The empirical analysis of strategic change across firms in the pharmaceutical industry concludes with a two-stage model of the timing and direction of second order change that provides insight into how a firm's strategic decisions are influenced by and subsequently influence the decisions of other firms in the industry. Strategic change at the firm level is assumed to be in response to two generalizable influences: organization stress arising from limitations inherent in the current strategy, inertia embodied in resource and institutional commitment to the current strategy, as mediated by strategic opportunity, defined in terms of the attractiveness/risk of alternatives demonstrated by other firms, and the firm's competitive position with respect to other firms in the industry.

The SIOP model (Stress, Inertia, Opportunity, Position) is designed to predict the timing of significant changes in strategy at the level of the firm, as well as the direction of change along strategic dimensions that are particularly salient to success in the industry. The model will be evaluated against the observed patterns of strategic change for a sample of 23 pharmaceutical firms over the period 1970–1990. Strategic change is defined in terms of changing resource allocation decisions, as reflected in observed changes in R&D effort and advertising effort, and changing scope decisions, as reflected in observed changes in product diversification across a firm's product portfolio.

The model first predicts the set of firms making second order changes in strategy along each strategic dimension for each of five time intervals, 1970–1974, 1974–1978, 1978–1982, 1982–1986, and 1986–1990. The second stage of the model predicts the content of the strategic changes (both first and second order changes) that the sample of pharmaceutical firms experienced over each of the time intervals in the sample.

Conceptually, the SIOP model of strategic change is quite simple and follows directly from earlier conceptualizations of the strategic change process. The decision to make a significant second order change in strategy is assumed to be driven by the interaction of organization stress and inertia. Firms experiencing high stress are assumed to be more likely to make second order changes in strategy; firms exhibiting high inertia are more likely to resist second order changes in strategy. A logistic regression model is used to evaluate the overall power of the model as a means of predicting which firms will make second order changes in strategy during a given time interval and along which strategic dimension the second order change will occur. The model is also used to evaluate the importance of industry-wide fluctuations in the propensity to make second order changes in strategy associated with shifts in the industry's competitive environment relative to the importance of variations in stress and inertia across the pharmaceutical firms in the sample.

The second stage of the model is conditional on the outcome of the first stage and is concerned with the problem of predicting both the magnitude and the direction of strategic change along each of three strategic dimensions for each of five time intervals for the pharmaceutical firms in the sample. The expectation is that the magnitude and direction of the change in strategy depend upon the firm's strategic position, reflecting its capabilities and resources relative to the distribution of attractive strategic opportunities. In particular, it is assumed that a firm will tend to move toward a strategic position that has a high performance potential and away from a strategic position with a low performance potential. It is also recognized that the entire industry may be drifting in a particular direction along a given strategic dimension; the importance of industry-wide fluctuations in strategic change from one time period to the next will be evaluated.

Stage 1: A Stress-Inertia Model of Strategic Change

The preceding discussion, coupled with the earlier analysis of stress and inertia as key forces in the strategic change process, set the stage for a predictive model of the timing and direction of second order change that provides insight into how a firm's strategic decisions are influenced by and subsequently influence the decisions of other firms in the industry. Second-order change as a function of stress and inertia may be formalized in the following hypothesis:

Hypothesis 5. *The decision to make a second order change in strategy is a function of the level of organization stress associated with the present strategy, $S_i(t)$, and the firm's strategic inertia, $I_i(t)$, such that the probability that firm i makes a second order change in strategy along dimension k, during time period t, $Y(i,k,t)$, is*

$$Y(i,k,t) = f_k(U) = f_k(S_{ik}(t), I_{ik}(t))$$

$$f_k(U) = \frac{e^{-\lambda_k U}}{1 + e^{-\lambda_k U}}$$

where U = column vector of independent variables measuring stress and inertia and λ_k = row vector of associated coefficients. The functional form of the model is the familiar logistic which lends itself to logit regression techniques.

The stress-inertia model just outlined is a general model of strategic change. To apply the model to the strategic behavior of firms within the pharmaceutical industry, the operational definition of second order change and the stress and inertia measures selected must be appropriate to the industry.

As in the previous empirical analysis, a firm's strategic position at time t is defined in terms of two strategic dimensions critical to firms in the pharmaceutical industry: research and development effort and advertising effort as measured by annual research and development expenditures as a percentage of sales (R&D) and annual advertising expenditures as a percentage of sales (advertising). To these two resource based dimensions, we add a scope dimension, Gini, designed to capture distinctions between firms with highly diversified portfolios (Gini values near 0) and firms with narrowly defined product lines concentrated in a small number of therapeutic classes (Gini values near 1). The measure of portfolio concentration is a simple index of concentration (Isard, 1960), requiring information on the number of products produced by the firm in each therapeutic class at six points in time: 1970, 1974, 1978, 1982, 1986, 1990. The product count data are compiled from the *Physician's Desk Reference* (PDR), containing a list of pharmaceutical products and producers grouped into 191 therapeutic classes. The 191 therapeutic classes have been grouped into 17 therapeutic classes used in the *Registered Nurses' Manual*. The resulting portfolio concentration measure ranges from 0 for a firm with a product portfolio identical in composition to the industry as a whole to near 1 for a firm with all of its products concentrated in a single therapeutic class.

The strategic positions of the 21 firms for which data are available are observed at 4-year intervals over the 20-year period 1970–1990, resulting in a total of 104 observed changes in strategic position along each of the three strategic dimensions over the period. To identify firms experiencing second order changes in strategy along key strategic dimensions, it is necessary to specify minimum threshold values such that any strategic change (on a given dimension) whose magnitude exceeds a pre-set threshold is classed as a second order change. In the present analysis, the thresholds are defined as 15% of the average range for each of the three strategic dimensions. These threshold values also are approximately 1.5 standard deviations beyond the mean change in strategic position along each strategic dimension.

There were a total of 46 second order changes for the sample over the four time intervals in the study: 16 second order changes on the R&D dimension, 12 second order changes on the advertising dimension, and 18 second order changes on the portfolio concentration dimension. In the analysis that follows, each of the dependent variables takes on a value of 1 if a second order change occurs during time interval t and is 0 otherwise. The dependent variables are **R&D Change(t),** which monitors second order change in R&D activity for each of the firms in the sample; **Advertising Change(t),** which monitors second order change in advertising activity; **Gini Change(t),** which monitors second order change in portfolio concentration; and **Combined Change(t),** monitoring the decision to make a second order change in any one of the three strategic dimensions.

Operational Definitions of Stress and Inertia

In the present model, it is assumed that stress is associated with very high performance conditions as well as very low performance conditions. Consequently, for two performance measures, the firm's annual return on sales **(ROS)** in the base year and the firm's annual sales growth **(SalesGrowth)** in the base year, we introduce a second set of performance variables, **ROS^2** and **SalesGrowth^2,** defined as the squared deviation in a firm's ROS and SalesGrowth, relative to the mean ROS and SalesGrowth for the sample as a whole. Strong performance in either area is expected to be associated with strategic change.

Firms positioned on the competitive frontier of the industry (prospectors in Miles and Snow's 1978 terminology) are expected to make second order changes in strategy. In this analysis, we focus especially on firms that are stretching the envelope in a way that entails considerable commitment of resources **(R&D** and/or **advertising)** within a narrowly focused product line **(Gini).** These firms are operating in atypical ways that are assumed to be high risk and stressful as a consequence.

The primary measure of inertia is a dummy variable, **Change($t-1$),** which takes on a value of 1 if the firm made a second order change in strategy (on the dimension in question) during the prior 4-year time period; otherwise, the variable = 0.

A second measure of inertia is future oriented and related to the potential of the firm's current product portfolio. The measure used is **Portfolio Potential,** the relative concentration of the firm's products in high growth therapeutic classes such that

$$\text{Portfolio Potential } (i,t) = \sum [N(i, j, t)/N(i, ., t)][\Delta N(., j, t)/N(., ., t)].$$

$N(i, j, t)$, $N(i, ., t)$, and $N(., ., t)$ are the number of drugs in therapeutic class j produced by firm i, the total number of drugs in all therapeutic classes produced by firm i, and the total number of drugs produced in all therapeutic classes by all firms in the sample at the beginning of time period t. The term $\Delta N(., j, t)$ is the observed change in the number of drugs produced in therapeutic class j from the beginning to the end of time period t across the entire set of firms in the sample.

Stage I Results: Predictions of Second Order Change in Strategy

The results from Stage I are reported in Table 8.6. Note that the coefficients are reported with their associated standard errors. These findings are very encouraging in that the four submodels perform well as predictors of second order change and the hypothesized relationships between the independent variables and the dependent variables are as expected. The log likelihood ratio tests, as well as the pseudo R-squares, indicate that the models are significant improvements over the null case. Even though the pseudo R-square values may appear to be rather low, they are actually quite respectable when compared against other efforts to predict the timing of significant changes in strategy (Olivia, Day & MacMillan, 1988).

Table 8.6 contains a number of interesting results that confirm many theoretical conjectures that heretofore have been based on very limited empirical evidence. In particular, the logic of our original stress-inertia model of second order strategic change is strongly supported by the results. Firms experiencing high stress tend to move, and the greatest change is along the strategic dimension where stress is greatest. Firms experiencing high inertia tend to retain the present strategy, making incremental adjustments rather than second order changes in strategy. Movers in the previous time period are more likely to make a second order change in strategy in the current time period, and this mover-stayer distinction is particularly marked on the advertising dimension and in the case of the combined model. The model's capacity to distinguish between movers and stayers on each of the three dimensions is particularly important because the subsequent analysis is predicated on our ability to accurately predict the set of firms making second order changes during each time period.

The relative attractiveness of the current strategy is also clearly in evidence in the consistently negative effects of portfolio potential on the firm's decision to make second order changes in the current strategy. Firms with portfolios that are well positioned with respect to changing market conditions exhibit a strong tendency to maintain their current strategy. The relationship is particularly important when predicting second order changes in advertising.

The stress-related variables all perform as expected. Firms with high resource commitments on a particular dimension and firms with narrowly focused product lines are

Table 8.6 A LOGIT Model of Second Order Change in Strategy for Pharmaceutical Firms, 1970–1990

Independent Variables	Dependent Variables			
	R&D Change	Advertising Change	Gini Change	Combined Change
Change($t-1$)	1.24	**4.74**	−1.91	**1.75**
	(.79)	(1.43)	(1.54)	(.59)
R&D	**28.83**	—	—	10.43
	(12.88)			(9.69)
Advertising	—	**12.47**	—	1.76
		(7.35)		(4.42)
Gini	—	—	**7.19**	2.53
			(2.15)	(1.72)
ROS	8.58	16.53	−.16	.34
	(7.76)	(14.68)	(7.12)	(5.92)
ROS^2	**96.83**	−537.04	67.47	79.29
	(50.32)	(448.49)	(55.62)	(63.65)
SalesGrow	−4.80	−13.07	.40	−4.0
	(4.84)	(9.43)	(3.99)	(3.79)
SalesGrow^2	**18.59**	−1.57	26.02	21.36
	(8.85)	(22.38)	(17.02)	(16.76)
Portfolio	−.13	**−7.83**	−2.90	−2.26
Position	(2.74)	(3.62)	(2.04)	(1.93)
Constant	**−4.59**	**−3.46**	**− 4.90**	**−3.10**
	(1.06)	(1.01)	(1.12)	(1.10)

Note: estimates in bold are significant at .05 level; standard errors are reported in parentheses.

LRT	22.26/7 df	33.68/7 df	21.99/7 df	27.79/9 df
Chow R-sq	.24	.48	.25	.26
% Correct	88%	93%	86%	76%

found to be strong candidates for second order change on that dimension. The relationship between performance and the decision to make a second order change is particularly important in considering second order changes in R&D activity, and the relationship is decidedly nonlinear. As hypothesized but not widely discussed in the literature on strategic change, both positive and negative extremes in performance tend to precipitate second order changes in overall strategy and are specifically related to changes in R&D.

Stage 2: An Opportunity and Positioning Model

The second stage of the strategic change model is designed to predict the magnitude and direction of strategic change along a particular strategic dimension for a specific firm, based on the outcome of the first stage of the decisioning process, as described in Stage 1, coupled with information on the firm's competitive position relative to the attraction of alternative strategic positions. Given that we can predict the timing of second order changes in strategy and hence the set of firms making such changes during a particular time period, we are then in a position to predict the direction (positive or negative changes along key strategic dimensions) of these changes. Whereas stress and inertia figure prominently in the decision to make a second order change in strategy, opportunity and positioning are the key factors affecting the direction of second order change.

Hypothesis 6. *Given that a firm makes a second order change in strategy, the direction of that change depends upon the distribution of attractive strategic opportunities, $O_i(t)$, relative to the firm's strategic position, $P_i(t)$, such that the conditional probability, $Z(i, k, t)$, that the firm makes a **positive change** in strategic position on dimension k during time t is*

$$Z(i,\ k,\ t) = g_k(V) = g_k(O_i(t),\ P_i(t))$$

$$g_k(V) = \frac{e^{-\lambda V}}{1 + e^{-\lambda V}}$$

where V = column vector of independent variables measuring opportunity and strategic position and λ = row vector of associated coefficients.

Given that a firm makes a second order change in strategy along one of the three strategic dimensions identified in Stage 1 of the model, the relevant indicator variable— **Positive R&D Change(*t*)**, **Positive Advertising Change(*t*)**, or **Positive Gini Change(*t*)**—is assigned a value of 1 if there is a positive change along the dimension in question or 0 if the second order change involves a significant contraction along the dimension (i.e., a negative change).

In Stage 2 of the strategic change model, we assume that a firm will move toward strategic positions that have a high performance potential and away from strategic positions with a low performance potential, which suggests that the slope of the performance potential surface evaluated at the location of the firm's current strategy in strategic space should be a reasonably good measure of the direction and the intensity of the aggregate attractiveness of strategic opportunities.

The direction of strategic change should be in the direction of increasing performance potential, as indicated by the partial derivatives of the ROS or the sales growth opportunity surfaces with respect to R&D, advertising, and scope. In the present analysis, decisions pertaining to R&D are assumed to be particularly sensitive to differences in performance potential, as measured in terms of a return on sales performance surface and the associated partial derivative, **dROS/dRAD.** For advertising and scope decisions, the sales growth performance surface and the associated partial derivatives are assumed to be the best indicators of performance potential, **dGrowth/dADS,** and **dGrowth/dGini.**[2]

Three positioning or capability measures highlight different aspects of the firm's capacity to respond to attractive opportunities:

- *Strategic Position.* The firm's prior position on each of the three strategic dimensions, **R&D(*t* − 1)**, **Advertising(*t* − 1)**, and **Gini(*t* − 1)**, is assumed to have a significant effect upon the direction of strategic change.

- *Market Positioning.* Firms that are well positioned with respect to changing market conditions are expected to enhance their already strong position in expanding therapeutic classes through increasing expenditure on R&D in those therapeutic classes thereby increasing portfolio concentration. We use the growth potential of a firm's portfolio, **Portfolio Potential** (as described in the previous section of the chapter), to measure the effects of market positioning on the firm's strategic repositioning decision.
- *Capital Limitations.* The expectation is that in the absence of capital resources, as measured by the **Debt/Equity** ratio, firms will be more likely to curtail expenditures on R&D while increasing expenditures on advertising.

The final independent variable recognizes the influence of the firm's

- *Portfolio Growth Rate* on changes in portfolio concentration. The rate of growth in the size of the firm's portfolio is measured by the change in the number of pharmaceutical products over the time period, divided by the number of products at the beginning of the period, **dRtot/Rtot**. Rapid growth in a firm's portfolio is assumed to create the conditions for the diversification of a firm's portfolio. The portfolio growth rate does not enter as an independent variable in either the R+D Change model or the Advertising Change model.

Stage 2 Results: Predicting the Direction of Second Order Change

The results of the analysis for Stage II are summarized in Table 8.7. The model's ability to predict the direction of a second order change in strategy is quite good, as can be seen from the summary statistics at the bottom the table. The model correctly predicts the direction of 41 of the 46 second order changes in the analysis and does especially well for second order changes in advertising expenditures and second order changes in portfolio concentration.

The strategic positioning of the firm is found to be a significant factor in the direction of change for firms making second order changes in advertising expenditures and in portfolio concentration. As shown in the previous analysis of second order change, firms with portfolios that are well positioned to take advantage of changing market conditions tend to avoid second order changes in strategy; within the set of firms that do change strategy, those with relatively well positioned portfolios tend to divert resources from advertising while increasing portfolio concentration in high-growth therapeutic classes.

As expected, firms are responsive to the underlying distribution of opportunities relative to their current strategic position, as reflected in the positive coefficients associated with the partial differentials of ROS with respect to R&D and of sales growth with respect to advertising and to the concentration of the firm's product portfolio (dROS/dRAD, dGROW/dAD, dGROW/dGini).

The firm's capacity to make desired changes in strategy is found to play important but qualitatively different roles in the three models. As expected, a low debt/equity ratio encourages investment in R&D and increasing portfolio specialization; however, a high debt/equity ratio is associated with increasing expenditures on advertising. As expected,

Table 8.7 Predicting the Direction of Second Order Change in
Strategy for Pharmaceutical Firms, 1970–1990

Independent Variables	Dependent Variables		
	Positive R&D Change	Positive Advertising Change	Positive Gini Change
R&D	−29.00		
	(33.42)		
Advertising		−**47.81**	
		(22.23)	
Gini			−11.07
			(15.14)
dROS/dRAD	1.42		
	(1.00)		
dGrow/dAD		2.14	
		(1.56)	
dGrow/dGini			**93.60**
			(50.90)
Debt/equity	−1.95	**18.17**	50.32
	(1.56)	(8.34)	(30.90)
Portfolio position	5.52	**11.76**	19.85
	(6.92)	(5.96)	(15.44)
dRtot/Rtot			−**16.76**
			(7.09)
Constant	2.90	**4.05**	−5.71
	(2.78)	(2.68)	(6.43)

Note: estimates in **bold** are significant at .05 level; standard errors in parentheses.

LRT	11.66/4 df	11.86/4 df	20.86/5 df
Chow R-sq	.50	.90	.96
% Correct	83%	100%	100%

percentage change in size of the firm's portfolio is positively associated with increasing diversification of the portfolio.

Predicting the Magnitude and Direction of Strategic Change in the Pharmaceuticals Industry

The SIOP model of second order change sets the stage for a more general regression model of strategic change in which we predict the magnitude and direction of change along each strategic dimension for every firm in the sample for each of five time periods. This model includes a subset of the stress, inertia, opportunity, and positioning variables introduced in the two preceding models—variables that are expected to influence the magnitude and direction of strategic change independent of the firm's decision to make a second order change in strategy; however, the direct effects of these variables are

Table 8.8 Predicting Strategic Change for Firms in the Pharmaceutical Industry, 1970–1990

Independent Variables	Dependent Variables		
	R&D Change	Advertising Change	Gini Change
R&D	−.026	−.018	.083
Advertising	−.022	**−.071** (−2.36)	−.022
Gini	−.005	.014	−.046
ROS	.036	.024	−.022
Sales Growth	**−.024** (−1.78)	−.022	**−.110** (−1.90)
dROS/dRAD	.0004		
dGrow/dAD		**.0002** (2.02)	
dGrow/dGini			.002
Plus Move	**.031** (9.26)	**.052** (9.85)	**.182** (8.42)
Neg Move	**−.037** (−5.57)	**−.052** (−9.07)	**−.136** (−7.13)
Constant	**.011** (2.14)	−.001	.027
R^2 =	**.65**	**.73**	**.66**

Note: estimates in **bold** are significant at .05 level; t statistics in parentheses.

expected to be small, relative to the indirect effects that such variables exert through their influence on the firm's decisions relating to second order changes in strategy. These indirect effects were modeled separately in the SIOP model, and the combined indirect effects are captured in the explanatory power of the indicator variables identifying the firm's decision to make a positive or a negative second order change along a given dimension during time period t, **Plus Move**(t), **Neg Move**(t).

Table 8.8 summarizes the results from the three regression models. As expected, the indicator variables are critical to the analysis; when the indicator variables associated with second order change are included in the model, the model's predictive power is quite high, with more than 60% of the variance explained in all three cases.

CONCLUSION

The central question driving this investigation is deceptively simple: why do firms within the same industry and operating within the same competitive environment adopt qualitatively different strategic responses to changing environmental conditions? This general question encompasses a series of more specific questions of concern to theorists and practitioners alike. Why do some firms within an industry retain the same basic strategy over long periods of time, whereas other firms in the same competitive environment make numerous changes in strategy? Is it possible to predict which firms are likely to make major changes in strategy, given prevailing environmental conditions? How do the past experiences of the firm affect present and future strategic decisions?

Longitudinal data on key strategic variables for firms in the pharmaceutical industry show that firms experiencing significantly higher or significantly lower performance than the industry average changed strategies more frequently than their compatriots. Firms that followed the same strategy for a period of time were much less likely to change strategy in the future. The results reiterate the importance of inertia in understanding industry evolution. While the pharmaceutical industry in the period studied is not perhaps one in which Shumpeterian gales of change would be expected, it is nonetheless startling how long firms stay in the same strategic position.

The empirical analysis of the mover-stayer distinction highlighted in chapter 4 is summarized in a Markov model of the transitions between high and low stress and inertia states for individual pharmaceutical firms over the 20-year period 1970–1990. The analysis provides a strong empirical basis for making a distinction between movers and stayers within the set of pharmaceutical firms in our study. Two thirds of the cases fall into either the high stress, low inertia (mover) category or the low stress, high inertia (stayer) category. Once in this mover or stayer state, firms have a high probability of remaining in that state. Of particular interest, our research shows that firms that change strategy in the pharmaceutical industry tend to show subsequent performance improvements as the result of changing strategy. The results from the empirical analysis of the evolving stress and inertia conditions and the resulting histories of strategic change closely parallel the predicted changes arising out of the theoretic model of strategic change dynamics.

Much of the work in the field of strategic management has been static in nature, seeking to provide snapshots of strategic postures through the weaponry of multivariate analysis. In contrast, the conceptual power of the models outlined in this chapter stem from the observation that the probability of changing strategic position may differ significantly from one firm to the next, depending upon differences in organizational stress, differences in inertia surrounding each firm's current strategy, and differences in the relative attractiveness of strategic alternatives accessible to each firm. At the same time, the strategic positions of all other firms in the industry and the associated performance of those firms (which we capture as an industry "performance surface") contribute to the change anticipated for each firm.

The findings from the SIOP models support the general logic proposed in the introductory discussion of this chapter and draw together several current themes in the strategy literature. The results reported reiterate the importance of inertia in understanding industry evolution. At the same time, the study supports the logic that focuses on stress as the countervailing influence that leads to strategic change. It also introduces the idea that stress comes from positive as well as negative sources. More specifically, the data show that firms are as likely to change strategic position when overperforming industry averages as when underperforming. In other words, there appears to be an upward spiral of industry activity that mirrors in an interesting way the "downward spiral" reported by and Hambrick D'Aveni (1988). Firms that do well don't stand still. Moreover, they make moves along strategic dimensions where they already have significant resource commitments, both increasing and decreasing their activity in these areas.

The SIOP model includes the classic idea that strategy is essentially a response to opportunity in the environment, but it operationalizes this idea in terms of observable industry indicators, an idea that has received little attention until recently but one that is becoming more salient given recent attention to mimetic behavior as the basis for institutionalization. The idea that observable industry indicators signal new opportunities is an important one that moves us away from a Horatio Alger view of firm strategists who independently invent strategy. This chapter demonstrates fundamental behavioral links between the firm and its industry; it suggests that "borrowed experience" (Huff, 1982) rather that direct experimentation is the major fuel of industry evolution.

Finally, this chapter's discussion of positioning has many links to the resource-based theory of the firm, but our analysis does suggest an area where further resource-based explanation is needed. It is important to recognize that the models we develop are designed to explain *both* the strategic behavior of an individual firm and the changing configuration of firms within the industry. The model allows us to predict not only which firms will move when but also where they will move. It therefore is possible to trace the impacts of firm-level decisions on more macro-level systems because the impact of any given relocation can be linked to subsequent relocation decisions by other firms in the industry. More broadly, the models and the mapping methods outlined in this chapter graphically illustrate a changing picture of industry evolution and competitive opportunity as firms by their actions demonstrate the viability or lack of viability of new strategic positions. This work thus helps construct a dynamic view of strategic interaction—a perspective often desired but rarely available in the strategic management literature.

APPENDIX 1: FIRMS IN SAMPLE

ABB Abbott	JJ Johnson & Johnson	SCH Schering
ACY American Cyanamid	ML Marion Labs	SRL Searle
AH American Home Products	MRK Merck	S-K SmithKline
B-D Becton-Dickenson	NOV Novo Nordisk	SQ Squibb
B-M Bristol-Myers	PF Pfizer	STL Sterling
C-W Carter-Wallace	RHO Rhone	SYN Syntex
E-L Eli Lilly	ROB Robins	UP Upjohn
GLX Glaxo	ROR Rorer	W-L Warner-Lambert

APPENDIX 2. ESTIMATING THE OPPORTUNITY SURFACE

The estimation of the opportunity surface involves OLS regression of a performance measure ($ROS(t)$, $SALGRO(t)$) at a given time t against a set of independent variables that are power functions of: $RADS(t)$, the firm's R&D expenditures as a percentage of sales; $ADS(t)$, the firm's advertising expenditures as a percentage of sales; and $GINI(t)$, the scope of the firm's product portfolio. In the present analysis, we fit a second order polynomial surface to the data for four overlapping time periods, 1970–1974, 1974–1978, 1978–1982, and 1982–1986, with an average of 42 observations per time period such that:

$$Y_i = AX_i$$

where A is a row vector of coefficients and X is a column vector containing the following variables:

x1—RADS(t)	x4—RADS(t)**2	x7—RADS(t)*ADS(t)
x2—ADS(t)	x5—ADS(t)**2	x8—RADS(t)*GINI(t)
x3—GINI(t)	x6—GINI(t)**2	x9—ADS(t)*GINI(t).

Because the variables are highly correlated, a standard table of the regression coefficients and the associated standard errors would be very misleading. Recall, however, that our objective is simply to describe a performance surface that fits the data reasonably well. The following table summarizes the degree to which the second order performance surface fits the data for each time period and for both performance measures.

Percentage of the Variance Explained by the Regression Model

Dependent Variable	Time Period			
	1970–1974	1974–1978	1978–1982	1982–1986
ROS	.58	.56	.46	.24
SALGRO	.32	.41	.16	.57

Once the coefficients of the opportunity surface are estimated, it is a simple matter to calculate the partial derivatives of the surface with respect to each of the three strategic dimensions and then to evaluate the partial derivatives at each firm's strategic position. We used the SHAZAM "derive" routine to perform the actual calculations.

Notes

1. The 24 pharmaceutical firms included in the sample are given in appendix 1. Because of the limitations of the COMPUSTAT database and merger and acquisition decisions, strategic change data were not available for all 24 firms over the entire time interval, 1966-1990; however, all firms in the sample reported strategic change information for at least three 4–year strategic time periods.

2. Performance measures based on the sales growth performance surface are highly correlated with performance measures based on the ROS performance surface for firms making second order changes in strategy; consequently, only one set of performance measures is used in the analysis.

9

The Structuration of Industries

with Larry Stimpert

In this concluding chapter,[1] we draw upon structuration theory, as outlined by the sociologist Anthony Giddens (1979, 1984), as a theoretic framework for extensions to the cognitively anchored theory of strategic change developed in Part I of this book. We are particularly interested in extending our theoretic arguments in ways that recognize the interdependencies between the actions of firms as knowledgeable actors and the structural conditions prevailing within an industry that influence and are influenced by the actions of firms both inside and outside the industry. Structuration theory is particularly well suited to structure-agency dualities of this sort and has received increasing attention in the management literature (Pettigrew, 1987; Ransom, Hinings & Greenwood, 1980; Orlikowski, 1992; Whittington, 1992; Gibbons, Prescott & Ganesh, 1993) because it provides a means of going beyond the economic-behavioral debate that has recently preoccupied the strategy field. As an example, in this chapter we use structuration theory to explore the creative tension between incumbent firms and new entrants whose actions serve to transform the structure of the industry. The example illustrates the need to draw economic, behavioral, and cognitive theories together.

STRUCTURATION THEORY

Structuration theory asserts that individuals are active agents with the capacity to transform their setting through action (Giddens, 1984). The theory equally recognizes the strong influence of external structures on behavior, though the definition of structure differs from that used by most economists, as elaborated later in this chapter. Even more important from our point of view, structuration theory provides a means of integrating an interpretive, cognitive perspective on strategic change with structural approaches.

The discussion begins with a review of basic tenets of structuration theory, which are expressed diagrammatically in Figure 9.1.

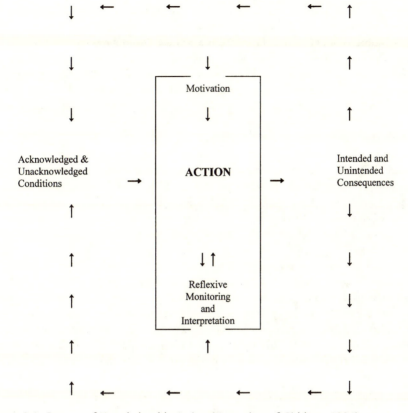

Figure 9.1 Context of Knowledgeable Action (Expansion of Giddens, 1984)

Agency

The bracketed, central part of the figure focuses on *agency*, which Giddens defines as a "a stream of actual or contemplated causal interventions" (1979, 55) in a "potentially malleable object-world" by actors who "could have acted otherwise" (1979, 56). Giddens insists that "every competent actor has a wide ranging, yet intimate and subtle, knowledge of the society of which he or she is a member" (1979, 73). This knowledge is practical and goes beyond what is consciously accessible to incorporate what Polanyi (1966) calls "tacit knowledge." Although bounded, because it relates to a specific time and place, Giddens notes that the individual's capacity to perform "in the diversity of contexts of social life is detailed and dazzling" (1984, 26).

Giddens' diagrams of the relationship between activity and the broader setting (1979: 56; 1984:5) include only unacknowledged conditions and unintended consequences. But his writing on the knowledgeability of actors and his observation that "all social reproduction occurs in the context of 'mixes' of intended and unintended consequences of action" (1979:112), leads us to add to Figure 9.1 the idea that agency also responds to *acknowledged* conditions and often generates *intended* consequences.

In addition, complex, often conscious, motives are an important part of agency as Giddens defines it. He regards the actors described by traditional sociologists such as Talcott Parsons as "cultural dopes of . . . stunning mediocrity" (1979, 52). Presumably, he would apply similar language to principals and agents described by agency theory (Eisenhandt, 1989), and to the decision makers described in many other management theories.

Knowledge, motive, and even values change over time because agency is "grounded in the conscious monitoring of action which human beings display and expect others to display" (1984, 3). This monitoring includes "*the setting of interaction*, and not just the behavior of . . . particular actors taken separately" (1979, 57). The individual's capacity to change is thus broad but linked to experience. Giddens writes that "all social practices are *situated* activities in [three] senses" (1979, 54): they occur at a specific time and in a specific space and involve a specific "instantiation" of social structure, a concept that we define next.

By insisting upon the situated nature of individual knowledge, Giddens emphasizes that action is *not* synonymous with unconstrained choice. All actors are affected by larger, imperfectly known conditions, as shown in Figure 9.1. Giddens writes, "The flow of action continually produces consequences that are unintended by actors, and these unintended consequences also may form unacknowledged conditions of action in a feedback fashion" (1984, 27). Even when causal links are well understood, then, action tends to exceed the boundaries of the actor's knowledge, in both its antecedents and its consequences.

Structure

Giddens does not equate structure with a hidden skeleton or relational pattern (1984, 16) of the sort popularized in Porter's (1980) five forces of industry structure. Instead, relationship is a feature of *social systems*, which are "relations between actors or collectives" (such as firms and their various stakeholders) are "organized as regular social practices" (1984, 25). Social systems are patterned but transitory. They "only exist in and through structuration, as the outcome of the contingent acts of a multiplicity of human beings" (1982, 35).

Structure itself is more general. Giddens (1984, 23) defines it as (1) the availability of resources and (2) the "rules" governing access to resources that are embedded within a particular social system, such as an industry. He proposes, along with writers in many other social science fields (e.g., Berger & Luckman, 1967; Wittgenstein, 1972), that "the knowledgeable capacities of agents . . . [structure the] features" of social systems (1984, 28). Therefore, "structure is not to be conceptualized as a barrier to action," (1979, 70) as it tends to be in many theories, including IO economics and most process and content research in the strategy field.

Duality of Structure

Perhaps Giddens's greatest contribution to theory in the social sciences is the inseparable link between structure and agency, a link he labels the *duality of structure*: "agents and structures are not two independently given sets of phenomena . . . but represent a duality. . . . The structural properties of social systems are both medium and outcome of the practices they recursively organize" (Giddens, 1984, 25). Giddens (1984, 29) outlines three important modes of behavior that serve as socially important grounds for the interaction of agency and structure. The first of these is a link between individual, face-to-face 'communication' and broader, institutionally supported 'signification.' This is the interaction between structure and agency that is most germane to a cognitively anchored theory of the firm. But Giddens equally recognizes the importance of "domination." He subdivides this aspect of the duality of structure into "authoritative" control over actions and "allocative" control over resources—roughly equating the first with the interests of political science and the second with the subject matter of economics. Legal studies provide the most obvious source material for the third arena of interaction, "legitimation," which looks at how individual efforts to sanction others have the ultimate effect of regulatory control in the broader society.

Figure 9.2 uses these ideas to coordinate issues and vocabulary discussed throughout this book. Individual cognition, which we have put in an "anchoring position" can be found in the lower left corner of the figure. It influences, and is influenced by, every other cell. The outcome of this interaction is the firm as a dynamic social system. Giddens goes beyond a simple systems theory view of feedback loops by emphasizing "recursive organization" (1979, 75-76) in describing the duality that creates such systems. As a simple example, "When I utter a grammatical English sentence in a casual conversation, I contribute to the reproduction of the English language as a whole. This is an unintended consequence of my speaking the sentence, but one that is bound in directly to the recursiveness of the duality of structure" (1979, 77). By implication, firms and industries are always being modified by human actions, just as human language is constantly modified by use.

In contrast to institution theory (Powell & DiMaggio, 1991), Giddens emphasizes that a range of "ad hoc" considerations influence the duality of structure and the social systems it creates: "There is not a singular relation between 'an activity' and 'a rule,' as is sometimes suggested or implied by appeal to statements like 'the rules governing the Queen's move' in chess. Activities or practices are brought into being in the context of overlapping and connected sets of rules" (Giddens, 1979, 65). The appropriate analogy is to the rules of informal children's play, rather than the rules of formal games like chess (1979, 66-68). Even legally codified rules, Giddens writes, are contested in very diverse ways that exhibit the power of agency (1984, 18). Although affected by structure, every action therefore has its own unique character, and every social system is unique, and uniquely changing.

The subtleties of the duality of structure are well illustrated by Giddens's discussion of power. The resource-based view of the firm has insisted upon the importance of firm-level resources in establishing competitive advantage. Influenced by this framework, it is natural to think of power as a resource, but Giddens insists that power must be seen

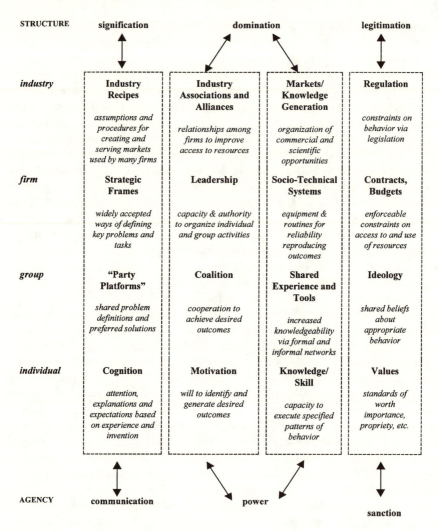

Figure 9.2 The Structuration of Strategic Change

as an aspect of *both* agency and structure. On the one hand, "power ... is centrally involved with human agency; a person or party who wields power *could* "have acted otherwise," and the person or party over whom power is wielded, the concept implies, *would* have acted otherwise if power had not been exercised" (1979, 91). On the other hand, Giddens also notes that "the resources which the existence of domination implies and the exercise of power ... must be seen as structural components of social systems. The exercise of power is not a type of act; rather power is instantiated in action, as a regular and active phenomenon" (1979, 91).

This broad definition of power is well suited to describing industry change and the acts of both incumbent firms and new entrants that often have consequences far beyond their initial intent. Whittington's (1992) review of structuration theory from a management standpoint further emphasizes that *differential* power in organizational settings often reflects differential access to and understanding of social structures. This insight is particularly relevant to the entry of new players in an established industry, an important source of strategic change we have not yet considered.

EXAMPLE: A STRUCTURATION PERSPECTIVE ON ENTRY

Structuration theory provides a useful theoretic basis for examining key interdependencies between strategic change and industry dynamics which goes beyond the insights from previous theoretic and empirical chapters. Through the lens of structuration theory, we will therefore revisit the ideas of industry, competitive position, opportunity, strategic change, stress and industry evolution with an emphasis on communication and signification.

The concept of an "industry" has always been problematic and is becoming more elusive in today's complicated world of interactions. Following Giddens's treatment of social systems as the instantiation of social structure, we argue that an industry is the instantiation of a commonly held set of beliefs and knowledge informing the strategies of firms, as agents, within the industry, as a social system.

Recent work in the cognitive field has shown that "commonly held" beliefs and knowledge are not easily identified (Johson, 1999). Yet, interaction among firms tends to have a homogenizing effect on the language, understanding, and strategies of firms. "Shared thinking" among firms within the same industry is reinforced by reading the same publications, by participating in the same trade associations, and by the movement of individuals from firm to firm as consultants, salespeople, and employees. We have argued in this book that over time, industry "recipes" for identifying and dealing with key strategic issues often develop from this social interaction (Spender, 1989). As suggested in Figure 9.2, these schema shared across firms play an important role in shaping industry standards, in encouraging consumer acceptance, and in facilitating incremental technological developments and improvements (Powell & DiMaggio, 1991). But cognition (at all levels of analysis) is just one piece of a much larger interacting puzzle. Industry associations, markets, and regulatory efforts are important, from a cognitive perspective, because firms within a given industry observe and learn. Their monitoring and copying serves as the primary knowledge base for subsequent strategic change.

In the discussion that follows, the focus is on entrepreneurial activity initiated from outside the industry and the ensuing incumbent response. The competitive position of "insiders" versus "outsiders" is seen as a critical distinction in attempting to understand subsequent strategic responses of the firms. We are particularly interested in framing the recursive transformation of industry structure as newcomers operate in response to new rules and resources. The discussion specifies in greater detail how interactions between structure and agency simultaneously influence, and are influenced by, events such as new entry.

Many observers have noted that radical innovations tend to be driven by new players, which is why we are interested in successful entry, but it is important to note that the insider's focus on known conditions and intended outcomes is a useful knowledge base for incumbents. Returning to our earlier stress-inertia arguments, as various actors (entrepreneurs, customers, scientists, etc.) change their desires and activities over time, the circumstances affecting the present and future viability of firms and their associated strategies necessarily change. Giddens's work helps us recognize that incumbents have the knowledge necessary to generate many desired outcomes, and thus a great deal of entrepreneurial activity should be expected from firms already established within the industry. Although this knowledge is inevitably incomplete, there are good reasons why incumbents tend to focus their attention on duplicating past success (Nelson & Winter, 1982). Past experience provides incumbent firms with the knowledge base for successfully satisfying many new desires and successfully responding to many new conditions and unexpected outcomes. These observations are summarized in the following proposition:

> *Proposition 9.1. As knowledgeable actors within the industry draw on past success to respond to new conditions, they draw primarily on familiar rules and resources. Because firms within the industry use knowledge gained from past experience in the industry, even when they are entrepreneurial, knowledgeable incumbents tend to reconstitute industry structures that are quite similar to previously existing industry structures.*

As widely observed, the result is that the preponderance of innovative activity by incumbents is *competence enhancing* (Tushman & Anderson, 1986) and tends to have rather small effects on current industry structure. *Competence-destroying* innovations with more dramatic structural consequences are much more likely to come from outsiders.

The irony is that the very industry structures that enhance and facilitate the performance of firms within the industry also act to inhibit entrepreneurial activity leading to second order change. The logic of chapter 2 can be moved to the industry level to suggest why incumbents do not rapidly respond. First, several years may pass before reductions in sales or profitability clearly signal the impact of changing conditions on the industry (Cooper & Schendel, 1976). In the meantime, relevant issues "do not present themselves to the decision maker in convenient ways; problems and opportunities in particular must be identified in the streams of ambiguous, largely verbal data" (Mintzberg, Raisinghani, & Théorêt, 1976, 253). Comprehension is further reduced when unfamiliar activity by new entrants increases the ambiguity of available data. The basic paradox of active information gathering under these circumstances is that monitoring may not lead to action; in fact, managers can end up *actively ignoring* a new rival or changed industry conditions (Staw, Sandelands, & Dutton, 1981).

Not all changes are equally easy for industry insiders to monitor and interpret. The attention of incumbent managers (and the attention of their buyers, suppliers, and distributors) is constrained by their past experience. Potential entrants from outside the industry *cannot* be limited in the same way, perhaps because they are not distracted by an ongoing business but primarily because, as outsiders, potential entrants are not embedded within the structure of the industry. The "same" stimuli indicating change (and potential change) in behavior will have—in fact, *must* have—a different significance for newcomers than they do for incumbents.[2]

In fact, new rivals would be foolish to work primarily with the rules and resources most closely associated with incumbent firms' activities when they have the possibility of instantiating alternative structures. The more successful new rivals typically offer novel products or services, use new or different technologies, or provide products or services in a new way. This pattern—of new entrants seeking (and trying to create) unoccupied "edges" and "holes" in the system—can be observed in Apple Computer's recognition and creation of a market for individual computing that had been ignored by virtually all other computer makers. Savin and Canon did the same thing in the copier industry. Philip Morris brought new ideas to the beer industry; Snapple, LaCroix, and other vendors surprised the soft drink industry. From an outsider's perspective,

Proposition 9.2. The motivation for entry increases as outsiders perceive opportunities in actual or contemplated activities that are ignored or perceived as trivial by industry insiders.

The *most* successful new entrants typically utilize unfamiliar "rules and resources" (Whittington, 1992) in more than one arena of activity. Howard Head brought new materials, new production techniques, new distribution channels, and new methods of promotion to the downhill ski industry. Japanese auto manufacturers focused on the unattractive small car segment and exploited the advantages of new production technologies. Wal-Mart stores not only provided customers in underserved locations with a broad product mix but also incorporated information technology and distribution systems that allowed operation with a very low cost structure. In the railroad locomotive industry, the arrival of new diesel electric technology was accompanied by the introduction of mass production techniques, while steam locomotives continued to be manufactured using job shop production techniques (Williamson, 1975). In summary,

Proposition 9.3. New entrants respond to system opportunity in novel ways by drawing on rules and resources that are unfamiliar to most industry participants.

This observation is equally applicable to such high-velocity industry environments as computing and software. Unlike Microsoft's proprietary Windows operating system, Linux and other "open-source" operating systems not only are designed to be compatible with nearly all types of hardware but also are freely distributed to any and all software developers (Seltzer & Graven, 1999). These deliberate strategies are important to understanding industry structuring.

It is also important that the structural effects of these differences are typically amplified over time. To act on their unique knowledge, new entrants are likely to seek (or be forced to seek) relationships with some actors who have not been a part of the industry and to make these ties in new ways. These additional newcomers bring their own novel perspectives because they, too, have not been a part of the systems that currently dominate the industry. They, too, "see" new things; they want and demand new things; they legitimate new things. Even the newcomers that seek relationships within the industry often find alliances with industry "mavericks" easier to forge, because these actors benefit less from the current distribution of industry resources. Linux, the open-source operating system software, has found eager and willing partners in both newer, maverick companies like Cisco and in more established companies like Corel that have been marginalized by the dominance of Microsoft's personal computer applications (Seltzer & Graven, 1999; Vizard, 1999).

The unacknowledged conditions and the unanticipated consequences of successful entry can be summarized in the following proposition:

Proposition 9.4. New activities by entrants, amplified by alliances with mavericks within the industry and/or actors not previously involved in the industry, modify the underlying structure (rules and available resources) of the industry.

In Giddens's terminology, an unintended consequence of entrepreneurial activity by those outside the mainstream of an industry is that their novel behavior generates yet more novel behavior. Because new entrants draw on different rules and resources, they create competitive conditions that are difficult to interpret and create even more opportunities for entrepreneurial behavior.

In fact, new activities by outsiders can alter industry structure even if the entrant fails or redeploys its assets outside the industry. New materials, alternative sourcing, lower prices, more generous warranties, and other new activities can become the tools used by existing competitors and the conditions demanded by customers. People Express provides just one example of an entrant that had such enduring effects on industry structure, even after its demise. Much of the airline industry's continuing turbulence is a legacy of its innovations (Banks, 1994).

New entrants, by contrast, are necessarily more vigilant than the typical incumbent because they are less aware of the industry structures influencing their activity. In less familiar circumstances, the newcomers' more active monitoring makes it more likely that they will quickly notice and effectively respond to further changes in industry structure. Although less knowledge of the setting can lead to disaster, first-mover advantages can accrue to new entrants and continue for many years (Urban, Carter, Gaskin & Mucha, 1986). Describing the early Japanese strategy for competing in the U.S. market, Yutaka Natayama, Nissan's representative in the United States, summarized the ideal scenario from the entrant's point of view: "What we should do is get better and creep up slowly, so we'll be good—and the customer will think we're good—before Detroit even knows about us" (quoted in Shapiro, 1991, 52-53).

Experience also suggests that successful new rivals are highly motivated by their achievements. It is not just economic opportunity that drives the new entrant. Observing Japanese automobile manufacturers' expansion, Nucor's growth as a steel producer, or Wal-Mart surpassing Sears and KMart suggests a compelling psychological argument: the positive reinforcement of closely monitored success breeds the desire for and increasing confidence in continued success. Though it is too early to declare that Linux or any other open-source operating system software will overtake Microsoft, its rapid growth has attracted the enthusiasm of many other companies that see Linux as a viable alternative to Microsoft's lock on the desktop operating system market (Seltzer & Graven, 1999). Furthermore, it is also likely that other firms that are less closely tied to established ways of doing will be able to imitate successful new rivals by adopting "me too" strategies (Haveman, 1994). In summary,

Proposition 9.5. Active monitoring and interpretation by entrants tends to quickly increase their relative knowledgeability and power. Strong niche performance motivates successful new entrants to expand their activities and invites further entry by imitators.

Shouldn't managers of incumbent firms at least respond to *major* changes in industry dimensions? After all, many firms employ sophisticated market research, forecasting, planning, and R&D departments that should alert managers to important new developments. Unfortunately, research findings and observations from practice support the conclusion that individual schema, shared problem definitions, strategic frames, and industry recipes remain relatively stable over time and are not easily changed, even when confronted by compelling evidence suggesting the need for change. The U.S. auto industry provides an early example of these problems. Brock Yates attributes delayed recognition of the threat posed by Japanese producers to "the Detroit Mind":

> If they [U.S. automobile executives] weren't isolated in Bloomfield Hills, driving their Cadillacs and Lincolns and Imperials, they'd understand why imported cars sell so well. Their automobiles are built to their life-styles, and they have no comprehension of why people in Los Angeles, San Francisco, Scarsdale, or Fairfield County, Connecticut, want Mercedes, BMW, and Hondas instead of Buicks and LeBarons. (1983, 80–81)

Observers of many other industries also record instances in which managers fail to see the implication of rivals' behavior for their own welfare (Barr, Stimpert, & Huff, 1992). Often, they assume that new products or services will not find a significant market because they are not made or do not perform in "the right way" (Porac, Thomas, & Baden-Fuller, 1989). Microsoft has so far largely ignored Linux and other open-source operating systems because it continues to dominate the market for personal computer operating systems, and the growing application of Linux in servers appears to pose little direct threat to Microsoft's core desktop software business (Seltzer & Graven, 1999; Vizard, 1999). Moreover, Linux remains beyond the technical capabilities of all but the most sophisticated desktop computer users (Dreyfuss, 1999). These examples from the automobile and software industries suggest that even if they are watching vigilantly for potential rivals, the managers of incumbent firms are likely to be watching for and concerned about potential rivals that look and behave very much as their firms do.

Proposition 9.6. Shared schema-based interpretations significantly decrease the likelihood that incumbent firms will quickly notice opportunities demonstrated by new entrants or clearly understand the threat of entrant activity.

The response to new circumstances is also delayed by dualities of domination and legitimation. Incumbent firms are often "structurally overbounded" (Alderfer, 1980) by internal bureaucracy or links to other firms. While some responses (e.g., changes in prices) may be made quickly, many others (such as developing new products or services) require considerably more time and investment for implementation (Bower, 1970a; Hayes & Abernathy, 1980; Hoskisson & Hitt, 1988). Regulation may be a problem, and existing contractual connections are even more likely to tie an incumbent to current ways of operating. Even alliances can be a conservative force (Buchko, 1994).

In summary:

Proposition 9.7. Structures of control and regulation limit the incumbents' power to respond to the circumstances that attract new entrants or to respond to subsequent opportunities associated with entry itself.

Effective response by the managers of incumbent firms is delayed further if decision makers perceive that the solution lies outside their control and thus look outside themselves for help (Barr et al., 1992; Bowman, 1976, 1978). The managers of incumbent firms frequently complain to the government about unfair competition, for example, as have executives who asked for quotas on imported textiles, automobiles, and steel. A number of studies offer different psychological explanations for why managers are quick to claim credit for positive results but reluctant to believe that their own actions are implicated in negative results (Bettman & Weitz, 1983; Salancik & Meindl, 1984; Staw, McKechnie & Puffer, 1983). Whatever the reason for this widely observed phenomenon, it is problematic because the search for external causes and solutions increases the elapsed time before incumbents change their own activity.

Established firms do not remain forever blind to new entrants, of course, but the first response to entrant success is often retreat to what incumbents believe are the most defensible areas in their competitive space (Harrigan, 1980). Though often described as "rationalization" or a "return to the core business," research suggests that these strategic retreats are rarely successful. In an early study, Cooper and Schendel (1976) document how incumbent firms pursue improvements in existing products or services just as they are being rendered obsolete by new innovations. Instead of adopting new diesel electric technology, for example, steam locomotive manufacturers sought to improve the efficiency of steam. In fact, the most efficient steam locomotives were built *after* the introduction of diesel electric technology. The result: not a single steam locomotive manufacturer builds diesel electric locomotives today.

The probability of disappointment or even failure is increased because competition often intensifies along two fronts: first from increased competition among other industry incumbents, who tend to retreat to smaller, overlapping arenas and must then compete more intensively for a smaller piece of the pie, and second from confrontations with new rivals seeking to expand from their initial "beachhead" into a more central position.

The steel industry provides an excellent example of the dangers of this situation for incumbent firms. Nearly all of the major integrated steel manufacturers abandoned the market for steel rod and other structural products, arguing that this segment of the market offered low margins and was subject to intense competition from foreign producers and domestic minimills such as Nucor Steel. In retreating to what their managers believed to be the more defensible and higher margin market for sheet steel, however, the major integrated mills have enjoyed very few benefits. Not only is the excess capacity of the major integrated producers now focused on a smaller segment of the total steel market, forcing sheet steel prices downward (Ansberry, 1991), but also the minimills have not been content to remain in the structural steel segment of the market. Nucor rather quickly began applying its minimill technology to manufacture flat-rolled steel, defying predictions that minimills would never be able to invade this segment of the market (Ansberry & Milbank, 1992). Following Giddens, the problem is that entry often has unintended consequences that go beyond even the entrepreneurial actors' intentions:

Proposition 9.8. Withdrawal to apparently "safer" or "stronger" strategies is often unsuccessful because new actors and activities are reconstituting industry structure. Strategic retreat by incumbent firms further changes industry structure, decreasing the utility of past knowledge and increasing opportunities for entrepreneurial activity.

Under the conditions just described, some incumbent firms are likely to fail or to exit the industry. Their "absorptive capacity" (Cohen & Levinthal, 1990; Nichols-Nixon, 1993) is insufficient to appropriate the new knowledge that is making old capabilities obsolete. At the same time, not all entrants remain in the industry, including some (as previously mentioned) who have influenced industry structure. In fact, Sharma (1993, 134) estimates that almost 60% of the firms diversifying into new industries exit within 4 years. The death or exit of less powerful firms has a positive side effect for survivors, in that it leaves a smaller number of firms competing in the industry. Early work by Porter (1980) and Harrigan (1980) established that firms can be profitable despite decreasing demand, if orderly exit occurs. The same logic would seem to apply to industries pressured by new entry.

Furthermore, surviving incumbents do not remain forever "blind" to successful entrants that become more and more important in the industry. This is particularly true as success by new entrants begins to affect performance indicators monitored by incumbent firms and by important stakeholders of those firms. It is logical that some important knowledge for more proactive incumbent responses will be gathered from their new rivals (Huff, 1982), and entrants cannot totally prevent this knowledge transfer, as their ways of understanding and acting increasingly become a part of the industry. New firms must acquire resources; they sell goods and services; they usually advertise; they use channels of distribution. Their buyers, suppliers, and distributors (as well as outside consultants, analysts, and the business press) carry information from these transactions to other firms. In other words:

Proposition 9.9. Over time, new entrants "train" an increasing number of actors within the industry to notice and understand their insights and behaviors, and it therefore becomes easier for incumbents to monitor and replicate the activities of new entrants.

We also suggest that the differences in monitoring and interpretation among incumbents and not-so-new entrants begin to shift. Entering firms become increasingly bound by the rules and resources that benefit them, and these causal connections root successful entrants more closely to their "new," but now aging, ways of acting. The strategic decisions of entrants can now bind *them* more closely to past behavior. They are increasingly tied to the external networks they must establish to do business and the internal routines they need to solidify early success. In short, new entrants begin to trade innovation and speed for the reliable reproduction of successful procedures (Nelson & Winter, 1982; Selznick, 1957).

Table 9.1 Key Assertions in the Cognitively Anchored Theory of the Firm

	Inertia ↔ Stress	First Order ↔ Second Order Change	Position ↔ Opportunity	Structure ↔ Agency
Individual	Inertia arises from the reuse of schema available in the social setting and developed from the individual's own experience. Stress rises if stimuli attracting attention cannot be interpreted by established or invented schematic frameworks.	*1ˢᵗ*: probable because many stimuli are ignored, existing schema efficiently use past experience, and schema can be fine-tuned. *2ⁿᵈ*: more likely as threatening anomalies cannot be overlooked or explained—if alternative frameworks are invented.	Each individual's unique history, position within the firm, will, skill, and values provide opportunities for improving that person's interests and the interests of others.	Rules and resources, instantiated by actors at many levels of analysis, tend to structure individual perceptions and actions. BUT, individuals have the power to act in ways that restructure the context of future actions.
Group	Inertia increases as other affiliated individuals reinforce confidence in "shared" interpretations and practices. Stress increases if mavericks, newcomers, or other groups plausibly challenge shared cognition.	*1ˢᵗ*: probable because established coalitions have satisfied their constituents in the past. *2ⁿᵈ*: more likely as stakeholders doubt the benefits of current activities—if they can identify satisficing alternatives.	Each coalition's activities and network of relationships provide opportunities for generating and controlling desired information and other resources.	Similarity of ideas and perceived power of actors affect the range and intensity of group influences. BUT, new ideas and new leaders can redefine similarity and power.
Firm	Inertia increases as the firm makes commitments and routinizes practices that allow individuals and groups to come and go without disrupting the status quo. Stress accumulates if the results of current strategy do not meet the performance expectations of key stakeholders.	*1ˢᵗ*: probable because organization outputs not only create some value but also involve activities that are costly for internal and external stakeholders to abandon or change. *2ⁿᵈ*: more likely as cumulative stress exceeds cumulative inertia—if an alternative strategy appears to reduce stress.	A firm's current resources and competitive position provide differential opportunities to more profitably interact with buyers, suppliers, competitors, and other actors.	The pattern of a firm's activities and performance over time affects the probability of future change attempts' success. BUT, astute managers can take advantage of discontinuities to reinterpret pattern and change the logic of firm activities.

Table 9.1 *(Continued)*

	Inertia ↔ Stress	First Order ↔ Second Order Change	Position ↔ Opportunity	Structure ↔ Agency
Industry	Inertia increases as recipes for success diffuse among organizations providing similar goods and services. Stress increases as mavericks and newcomers achieve success by drawing on unfamiliar recipes.	*1st*: probable because interacting firms in an industry have routinized ways of generating and allocating resources. *2nd*: more likely as entrepreneurial success becomes apparent—if supportive infrastructures develop.	Industry networks create larger social, economic, and legal environments that can change the valuation of their members' inputs and outputs.	Networks of firms affect the timing, direction, and success of firm activities. BUT, strategic moves and subsequent outcomes across the industry can recalibrate assumptions, resources, and boundaries.

Proposition 9.10. Efforts to institutionalize their success begin to structure entrant activities, reduce their capacity to respond to subsequent changes in the industry, and thereby increase the opportunities for new entrepreneurial activity by others.

The preceding discussion is not intended to exhaustively cover either the details of structuration theory or the many nuances of entrepreneurial activity. It does emphasize how cognition affects the ongoing shifts in the motives and monitoring capabilities of industry participants. The basic argument of this chapter is that there is no static industry *structure*, only the ongoing conditions of industry *structuring* and cognition plays an important role in that drama.

CONCLUSION

Academic understanding of industry evolution and many other phenomena has been constrained by a tendency to focus either on agency or on structure. This is perhaps understandable, given the structures that have influenced us. For many years, business policy scholars recognized external opportunities and threats but tended to focus on firms and the managers who "ran" them. By the late 1970s, those in the field began talking about "strategy" rather than "policy," and strategy researchers were moving away from the specific case studies that supported a managerial or agency- oriented focus to search for generic conditions that could predict success or failure across firms. Abetted by theory imported first from economics and more recently from sociology, the vocabulary turned to how economic and institutional structures determined performance, de-emphasizing the role of strategic choice.

Changes in the larger environment in which firms and managers must navigate help explain a new pendulum swing in academic attention. Conditions in most of the twentieth century have been generally kind, especially to U.S. companies. With the notable

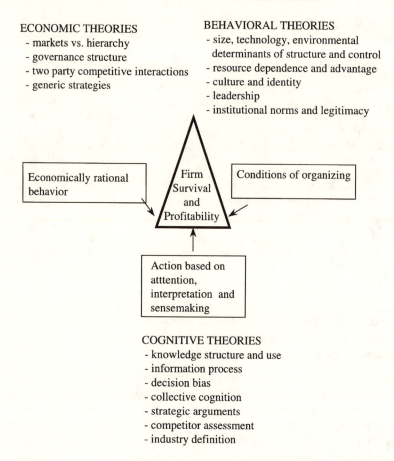

ECONOMIC THEORIES
- markets vs. hierarchy
- governance structure
- two party competitive interactions
- generic strategies

BEHAVIORAL THEORIES
- size, technology, environmental determinants of structure and control
- resource dependence and advantage
- culture and identity
- leadership
- institutional norms and legitimacy

Economically rational behavior

Firm Survival and Profitability

Conditions of organizing

Action based on atttention, interpretation and sensemaking

COGNITIVE THEORIES
- knowledge structure and use
- information process
- decision bias
- collective cognition
- strategic arguments
- competitor assessment
- industry definition

Figure 9.3 Economic, Behavioral, and Cognitive Contributions to Understanding Strategic Change

exception of the Great Depression, our collective fortunes have steadily risen. As long as the environment remained relatively hospitable, it made sense for academics and practitioners to focus on individual efforts. By the end of the century, however, firms around the world have encountered a much more demanding environment. Growth has slowed and become more volatile; a larger share of profits has gone to global competitors. Many U.S. and European companies have sought both structural explanations and structural solutions. It is not surprising that Western academics followed suit.

In our view, researchers and practicing managers are now searching for new frameworks that provide a more balanced and more dynamic view of the ongoing process of industry structuring (Baum, Korn, & Kotha, 1993; Chen, Loree, & Brittain, 1993). The shift in attention toward structure was needed but went too far, and our language of inquiry has been too static. The strategy field's basic concern with firm survival and profitability requires multiple approaches.

As suggested in Figure 9.3, we are convinced that a cognitively anchored theory of strategic change provides an important perspective which is missing in existing theoretical arguments derived from economic and behavioral assumptions. As a first step in the development of a cognitively anchored theory of strategic change, we have chosen to focus on the fundamental tension between stress and inertia as a key to understanding the strategic change process. Both stress and inertia are constructs rooted in a cognitive paradigm and both are under theorized in existing theories of strategic change.

The first column in Table 9.1 provides a brief summary of the progression in the theoretical development of the stress and inertia constructs beginning with the stress/inertia tensions within individuals that arise from schema based modes of knowledge acquisition and interpretation. These arguments are fully developed in chapter 2 and are the basis of an empirical study of schema formation among firms in the pharmaceuticals industry described in chapter 6.

Chapter 3 focuses on the group dynamics within the firm associated with changes in both stress (dissatisfaction with the current strategy) and inertia (commitment to the current strategy). The key theoretical issue from a cognitive perspective is how shared interpretations and practices are created and/or challenged within and across organizations. The empirical study of strategic change among firms in the biotech industry described in chapter 7 serves as an interesting example of the group dynamics surrounding development and change of shared strategic recipes for contracts, collaboration, and alliances.

The group level arguments translate directly into conjectures about stress/inertia dynamics at the level of the firm and across firms with an industry, as formally modeled in chapter 4 and evaluated empirically in chapter 8. The key insight is that changes in stress and inertia are interdependent and historically contingent. The effectiveness of homeostatic mechanisms designed to reduce stress incrementally depends directly on the level of commitment (inertia) associated with the current strategy whereas inertia rises or falls depending upon the level of stress *relative to* the level of inertia surrounding the current strategy. The stress/inertia dynamics are such that two behaviorally distinct classes of firms evolve: movers and stayers. Firms that have retained the same strategy for some time (stayers) tend to continue with the same strategy—inertia is high and stress is relatively low; whereas firms that make second order changes in strategy (movers) have a much greater change of moving again—inertia surrounding the new strategy is low, while stress may grow rapidly.

Finally, it is important to emphasize that strategic change decisions at all levels are embedded within and contingent upon a particular decision context as outlined in columns 3 and 4 of Table 9.1. The position—opportunity duality discussed in chapter 8 emphasizes the importance of a firm's strategic position in the decision to make a second order change in strategy as well as in the choice of direction for that change. At the industry level, the resulting second order changes in strategy also are found to have a significant effect upon the decision contest of other firms in the industry. These insights are extended and formalized in the structuration arguments presented in chapter 9. The key theoretical contribution from a cognitive perspective is that every individual, and by extension every firm, "sees" the opportunities for action differently. Every actor is drawing on a set of unique experiences and resources which uniquely influence thought and action.

Notes

1. This chapter is based on a paper presented at the ESSEC workshop on Action, Structure, and Organizations, Paris, May 10–12, 1995.

2. A significant number of entrants are managed by individuals with prior experience in incumbent firms. The perceptions of these entrepreneurs are channeled by previous experience in the industry, but the individuals involved are often mavericks who did not agree with the prevailing wisdom.

References

Abrahamson, E. 1991. Managerial fads and fashions: The diffusion and rejection of innovations. *Academy of Management Review*, 16: 586–612.

Ackermann, F. 1992. Strategic direction through burning issues using SODA as a strategic decision support system. *OR Insight*, 5: 24–28.

Adler, E., & Haas, P. M. 1992. Conclusion: Epistemic communities, world order, and the creation of a reflective research program. *International Organization,* 46(1): 367–390.

Alderfer, C. P. 1980. Consulting to underbounded systems. In C. P. Alderfer & C. L. Cooper (Eds.), *Advances in experiential social processes*, 2: 267–295. New York: Wiley.

Aldrich, H. E. 1999. *Organizations evolving.* London: Sage.

Alexander, J. C., Giesen, B., Munch, R., & Smelser, N. J. 1987.*The micro-macro link.* Berkeley: University of California Press.

Allard Poesi, F. 1994. From individual causal maps to a collective causal map. *Second international workshop on managerial and organizational cognition proceedings*: 26–27. Brussels, Belgium.

Allison, G. 1971. *Essence of decision.* Boston: Little, Brown.

Alvarez, S. A. 1999. *Entrepreneurial alliances: Prescriptions for alliance success with larger firms.* Unpublished doctoral dissertation, University of Colorado, Boulder.

Ambrosini, V., & Bowman, C. 1998. *The dilemma of tacit knowledge: Tacit routines as a source of sustainable competitive advantage.* Paper presented at the annual British Academy of Management meeting, Nottingham.

Amburgey, T. L., & Dacin, T. 1994. As the left foot follows the right: The dynamics of strategic and structural change. *Academy of Management Journal*, 37(6): 1427–1452.

Amburgey, T. L., Kelly, D., & Barnett, W. P. 1993. Resetting the clock: The dynamics of organizational change and failure. *Administrative Science Quarterly*, 38: 51–73.

Amburgey, T. L., & Miner, A. S. 1992. Strategic momentum: The effects of repetitive, positional, and contextual momentum on merger activity. *Strategic Management Journal*, 13(5): 335–348.

American Heritage Dictionary, Second College Edition. Boston: Houghton Mifflin.

Amit, R., & Schoemaker, P. J. H. 1993. Investments in strategic assets: Industry and firm-level perspectives. In P. Shrivastava, A. S. Huff & J. Dutton (Eds.), *Advances in strategic management*, 3–34. Greenwich, CT: JAI Press.

Anderson, C., Lepper, M., & Ross, L. 1980. Perseverance of social theories: The role of explanation in the persistence of discredited information. *Journal of Personality and Social Psychology*, 39: 1037–1049.

Anderson, J. R. 1983. *The architecture of cognition.* Cambridge, MA: Harvard University Press.

Andrews, K. R. 1971. *The concept of corporate strategy.* Homewood, IL: Dow-Jones Irwin.

Ansberry, C. 1991. Men of steel see no end to leaden prices. *Wall Street Journal*, March 19: A2.

Ansberry, C., & Milbank, D. 1992. Small, midsize steelmakers are ripe for a shakeout. *Wall Street Journal*, March 4: B4.

Argote, L. 1999. *Organizational learning: Creating, retaining and transferring knowledge.* Boston: Kluwer Academic.

Argote, L., & Epple, D. 1990. Learning curves in manufacturing. *Science*, 247: 920–924.

Argyris, C. 1977. Double-loop learning in organizations. *Harvard Business Review*, 55(5): 115–125.

Argyris, C., & Schön, D. A. 1978. *Organizational learning: A theory of action perspective.* Reading, MA: Addison-Wesley.

Armenakis, A. A., Harris, S. G., & Mossholder, K. W. 1993. Creating readiness for organizational change. *Human Relations*, 46(4): 681–703.

Asch, S. E. 1946. Forming impressions of personality. *Journal of Personality and Social Psychology*, 41: 1230–1240.

Axelrod, R. 1976. *Structure of decision.* Princeton, NJ: Princeton University Press.

Baird, I. S., Sudharshan, D., & Thomas, H. 1988. Addressing temporal change in strategic groups analysis: A three-mode factor analysis approach. *Journal of Management*, 14: 425–439.

Baker, D. D., & Cullen, J. G. 1993. Administrative reorganization and configurational content: The contingent effects of age, size, and change in size. *Academy of Management Journal*, 36: 1251–1277.

Balogun, J. 1999. *The role of obstructing and facilitating processes in change.* Unpublished doctoral dissertation, Cranfield School of Management, Cranfield, England.

Banks, H. 1994. A sixties industry in a nineties economy. *Forbes*, May 9: 107–112.

Barker, V. L. 1991. *Corporate turnarounds as strategic reorientations.* Unpublished doctoral dissertation, University of Illinois, Urbana-Champaign.

Barley, S.R. 1986. Technology as an occasion for structuring: Evidence from observations of CT scanners and the social order of radiology departments. *Administrative Science Quarterly*, 31: 78–108.

Barnard, C. I. 1938. *The functions of the executive.* Cambridge, MA: Harvard University Press.

Barnes, J. H., Jr. 1984. Cognitive biases and their impact on strategic planning. *Strategic Management Journal*, 5: 129–137.

Barnett, W. P., Breve, H. R., & Park, D. Y. 1994. An evolutionary model of organizational performance. *Strategic Management Journal*, 15: 11–28.

Barney J. B. 1986a. Organizational culture: Can it be a source of sustained competitive advantage? *Academy of Management Review*, 11: 656–665.

Barney, J. B. 1986b. Strategic factor markets: Expectations, luck, and business strategy. *Management Science*, 32: 1512–1514.

Barney, J. B. 1991. Firm resources and sustained competitive advantage. *Journal of Management*, 7: 99–120.

Barney, J. B. 1995. Looking inside for competitive advantage: A resource-based analysis. *Academy of Management Executive*, 9(4): 49–61.

Barney, J. B. 1997. *Gaining and sustaining competitive advantage.* Reading, MA. Addison-Wesley.

Barney, J. B., & Ouchi, W. G. 1986. *Managerial economics.* San Francisco: Jossey-Bass.

Barney, J. G., & Zajac, E. J. 1994. Competitive organizational behavior: Toward an organizationally-based theory of competitive advantage. *Strategic Management Journal*, 15: 5–9.

Barr, P. S. 1991. *Organization stress and mental models.* Unpublished doctoral dissertation, University of Illinois, Urbana-Champaign.

Barr, P. S., & Huff, A. S. 1997. Seeing isn't believing: Understanding diversity in the timing of strategy response. *Journal of Management Studies*, 34(3): 337–370.

Barr, P. S., Stimpert, J. L., & Huff, A. S. 1992. Cognitive change, strategic action, and organizational renewal. *Strategic Management Journal*, 13: 15–36.

Barry, D., & Elmes, M. 1997. Strategy retold: Toward a narrative view of strategic discourse. *Academy of Management Review*, 22: 429–452.

Bartholini, G. 1983. Organization of industrial drug research. In F. Gross (Ed.), *Decision making in drug research*: 123–146. New York: Raven Press.

Bartlett, C. A., & Ghoshal, S. 1993. Beyond the M-form: Toward a managerial theory of the firm. *Strategic Management Journal*, 14: 23–46.

Bartlett, F. C. 1932. *Remembering: A study in experimental and social psychology.* Cambridge: Cambridge University Press.

Bartlett, F. C. 1958. *Thinking: An experimental and social study.* London: Unwin.

Bartunek, J. 1984. Changing interpretive schemes and organizational restructuring: The example of a religious order. *Administrative Science Quarterly*, 29: 355–372.

Bartunek, J., Kolb, D., & Lewicki, R. 1992. Bringing conflict out from behind the scenes: Private informal and non-rational dimensions of conflict in organizations. In D. Kolb & J. Bartunek (Eds.), *Hidden conflict in organizations: Uncovering behind the scenes disputes.* Thousand Oaks, CA: Sage.

Bartunek, J. M., & Moch, M. K. 1987. First-order, second-order, and third-order change and organization development interventions: A cognitive approach. *Journal of Applied Behavioral Science*, 23(4): 483–500.

Bateman, T., & Zeithaml, C. 1989. The psychological context of strategic decisions: A model and convergent experimental findings. *Strategic Management Journal*, 10: 59–74.

Bateson, G. 1972. *Steps to an ecology of mind.* New York: Ballantine.

Baum, J. A. C. 1998. Introduction: Strategic management as a fish-scale multiscience. In J. Baum (Ed.), *Advance in strategic management*: 1–18. Greenwich, CT: JAI Press.

Baum, J. A. & Mezias, S. J. 1992. Localized competition and organizational failure in the Manhattan hotel industry. *Administrative Science Quarterly*, 37: 580–604.

Baum, J. A. C., Korn, H. J., & Kotha, S. B. 1993. *Technological evolution and the dynamics of an organizational population: Founding and failure of facsimile transmission service organizations, 1965–1992.* Paper presented at the annual meeting of the Academy of Management, Atlanta.

Baum, J. A. C., & Singh, J. V. (Eds.). 1994. *Evolutionary dynamics of organizations.* Oxford: Oxford University Press.

Bechtel, W., & Abrahamsen, A. 1991. *Connectionism and the mind: An introduction to parallel processing in networks.* Oxford: Blackwell.

Becker, H. 1964. Personal change in adult life. *Sociometry*, 27: 40–53.

Beehr, T. A., & Bhagat, R. S. (Eds.). 1985. *Human stress and cognition in organizations*. New York: Wiley.

Beer, M., Eisenstat, R. A., & Spector, B. 1990. Why change programs don't produce change. *Harvard Business Review*, 68(6): 158–166.

Berger, P., & Luckman, T. 1967. *The social construction of reality*. New York: Penguin.

Bettis, R. A. 1991. Strategic management and the straightjacket: An editorial essay. *Organization Science*, 2(3): 315–319.

Bettis, R. A., & Hitt, M. A. 1995. The new competitive landscape. *Strategic Management Journal*, 16: 7–19.

Bettis, R. A., & Prahalad, C. K. 1995. The dominant logic: Retrospective and extension. *Strategic Management Journal*, 16: 5–14.

Bettman, J. R., & Weitz, B. A. 1983. Attributions in the board room: Causal reasoning in corporate annual reports. *Administrative Science Quarterly*, 28: 165–183.

Beyer, J. M., Chattopadhyay, P., George, E., Glick, W. H., Ogilvie, D.T., & Pugliese, D. 1997. The selective perception of managers revisited. *Academy of Management Journal*, 40: 716–737.

Bibeault, D. B. 1982. *Corporate turnaround*. New York: McGraw-Hill.

Bigelow, J. 1982. A catastrophe model of planned organizational change. *Behavioral Science*, 27: 26–42.

Biggadike, R. E. 1979. *Corporate diversification: Entry, strategy, and performance*. Cambridge, MA: Harvard University Press.

BioPharm. 1988, Volume 1; 1991, Volume 4; 1994, Volume 7; 1997, Volume 10. Eugene, OR: Aster Publishing.

BioVenture View. 1989, Volume 4; 1990 Volume 5. San Mateo, CA: Bioventure Publishing.

Birnbaum-More, P. H., & Weiss, A. R. 1990. Discovering the basis of competition in 12 industries: Computerized content analysis of interview data from the US and Europe. In A. S. Huff (Ed.), *Mapping strategic thought*: 53–69. Chichester, England: Wiley.

Bogner, W. C., & Thomas, H. 1992. Competitive positions of European firms in the U.S. pharmaceutical market. In C. Huttin & N. Bosanquet (Eds.), *The prescription drug market: International perspectives and challenges for the future*: 205–231. Netherlands: Elsevier Science Publishers.

Bogner, W. C., & Thomas, H. 1993. The role of competitive groups in strategy formulation: A dynamic integration of two competing models. *Journal of Management Studies*, 30(1): 51–67.

Boje, D. M. 1991. The storytelling organization: A study of story performance in an office-supply firm. *Administrative Science Quarterly*, 36: 106–126.

Borgida, E., & Campbell, B. 1982. Attitude-behavior consistency: The moderating role of personal experience. *Journal of Personality and Social Psychology*, 42: 239–247.

Borys, B. & Jemison, D. 1989. Hybrid arrangements as strategic alliances: Theoretical issues in organizational combinations. *Academy of Management Review*, 14(2): 234–249.

Bougon, M. G. 1983. Uncovering cognitive maps: The self-Q technique. In G. Morgan (Ed.), *Beyond methods: Strategies for social research*. Beverly Hills, CA: Sage.

Bougon, M. G., Weick, K. E., & Binkhorst, D. 1977. Cognition in organizations: Analysis of the Utrecht Jazz Orchestra. *Administrative Science Quarterly*, 22: 609–632.

Bower, J. L. 1970a. Planning within the firm. *American Economic Review*, 60(2): 186–194.

Bower, J. L. 1970b. *Managing the resource allocation process*. Homewood, IL: Irwin.

Bowman, C., & Daniels, K. 1995. The influence of functional experience on perceptions of strategic priorities. *British Journal of Management*, 6: 157–167.

Bowman, E. H. 1976. Strategy and the weather. *Sloan Management Review*, 17(2): 49–62.

Bowman, E. H. 1978. Strategy, annual reports, and alchemy. *California Management Review*, 20(3): 64–71.

Bowman, E. H. 1984. Content analysis of annual reports for corporate strategy and Risk. *Interfaces*, 14: 61–71.

Bowman, E. H. 1995. Strategic history: Through different mirrors. In P. Shrivastava, A. S. Huff & J. Dutton (Eds.), *Advances in Strategic Management*, 11: 25–45. Greenwich, CT: JAI Press.

Bowman, E. H., & Hurry, D. 1993. Strategy through the options lens: An integrated view of resource investments and the incremental-choice process. *Academy of Management Review*, 18: 760–782.

Boyce, M. E. 1995. Collective centering and collective sense-making in the stories and storytelling of one organization. *Organization Studies*, 16: 107–137.

Bransford, J. D., & Johnson, M. K. 1972. Contextual prerequisites for understanding: Some investigations of comprehension and recall. *Journal of Verbal Learning and Verbal Behavior*, 11: 717–726.

Braybrooke, D., & Lindblom, C. E. 1963. *A strategy of decision*. New York: Free Press.

Brown, G. W., & Harris, T. O. 1978. *Social origins of depression: A study of psychiatric disorder in women*. London: Tavistock.

Brown, J. S. 1988. *Seeing differently: Insights on innovation*. Boston, MA: Harvard Business School.

Brown, S. L., & Eisenhardt, K. M. 1997. The art of continuous change: Linking complexity theory and time-paced evolution in relentlessly shifting organizations. *Administrative Science Quarterly*, 42: 1–34.

Brown, S. L., & Eisenhardt, K. M. 1998. *Competing on the edge: Strategy as structured chaos*. Boston: Harvard Business School Press.

Buchko, A. A. 1994. Conceptualization and measurement of environmental uncertainty: An assessment of the Miles and Snow perceived environmental uncertainty scale. *Academy of Management Journal*, 37: 410–425.

Bukszar, E., & Connolly, T. 1988. Hindsight bias and strategic choice: Some problems in learning from experience. *Academy of Management Journal*, 31: 628–642.

Burgleman, R. A. 1983. A process model of internal corporate venturing in the diversified major firm. *Administrative Science Quarterly*, 28: 223–244.

Burgelman, R. A. 1994. Fading memories: A process theory of strategic business exit in dynamic environments. *Administrative Science Quarterly*, 39: 24–56.

Burgelman, R. A. 1996. A process model of strategic business exit: Implications for an evolutionary perspective on strategy. *Strategic Management Journal*, 17: 193–214.

Burrell G., & Morgan, G. 1979. *Sociological paradigms and organisational analysis*. London: Heinemann.

Burrill, S. G. (Ed.). 1987. *Biotech 86: At the crossroad*. San Francisco: Arthur Young High Technology Group.

Burrill, S. G. (Ed.). 1988a. *Biotech 88: Into the next decade*. San Francisco: Arthur Young High Technology Group.

Burill, S. G. 1988b. Biotechnology financing: Strategies after the crash. *BioPharm*, April. Vol. 1, No. 4.

Burrill, S. G. (Ed.). 1989. *Biotech 89: Commercialization*. San Francisco: Arthur Young High Technology Group.

Burrill, S. G. (Ed.). 1990. *Biotech 90: Into the next decade*. San Francisco: Ernst & Young High Technology Group.

Burrill, S. G., & Lee, K. B., Jr. (Eds.). 1991. *Biotech 91: A changing environment.* San Francisco: Ernst & Young High Technology Group.

Burrill, S. G., & Lee, K. B., Jr. (Eds.). 1992. *Biotech 92: Promise to reality.* San Francisco: Ernst & Young High Technology Group.

Burrill, S. G., & Lee, K. B., Jr. (Eds.). 1993. *Biotech 93: Accelerating commercialization.* San Francisco: Ernst & Young High Technology Group.

Burrill, S. G., & Lee, K. B., Jr. (Eds.). 1994. *Biotech 94: Long-term value, short-term hurdles.* San Francisco: Ernst & Young High Technology Group.

Burrill, S. G., & Lee, K. B., Jr. (Eds.). 1995. *Biotech 95: Reform, restructure, renewal.* San Francisco: Ernst & Young High Technology Group.

Calori, R., Johnson, G., & Sarnin, P. 1992. French and British top managers' understanding of the structure and dynamics of their industries: A cognitive analysis and comparison. *British Journal of Management,* 3: 61–78.

Calori, R., Johnson, G., & Sarnin, P. 1994. CEO's cognitive maps and the scope of the organization. *Strategic Management Journal,* 15: 437–457.

Camerer, C. F. 1991. Does strategy research need game theory? *Strategic Management Journal,* 12: 137–152.

Cameron, K., Sutton, R., & Whetten, D. 1988. *Readings in organizational decline.* Cambridge, MA: Ballinger.

Cantor, N., & Mischel, W. 1977. Traits as prototypes: Effects on recognition memory. *Journal of Personality and Social Psychology,* 35(1): 38–48.

Carroll, G. R. 1993. A sociological view on why firms differ. *Strategic Management Journal,* 14: 237–249.

Chaganti, R., & Sambharya, R. 1987. Strategic orientation and characteristics of upper management. *Strategic Management Journal,* 8: 393–401.

Chakravarthy, B. 1982. Adaptation: A promising metaphor for strategic management. *Academy of Management Review,* 7: 33–44.

Chakravarthy, B. 1986. Measuring Strategic Performance. *Strategic Management Journal,* 7: 437–458.

Chandler, A. D. 1962. *Strategy and structure.* Garden City, NJ: Doubleday.

Chang, S. J. 1996. An evolutionary perspective on diversification and corporate restructuring: Entry, exit, and economic performance during 1981-1989. *Strategic Management Journal,* 17: 587–611.

Chen, R. X., Loree, D., & Brittain, J. 1993. *Learning from organizational change episodes: A punctuated learning model.* Paper presented at the annual meeting of the Academy of Management, Atlanta, GA.

Chesley, J. A., & Huff, A. S. 1998. Anticipating strategic turnaround: The systems and structures that enable/constrain change. *Advances in Applied Business Strategy,* 5: 177–204. Greenwich, CT: JAI Press.

Child, J. C. 1972. Organization, structure, environment and performance: The role of strategic choice. *Sociology,* 6: 1–22.

Christensen, C. R., Andrews, K. R., Bower, J. L., Hamermesh, R. G., & Porter, M. E. 1985. *Business policy: Text and cases.* Homewood, IL: Irwin.

Clapham, S., & Schwenk, C. 1991. Self-serving attributions, managerial cognition, and company performance. *Strategic Management Journal,* 12: 219–229.

Clark, B. R. 1970. *The distinctive college.* Chicago: Aldine.

Clark, W. A. V. 1986. *Human migration.* Beverly Hills, CA: Sage.

Cohen, M. D. 1991. Individual learning and organizational routine: Emerging connections. *Organization Science,* 2: 135–139.

Cohen, M. D., March, J. G., & Olsen, J. P. 1972. A garbage can model of organizational choice. *Administrative Science Quarterly*, 17: 1–25.

Cohen, M. D., & Sproull, L. S., 1991. Editors' introduction. *Organization Science*, 2: i–iii.

Cohen, W., & Levinthal, D. 1990. Absorptive capacity: A new perspective on learning and innovation. *Administrative Science Quarterly*, 35: 128–152.

Collis, D. J. 1993. *The evolution of firm boundaries: The case of the Baby Bells*. Paper presented at the annual meeting of the Academy of Management, Atlanta.

Comanor, W. S. 1986. The political economy of the pharmaceutical industry. *Journal of Economic Literature*, 24(3): 1178–1217.

Conner, K. R., & Prahalad, C. K. 1996. A resource-based theory of the firm: Knowledge versus opportunism. *Organization Science*, 7(5): 477–501.

Cool, K. O., Dierickx, I., & Jemison, D. 1989. Business stragegy, market structure and risk-return relationships: A structural approach. *Strategic Management Journal*, 10(6): 507–522.

Cool, K. O. 1985. *Strategic group formation and strategic group shifts: A longitudinal analysis of the U.S. pharmaceutical industry, 1963–1982*. Unpublished doctoral dissertation, Purdue University, West Lafayette, IN.

Cool, K. O., & Dierickx, I. 1993. Rivalry, strategic groups and firm profitability. *Strategic Management Journal*, 14: 47–59.

Cool, K. O., & Schendel D. 1987. Strategic group formation and performance: The case of the U.S. pharmaceutical industry, 1963–1982. *Management Science*, 33(9): 1102–1124.

Cool, K. O., & Schendel, D. 1988. Performance differences among strategic group members. *Strategic Management Journal*, 9: 207–233.

Cooper, A. C., & Schendel, D. 1976. Strategic responses to technological threats. *Business Horizons*, 19(1): 61–69.

Cooper, C. L., & Marshal, J. 1976. Occupational sources of stress: A review of the literature relating to coronary heart disease and mental health. *Journal of Occupational Psychology*, 49: 11–28.

Corner, P. D., Kinicki, A. J., & Keats, B. W. 1994. Integrating organizational and individual information processing perspectives on choice. *Organization Science*, 3: 294–308.

Covin, T. J., & Kilmann, R. H. 1990. Participant perceptions of positive and negative influences on large-scale change. *Group and Organization Studies*, 15: 233–248.

Crossan, M., & Sorrenti, M. 1997. Making sense of improvisation. In J. Walsh & A. S. Huff (Eds.), *Advances in Strategic Management*, 14: 155–180. Stamford, CT: JAI Press.

Crossan, M. M., Lane, H. W., & White R. E. 1999. An organizational learning framework: From intuition to institution. *Academy of Management Review*, 24: 522–537.

Crozier, M. 1964. *The bureaucratic phenomenon*. London: Tavistock.

Cummings, T. G., & Cooper, C. L. 1979. A cybernetic theory of organizational stress. *Human Relations*, 32: 395–418.

Cummings, T. G., & Cooper, C. L. 1998. A cybernetic theory of organizational stress. In C. L. Cooper (Ed.), *Theories of organizational stress*. Oxford: Oxford University Press, 101–121.

Cummings, T. G., & Worley, C. G. 1993. *Organization development and change* (5th ed.). Minneapolis/St. Paul, MN: West Publishing.

Cyert, R. M., & March, J. 1963. *A behavioral theory of the firm*. Englewood Cliffs, NJ: Prentice-Hall.

Czarniawska, B. 1997. *Narrating the organization*. Chicago: University of Chicago Press.

Daft, R. L., & Steers, R. M. 1986. *Organizations*. Glenview, IL: Scott, Foresman.

Daft, R. L., & Weick, K. E. 1984. Toward a model of organizations as interpretive systems. *Academy of Management Review*, 9: 284–295.

Dandoy, A. C., & Goldstein, A. G. 1990. The use of cognitive appraisal to reduce stress reactions: A replication. *Journal of Social Behavior and Personality*, 5(4): 275–285.

Daniels, K. 1998. Toward integrating emotions into strategic management research: trait affect and perceptions of the strategic environment. *British Journal of Management*, 9: 163–168.

Daniels, K., de Chernatony, L., & Johnson, G. 1995. Validating a method for mapping manager's mental models of competitive industry structures. *Human Relations*, 48(9): 975–991.

Das, P., & Moch, M. 1998. *Pressures for and resistance to change: Interacting determinants of the abruptness of strategic change in product diversity.* Working paper, University of Arkansas.

Das, T. K. 1986. *The subjective side of strategy making: Future orientations and perceptions of executives.* New York: Praeger.

Das T. K., & Teng B-S. 1999. Cognitive biases and strategic decision processes: An integrative perspective. *Journal of Management Studies*, 36.

D'Aveni, R. 1994. *Hypercompetition.* New York: Free Press.

Dawson, P. 1994. *Organizational change: A processual approach.* London: Chapman.

Day, D. V., & Lord, R. G. 1992. Expertise and problem categorization: The role of expert processing in organizational sense-making. *Journal of Management Studies*, 29:35–47.

Deal, T., & Kennedy, A. 1982. *Corporate cultures: The rites and rituals of corporate life.* Reading, MA: Addison-Wesley.

Dearborn, D. C., & Simon, H. A. 1958. Selective perception: A note on the departmental identifications of executives. *Sociometry,* 21:140–144.

Deeds, D. L., & Hill, C. W. L. 1996. Strategic alliances and the rate of new product development: An empirical study of entrepreneurial biotechnology firms. *Journal of Business Venturing*, 11(1): 41–55.

Demsetz, H. 1991. The theory of the firm revisited. In O. E. Williamson & W. Winter (Eds.), *The nature of the firm*, 159–178. New York: Oxford University Press.

Denis, J. L., Langley, A., & Cazale, L. 1996. Leadership and strategic change under ambiguity. *Organization Studies*, 17(4): 673–699.

DeNisi, A., Cafferty, T., & Meglino, G. 1984. Dimensions of organizational task environments. *Organizational Behavior and Human Performance*, 33: 360–396.

Dewar, R. D., & Dutton, J. E. 1986. The adoption of radical and incremental innovations. *Management Science*, 32: 1422–1433.

Dibner, M. D. 1993. Blood brothers. *Bio/Technology*, 11: 1120–1123.

Dierickx, I., & Cool, K. 1987. *Strategic flows versus stocks: A framework for analysing business strategy and competitive advantage.* Working paper, INSEAD.

Dierickx, I., & Cool, K. 1989. Asset stock accumulation and sustainability of competitive advantage. *Management Science*, 35: 1504–1511.

DiMaggio, P. J. 1988. Interest and agency in institutional theory. In L. G. Zucker (Ed.), *Institutional patterns and organizations:* 3–21. Cambridge, MA: Ballinger.

DiMaggio, P. J., & Powell, W. W. 1983. The iron cage revisited: Institutional isomorphism and collective rationality in organizational fields. *American Sociological Review*, 48: 147–160.

DiMaggio, P. J., & Powell, W. W. 1991. Introduction. In W. W. Powell & P. J. DiMaggio, *The new institutionalism in organizational analysis:* 1–38. Chicago: University of Chicago Press.

Donaldson, L. 1986. *In defense of organization theory.* Cambridge: Cambridge University Press.

Donnellon, A., Gray, B., & Bougon, M. G. 1986. Communication, meaning, and organizational action. *Administrative Science Quarterly,* 31: 43–55.

Dougherty, D. 1992. A practice-centered model of organizational renewal through product innovation. *Strategic Management Journal,* 13: 77–92.

Dowie, J., & Elstein, A. 1988. *Professional judgement: A reader in clinical decision making.* Cambridge: Cambridge University Press.

Doz, Y. L. 1996. The evolution of cooperation in strategic alliances: Initial conditions or learning processes? *Strategic Management Journal,* 17: 55–83.

Dreyfus, J. 1999. Linux holds promise, but Microsoft doesn't have to worry—yet. *Fortune,* April 26, 139(8): 395–396.

Duhaime, I. M., & Schwenk, C. R. 1985. Conjectures on cognitive simplification in acquisition and divestment decision making. *Academy of Management Review,* 10: 287–295.

Dutton, J., Fahey, L., & Narayanan, V. K. 1983. Toward understanding strategic issue diagnosis. *Strategic Management Journal,* 4: 307–23.

Dutton, J., & Jackson, S. 1987. Categorizing strategic issues: Links to organizational action. *Academy of Management Review,* 12: 76–90.

Dutton, J., & Thomas, A. 1985. Relating technological change and learning by doing. In R. S. Rosenbloom (Ed.), *Research on technological innovation management and policy.* Greenwich, CT: JAI Press.

Dutton, J. E., & Dukerich, J. M. 1991. Keeping an eye on the mirror: The role of image and identity in organizational adaptation. *Academy of Management Journal,* 34:517–554.

Dutton, J. E., Walton, E. J., & Abrahamson, E. 1989. Important dimensions of strategic issues: Separating the wheat from the chaff. *Journal of Management Studies,* 26: 379–396.

Eccles, R. G., & Nohria, N. 1992. *Beyond the hype: Rediscovering the essence of management.* Cambridge, MA: Harvard Business School Press.

Eden, C. 1990a. Strategic thinking with computers. *International Journal of Strategic Management,* 23: 35–43.

Eden, C. 1990b. Working on problems using cognitive mapping. In S. C. Littlechild & M. Shutler (Eds.), *Operations research in management.* London: Prentice-Hall.

Eden, C. 1992. Strategy development as a social process. *Journal of Management Studies,* 29(6): 799–811.

Eden, C. 1993. Strategy development and implementation: Cognitive mapping for group support. In J. Hendrix, G. Johnson, & J. Newton (Eds.), *Strategic thinking.* Chichester, England: Wiley.

Eden, C., & Ackermann, F. 1998. *Making strategy: The journey of strategic management.* London: Sage.

Eden, C., Ackermann, F., & Tait, A. 1993. *Comparing cognitive maps: Methodological issues.* Paper presented at the First international workshop on managerial and organizational cognition, Brussels, Belgium.

Eden, C., Jones, S., & Sims, D. 1979. *Thinking in organizations.* London: Macmillan.

Eden, C., & Spender, J.-C. (Eds.). 1998. *Managerial and organizational cognition.* London: Sage.

Edwards, J. R. 1998. Cybernetic theory of stress, coping, and well-being: Review and extension to work and family. In C. L. Cooper (Ed.), *Theories of organizational stress.* Oxford: Oxford University Press.

Edwards, M. 1994. Roundtable: Partnering along the value chain. In S. G. Burrill, & K. B. Lee (Eds.), *Biotech 94: Long-term, short-term hurdles*. San Francisco: Ernst & Young High Technology Group.

Ehlinger, S. 1994. How do centre's and peripheral units' cognitions interact during the strategic planning process? *Second international workshop on managerial and organizational cognition proceedings:* 151–178. Brussels, Belgium.

Einstein, A., & Infeld, L. 1938. *The evolution of physics*. New York: Simon & Schuster.

Eisenhardt, K. M. 1989. Agency theory: An assessment and review. *Academy of Management Review*, 14: 57–74.

Eisenhardt, K. M. 1990. Speed and strategic choice: How managers accelerate decision making. *California Management Review*, 32(3): 39–54.

Eisenhardt, K. M., & Bourgeois, L. J. 1988. Politics of strategic decision making in high-velocity environments: Toward a midrange theory. *Academy of Management Journal*, 31(4): 737–770.

Eisenhardt, K. M., & Schoonhoven, C. B. 1996. Resource-based view of strategic alliance formation: Strategic and social effects in entrepreneurial firms. *Organization Science*, 7(2): 136–150.

Eisenhardt, K. M., & Zbaracki, M. J. 1992. Strategic decision making. *Strategic Management Journal*, 13: 17–37.

Eliasmith, C. 1996. The third contender: A critical examination of the dynamicist theory of cognition. *Philosophical Psychology* 9: 441–463.

El Sawy, O. A., & Pauchant, T. C. 1988. Triggers, templates, and twitches in the tracking of emerging strategic issues. *Strategic Management Journal*, 9: 455–474.

Evritt, B. 1980. *Cluster analysis* (2nd edition). London: Heinemann Educational.

Fahey, L., & Narayanan, V. K. 1989. Linking changes in revealed causal maps and environmental change: An empirical study. *Journal of Management Studies*, 26: 361–378.

Fay, D., Sonnentag, S., & Frese, M. 1998. Stressor, innovation, and personal initiative. In C.L. Cooper (Ed.), *Theories of organizational stress*: 170–189. Oxford: Oxford University Press.

Festervand, T. A., & Tucker, G. K. 1990. Direct-to-consumer promotion of prescription drug products: Chronic condition or enduring opportunity? *Health Marketing Quarterly*, 7: 21–36.

Festinger, L. 1957. *A theory of cognitive dissonance*. Stanford, CA: Stanford University Press.

Feyerabend, P. 1970. Consolations for the specialist. In I. Lakatos & A. Musgragve, (Eds.), *Criticism and the growth of knowledge*: 197–230. Cambridge: Cambridge University Press.

Fiegenbaum, A. 1987. *Dynamic aspects of strategic groups and competitive strategy: Concepts and empirical examination in the insurance industry*. Unpublished doctoral dissertation, University of Illinois, Urbana-Champaign.

Fiegenbaum, A., Hart, S., & Schendel, D. 1996.Strategic reference point theory. *Strategic Management Journal*, 17: 219–235.

Fiegenbaum, A., Sundharshan, D., & Thomas, H. 1987. The concept of stable strategic time periods in strategic group research. *Managerial and Decision Economics*, 8(2): 139–148.

Fiegenbaum, A., Sundharshan, D., & Thomas, H. 1990. Strategic time periods and strategic groups research: Concepts and an empirical example. *Journal of Management Studies*, 27(2): 133–148.

Fiegenbaum, A., & Thomas, H. 1995. Strategic groups as reference groups: Theory, modeling and empirical examination of industry and competitive strategy. *Strategic Management Journal*, 16(6): 461–476.

Fildes, R. A. 1990. Strategic challenges in commercializing biotechnology. *California Management Review,* 32(3): 63–72.

Fiol, C. M. 1989. A semiotic analysis of corporate language: Organizational boundaries and joint venturing. *Administrative Science Quarterly,* 34(2): 277–303.

Fiol, C. M. 1991. Managing culture as a competitive resource: An identity-based view of sustainable competitive advantage. *Journal of Management,* 17(1): 191–211.

Fiol, C. M. 1994. Consensus, diversity, and learning in organizations. *Organization Science,* 5: 403–419.

Fiol, C. M., & Huff, A. S. 1992. Maps for managers: Where are we? Where do we go from here? *Journal of Management Studies,* 29(3): 267–285.

Fiol, C. M., & Lyles, M. A. 1985. Organizational learning. *Academy of Management Review,* 10(4): 803–813.

Fiske, S. T., & Linville, P. W. 1980. What does the schema concept buy us? *Personality and Social Psychology Bulletin,* 6: 543–557.

Fiske, S. T., & Taylor, S. E. 1991. *Social cognition* (2nd ed.). New York: Random House.

Flood, R. L., & Jackson, M. C. 1991. *Creative problem solving.* Chichester, England: Wiley.

Floyd, S. W., & Wooldridge, B. 1992. Managing strategic consensus: The foundation of effective implementation. *Academy of Management Executive,* 6(3): 27–39.

Floyd, S. W., & Wooldridge, B. 2000. *Building strategy from the middle: Reconceptualizing strategy process.* Thousand Oaks, CA: Sage.

Folkman, S., & Lazarus, R. S. 1983. *Folkman-Lazarus ways of coping checklist.* Princeton, NJ: Educational Testing Service.

Fombrun, C., & Shanley, M. 1990. What's in a name? Reputation building and corporate strategy. *Academy of Management Journal,* 33: 233–258.

Fombrun, C. J. 1994. Taking on strategy, 1-2-3. In J. A. C. Baum & J. V. Singh (Eds.), *Evolutionary dynamics of organizations.* Oxford: Oxford University Press.

Fombrun, C. J., & Ginsberg, A. 1990. Shifting gears: Enabling change in corporate aggressiveness. *Strategic Management Journal,* 11(4): 297–308.

Fondas, N., & Wiersema, M. 1997. Changing of the guard: The influence of CEO socialization on strategic change. *Journal of Management Studies,* 34(4): 561–584.

Ford, J., & Baucus, D. 1987. Organizational adaptation to performance downturns. *Academy of Management Review,* 12: 366–380.

Foreman, C. H. 1991. The fast track: Federal agents and the political demand for AIDS drugs. *Brookings Review,* 9(2): 30–37.

Fox-Wolfgramm, S. J., Boal, K. B., & Hunt, J. G. 1998. Organizational adaptation to institutional change: A comparative study of first-order change in prospector and defender banks. *Administrative Science Quarterly,* 43: 87–126.

Fredrickson, J., & Iaquinto, A. L. 1989. Inertia and creeping rationality in strategic decision processes. *Academy of Management Journal,* 32: 516–542.

Freeman, R. E. 1984. *Strategic management: A stakeholder approach.* Cambridge, MA: Ballinger.

Frost, P. J., & Morgan, G. 1983. Symbols and sensemaking: The realization of a framework. In L. R. Pondy, P. J. Frost, G. Morgan & T. C. Dandridge (Eds.), *Organizational symbolism:* 207–236. Greenwich, CT: JAI Press.

Gaeta, L. 1991. Japan: New competitor for the U.S. doctor's scripts. *Medical Marketing and Media,* 26(6): 16–29.

Galambos, J., & Rips, L. 1982. Memory for routines. *Journal of Verbal Learning and Verbal Behavior,* 21: 260–281.

Galaskiewicz, J., & Wasserman, S. 1989. Mimetic processes within an interorganizational field: An empirical test. *Administrative Science Quarterly,* 34: 454–479.

Garud, R. 1997. On the distinction between know-how, know-why, and know-what. In J. Walsh & A. S. Huff (Eds.), *Advances in Strategic Management,* 14: 81–101. Greenwich, CT: JAI Press.

Garud, R., & Kumarswamy, A. 1993. Changing competitive dynamics in network industries: An exploration of Sun Microsystems' open systems strategy. *Strategic Management Journal,* 14: 351–369.

Garud, R., & Nayyar, P. 1994. Transformative capacity: Continual restructuring by intertemporal technology transfer. *Strategic Management Journal,* 15: 365–385.

Garud, R., & Van de Ven, A. H. 1989. *Development of the cochlear implant program at 3M.* Strategic Research Center, University of Minnesota.

Gersick, C. 1991. Revolutionary change theories: A multilevel exploration of the punctuated equilibrium paradigm. *Academy of Management Review,* 16(1): 10–36.

Gersick, C. 1994. Pacing strategic change: The case of a new venture. *Academy of Management Journal,* 37(1): 9–45.

Ghemawat, P., & Ricarti Costa, J. E. 1993. The organizational tension between static and dynamic efficiency. *Strategic Management Journal,* 14: 59–73.

Gibbons, P. T., Prescott, J. E., & Ganesh, U. 1993. *Structuration theory and the strategy process.* Paper presented at the annual meeting of the Academy of Management, Atlanta.

Giddens, A. 1979. *Central problems in social theory: Action, structure and contradictions in social analysis.* London: Macmillan.

Giddens, A. 1981. *A contemporary critique of historical materialism.* Berkeley: University of California Press.

Giddens, A. 1982. On the relation of sociology to philosophy. In P. Secord (Ed.), *Explaining human behavior: Consciousness, human action and social structures:* 175–187. Beverly Hills, CA: Sage.

Giddens, A. 1984. *The constitution of society: Outline of the theory of structuration.* Berkeley: University of California Press.

Giddens, A. 1987. *Social theory and modern sociology.* Cambridge, MA: Polity.

Giddens, A. 1991. Structuration theory: Past, present and future. In C. G. A. Bryant & D. Jary (Eds.), *Giddens' theory of structuration: A critical perspective:* 201–221. London: Routledge.

Giere, R. 1988. *Explaining social science: A cognitive approach.* Chicago: University of Chicago Press.

Gilbert, M. 1989. *On social facts.* Princeton, NJ: Princeton University Press.

Ginsberg, A. 1988. Measuring and modeling changes in strategy. *Strategic Management Journal,* 9: 559–575.

Ginsberg, A. 1994. Minding the competition: From mapping to mastery. *Strategic Management Journal,* 15: 153–174.

Ginsberg, A., & Buchholtz, A. 1990. Converting to for-profit status: Corporate responsiveness to radical change. *Academy of Management Journal,* 33: 445–477.

Ginsberg, A., & Venkatraman, N. 1992. Investing in new information technology: The role of competitive postures and issue diagnosis. *Strategic Management Journal,* 13: 37–54.

Gioia, D. 1986. Conclusion: The state of the art in organizational social cognition. In H. Sims & D. Gioia. (Eds.), *The thinking organization:* 336–355. San Francisco: Jossey-Bass.

Gioia, D. A., & Chittiipeddi, K. 1991. Sensemaking and sensegiving in strategic change initiation. *Strategic Management Journal*, 12: 433–448.

Gioia, D. A., Donnellon, A., & Sims, H., Jr. 1989. Communication and cognition in appraisal: A tale of two paradigms. *Organization Studies*, 10: 503–530.

Gioia, D. A., & Mantz, C. C. 1985. Linking cognition and behavior: A script processing interpretation of vicarious learning. *Academy of Management Review*, 10: 527–539.

Gioia, D. A., & Sims, H., Jr. (Eds.). 1986a. *The thinking organization*. San Francisco: Jossey-Bass.

Gioia, D. A., & Sims, H., Jr. 1986b. Social cognition in organizations. In H. Sims & D. Gioia. (Eds.), *The thinking organization:* 1–19. San Francisco: Jossey-Bass.

Gioia, D. A., & Thomas, J. B. 1996. Identity, image and issue interpretation: Sensemaking during strategic change in academia. *Administrative Science Quarterly*, 41: 370–403.

Glasgow, J., & Papadias, D. 1992. Computational imagery. *Cognitive Science*, 16: 355–394.

Glazer, R., Stekel, J. H., & Winer, R. S. 1992. Locally rational decision-making: The distracting effect of information on managerial performance. *Management Science*, 38(2): 212–226.

Glynn, M. A., Milliken, F. J., & Lant, T. 1994. Mapping learning processes in organizations. In C. Stubbart, J. Meindl & J. Porac (Eds.), *Advances in managerial cognition and organizational information processing:* 43–83. Greenwich, CT: JAI Press.

Goffman, E. 1974. *Frame analysis: An essay on the organization of experience*. Cambridge, MA: Harvard University Press.

Golden, B. 1992. The past is past—or is it? The use of retrospective accounts as indicators of past strategy. *Academy of Management Journal*, 35: 848–857.

Gottlieb, B. H. 1981. *Social networks and social support*. Beverly Hills, CA: Sage.

Gottlieb, B. H. 1983. *Social support strategies: Guidelines for mental health practice*. Beverly Hills, CA: Sage.

Grabowski, H. G., & Vernon, J. M. 1992. Brand loyalty, entry, and price competition in pharmaceuticals after the 1984 drug act. *Journal of Law and Economics*, 35(2): 331–350.

Grabowski, H. G., Vernon, J., & Thomas, L. 1978. Estimating the effects of regulation on innovation: An internal comparative analysis of the pharmaceutical industry. *Journal of Law and Economics*, April: 133–163.

Granovetter, M. 1973. The strength of weak ties. *American Journal of Sociology*, 78: 1360–1380.

Grant, R. M. 1991a. *Contemporary strategy analysis*. Oxford: Blackwell.

Grant, R. M. 1991b. The resource-based theory of competitive advantage: Implications for strategy formulation. *California Management Review*, 33(3): 114–135.

Grant, R. M. 1996. Toward a knowledge-based theory of the firm. *Strategic Management Journal*, 17: 109–122.

Gray, B., & Ariss, S. S. 1985. Politics and strategic change across organizational life cycles. *Academy of Management Review*, 10: 707–723.

Greenwood, R., & Hinings, C. R. 1988. Organization design types, tracks and the dynamics of strategic change. *Organization Studies*, 9(3): 293–316.

Greenwood, R., & Hinings, C. R. 1993. Understanding strategic change: The contribution of archetypes. *Academy of Management Journal*, 36: 1053–1081.

Greenwood, R., & Hinings, C. R. 1996. Understanding radical organizational change: bringing together the old and new institutionalism. *Academy of Management Review*, 21: 1022–1054.

Greiner, L. E. 1972. Evolution and revolution as organizations grow. *Harvard Business Review*, 50(4): 37–46.

Greiner, L. E., & Bhambri, A. 1989. New CEO intervention and dynamics of deliberate strategic change. *Strategic Management Journal,* 10: 67–86.

Greve, H. R. 1998. Managerial cognition and the mimetic adoption of market positions: What you see is what you do. *Strategic Management Journal,* 19: 967–988.

Grinyer, P. H., Mayes, D., & McKiernan, P. 1988. *Sharpbenders: The secrets of unleashing corporate potential.* Oxford: Basil Blackwell.

Grinyer, P. H., & McKiernan, P. 1990. Generating major change in stagnating companies. *Strategic Management Journal,* 11: 131–146.

Grinyer, P. H., & Spender, J.-C. 1979. Recipes, crises and adaptation in mature businesses. *International Studies of Management and Organization,* 9: 113–133.

Grove, A. S. 1996. *Only the paranoid survive.* New York: Currency Doubleday.

Haas, P. M. 1992. Introduction: Epistemic communities and international policy coordination. *International Organization,* 46: 1–35.

Hagendorn, J. 1995. A note on international market leaders and networks of strategic technology partnering. *Strategic Management Journal,* 16: 241–250.

Hall, D. T., & Mansfield, R. 1971. Organizational and individual response to external stress. *Administrative Science Quarterly,* 20: 533–547.

Hall, R. 1984. The natural logic of management policy making: Its implications for the survival of an organization. *Management Science,* 30: 905–927.

Hambrick, D. C. 1981. Environment, strategy and power within top management teams. *Administrative Science Quarterly,* 26: 253–276.

Hambrick, D. C. 1982. Environmental scanning and organizational strategy. *Strategic Management Journal,* 3: 159–174.

Hambrick, D. C. 1984. Taxonomic approaches to studying strategy: Some conceptual and methodological issues. *Journal of Management,* 10: 27–42.

Hambrick, D. C., & D'Aveni, R. 1988. Large corporate failures as downward spirals. *Administrative Science Quarterly,* 33(1): 1–23.

Hambrick, D. C., & Mason, P. A. 1984. Upper echelons: The organization as a reflection of its top managers. *Academy of Management Review,* 9: 193–206.

Hamel, G., & Prahalad, C. K. 1994. *Competing for the future.* Boston: Harvard Business School Press.

Hamilton, V., & Warburton, D. M. 1979. *Human stress and cognition: An information processing approach.* Chichester, England: Wiley.

Hamilton, W. F., & Singh, H. 1991. Strategic alliances in technical innovation: Cooperation in biotechnology. *Journal of High Technology Management Research,* 2(2): 211–221.

Hampden-Turner, C.A. 1993. Dilemmas of strategic learning loops. In J. Hendry, G. Johnson, & J. Newton (Eds.), *Strategic thinking, leadership and the management of change:* 337–346. Chichester, UK: Wiley.

Hannan, M. T., & Freeman, J. 1977. The population ecology of organizations. *American Journal of Sociology,* 83: 929–964.

Hannan, M. T., & Freeman, J. 1984. Structural inertia and organization change. *American Sociological Review,* 49: 149–164.

Hardy, C. 1996a. Understanding power: Bringing about strategic change. *British Journal of Management,* 7: S3–S16.

Hardy C. 1996b. *The politics of collegiality: Retrenchment strategies in Canadian universities.* Montreal: McGill-Queen's University Press.

Harrigan, K. R. 1980. Strategy formulation in declining industries. *Academy of Management Review,* 5: 599–604.

Harrigan, K. R. 1985. An application of clustering for strategic group analysis. *Strategic Management Journal,* 6: 55–74.

Harrigan, K. R. 1988. Joint ventures and competitive strategy. *Strategic Management Journal*, 9: 141–158.

Harrison, R. V. 1985. The person-environment fit model and the study of job stress. In T. A. Beehr & R. S. Bhagat (Eds.), *Human stress and cognition in organizations*. New York: Wiley.

Hart, S. L. 1992. An integrative framework for strategy-making processes. *Academy of Management Review*, 17(2): 327–351.

Hartigan, J. A. 1976. *Clustering algorithms*. New York: John Wiley.

Hastie, R. 1984. Causes and effects of causal attributions. *Journal of Personality and Social Psychology*, 46: 44–56.

Hatch, M. J. 1997. *Organization theory: Modern, symbolic and postmodern perspectives*. Oxford: Oxford University Press.

Hatten, K. J., & Schendel, D. E. 1977. Heterogeneity within the industry: Firm conduct in the U.S. brewing industry. *Journal of Industrial Economics*, 26: 97–113.

Haugeland, J. (Ed.). 1997. *Mind design II*. Cambridge: MIT Press.

Haveman, H. 1992. Between a rock and a hard place: Organizational change and performance under conditions of fundamental environmental transformation. *Administrative Science Quarterly*, 37: 48–75.

Haveman, H. 1994. Follow the leader: Mimetic isomorphism and entry into new markets. *Administrative Science Quarterly*, 38: 593–627.

Hayes, R. H., & Abernathy, W. J. 1980. Managing our way to economic decline. *Harvard Business Review*, 58(4): 67–77.

Hedberg, B. 1981. How organizations learn and unlearn. In P. C. Nystrom & W. H. Starbuck (Eds.), *Handbook of organizational design*: 3–27. New York: Oxford University Press.

Hedberg, B. 1990. *Exit, voice and loyalty in knowledge-intensive firms*. Paper presented at the annual meeting of the Strategic Management Association, Stockholm.

Hedberg, B., & Jönsson, S. 1977. Strategy formulation as a discontinuous process. *International Studies of Management and Organization*, 88–109.

Hedberg, B., & Jönsson, S. 1978. Designing semi-confusing information systems for organizations in changing environments. *Accounting, Organizations and Society*, 3(1): 47–64.

Hedberg, B., Nystrom, P. C., & Starbuck, W. H. 1976. Camping on seesaws: Prescriptions for a self-designing organization. *Administrative Science Quarterly*, 21: 41–65.

Helfat, C. E. 1997. Know-how and asset complementarity and dynamic capability accumulation: The case of R&D. *Strategic Management Journal*, 18: 339–360.

Henderson, R. M., & Clark, K. B. 1990. Architectural innovation: the reconfiguration of existing product technologies and the failure of established firms. *Administrative Science Quarterly*, 35: 9–30.

Henderson, R. M. 1993. Underinvestment and incompetence as responses to radical innovation. *Rand Journal of Economics*, 24: 248–269.

Hertz, D. B., & Thomas, H. 1983. New strategic analysis: Total organizational behavior strategies; strategic risk assessment. In R. Lamb (Ed.), *Advances in strategic management*: 145–158. Greenwich, CT: JAI.

Hill, C. W. L., & Hansen, G. S. 1991. A longitudinal study of the cause and consequences of changes in diversification in the U.S. pharmaceutical industry. *Strategic Management Journal*, 12(3): 187–199.

Hill, R. C., & Levenhagen, M. 1995. Metaphors and mental models: Sensemakng and sensegiving in innovative and entrepreneurial activities. *Journal of Management*, 21: 1057–1074.

Hinings, C. R., & Greenwood, R. 1988. *The dynamics of strategic change*. Oxford, England: Basil Blackwell.

Hirsch, P. M. 1975. Organizational effectiveness and the institutional environment. *Administrative Science Quarterly*, 20: 327–344.

Hirschman, A. O. 1970. *Exit, voice, and loyalty*. Cambridge, MA: Harvard University Press.

Hodgkinson, G. P., & Johnson, G. 1994. Exploring the mental models of competitive strategists. *Journal of Management Studies*, 31: 525–549.

Hofer, C., & Schendel, D. 1978. *Strategy formulation: Analytical concepts*. St. Paul, MN: West Publishing.

Hofstede, G. 1980. Motivation, leadership, and organization: Do American theories apply abroad? *Organizational Dynamics*, 9(1): 42–63.

Holmes, T., & Rahe, R. 1967. The social readjustment rating scale. *Journal of Psychosomatic Research*, 11: 213–218.

Holsti, O. R. 1971. Crisis, stress, and decision-making. *International Social Science Journal, UNESCO*, 23: 53–67.

Horowitz, J. 1986. *Stress response syndromes* (second edition). Northvale, N.J.: J. Aronson.

Hosking, D. M., & Morley, I. E. 1991. *A social psychology of organizing: People, processes and contexts*. Hempel Hempsted, UK: Prentice Hall/Harvester Wheatsheaf.

Hoskisson, R. E., & Hitt, M. A. 1988. Strategic control systems and relative R&D investment in large, multiproduct firms. *Strategic Management Journal*, 9: 605–621.

Hoskisson, R. E., & Johnson, R. A. 1992. Corporate restructuring and strategic change: The effect on diversification strategy and R&D intensity. *Strategic Management Journal*, 13: 625–634.

House, R., Rousseau, D. M., & Thomas-Hunt, M. 1995. The meso paradigm: A framework for the integration of micro and macro organizational behavior. *Research in Organizational Behavior*, 17: 71–114.

Hrebiniak, L., & Joyce, W. 1985. Organizational adaptation: Individual choice and environmental determinism. *Administrative Science Quarterly*, 23: 119–131.

Huber, G. P. 1991. Organizational learning: The contributing processes and the literatures. *Organization Science*, 2: 88–115.

Huff, A. S. 1980a. Evocative metaphors. *Human Systems Management*, 1: 219–228.

Huff, A. S. 1980b. Organizations as political systems: Implications for diagnosis, change, and stability. In T. G. Cummings (Ed.), *Systems theory for organization development*: 163–180. London: Wiley.

Huff, A. S. 1981. Multilectic methods of inquiry. *Human Systems Management*, 2: 83–94.

Huff, A. S. 1982. Industry influences as strategy reformulation. *Strategic Management Journal*, 3: 119–131.

Huff, A. S. 1983. A rhetorical examination of strategic change. In L. R. Pondy, P. J. Frost, G. Morgan & T. C. Dandridge (Eds.), *Organizational Symbolism*: 167–183. Greenwich, CT: JAI Press.

Huff, A. S. 1985. Managerial implications of the emerging paradigm. In Y. S. Lincoln (Ed.), *Organization theory and inquiry: The paradigm revolution*. Newbury Park, CA: Sage.

Huff, A. S. 1988. Politics and argument as a means of coping with ambiguity and change. In L. R. Pondy, R. J. Boland, Jr., & H. Thomas (Eds.), *Managing ambiguity and change*: 79–90. New York: Wiley.

Huff, A. S. (Ed.). 1990. *Mapping strategic thought*. Chichester, England: Wiley.

Huff, A. S., & Chappell, D. S. 1993. *Party politics' contribution to organization learning*. Paper presented at the annual meeting of the Academy of Management, Atlanta.

Huff, A. S., Huff, J. O., & Thomas, H. 1994. The dynamics of strategic change. In H. Daems & H. Thomas (Eds.), *Strategic Groups, strategic moves and competitive strategy.* London: Pergamon Press.

Huff, A. S., Narapareddy, V., & Fletcher, K. E. 1990. Coding the association of concepts. In A. S. Huff (Ed.), *Mapping strategic thought:* 211–325. Chichester, England: Wiley.

Huff, A. S., & Schwenk, C. R. 1990. Bias and sensemaking in good times and bad. In A. S. Huff (Ed.), *Mapping strategic thought:* 89–108. Chichester, England: Wiley.

Huff, A. S., Thomas, H., & Feigenbaum, A. 1983. *Modeling strategic group formation.* Paper presented at the annual meeting of the Strategic Management Society, Paris.

Huff, J. O., & Clark, W. A. V. 1978. Cumulative stress and cumulative inertia: A behavioral model of the decision to move. *Environment & Planning,* 10: 1101–1119.

Huff, J. O., Huff, A. S., & Thomas, H. 1992. Strategic renewal and the interaction of cumulative stress and inertia. *Strategic Management Journal,* 13: 55–75.

Hunt, M. S. 1972. *Competition in the major home appliance industry, 1960–1970.* Unpublished doctoral dissertation, Harvard University, Cambridge, MA.

Hurst, D. K. 1995. *Crisis and renewal: Meeting the challenge of organization change.* Boston: Harvard Business School Press.

Inkpen, A., & Choudhury, N. 1995. The seeking of strategy where it is not: Towards a theory of strategy absence. *Strategic Management Journal,* 16: 313–323.

InVivo, 1990, 1991, 1992, 1994.

Isabella, L. A. 1990. Evolving interpretations as a change unfolds: How managers construe key organizational events. *Academy of Management Journal,* 33(1): 7–41.

Isard, W. 1960. *Methods of regional analysis.* Cambridge, MA: MIT Press.

Itami, H. 1987. *Mobilizing invisible assets.* Cambridge, MA: Harvard University Press.

Jablin, F., Putnam, L., Roberts, K., & Porter, L. (Eds.). 1987. *Handbook of organizational communication.* Newbury Park, CA: Sage.

Jackson, S., & Dutton, J. 1991. Discerning threats and opportunities. *Administrative Science Quarterly,* 33: 370–387.

James, B. G. 1994. The pharmaceutical industry in 2010. In C. Bezold & K. Knabner (Eds.), *Health care 2010: Health care delivery, therapies and the pharmaceutical industries:* 49–65. Berlin: Springer-Verlag.

James, G. E. 1995. *Strategic alliances as virtual integration: A longitudinal exploration of biotech industry-level learning.* Paper presented at the annual meeting of the Academy of Management.

James, G. E. 1996. *Strategic alliances: Elixers, poison pills or virtual integration? A longitudinal exploration of industry-level learning in biotech.* Unpublished doctoral dissertation, University of Colorado, Boulder, CO.

Janis, I. L. 1982. *Stress, attitudes, and decisions.* New York: Praeger.

Janis, I. L., & Leventhal, H. 1968. Human reaction to stress. In E. F. Borgatta & W.W. Lamberts (Eds.), *Handbook of personality theory and research.* Chicago: Rand McNally.

Janis, I. L., & Mann, L. 1977. *Decision making: A psychological analysis of conflict, choice, and commitment.* New York: Free Press.

Jemison, D. B. 1981. The importance of an integrative approach to strategic management research. *Academy of Management Review,* 6: 601–608.

Jenkins, M. 1994. Creating and comparing strategic causal maps. *Second international workshop on managerial and organizational cognition proceedings:* 26–27. Brussels, Belgium.

Johnson, G. 1987. *Strategic change and the management process.* Oxford: Basil Blackwell.

Johnson, G. 1988. Rethinking incrementalism. *Strategic Management Journal,* 9: 75–91.

Johnson, G. 1990. Managing strategic change: The role of symbolic action. *British Journal of Management,* 1: 183–200.

Johnson, G. 1992. Managing strategic change. *Long Range Planning,* 25: 28–36.

Johnson, G., & Huff, A. S. 1998. Everyday innovation/everyday strategy. In G. Hamel, C. K. Prahalad, H. Thomas & D. O'Neil (Eds.), *Strategic flexibility: Managing in a turbulent environment.* Chichester, England: Wiley.

Johnson, G., & Scholes, K. 1999. *Exploring corporate strategy.* London: Prentice-Hall Europe.

Johnson, P. 1999. *A study of cognition and behaviour in top management team interaction.* Unpublished doctoral dissertation, Cranfield University, Cranfield, England.

Johnson, P., Daniels, K., & Asch, R. 1998. Mental models of competition. In C. Eden & J.-C Spender (Eds.), *Managerial and organizational cognition.* London: Sage.

Johnson-Laird, P. N. 1983. *Mental models.* Cambridge, MA: Harvard University Press.

Johnson-Laird, P. N. 1988. *The computer and the mind.* London: Fontana Press.

Kahn, R., & Byosiere, P. 1991. Stress in organizations. In M. D. Dunnette & L. M. Hough (Eds.), *Handbook of industrial and organizational psychology:* 571–650. Palo Alto, CA: Consulting Psychologists Press.

Kanter, R., Stein, B. A., & Jick, T. D. 1992. *The challenge of organizational change: How companies experience it and leaders can guide it.* New York: Free Press.

Keats, B. W., & Hitt, M. A. 1988. A causal model of linkages among environmental dimensions, macro organizational characteristics, and performance. *Academy of Management Journal,* 31: 570–598.

Keck, S. L., & Tushman, M. L. 1993. Environmental and organizational context and executive team structure. *Academy of Management Journal,* 36: 1314–1344.

Kelley, H. H. 1972. Causal schemata and the attribution process. In E. E. Jones, D. E. Kanouse, H. H. Kelley, R. E. Nisbett, S. Valins & B. Weiner (Eds.), *Attribution: Perceiving the causes of behavior.* Morristown, NJ: General Learning Press.

Kelly, D., & Amburgey, T. L. 1991. Organizational inertia and momentum. *Academy of Management Journal,* 34: 591–612.

Kelly, G. 1955. *The psychology of personal constructs,* Volumes 1 and 2. New York: Norton.

Kiesler, S., & Sproull, L. 1982. Managerial response to changing environments: Perspectives on problem sensing from social cognition. *Administrative Science Quarterly,* 27: 548–570.

Kimberly, J. R. 1979. Issues in the creation of organizations: Initiation, innovation, and institutionalization. *Academy of Management Journal,* 22: 437–457.

Klimoski, R., & Mohammed, S. 1994. Team mental model: Construct or metaphor? *Journal of Management,* 20(2): 403–437.

Kogut, B., & Zander, U. 1996. What firms do? Coordination, identity, and learning. *Organization Science,* 7(5): 502–518.

Kosslyn, S. M. 1980. *Image and mind.* Cambridge, MA: Harvard University Press.

Kotter, J. P. 1995. Leading change: Why transformation efforts fail. *Harvard Business Review,* 73(2): 59–67.

Kotter, J. P. 1996. *Leading change.* Cambridge, MA: Harvard Business School Press.

Krackhardt, D. 1990. Assessing the political landscape: Structure, cognition, and power in organizations. *Administrative Science Quarterly,* 35(2): 342–369.

Kuhn, T. S. 1970. *The structure of scientific revolutions.* Chicago: University of Chicago Press.

Lam, A. 1997. *The social embeddedness of knowledge.* Paper presented at the annual British Academy of Management meeting, London.

Lane, P. J., & Lubatkin, M. 1998. Relative absorptive capacity and interorganizational learning. *Strategic Management Journal,* 19: 461–477.

Langer, E. J., & Abelson, R. P. 1974. Patient by any other name: Clinician group difference in labeling bias. *Journal of Consulting and Clinical Psychology*, 42(1): 4–9.

Langfield-Smith, K. 1992. Exploring the need for a shared cognitive map. *Journal of Management Studies*, 29(3): 349–368.

Lant, T. K., & Mezias, S. J. 1992. An organizational learning model of convergence and reorientation. *Organization Science*, 3: 47–71.

Lant, T. K., Milliken, F. J., & Batra, B. 1992. The role of managerial learning and interpretation of strategic persistence and reorientation: An empirical exploration. *Strategic Management Journal*, 13: 585–608.

Lasagna, L., & Wardell, W. 1975. The rate of new drug discovery. In R. Helms (Ed.), *Drug development and marketing*. Washington D.C.: The American Institute for Public Policy Research.

Laukkanen, M. 1994. Comparative cause mapping of organizational cognitions. *Organization Science*, 5: 322–343.

Lave, C. A., & March, J. G. 1975. *An introduction to models in the social sciences*. New York: Harper & Row.

Lave, J., & Wenger, E. 1991. *Situated learning*. Cambridge: Cambridge University Press.

Lazarus, R. S. 1966. *Psychological stress and the coping process*. New York: McGraw-Hill.

Lazarus, R. S., & Folkman, S. 1984. *Stress, appraisal, and coping*. New York: Springer.

Learned, E. P., Christensen, C. R., Andrews, K. R., & Guth, W. D. 1965. *Business policy*. Homewood, IL: Irwin.

Leavy, 1983. Social support and psychological disorder: A review. *Journal of Community Psychology*, 11: 3–21.

Leonard-Barton, D. 1992. Core capabilities and core rigidities: A paradox in managing new product development. *Strategic Management Journal*, 13: 111–125.

Levi, I. 1983. *The enterprise of knowledge*. Cambridge, MA: MIT Press.

Levi, L. 1998. Stress in organizations—theoretical and empirical approaches. In C. L. Cooper (Ed.), *Theories of organizational stress*. Oxford: Oxford University Press.

Levine, D. 1993. What do wages buy? *Administrative Science Quarterly*, 38: 462–83.

Levinthal, D. A., & March, J. G. 1993. The myopia of learning. *Strategic Management Journal*, 14: 95–112.

Lewin, A. Y. 1993. *The emergence of strategic leaders through competitive advantage and the potential formation of strategic groups*. Paper presented at the annual meeting of the Academy of Management, Atlanta.

Lewin, K. 1947. Frontiers in group dynamics. *Human Relations*, 1: 5–41.

Lewin, K. 1951. *Field theory in social science*. New York: Harper & Row.

Lewis, L., & Siegelman, S. 1993. The pharmaceutical industry. *Business and Health*, 11: 42–49.

Lippman, S. A., & Rumelt, R. P. 1982. Uncertain imitability: An analysis of interfirm differences in efficiency under competition. *Bell Journal of Economics*, 13(2): 418–438.

Loesel, A. 1993. Pharmaceuticals '93: Generics—finger in the dike. *Chemical Marketing Reporter*, 243(10): SR14–SR18.

Lord, R. G., & Foti, R. J. 1986. Schema theories, information processing, and organizational behavior. In H. P. Sims, Jr. & D. A. Gioia (Eds.), *The thinking organization*. San Francisco: Jossey-Bass.

Lord, R. G., Foti, R. J., & DeVader, C. L. 1984. A test of leadership categorization theory: Internal structure, information processing, and leadership perceptions. *Organizational Behavior and Human Performance*, 34: 343–378.

Lowstedt, J. 1993. Organizing frameworks in emerging organizations: A cognitive approach to the analysis of change. *Human Relations*, 46: 501–526.

Louis, M. 1980. Surprise and sensemaking: What newcomers experience in entering unfamiliar organizational settings. *Administrative Science Quarterly*, 25: 226-251.

Louis, M. R., & Sutton, R. I. 1991. "Switching cognitive gears:" From habits of mind to active thinking. *Human Relations*, 44: 55-76.

Lundberg, C. C. 1984. Strategies for organizational transitioning. In J. R. Kimberly & R. E. Quinn (Eds.), *New Futures:* 60-82. Homewood, IL: Dow Jones-Irwin.

Lurigio, A. J., & Carroll, J. S. 1985. Probation officers' schemata of offenders: Content, development, and impact on treatment decisions. *Journal of Personality and Social Psychology*, 48: 1112-1126.

Lyles, M. 1981. Formulating strategic problems: Empirical analysis and model development. *Strategic Management Journal*, 2: 61-75.

Lyles, M. A. 1990. A research agenda for strategic management in the 1990s. *Journal of Management Studies*, 27(4): 363-375.

Lyles, M. A., & Mitroff, I. I. 1980. Organization problem formulation: An empirical study. *Administrative Science Quarterly*, 25: 109-119.

Lyles, M. A., & Schwenk, C. R. 1992. Top management, strategy and organizational knowledge structures. *Journal of Management Studies*, 29: 155-174.

Lyles, M. A., & Thomas, H. 1988. Strategic problem formulation: Biases and assumptions embedded in alternative decision making models. *Journal of Management Studies*, 9: 131-147.

Lyons, P. D., Lang, J., & Guzzo, M. A. 1993. Consolidating alliances: How biotechnology and pharmaceutical companies are finding ways to prosper together. *Bio/Technology*, 11: 1529-1532.

MacMillan, I. C. 1978. *Strategy formulation: Political concepts*. St. Paul, MN: West.

MacMillan, I. C. 1983a. The politics of new venture management. *Harvard Business Review*, 61(6): 8-16.

MacMillan, I. C. 1983b. Corporate ideology and strategic delegation. *Journal of Business Strategy*, 3(3): 71-76.

MacMillan, I. C. 1987. Corporate ventures into industrial markets: Dynamics of aggressive entry. *Journal of Business Venturing*, 2: 29-39.

MacMillan, I. C. 1988. Controlling competitive dynamics by taking strategic initiative. *Academy of Management Executive*, 2(2): 111-118.

MacMillan, I. C., McCaffrey, M. L., & Van Wijk, G. 1985. Competitors' responses to easily imitated new products: Exploring commercial banking product introductions. *Strategic Management Journal*, 6: 75-86.

Mahoney, J. T. 1992. Organizational economics within the conversation of strategic management. In P. Shrivastava, J. Dutton & A. S. Huff (Eds.), *Advances in Strategic Management*, 8: 103-155. Greenwich, CT: JAI Press.

Mahoney, J. T., & Pandian, J. R. 1992. The resource-based view of the firm within the conversation of strategic management. *Strategic Management Journal*, 13: 363-380.

Makridakis, S. 1990. Sliding simulation: A new approach to time series forecasting. *Management Science*, 36(4): 505-512.

Malnight, T. W. 1995. Globalization of an ethnocentric firm: An evolutionary perspective. *Strategic Management Journal*, 16: 119-141.

Mamer, J., & McCardle, K. 1987. Uncertainty, competition, and adoption of new technology. *Management Science*, 33: 161-177.

March, J. G. 1991. Exploration and exploitation in organizational learning. *Organization Science*, 2: 71-87.

March, J. G., & Olsen, J. P. 1976. *Ambiguity and choice in organizations*. Bergen, Norway: Universitetsforlaget.

March, J. G., & Sevon, G. 1984. Gossip, information and decision making. In L. S. Sproull & P. D. Larkey (Eds.), *Advances in information processing in organizations*, 1: 95–107. Greenwich, CT: JAI Press.

March, J. G., & Simon, H. 1958. *Organizations.* New York: Wiley.

March, J. G., Sproull, L. W., & Tamuz, M. 1991. Learning from samples of one or fewer. *Organization Science*, 2: 1–13.

Markóczy, L., & Goldberg, J. 1995. A method for eliciting and comparing causal maps. *Journal of Management*, 21: 305–333.

Markóczy, L., & Goldberg, J. 1998. Woman and taxis and dangerous judgments: Content sensitive use of base-rate information. *Managerial & Decision Economics*, 19: 481–493.

Marshall, S. P., Van de Ven, A. H., & Dooley, K. 1999. *Theory and methods for the study of organizational change and development.* New York: Oxford University Press.

Martin, J., & Siehl, C. 1983. Organizational culture and counterculture: An uneasy symbiosis. *Organizational Dynamics*, 12(2): 52–64.

Maruyama, M. 1992. Changing dimensions in international business. *Academy of Management Executive*, 6(3): 88–96.

Maruyama, M. 1994. *Mindscapes in management.* Hants, England: Dartmouth.

Maybury-Lewis, D., & Almajor, J. (Eds.). 1989. *The attraction of opposites: Thought and society in the dualistic mode.* Ann Arbor: University of Michigan Press.

McArthur, L. S. 1981. What grabs you? The role of attention in impression formation and causal attribution. In E. T. Higgins, C. P. Herman, & M. P. Zanna (Eds.), *Social cognition: The Ontario symposium*, 1: 201–246. Hillsdale, NJ: Erlbaum.

McCaskey, M. B. 1982. *The executive challenge: Managing change and ambiguity.* Marshfield, MA: Pitman.

McCutcheon, W. W. 1993. Strategy changes as a response to alterations in tax policy. *Journal of Management*, 19(3): 575–593.

McFadden, D. 1978. Modelling the choice of residential location. In A. Darlqvist et al. (Eds.), *Spatial interaction theory and planning models:* 75–96. Amsterdam: North-Holland.

McGee, J., & Thomas, H. 1986. Strategic groups: Theory, research and taxonomy. *Strategic Management Journal*, 7: 141–161.

McGrath, J. 1982. Dilemmatics: The study of research choices and dilemmas. In J. E. McGrath, J. Martin & R. A. Kilka (Eds.), *Judgment calls in research.* Beverly Hills, CA: Sage.

McGrath, R. G., MacMillan, I. C., & Tushman, M. L. 1992. The role of executive team actions in shaping dominant designs: Towards the strategic shaping of technological progress. *Strategic Management Journal*, 13: 137–161.

McKelvey, W. 1982. *Organizational systematics: Taxomony, evolution and classification.* Berkeley: University of California Press.

McPhee, R. D., & Thompkins, P. K. (Eds.). 1985. *Organizational communication: Traditional themes and new directions.* Beverly Hills, CA: Sage.

Melin, L. 1992. Internationalization as a strategy process. *Strategic Management Journal*, 13: 99–118.

Meyer, A. D. 1982a. Adapting to environmental jolts. *Administrative Science Quarterly*, 27: 515–538.

Meyer, A. D. 1982b. How ideologies supplant formal structures and shape responses to environment. *Journal of Management Studies*, 19: 45–61.

Meyer, A. D., Tsui, A. S., & Hinings, C. R. 1993. Configurational approaches to organizational analysis. *Academy of Management Journal*, 36(6): 1175–1195.

Meyer, J., & Rowan, B. 1977. Institutionalized organizations: Formal structure as myth and ceremony. *American Journal of Sociology*, 83: 240–263.

Mezias, S. J., & Lant, T. K. 1994. Mimetic learning and the evolution of organizational populations. In J. Baum & J. Singh (Eds.) *Evolutionary dynamics in organizations*, 179–198. New York: Oxford University Press.

Mikhail, 1985. Stress: A psycholphysiological conception. In A. Monat & R. S. Lazarus (Eds.) *Stress and coping: An anthology* (second edition). New York: Columbia University Press.

Milburn, T. W., Schuler, R. S., & Watman, K. H. 1983. Organizational crisis. *Human Relations*, 36: 1141–1179.

Miles, R. E., & Snow, C. C. 1978. *Organizational strategy, structure, and process*. New York: McGraw-Hill.

Miles, R. E., Snow, C. C., Mathew, J. A., Miles, G., & Coleman, H. J., Jr. 1997. Organizing in the knowledge age: Anticipating the cellular form. *Academy of Management Executive*, 11(4): 7–20.

Miller, D. 1996. Configurations revisited. *Strategic Management Journal*, 17(7): 505–512.

Miller, D., & Friesen, P. H. 1980. Momentum and revolution in organizational adaptation. *Academy of Management Journal*, 22: 591–614.

Miller, D., & Friesen, P. H. 1984. *Organizations: A quantum view*. Englewood Cliffs, NJ: Prentice-Hall.

Miller, D., & Shamsie, J. 1996. The resource-based view of the firm in two environments: The Hollywood film studios from 1936 to 1965. *Academy of Management Journal*, 39(3): 519–543.

Milliken, F. 1987. Three types of uncertainty about the environment: State, effect, and response uncertainty. *Academy of Management Review*, 12: 133–143.

Milliken, F. 1990. Perceiving and interpreting environmental change. *Academy of Management Journal*, 33: 42–63.

Minsky, M. 1975. A framework for representing knowledge. In P. H. Winston (Ed.), *The psychology of computer vision*. New York: McGraw-Hill.

Mintzberg, H. 1973a. *The structuring of organizations: A synthesis of research*. Englewood Cliffs, NJ: Prentice-Hall.

Mintzberg, H. 1973b. *The nature of managerial work*. New York: Harper & Row.

Mintzberg, H. 1978. Patterns of strategy formation. *Management Science*, 24: 934–948.

Mintzberg, H. 1983. *Power in and around organizations*. Englewood Cliffs, NJ: Prentice-Hall.

Mintzberg, H. 1990. The design school: Reconsidering the basic premises of strategic management. *Strategic Management Journal*, 11: 171–195.

Mintzberg, H. 1991. Strategy formulation: Schools of thought. In J. W. Fredrickson (Ed.), *Perspectives on strategic management*. New York: Harper & Row.

Mintzberg, H. 1994. *The rise and fall of strategic planning: Reconceiving roles for planning, plans, planners*. New York: Free Press.

Mintzberg, H., Ahlstrand, B., & Lampel, J. 1998. *Strategy safari*. New York: Free Press.

Mintzberg, H., Raisinghani, D., & Théorêt, A. 1976. The structure of unstructured decision processes. *Administrative Science Quarterly*, 21: 246–275.

Mintzberg, H., & Waters, J. A. 1982. Tracking strategy in an entrepreneurial firm. *Academy of Management Journal*, 25: 465–499.

Mintzberg, H., & Waters, J. A. 1984. Researching the formation of strategies: The history of Canadian Lady 1939–1976. In R. B. Lamb (Ed.), *Competitive strategic management*: 62–93. Englewod Cliffs, NJ: Prentice Hall.

Mintzberg H., & Waters, J. A. 1985. Of strategies, deliberate and emergent. *Strategic Management Journal*, 6: 257–272.

Mintzberg, H., & Waters, J. 1990. Does decision get in the way? *Organization Science*, 1: 1-6.

Mintzberg, H., Waters, J., Pettigrew, A. M., & Butler, R. 1990. Studying deciding: An exchange of views between Mintzberg and Waters, Pettigrew, and Butler. *Organization Studies*, 11(1): 1-16.

Mintzberg, H., & Westley, F. 1992. Cycles of organizational change. *Strategic Management Journal*, 13: 39-59.

Mitroff, I. I. 1983. Archetypal social systems analysis: On the deeper structure of human systems. *Academy of Management Review*, 8(3): 387-397.

Monat, A., & Lazarus, R. S. 1977. *Stress and coping: An anthology.* New York: Columbia University Press.

Monat, A., & Lazarus, R. S. 1985. *Stress and coping: An anthology* (2nd ed.) New York: Columbia University Press.

Morgan, G., Frost, P. J., & Pondy, L. R. 1983. Organizational symbolism. In L. R. Pondy, P. J. Frost, G. Morgan & T. C. Dandridge (Eds.), *Organizational symbolism:* 3-35. Greenwich, CT: JAI Press.

Morris, W. (Ed.). 1985. *American heritage dictionary.* Boston: Houghton Mifflin.

Murtha, T. P., Lenway, S. A., & Bagozzi, R. P. 1998. Global mind-sets and cognitive shift in a complex multinational corporation. *Strategic Management Journal*, 19: 97-114.

Myllys, K. 1994. Cognitive approach to managerial work: An empirical study of Finnish bank managers in crisis situation. *Second international workshop on managerial and organizational cognition proceedings:* 26-27. Brussels, Belgium.

Narayanan, V. K., & Fahey, L. 1982. The politics of strategy reformulation. *Academy of Management Review*, 7: 25-34.

Narayanan, V. K., & Fahey, L. 1990. Evolution of revealed causal maps during decline: A case study of Admiral. In A. S. Huff (Ed.), *Mapping strategic thought:* 109-133. Chichester, England: Wiley.

Nath, D., & Sudharsan. D. 1994. Measuring strategic coherence through patterns of strategic choices. *Strategic Management Journal*, 15: 43-61.

Nayyar, P. R., & Kazanjian, R. K. 1993. Organizing to attain potential benefits from information asymmetries and economics of scope in related diversified firms. *Academy of Management Review*, 18: 735-759.

Neisser, U. 1967. *Cognitive psychology.* Englewood Cliffs, NJ: Prentice-Hall.

Neisser, U. 1983. Toward a skillful pyschology. In D. R. Rogers & J. A. Slobada (Eds.), *The acquisition of symbolic skills.* New York: Plenum.

Nelson, R. R. 1991. Why do firms differ, and how does it matter? *Strategic Management Journal*, 12: 61-74.

Nelson, R. R., & Winter, S. G. 1982. *An evolutionary theory of economic change.* Cambridge: Cambridge University Press.

Nichols-Nixon, C. L. 1993. *Absorptive capacity and technology sourcing: Implications for responsiveness of established firms.* Unpublished doctoral dissertation, Purdue University, West Lafayette, IN.

Nichols-Nixon, C. L. 1997. Commentary: The importance of know-where and know-when. In James Walsh & Anne Huff (Eds.), *Advances in strategic management*, 14: 103-109. Greenwich, CT: JAI Press.

Nisbett, R. E., & Ross, L. 1980. *Human inference.* Englewood Cliffs, NJ: Prentice-Hall.

Nonaka, I., & Takeuchi, H. 1995. *The knowledge-creating company: How Japanese companies create the dynamics of innovation.* New York: Oxford University Press.

Nooteboom, B. 1996. Towards a cognitive theory of the firm. Working paper, School of Management and Organization, Groningen University, The Netherlands.

Northcraft, G. B., Neale, M. A., & Huber, V. L. 1988. The effects of cognitive bias and social influence on human resource management decisions. *Research in Personnel and Human Resources Management,* 6: 157–189.

Nutt, P. 1984. Types of organizational decision processes. *Administrative Science Quarterly,* 29: 414–450.

Nystrom, P. C., & Starbuck, W. H. 1984. To avoid organizational crises, unlearn. *Organizational Dynamics,* 12(4): 53–65.

Office of Technology Assessment. 1984. *Commercial biotechnology: An international analysis.* Washington, DC: U.S. Congress, Government Printing Office.

Oliva, T., Day, D., & DeSarbo, W. 1987. Selecting competitive tactics: Try a strategy map. *Sloan Management Review,* 28: 5–17.

Oliver, C. 1990. Determinants of interorganizational relationships: Integration and future directions. *Academy of Management Review,* 15: 241–265.

Oliver, C. 1997. Sustainable competitive advantage: Combining institutional and resource-based views. *Strategic Management Journal,* 18: 697–713.

Olivia, T., Day, D., & MacMillan, I. C. 1988. A generic model of competitive dynamics. *Academy of Management Review,* 13: 374–389.

Omta, S. W. F., Bouter, L. M., & Engelen, J. M. L. 1994. Managing industrial pharmaceutical R&D: A comparative study of management control and innovative effectiveness in European and Anglo-American companies. *R&D Management,* 24(4): 303–315.

O'Neill, H. M., Pouder, R. W., & Buchholtz, A. K. 1998. Patterns of diffusion of strategies across organizations: Insights from the innovation diffusion literature. *Academy of Management Review,* 23(1): 98–114.

Orlikowski, W. J. 1992. The duality of technology: Rethinking the concept of technology in organizations. *Organization Science,* 3: 398–427.

Oster, S. 1982. Intraindustry structure and the ease of strategic change. *Review of Economics and Statistics,* 64: 376–383.

Oxford English dictionary. 1971. Oxford: Oxford University Press.

Papadakis, V. M., Lioukas, S., & Chambers, D. 1998. Strategic decision-making processes: The role of management and context. *Strategic Management Journal,* 19: 115–147.

Park, O. S., Sims, H. P., Jr., & Motowidlo, S. J. 1996. Affect in organizations: How feelings and emotions influence managerial judgment. In H. P. Sims, Jr. & D. A. Gioia (Eds.), *The thinking organization.* San Francisco: Jossey-Bass.

Pearlin, L. I., Meneghan, E. G., Lieberman, M. A., & Mullan, J. T. 1981. *The stress process.* Washington, DC: American Sociological Association.

Pearlin, L. I., & Schooler, C. 1978. Structure of coping. *Journal of Health and Social Behavior,* 19(1): 2–21.

Penrose, E. T. 1959. *The theory of the growth of the firm.* New York: Wiley.

Pentland, B. T., & Rueter, H. H. 1994. Organization routines as grammars of action. *Administrative Science Quarterly,* 39: 484–510.

Perls, F., Hefferline, R. F., & Goodman, P. 1951. *Gestalt therapy: Excitement and growth in the human personality.* New York: Dell.

Peteraf, M. A. 1993. The cornerstone of competitive advantage: A resource-based view. *Strategic Management Journal,* 14(3): 179–191.

Peteraf, M. A. & Shanley, M. 1994. *Getting to know you: A theory of strategic group identity.*

Discussion Paper #94-67 presented at the Social Construction of Industries and Markets Conference, University of Illinois, Champaign, IL.

Pettigrew, A. M. 1973. *The politics of organizational decision-making.* London: Tavistock.

Pettigrew, A. 1979. On studying organizational culture. *Administrative Science Quarterly,* 24: 570–581.

Pettigrew, A. M. 1987. Context and action in the transformation of the firm. *Journal of Management Studies,* 24: 649–670.

Pettigrew, A. M. 1990. Longitudinal field research on change: Theory and practice. *Organization Science,* 1: 267–292.

Pettigrew, A. M. 1991. *Managing change for competitive success.* Oxford: Oxford University Press.

Pettigrew, A. M. 1992. The character and significance of strategy process research. *Strategic Management Journal,* 13: 5–16.

Pettigrew, A., Ferlie, E., & McKee, L. 1992. *Shaping strategic change.* London: Sage.

Pettigrew, A. M., & Whipp, R. 1991. *Managing change for competitive success.* Oxford: Blackwell.

Pfeffer, J. 1981a. *Power in organizations.* Marshfield, MA: Pitman.

Pfeffer, J. 1981b. Management as symbolic action: The creation and maintenance of organization paradigms. In L. L. Cummings & B. M. Staw (Eds.), *Research in organization behavior:* 1–15. Greenwich, CT: JAI Press.

Pfeffer, J. 1992. *Managing with power.* Boston: Harvard Business School Press.

Pfeffer, J., & Salancik, G. R. 1978. *The external control of organizations: A resource dependence perspective.* New York: Harper & Row.

Phillips, M. E. 1990. *Industry as a cultural grouping.* Unpublished doctoral dissertation, University of California, Los Angeles.

Pisano, G. P. 1990. The R&D boundaries of the firm: An empirical anaylsis. *Administrative Science Quarterly,* 35(1): 153–176.

Pitt, M., & Johnson, G. 1987. Managing strategic change. In G. Johnson (Ed.), *Business strategy and retailing.* Chichester, England: Wiley.

PMA (Pharmaceutical Manufacturers' Association). 1995a. Important new medicines were approved in 1995 as the cost of innovation continues to increase. *PharmFacts,* February 1995B (*http://www.phrma.org/facts/phfacts/2_96b.html*).

PMA (Pharmaceutical Manufacturers' Association). 1995b. World leader. *PharmFacts,* March 1995B (*http://www.phrma.org/facts/phfacts/3_95b.html*).

PMA (Pharmaceutical Manufacturers' Association). 1995c. The time Americans must wait for new drugs has nearly doubled! *PharmFacts,* August 1995B (*http://www.phrma.org/facts/phfacts/8_95b.html*).

PMA (Pharmaceutical Manufacturers' Association). 1995d. R&D as a percent of U.S. sales, ethical pharmaceuticals, PhRMA Member Companies, 1970–1995. *PharmFacts* (*http://www.phrma.org/facts/data/R&Dsales.html*).

PMA (Pharmaceutical Manufacturers' Association). 1996a. Drug companies once again achieve a record in R&D spending—$15.8 billion. *PharmFacts,* January 1996B (*http://www.phrma.org/facts/phfacts/1_96b.html*).

PMA (Pharmaceutical Manufacturers' Association). 1996b. 1984 Hatch-Waxman law helps generic drug makers at the expense of brand name manufacturers. *PharmFacts,* April 1996A (*http://www.phrma.org/facts/phfacts/4_96a.html*).

PMA (Pharmaceutical Manufacturers' Association). 1996c. Executive summary. *Industry profile 1996* (http://www/phrma.org/fact/industry/exec.html).

PMA (Pharmaceutical Manufacturers' Association). 1996d. Lengthy U.S. drug development times have convinced U.S. to firms to move testing overseas. *PharmFacts,* March 1996A (*http://www.phrma.org/facts/phfacts/3_96a.html*).

PMA (Pharmaceutical Manufacturers' Association). 1996e. Mean approval times for new drugs, 1985–1995. *PharmFacts* (*http://www.phrma.org/facts/industry/figures/3–2.html*).

PMA (Pharmaceutical Manufacturers' Association). 1996f. The changing pharmaceutical marketplace. *Industry Profile 1996* (http://www.phrma.org/facts/industry/chap5.html).

PMA (Pharmaceutical Manufacturers' Association). 1996g. The global perspective. *Industry Profile 1996* (http://www.phrma.org/facts/industry/chap5.html).

PMA (Pharmaceutical Manufacturers' Association). 1996h. Intellectual property protection and trade. *Industry Profile 1996* (http://www.phrma.org/facts/industry/chap8.html).

PMA (Pharmaceutical Manufacturers' Association). 1996i. Prescription drugs in the healthcare system. *Industry Profile 1996* (*http://www.phrma.org/facts/industry/chap4.html*).

Polanyi, M. 1966. *The tacit dimension.* Garden City, NY: Doubleday.

Pondy, L. R. 1978. Leadership is a language game. In M. McCall & M. Lombardo (Eds.), *Leadership: Where else can we go?* Durham, NC: Duke University Press.

Pondy., L. R., Frost, P. J., Morgan, G., & Dandridge, T. C. (Eds.). 1983. *Organizational symbolism.* Greenwich, CT: JAI Press.

Pondy, L. R., & Huff, A. S. 1985. Achieving routine in organizational change. *Journal of Management,* 11(2): 103–116.

Pondy, L. R., & Huff, A. S. 1988. Budget cutting in Riverside: Emergent policy reframing as a process of conflict minimization. In L. R. Pondy, R. J. Boland, Jr. & H. Thomas (Eds.), *Managing ambiguity and change:* 177–200. New York: Wiley.

Pondy, L. R., & Mitroff, I. I. 1979. Beyond open systems models of organizations. In B. M. Staw (Ed.), *Research in organizational behavior:* 3–39. Greenwich, CT: JAI Press.

Poole, M. S., Gioia, D. A., & Gray, B. 1989. Influence modes, schema change, and organizational transformation. *Journal of Applied Behavioral Science,* 25: 271–289.

Poole, M. S.,Van De Ven, A. H., Dooley, K. J., & Holmes, M. 1999. *Studying processes of organizational change and development: Theory and methods.* New York: Oxford University Press.

Porac, J. F., & Thomas, H. 1990. Taxonomic mental models in competitor definition. *Academy of Management Review,* 15(2): 224–240.

Porac, J. F., Thomas, H., & Baden-Fuller, C. 1989. Competitive groups as cognitive communities: The case of Scottish knitwear manufacturers. *Journal of Management Studies,* 26: 397–416.

Porac, J. F., Thomas, H., & Emme, B. 1987. Knowing the competition: The mental models of retailing strategists. In G. Johnson (Ed.), *Business strategy and retailing.* New York: Wiley.

Porter, M. E. 1980. *Competitive strategy.* New York: Free Press.

Porter, M. E. 1990. *The competitive advantage of nations.* New York: Free Press.

Porter, M. E. 1991. Towards a dynamic theory of strategy. *Strategic Management Journal,* 12: 95–117.

Porter, M. E. 1994. Toward a dynamic theory of strategy. In R. P. Rumelt, D. E. Schendel, & D. J. Teece (Eds.), *Fundamental issues in strategy,* 423–461. Boston: Harvard Business School Press.

Porter, M. E. 1996. What is strategy? *Harvard Business Review,* 74(6): 61–78.

Powell, W. W., & Brantley, P. 1992. Competitive cooperation in biotechnology: Learning through networks? In N. Nohria & R. G. Eccles (Eds.), *Networks and organizations: Structure, form, and action:* 366–394. Boston: Harvard Business School Press.

Powell, W. W., & DiMaggio, P. J. (Eds.). 1991. *The new institutionalism in organizational analysis.* Chicago: University of Chicago Press.

Prahalad, C. K. 1996. A resource-based theory of the firm: Knowledge versus opportunism. *Organization Science,* 7(5): 477–501.

Prahalad, C. K., & Bettis, R. A. 1986. The dominant logic: A new linkage between diversity and performance. *Strategic Management Journal,* 7: 485–502.

Prahalad, C. K., & Hamel, G. 1994. Strategy as a field of study: Why search for a new paradigm? *Strategic Management Journal,* 15: 5–16.

Prasad, P. 1993. Symbolic processes in the implementation of technological change: A symbolic interactionist study of work computerization. *Academy of Management Journal,* 36: 1400–1429.

Praveen, N. R., & Kazanjian, R. K. 1993. Organizing to attain potential benefits from information asymmetries and economies of scope in related diversified firms. *Academy of Management Review,* 18(4): 735–759.

Pred, A. 1985. The social becomes the spatial: Enclosures, social change, and the becoming of places in the Swedish province of Skåne. In D. Gregory & J. Urry (Eds.), *Social relations and spatial structures.* London: Macmillan.

Press, S. J. 1972. *Applied multivariate analysis.* New York: Holt, Rinehart & Winston.

Quinn, J. B. 1978. Strategic change: "Logical incrementalism." *Sloan Management Review,* 20(1): 7–21.

Quinn, J. B. 1980. *Strategies of change: Logical incrementalism.* Homewood, IL: Irwin.

Rajagopalan, N., & Spreitzer, G. M. 1996. Toward a theory of strategic change: A multilens perspective and integrative framework. *Academy of Management Review,* 22: 48–79.

Ransom, S., Hinings, G., & Greenwood, R. 1980. The structuring of organizational structures. *Administrative Science Quarterly,* 25: 1–17.

Redwood, H. 1989. The future for pharmaceuticals in a health care crisis. *Long Range Planning,* 22(1): 18–27.

Reger, R. K. 1988. *Competitive positioning in the Chicago banking market: Mapping the mind of the strategist.* Unpublished doctoral dissertation, University of Illinois, Urbana-Champaign.

Reger, R. K. 1990. Managerial though structures and competitive positioning. In A. S. Huff (Ed.) *Mapping Strategic Thought.* Chichester, U.K.: Wiley.

Reger, R. K., Gustafson, L. T., DeMarie, S. M., & Mullane, J. V. 1994. Reframing the organization: Why implementing total quality is easier said than done. *Academy of Management Review,* 13(3): 565–584.

Reger, R. K., & Huff, A. S. 1993. Strategic groups: A cognitive perspective. *Strategic Management Journal,* 14: 103–124.

Reger, R. K., & Palmer, T. B. 1996. Managerial categorization of competitors: Using old maps to navigate new environments. *Organization Science,* 7(1): 22–39.

Reich, M. R. 1990. Why the Japanese don't export more pharmaceuticals: Health policy as industrial policy. *California Management Review,* 32(2): 124–150.

Rich, P. 1992. The organizational taxonomy: Definition and design. *Academy of Management Review,* 17: 758–781.

Ring, P. S., & Rands, G. P. 1989. Sensemaking, understanding, and committing: Emergent interpersonal transaction processes in the evolution of 3M's microgravity research program. In A. J. Van de Ven, H. L. Angle & M. S. Poole (Eds.), *Research on the management of innovation: The Minnesota studies*. New York: Ballinger.

Robinson, W. 1957. The statistical measure of agreement. *American Sociological Review*, 22: 17–25.

Rogers, E. M. 1962. *Diffusion of innovations*. New York: Free Press.

Rogers, E. M. 1995. *Diffusion of innovations* (4th ed.). New York: Free Press.

Romanelli, E., & Tushman, M. L. 1988. Executive leadership and organizational outcomes: An evolutionary perspective. In D. C. Hambrick (Ed.), *The executive effect: concepts and methods for studying top managers*: 129–146. Greenwich, CT: JAI Press.

Romanelli, E., & Tushman, M. L. 1994. Organizational transformation as punctuated equilibrium: An empirical test. *Academy of Management Journal*, 37: 1141–1166.

Ross, L., Lepper, M., & Hubbard, M. 1975. Perseverance in self-perception and social perception. *Journal of Personality and Social Psychology*, 32: 880–892.

Rothbart, M., Evans, M., & Fulero, S. 1979. Recall for confirming events: Memory processes and the maintenance of social stereotypes. *Journal of Experimental Social Psychology*, 15(4): 343–355.

Ruef, M. 1997. Assessing organizational fitness on a dynamic landscape: An empirical test of the relative inertia thesis. *Strategic Management Journal*, 18: 837–853.

Rumelhart, D. E. 1977. *Introduction to human information processing*. New York: Wiley.

Rumelhart, D. E. 1980. Schemata: The building blocks of cognition. In R. J. Spiro, B. C. Bruce & W. F. Brewer (Eds.), *Theoretical issues in reading comprehension*. Hillsdale, NJ: Erlbaum.

Rumelhart, D. E. 1989. The architecture of mind: A connectionist approach. In M. I. Posner (Ed.), *Foundation of cognitive science*. Cambridge, MA: MIT Press.

Rumelhart, D. E., & Norman, D. E. 1975. *Explorations in cognition*. San Francisco: W. H. Freeman.

Rumelhart, D. E., & Norman D. E. 1978. Accretion, tuning, and restructuring: Three modes of learning. In J. W. Cotton & R. L. Klatzky (Eds.), *Semantic factors in cognition*, 37–53. Hillsdale, NJ: Erlbaum.

Rumelt, R. P. 1984. Towards a strategic theory of the firm. In R. Lamb (Ed.), *Competitive strategic management*. Englewood Cliffs, NJ: Prentice-Hall.

Rumelt, R. P., Schendel, D. E., & Teece, D. J. 1994. Fundamental issues in strategy. In R. P. Rumelt, D. E. Schendel & D. J. Teece (Eds.), *Fundamental issues in strategy*: 9–54. Boston: Harvard Business School Press.

Russo, M. V. 1992. Power plays: Regulation, diversification and backward integration in the electric utility industry. *Strategic Management Journal*, 13(1): 13–27.

Sackman, S. A. 1991. *Cultural knowledge in organizations: Exploring the collective mind*. Newbury Park, CA: Sage.

Salancik, G. R., & Meindl, J. 1984. Corporate attributions as strategic illusions of management control. *Administrative Science Quarterly*, 29: 583–600.

Saloner, G. 1991. Modeling, game theory, and strategic modeling. *Strategic Management Journal*, 12 : 119–136.

Sanchez, R. 1993. Strategic flexibility, firm organization, and managerial work in dynamic markets: A strategic-options perspective. In P. Shrivastava, J. Dutton & A. S. Huff (Eds.), *Advances in Strategic Management*, 9: 251–291. Greenwich, CT: JAI Press.

Sanchez, R. 1994. Higher-order organization and commitment in strategic options theory. In P. Shrivastava, J. Dutton & A. Huff, (Eds.), *Advances in Strategic Management,* 10: 551–559.

Sanford, A. J. 1983. *Models, mind, and man.* Pressang: Glasgow University.

Sanford, A. J., & Garrod, S. C. 1981. *Understanding written language: Explorations of comprehension beyond the sentence.* Chichester: Wiley.

Sapienza, A. M. 1989. R&D collaboration as a global competitive tactic: Biotechnology and the ethical pharmaceutical industry. *R&D Management,* 19(4): 285–295.

SAS Institute, Inc. (1990). *SAS users guide: Basics, version 6* (4th ed.). Chapter 6, 53–101.

Sastry, M. A. 1997. Problems and paradoxes in a model of punctuated organizational change. *Administrative Science Quarterly,* 42: 237–275.

Schank, R. C. 1984. *The cognitive computer: On language, learning, and artificial intelligence.* Reading, MA: Addison-Wesley.

Schank, R. C., & Abelson, R. P. 1977. *Script, plans, goals and understanding.* Hillsdale, NJ: Erlbaum.

Scheid-Cook, T. 1992. Organizational enactments and conformity to environmental prescriptions. *Human Relations,* 45:537–554.

Schein, E. H. 1985. *Organizational culture and leadership.* San Francisco: Jossey-Bass.

Schelling, T. C. 1978. *Micromotives and macrobehavior.* New York: Norton.

Schendel, D. 1995. Editor's introduction to the 1995 summer special issue: Technological transformation and the new competitive landscape. *Strategic Management Journal,* 16: 1–6.

Schendel, D. E., Patton, G., & Riggs, J. 1976. Corporate turnaround strategies. *Journal of General Management,* 3: 3–11.

Schmalensee, R. 1978. Entry deterrence in the ready-to-eat breakfast cereal industry. *Bell Journal of Economics,* 9: 305–327.

Schneider, S., & Angelmar, R. 1993. Cognition in organizational analysis: Who's minding the store? *Organizational Studies,* 14: 347–374.

Schoemaker, P. J. H. 1993. Strategic decisions in organizations: Rational and behavioural views. *Journal of Management Studies,* 30(1): 107–129.

Schön, D. A. 1967. *Invention and the evolution of ideas.* London: Tavistock.

Schön, D. A. 1983. Organizational learning. In G. Morgan (Ed.), *Beyond method: Strategies for social research.* Beverly Hills, CA: Sage.

Schwenk, C. R. 1984. Cognitive simplification processes in strategic decision-making. *Strategic Management Journal,* 5: 111–128.

Schwenk, C. R. 1988. The cognitive perspective on strategic decision making. *Journal of Management Studies,* 25(1): 41–55.

Schwenk, C. R. 1989. Linking cognitive, organizational and political factors in explaining change. *Journal of Management Studies,* 26(2): 177–187.

Schwenk, C. R., & Tang, M. 1989. Economic and psychological explanations for strategic persistence. *Omega—International Journal of Management Science,* 17: 559–570.

Scott, W. R. 1995. *Institutions and organizations.* Thousand Oaks, CA: Sage.

Scott, W. R., & Meyer, J. W. 1983. The organization of societal sectors. In J. W. Meyer & W. R. Scott (Eds.), *Organizational environments: Ritual and rationality:* 129–153. Beverly Hills, CA: Sage.

Seigelman, S. 1989. Pharmaceuticals: A fast growth track. *Chemical Week,* 145(5): 32–42.

Seigelman, S. 1992. An "expensive" drug may be the most cost effective. *Business and Health,* January: 8–14.

Selye, H. 1956. *The stress of life.* New York: McGraw-Hill.

Selye, H. 1964. *From dream to discovery: On being a scientist.* New York: McGraw-Hill.

Selye, H. 1974. *Life without distress.* Philadelphia: Lippincott.

Selye, H. 1976. *Stress in health and disease.* Boston: Butterworths.

Seltzer, L., & Graven, M. 1999. Software returns to its source. *PC Magazine,* March 23, 18(6): 166–169.

Selznick, P. 1957. *Leadership in administration.* Evanston, IL: Row, Peterson & Co.

Senge, P. 1990. *The fifth discipline: The art and practice of the learning organization.* New York: Doubleday

Senge, P. 1992a. Building learning organizations. *Journal of Quality and Participation,* 15(2): 30–38.

Senge, P. 1992b. Mental models. *Planning Review,* 20(2): 4–10.

Senior, B. 1997. *Organisational Change.* London: Pitman.

Seth, A., & Thomas, H. 1994. Theories of the firm: Implications for strategy research. *Journal of Management Studies,* 31(2): 165–191.

Shapiro, E. C. 1991. *How corporate truths become competitive traps.* New York: Wiley.

Sharma, A. 1993. *Diversifying entry.* Unpublished doctoral dissertation, University of North Carolina at Chapel Hill.

Sheffet, M. J., & Kopp, S. W. 1990. Advertising prescription drugs to the public: Headache or relief? *Journal of Public Policy and Marketing,* 9: 42–61.

Sheldon, A. 1980. Organizational paradigms. *Organization Dynamics,* 8: 61–71.

Sherif, M., & Sherif, C. W. 1969. *Social psychology.* New York: Harper & Row.

Shrivastava, P., & Lin, G. 1984. *Alternative approaches to strategic analysis of environments.* Paper presented at the annual meeting of the Strategic Management Society, Philadelphia.

Shrivastava, P., & Mitroff, I. I. 1983. Frames of reference managers use: A study in the applied sociology of knowledge. In R. Lamb (Ed.), *Advances in strategic management.* Greenwich, CT: JAI Press.

Shrivastava, P., & Schneider, S. 1984. Organizational frames of reference. *Human Relations,* 37: 795–809.

Siehl, C., & Martin, J. 1984. The role of symbolic management: how can managers effectively transmit organizational culture? In J. D. Hunt, D. Hosking, C. Schriesheim, & R. Steward (Eds.), *Leaders and managers: International perspectives on managerial behavior and leadership.* New York: Pergamon: 227–39.

Silver, W. S., & Mitchell, T. R. 1990. The status quo tendency in decision making, *Organization Dynamics,* 18(4): 34–46.

Simon, H. A. [1947] 1976. *Administrative behavior.* 3rd ed. New York: Free Press.

Simon, H. A. 1957. *Models of man.* New York: Wiley.

Simon, H. A. 1987. Making management decisions: The role of intuition and emotion. *Academy of Management Executive,* 1: 57–64.

Sims, D., & Eden, C. 1984. Future research: Working with management teams. *Long Range Planning,* 17: 51–59.

Sims, H., Jr., & Gioia, D. (Eds.) 1986. *The thinking organization.* San Francisco: Jossey-Bass.

Slatter, S. 1984. *Corporate recovery.* Harmondsworth, England: Penguin.

Smircich, L., & Stubbart, C. 1985. Strategic management in an enacted world. *Academy of Management Review,* 10: 724–736.

Smith, A. 1993. *A punctuated equilibrium model of organizational transformation: A case study of the regional Bell operating companies and their international expansion, 1984–1991.* Unpublished doctoral dissertation, University of North Carolina at Chapel Hill, Kenan-Flagler Business School.

Smith, K. G., & Grimm, C. M. 1987a. Environmental variation, strategic change and firm performance: A study of railroad deregulation. *Strategic Management Journal*, 8(4): 363–376.

Smith, K. G., & Grimm, C. M. 1987b. *Gambit and repartee: A theory of competitive action and response.* Paper presented at the annual meeting of the Academy of Management, New Orleans, LA.

Smith, K. G., Grimm, C. M., & Gannon, M. J. 1992. *Dynamics of competitive strategy.* Newbury Park, CA: Sage.

Smith, T., Clark, W. A. V., Huff, J. O., & Shapiro, P. 1979. A decision making and search model for intraurban migration. *Geographical Analysis*, 11: 1–22.

Spender, J.-C. 1980. *Strategy making in business.* Unpublished doctoral dissertation, Manchester University, Manchester, England.

Spender, J.-C. 1989. *Industry recipes: An enquiry into the nature and sources of managerial judgement.* Oxford: Blackwell.

Spender, J.-C. 1993. Some frontier activities around strategy theorizing. *Journal of Management Studies*, 30(1): 11–30.

Spender, J.-C. 1998. The dynamics of individual and organizational knowledge. In C. Eden & J.-C. Spender (Eds.), *Managerial and organizational cognition.* London: Sage.

Spender, J.-C., & Eden, C. 1998. Introduction. In C. Eden & J.-C. Spender (Eds.), *Managerial and organizational cognition.* London: Sage.

Spilker, B. 1994. *Multinational pharmaceutical companies: Principles and practices.* New York: Raven Press.

Spinello, R. A. 1992. Ethics, pricing and the pharmaceutical industry. *Journal of Business Ethics*, 11(8): 617–626.

Sproull, L. S., & Hofmeister, K. R. 1986. Thinking about implementation. *Journal of Management*, 12: 43–60.

Stacey, R. D. 1995. The science of complexity. *Strategic Management Journal*, 16: 477–495.

Standard and Poors Industry Survey, October 6, 1994, 162: H1–6.

Standard and Poors Industry Survey, January 5, 1995, 163(1): H1–6.

Standard and Poors Industry Survey, May 4, 1995, 163(18): H1–6.

Starbuck, W. H. 1983. Organizations as action generators. *American Sociological Review*, 48: 91–102.

Starbuck, W. H. 1992. Learning by knowledge-intensive firms. *Journal of Management Studies*, 29(6): 713–740.

Starbuck, W. H. 1999. *Plenary session speech.* Presented at the annual meeting of the British Academy of Management, Manchester.

Starbuck, W. H., & Milliken, F. J. 1988. Executives' perceptual filters: What they notice and how they make sense. In D. C. Hambrick (Ed.), *The executive effect: Concepts and methods for studying top managers*: 35–65. Greenwich, CT: JAI Press.

Staw, B. M., McKechnie, P., & Puffer, S. 1983. The justification of organizational performance. *Administrative Science Quarterly*, 28: 582–600.

Staw, B. M., Sandelands, L. E., & Dutton, J. E. 1981. Threat-rigidity effects in organizational behavior: A multilevel analysis. *Administrative Science Quarterly*, 26: 501–524.

Stein, J. (Ed.). 1966. *The Random House dictionary of the English language.* New York: Random House.

Steinberg, R. J. 1985. Implicit theories of intelligence, creativity, and wisdom. *Journal of Personality and Social Psychology*, 49: 607–627.

Steinberg, R. J. 1990. *Metaphors of mind: Conceptions of the nature of intelligence.* Cambridge: Cambridge University Press.

Steinberg, R. J. 1994. PRSVL: An integrative framework for understanding mind in context. In R. J. Steinberg & R. K. Wagner (Eds.), *Mind in context: interactionist perspectives on human intelligence*. Cambridge: Cambridge University Press.

Steinbruner, J. D. 1974. *The cybernetic theory of decision*. Princeton, NJ: Princeton University Press.

Stetler, C. J. 1991. The pharmaceutical industry in review: How we got to where we are. *Medical Marketing and Media*, 26(11): 40–51.

Stimpert, J. L., & Duhaime, I. M. 1997. In the eyes of the beholder: Conceptualizations of relatedness held by the managers of large diversified firms. *Strategic Management Journal*, 18: 111–125.

Stinchcomb, A. L. 1990. *Information and organizations*. Berkeley: University of California Press.

Stjernberg, T., & Ullstad, C. 1994. Organization images: Organizational diagnosis by transformation of individuals' cognitive maps into shared local theories. *Second international workshop on managerial and organizational cognition proceedings*: 601–622. Brussels, Belgium.

Strati, A. 1998. Organizational symbolism as a social construction: A perspective from the sociology of knowledge. *Human Relations*, 15(11): 1379–1402.

Strauss, A., Schatzman, L., Ehrlich, D., Bucher, R., & Sabshin, M. 1963. The hospital and its negotiated order. In E. Friedson (Ed.), *The hospital in modern society*. New York: Free Press.

Stubbart, C. I. 1989. Managerial cognition: A missing link in strategic management research. *Journal of Management Studies*, 26(4): 325–347.

Takahashi, S. 1994. Japan's pharmaceutical industry. *Japan 21st*, 39(8): 18–23.

Tang, M. J., & Thomas, H. 1992. The concept of strategic groups: Theoretical construct or analytical convenience. *Managerial and Decision Economics*, 13(4): 323–329.

Tarabusi, C. C., & Vickery, G. 1994. Globalisation and pharmaceuticals. *OECD Observer*, 185: 41–44.

Taylor, S. E., & Crocker, J. 1981. Schematic basis of social information processing. In E. T. Higgins, C. P. Herman, & M. P. Zanna (Eds.), *Social cognition: The Ontario symposium*, 1: 89–134. Hillsdale, NJ: Erlbaum.

Taylor, J. R., & Lerner, L. 1996. Making sense of sensemaking: How managers construct their organisation through talk. *Studies in culture, organizations and sociology*, 2: 257–286.

Taylor, S. E., Lichtman, R. R., & Wood, J. V. 1984. Attributions, beliefs about control, and adjustments to breast cancer. *Journal of Personality and Social Psychology*, 46(3): 489–502.

Taylor, S. E., Wood, J. V., & Lichtman, R. R. 1983. It could be worse: Selective evaluation as a response to victimization. *Journal of Social Issues*, 39(2): 19–40.

Teece, D. J., Pisano, G., & Shuen, A. 1997. Dynamic capabilities and strategic management. *Strategic Management Journal*, 18: 509–533.

Teitelman, R., Siwolop, S., & Baldo, A. 1989. Global report on pharmaceuticals. *Financial World*, 158(11): 53–80.

Temin, P. 1980. *Taking your medicine: Drug regulation in the United States*. Cambridge, MA: Harvard University Press.

Tenbrunsel, A. E., Galvin, T. L., Neale, M. A., & Bazerman, M. H. 1996. Cognitions in organizations. In S. Clegg, C. Hardy & W. Nord (Eds.), *Handbook of organization studies*: 313–337. London, Sage.

Tenkasi, R. V., & Boland, R. J., Jr. 1993. Locating meaning making in organizational learning: The narrative basis of cognition. *Organization change and development,* 7: 77–103. Greenwood, CT: JAI Press.

Thagard, P. (Ed.). 1998. *Mind readings.* Cambridge, MA: MIT Press.

Thayer, A. M. 1993. Biotechnology industry looks to more creative financing options. *C&EN,* August 23: 10–13.

Thomas, H. 1984. Strategic decision analysis: Applied decision analysis and its role in strategic management. *Strategic Management Journal,* 5(2): 139–156.

Thomas, H., & Venkatraman, R. 1988. Research on strategic groups: Progress and prognosis. *Journal of Management Studies,* 25(6): 537–555.

Thompson, J. 1967. *Organizations in action.* New York: McGraw-Hill.

Thomas, J., Clark, S., & Gioia, D. 1993. Strategic sensemaking and organizational performance: Linkages among scanning, interpretation, action, and outcomes. *Academy of Management Journal,* 36: 239–270.

Thomas, J. B., Clark, S. M., & Gioia, D. A. 1997. Strategic sensemaking and organizational performance: Linkages among scanning, interpretation, action, and outcomes. *Academy of Management Journal,* 36: 239–270.

Thomas, J. B., & McDaniel, R. R. Jr. 1990. Interpreting strategic issues: Effects of strategy and information-processing structure of top management teams. *Academy of Management Journal,* 33(2): 286–306.

Tichy, N. 1983a. The essentials of strategic change management. *Journal of Business Strategy,* 3(4): 55–67.

Tichy, N. 1983b. *Managing strategic change: Technical, political, and cultural dynamics.* New York: John Wiley.

Tichy, N., & Ulrich, D. 1984. Revitalizing organizations: The leadership role. In J. Kimberly & R. Quinn (Eds.), *Managing organizational transitions:* 240–264. Homewood, IL: R. D. Irwin.

Tushman, M. L., & Anderson, P. 1986. Technological discontinuities and organizational environments. *Administrative Science Quarterly,* 31: 439–465.

Tushman, M. L., & Anderson, P. 1997. *Managing strategic innovation and change.* Oxford: Oxford University Press.

Tushman, M. L., Newman, W., & Romanelli, E. 1986. Technological discontinuities and organizational environments. *Administrative Science Quarterly,* 31: 439–465.

Tushman, M. L., & Romanelli, E. 1985. Organizational evolution. In B. M. Staw & L. L. Cummings (Eds.), *Research in organization behavior,* 7: 171–222.

Tversky, A., & Kahneman, D. 1974. Judgment under uncertainty: Heuristics and biases. *Science,* 185: 1124–1131.

Tversky, A., & Kahneman, D. 1981. The framing of decisions and the psychology of choice. *Science,* 211: 453–458.

Urban, G. L., Carter, T., Gaskin, S., & Mucha, Z. 1986. Market share rewards to pioneering brands: An empirical analysis and strategic implications. *Management Science,* 32: 645–659.

Uzzi, B. 1997. Social structure and competition in interfirm networks: The paradox of embeddedness. *Administrative Science Quarterly,* 42: 35–67.

Vagelos, P. R. 1991. Are prescription drug prices high? *Science,* 252: 1080–1084.

Van de Ven, A. H. 1986. Central problems in the management of innovation. *Management Science,* 32: 590–607.

Van de Ven, A. H. 1990. Methods for studying innovation development in the Minnesota Innovation Research Program. *Organization Science,* 1(3): 313–335.

Van de Ven, A. H., Polley, D. E., Garud, R., & Venkataraman, S. 1999. *The innovation journey.* New York: Oxford University Press.

Van Gelder, T. 1966. Dynamics and cognition. In J. Haugeland (Ed.), *Mind design II:* 421–450. Cambridge, MA: MIT Press.

Van Gelder, T., Port, R. 1995. It's about time: an overview of the dynamical approach to cognition. In *Mind as motion: Explorations in the dynamics of cognition.* Cambridge, MA: MIT Press.

Van Gelder, T. 1996. Dynamics and cognition. In J. Haugeland (Ed.), *Mind design II.* Cambridge, MA: MIT Press.

Van Mannen, J., & Barley, S. R. 1984. Occupational communities: Culture and control in organizations. In B. M. Staw & L. L. Cummings (Eds.), *Research in organizational behavior.* Greenwich, CT: JAI Press.

Vizard, M. 1999. Linux barbarians at the Microsoft gate. *InforWorld,* March 1, 21(9): 5.

VonKrogh, G., & Roos, J. 1995. *Organizational epistemology.* London: Macmillan.

VonKrogh, G., & Roos, J. 1996. A tale of the unfinished. *Strategic Management Journal,* 17: 729–737.

Wagner, J. A., III, & Gooding, R. Z. 1997. Equivocal information and attribution: An investigation of patterns of managerial sensemaking. *Strategic Management Journal,* 18: 275–286.

Walsh, J. P. 1988. Selectivity and selective perception: An investigation of managers' belief structures and information processing. *Academy of Management Journal,* 31: 873–896.

Walsh, J. P. 1995. Managerial and organizational cognition: Notes from a trip down memory lane. *Organization Science,* 6(3): 280–321.

Walsh, J. P., Henderson, C. M., & Deighton, J. 1988. Negotiated belief structures and decision performance: An empirical investigation. *Organizational Behavior & Human Decision Processes,* 42(2): 194–216.

Walsh, J. P., & Ungson, G. R. 1991. Organizational memory. *Academy of Management Review,* 16: 57–91.

Wardell, W. 1971. Introduction of new therapeutic drugs in the US and Great Britain: An international comparison. *Clinical Pharmacology and Therapeutics,* 14: 773–790.

Watzlawick, P., Weakland, J. H., & Fisch, R. 1974. *Change.* New York: Norton.

Wegner, D. M., Giuliano, T., & Hertel, P. T. 1985. Cognitive interdependence in close relationships. In W. J. Ickes (Ed.), *Compatible and incompatible relationships:* 253–276. New York: Springer-Verlag.

Weick, K. E. 1969. *The social psychology of organizing.* Reading, MA: Addison-Wesley.

Weick, K. E. 1976. Educational organizations as loosely coupled systems. *Administrative Science Quarterly,* 21:1–19.

Weick, K. E. 1979. *The social psychology of organizing* (2nd ed.). Reading, MA: Addison-Wesley.

Weick, K. E. 1990. Cartographic myths in organizations. In A. S. Huff (Ed.), *Mapping strategic thought:* 1–10. Chichester, England: Wiley.

Weick, K. E. 1995. *Sensemaking in organizations.* Thousand Oaks, CA: Sage.

Weick, K. E., & Bougon, M. 1986. Organizations as cognitive maps: Charting ways to success and failure. In H. Sims & D. Gioia (Eds.), *The thinking organization:* 102–135. San Francisco: Jossey-Bass.

Weick, K. E., & Roberts, K. H. 1993. Collective mind in organizations: Heedful interrelating on flight decks. *Administrative Science Quarterly,* 38: 357–381.

Weick, K. E., & Westley, F. 1996. Organizational learning: Affirming an oxymoron. In S. Clegg, C. Hardy & W. Nord (Eds.), *Handbook of organization studies:* 440–458. London: Sage.

Wernerfelt, B. 1984. A resource-based view of the firm. *Strategic Management Journal,* 5(2): 171–180.

Wernerfelt, B. 1995. The resource-based view of the firm: Ten years after. *Strategic Management Journal,* 16: 171–174.

Westley, F. R. 1990. Middle managers and strategy: Microdynamics of inclusion. *Strategic Management Journal,* 11: 337–351.

Westley, F. R., & Mintzberg, H. 1989. Visionary leadership and strategic management. *Strategic Management Journal,* 10: 17–32.

Whetten, D. 1980. Organizational decline: A neglected topic in organizational science. *Academy of Management Review,* 5: 577–588.

Whetten, D. A., & Godfrey, P. C. 1998. *Identity in organizations: Building theory through conversations.* Thousand Oaks, CA: Sage.

Whittaker, E., & Bower, J. D. 1994. A shift to external alliances for product development in the pharmaceutical industry. *R&D Management,* 24(3): 249–260.

Whittington, R. 1992. Putting Giddens into action: Social systems and managerial agency. *Journal of Management Studies,* 29: 693–712.

Wilkins, A. L. 1983. Organizational stories as symbols which control the organization. In L. Pondy, P. Frost, G. Morgan & T. Dandridge (Eds.), *Organizational symbolism.* Greenwich, CT: JAI Press.

Williamson, O. E. 1975. *Markets and hierarchies: Analysis and antitrust implications.* New York: Free Press.

Williamson, O. E. 1979. Transaction-cost economics: The governance of contractual relations. *Journal of Law and Economics,* 22: 233–260.

Wilson, D., & Huff, J. O. 1994. *Marginalized places and populations: A structurationist agenga.* Westport, CT: Praeger.

Winograd, T., & Flores, F. 1986. *Understanding computers and cognition: A new foundation for design.* Norwood, NJ: Ablex.

Wirtlin, G. 1989. Interim measures. In S. G. Burrill (Ed.), *Biotech 89: Commercialization.* San Francisco: Ernst & Young High Technology Group.

Wittgenstein, L. 1972. *Philosophical investigations.* Oxford: Basil Blackwell.

Wood, M. 1996. Situating cognition: Organizations as communities-of-practice. In *Fourth international workshop on managerial and organizational cognition proceedings.* Stockholm.

Woodrum, E. 1984. Mainstreaming content analysis in social science: Methodological advantages, obstacles, solutions. *Social Science Research,* 13: 1–9.

Yates, B. 1983. *The decline and fall of the American automobile industry.* New York: Empire Books.

Yerkes, R. M., & Dodson, J. D. 1908. The relation of strength of stimulus to rapidity of habit-formation. *Journal of Comparative and Neurological Phychology,* 18: 459–482.

Yoshikawa, A. 1989. The other drug war: US-Japan trade in pharmaceuticals. *California Management Review,* 31(2): 76–90.

Zahra, S. A., & Chapels, S. S. 1993. Blind spots in competitive analysis. *Academy of Management Executive,* 7(2): 7–28.

Zajac, E. J. 1992. Relating economic and behavioral perspectives in strategy research. In P. Shrivastava, J. Dutton & A. Huff (Eds.), *Advances in Strategic Management,* 8: 69–96. Greenwich, CT: JAI Press.

Zajac, E. J., & Bazerman, M. H. 1991. Blind spots in industry and competitor analysis: Implications of interfirm (mis)perceptions for strategic decisions. *Academy of Management Review,* 16: 37–56.

Zajac, E. J., & Kraatz, M. S. 1993. A diametric forces model of strategic change: Assessing the antecedents and conseqences of restructuring in the higher education industry. *Strategic Management Journal,* 14: 83–102.

Zajac, E. J., & Shortell, S. M. 1989. Changing generic strategies: Likelihood, direction, and performance implications. *Strategic Management Journal,* 10(5): 413–430.

Zapt, D., Dormann, C., & Frese, M. 1996. Longitudinal studies in organizational stress research; a review of the literature with reference to methodological issues. *Journal of Occupational Health Psychology,* 2: 145–269.

Zeidner, M., & Hammer, A. 1990. Life events and coping resources as predictors of stress symptoms in adolescents. *Personality and Individual Differences,* 11(7): 693–703.

Zukav, G. 1979. *The dancing Wu Li masters: An overview of the new physics.* New York: Murrow.

Index